"研究生学术论文写作"丛书

语言学研究论文写作

案例与方法

◎ 主　编　唐青叶　张新玲
◎ 副主编　朱音尔　李晓媛

Paper Writing

上海大学出版社

图书在版编目(CIP)数据

语言学研究论文写作：案例与方法 / 唐青叶，张新玲主编；朱音尔，李晓媛副主编. -- 上海：上海大学出版社，2024.7. --（研究生学术论文写作）.
ISBN 978-7-5671-4981-6

Ⅰ. H0

中国国家版本馆 CIP 数据核字第 2024R39V04 号

责任编辑　贺俊逸
封面设计　缪炎栩
技术编辑　金　鑫　钱宇坤

"研究生学术论文写作"丛书

语言学研究论文写作：案例与方法

主　编　唐青叶　张新玲
副主编　朱音尔　李晓媛

上海大学出版社出版发行
（上海市上大路 99 号　邮政编码 200444）
（https://www.shupress.cn　发行热线 021-66135112）
出版人　戴骏豪

＊

南京展望文化发展有限公司排版
上海普顺印刷包装有限公司印刷　各地新华书店经销
开本 710mm×1000mm　1/16　印张 21.5　字数 362 千
2024 年 8 月第 1 版　2024 年 8 月第 1 次印刷
ISBN 978-7-5671-4981-6/H·434　定价　65.00 元

版权所有　侵权必究
如发现本书有印装质量问题请与印刷厂质量科联系
联系电话：021-36522998

"研究生学术论文写作"丛书编委会

主　任　张建华

副主任　张勇安　李常品　曾桂娥　戴骏豪
　　　　　姚　蓉

委　员　（按姓氏笔画为序）
　　　　　丁治民　丁敬达　于瀛洁　王　勇
　　　　　王廷云　王远弟　毛建华　方　勇
　　　　　卢志国　叶海涛　田立君　宁镇疆
　　　　　刘文光　闫坤如　严三九　李凤章
　　　　　李桂琴　李颖洁　吴　浩　沈　荟
　　　　　张恒龙　张新鹏　陆丹丹　陈　静
　　　　　陈　瑜　尚　新　姚　萱　聂永有
　　　　　唐青叶　黄晓春　梁　奇　曾　军
　　　　　廖大伟　阚怀未　戴世强

本书编委会

主　编　唐青叶　张新玲

副主编　朱音尔　李晓媛

专家委员会(按姓氏笔画为序)
　　　　　王文斌(北京外国语大学)
　　　　　王克非(北京外国语大学)
　　　　　王振华(上海交通大学)
　　　　　文　旭(西南大学)
　　　　　邓志勇(上海大学)
　　　　　田海龙(天津外国语大学)
　　　　　刘正光(湖南大学)
　　　　　杨信彰(厦门大学)
　　　　　束定芳(上海外国语大学)
　　　　　张　辉(南京师范大学)
　　　　　陈新仁(南京大学)
　　　　　尚　新(上海大学)
　　　　　罗选民(广西大学/清华大学)
　　　　　胡开宝(上海外国语大学)
　　　　　梁茂成(北京航空航天大学)

编　委(按姓氏笔画为序)

　　　　王仁强(四川外国语大学)
　　　　方　帆(汕头大学)
　　　　冯德正(香港理工大学)
　　　　朱永生(复旦大学)
　　　　刘建达(广东外语外贸大学)
　　　　张吉生(华东师范大学)
　　　　陆俭明(北京大学)
　　　　郑咏滟(复旦大学)
　　　　胡壮麟(北京大学)
　　　　俞理明(上海交通大学)
　　　　黄国文(华南农业大学)
　　　　董燕萍(浙江大学)
　　　　曾用强(广东外语外贸大学)
　　　　雷　蕾(上海外国语大学)
　　　　潘文国(华东师范大学)
　　　　魏在江(广东外语外贸大学)

总 序

教育部办公厅《关于进一步规范和加强研究生培养管理的通知》明确指出，研究生培养单位要加强学术规范和学术道德教育，把论文写作指导课程作为必修课纳入研究生培养环节。上海大学积极响应，安排各个学院组织开设相关课程并纳入研究生培养环节，取得良好效果。

为了进一步提升研究生培养质量，上海大学研究生院和上海大学出版社联合策划了"研究生学术论文写作"丛书，作为研究生学习学术写作的指导用书。本丛书内容涵盖文科、理科、工科、医学、经济、管理等多个学科，邀请各学科教授及学术骨干领衔担任主编，并根据学科特点，采用以下两种编纂模式：一是对已发表的高水平论文进行综合分析，归纳出写作要点；二是在已发表的论文案例基础上，论文原作者解析撰文过程和注意事项。这种"案例+方法"的编纂模式，通过论文作者现身说法的方式，从问题意识、论证方法、创新之处等方面揭示论文的成文之道，为研究生提供可参考、可借鉴的学术写作范例。

上海大学老校长钱伟长生前指出，研究生培养分为两个阶段，一个是课程学习阶段，另一个是论文写作阶段。钱校长非常重视研究生学术论文写作能力的培养，他曾经在研究生开学典礼的讲话中指出："论文很重要。写论文以前，你首先要到第一线找到人家的'肩膀'在哪儿。"本丛书的编纂，践行钱伟长教育思想，探索案例和方法相结合的教学途径，为研究生提供学术研究的"肩膀"，为各学科研究生提供学术论文写作的方法指导，也可为青年教师撰写学术论文提供思路启发。

我们真诚地希望使用本丛书的教师、学生以及广大读者对其中存在的问题提出修改意见或建议，交流互鉴，共彰学术。

"研究生学术论文写作"丛书编委会

2021 年 9 月

目 录

序 ··· 杨信彰　1

第一部分　千里之行,始于足下

社会符号学研究中的多模态化 ·· 胡壮麟　1
　　方法谈:如何选题并确保选题的理论价值和应用价值? ············· 15
韩礼德的语篇连贯标准
　　——外界的误解与自身的不足 ···································· 朱永生　19
　　方法谈:如何从质疑中萌生选题? ·· 27
从语言信息结构视角重新认识"把"字句 ···························· 陆俭明　31
　　方法谈:老问题如何才能出新意? ·· 51
渥太华依托式课程教学及其启示 ··························· 俞理明　韩建侠　55
　　方法谈:如何从实践中找到值得研究的问题? ··························· 60
论生态话语和行为分析的假定和原则 ································ 黄国文　67
　　方法谈:如何进行语言学的本土化研究? ·································· 78
关于外国语言学研究的几点思考 ······································ 潘文国　84
　　方法谈:如何反思西方语言学理论对中国语言现象的解释力? ······ 92

第二部分　专精覃思,审思明辨

认知语言学中的语境:定义与功能 ···································· 魏在江　96

方法谈：如何厘清文献综述的述与评？ ……………………… 108
也论汉语词重音 ……………………………………… 张吉生 112
　　方法谈：如何在理论框架下展开论证、提升思辨素养？ ……… 133
职业英语能力构念的实证研究 ………………………… 曾用强 137
　　方法谈：研究方案如何体现研究目的？ ……………………… 148
How does Consecutive Interpreting Training Influence Working
　　Memory: A Longitudinal Study of Potential Links between
　　the Two ……………… Yanping Dong, Yuhua Liu and Rendong Cai 151
　　方法谈：实证类研究如何做到不止于描述层面？ …………… 184
基于语料库的动词与构式关系研究
　　——以 sneeze 及物动词用法的规约化为例 …… 王仁强　陈和敏 187
　　方法谈：如何提升语言学论文讨论和结论部分的站位？ ……… 203

第三部分　欲善其事，先利其器

大规模计算机口试分析评分效果研究 …………… 刘建达　吕剑涛 206
　　方法谈：定量研究的优势是什么？数据会说谎吗？ …………… 219
"A More Inclusive Mind towards the World": English Language
　　Teaching and Study Abroad in China from Intercultural
　　Citizenship and English as a Lingua Franca Perspectives
　　……………………………… Fan (Gabriel) Fang, Will Baker 221
　　方法谈：质性研究的优势是什么？如何让人信服？ …………… 246
Syntactic Complexity in Adapted Extracurricular Reading Materials
　　………………………………………… Lei Lei, Yaqian Shi 251
　　方法谈：语料库语言学可以帮我们做什么？ …………………… 283
复杂理论视角下任务复杂度对二语口语表现的影响 …… 郑咏滟　刘飞凤 293
　　方法谈：跨学科研究方法如何助力语言学研究？ ……………… 306
基于多元读写理论的课堂教学设计：以英语语言学课程为例 …… 冯德正 312
　　方法谈：行动研究中如何基于问题阐释论文的研究价值？ …… 326

后记 ……………………………………………………………… 329

序

  论文是研究人员呈现研究成果的一个重要手段。论文写作是研究工作的一个重要环节,也是写作课程的一个重要组成部分。这本书汇集的16篇案例和方法谈聚焦语言学研究论文写作,从不同侧面向读者描述了语言学论文写作的方法,为语言学研究的论文写作实践提供了很好的指导作用。

  总体上看,本书具有以下五个显著特征。

  一是说明语言学研究论文写作是个复杂的过程,涉及许多的因素。研究工作是论文写作的基础,因此在着手写作时,论文作者需要确定所要研究的问题。作者对论文的选题需要有清晰的认识,了解有关的文献,确定自己的研究视角、研究框架和研究方法,体现研究的新意和意义。因此,论文作者在着手写作时需要考虑一系列的问题。在确定选题和研究框架时,作者需要确定研究方法、资料搜集和数据处理的方式、论文的宏观结构以及语言表达的方式。在论文的写作过程中,作者需要在描述数据的基础上,把研究问题和数据分析的结果联系起来,在理论层面进行阐释,对所涉及的研究领域有所贡献。

  二是说明语言学论文的选题是论文写作的关键。我们知道,随着新的研究视角和研究手段的出现,语言学研究发展迅速,其范围和角度发生了很大的变化,出现了跨学科、多学科、超学科的特征。语言学不再局限于研究语音、音系、词汇和句子,其研究范围已经扩展到探讨语言与其他相关因素之间的关系,研究语言学理论在相关领域的应用。正因如此,语言学出现了许多的分支。此外,由于意义表达的多模态特征,多模态也成为一个研究热点。语言研究既可对人类语言的普遍规律展开探索,也可对某种语言进行专门的研究。在这样的范围内

确立一个好的选题需要作者有宽广的学科基础,仔细研读相关的语言学理论,了解语言学的发展脉络和最新的发展动向。

三是说明理论框架是语言学论文写作的重要基础。理论框架为论文的选题提供支撑,能影响论文的研究视角和研究路径。理论框架通常包含了与论文研究相关的概念和理论。这些概念和理论形成一个逻辑严密和连贯的整体,为论文的论证和整体结构打下基础。理论框架与论文的整个研究工作有着紧密的联系,在写作过程中,论文的分析推理工作需要根据所确定的理论框架和研究目标,围绕研究问题,结合数据和语料分析展开论证,得出可靠的结论。

四是说明语言学研究论文呈现了作者所做的研究工作,因此在确立了选题之后就会涉及研究方法。研究方法有很多,如实证研究、量化研究、质性研究、个案分析、演绎归纳。近年来,许多研究通过使用实地观察、测试、问卷调查、访谈、实验、语料库、文献分析等手段来获取数据,在此基础上对数据和资料进行分析和统计,进而讨论并归纳出研究的发现。研究方法的使用与论文的研究问题和研究框架有很大的关系。每一种研究方法有其优势,但也有不足之处。由于人类语言的复杂性和多样化,语言交际涉及的语境因素有很多。在实际研究中,每一项研究都会用到一种或多种研究方法。近年来,随着计算机技术和网络技术的发展,语料库的优势得到了广泛认同,因此也出现了许多语料分析工具。许多语言学论文借助语料库数据对语言现象展开研究,以此来探索人类语言。这就需要研究者熟悉有关语料库分析工具,掌握语料收集、语料处理和语料分析的原则和方法。

五是说明语言学研究论文的作者需要有语类意识,能根据论文选题的性质和特点确定论文的语类结构。从话语的组织模式上看,论文通常由引言、文献综述、理论框架、研究方法、结果与讨论、结论、参考文献、摘要、致谢等语类成分组成。由于论文的类别和性质不一样,再加上语言学存在着许多分支,这些成分在论文的表现形式上不尽相同,有些成分也不一定出现。这些成分各具语类特点,例如引言主要介绍选题的依据、论文的研究问题等;文献综述主要根据经过全面搜集的相关文献,归纳和评析不同学者的研究和观点,从而指出新的研究亮点;研究方法部分描述研究所采用的方法、语料和数据、研究工具、研究步骤等。论文的最后部分通常是参考文献。不同出版单位对于参考文献的格式要求不同,作者需要注意。

随着技术的发展,许多语言学研究论文近年来使用了语言、图表等多种符号来呈现研究工作,因此运用多种符号的能力在语言学研究论文写作显得十分重要。此外,学术论文虽然都有一些共同点,但每个学科都有自己的一套话语习惯。由于学科内容上的差异,每个学科在语言手段的使用上会有一定的差异。语言学论文也不例外,有自己的一些结构特征和词汇语法特征,如时态、语态、语气、情态、引证、语法隐喻、人称代词、逻辑连接语、转述动词等语言手段的使用。

本书的方法谈可读性很强,紧扣语言学论文写作的实际,覆盖了语言学论文写作的重要方面。这些导读为我们展示了语言学论文写作的实例,阐释了写作要领,有助于提高语言学论文作者的学术写作能力和写作水平。语言学论文写作也需要作者熟悉语言学研究的话语,掌握语言学论文的词汇语法和修辞特点,关注语言学以及相关学科理论的新发展,在论文写作实践中研究语言问题。

杨信彰

2023 年 9 月 15 日

> 第一部分　千里之行，始于足下

社会符号学研究中的多模态化[*]

胡壮麟[**]

摘要：索绪尔对语言符号学的建立和对普通符号学的展望有其不可磨灭的贡献，但他的有些观点在符号学研究者中有不同反响。代表英美传统的皮尔斯发展了符号范畴，但他忽视了作为社会成员的人，因此仍不能摆脱形式主义的研究方法。随后的社会符号学发端于韩礼德的"语言是社会符号"的理论，关注的是特定于某一文化某一社团的符号实践。这一理论推动了多模态表达的研究，从而形成了多模态符号学。本文首先讨论多模态符号学和多媒体符号学的区别；进一步介绍具有媒体和模态双重特性的计算机符号学；对一些具体问题分别作了论述，如作为符号系统的符号资源、以屏幕代替书本的多模态符号的设计以及由话语参与者实现的连贯。最后指出，在人类进入社会符号学的多模态化的新世纪，对多模态识读能力的培养应引起重视。

关键词：社会符号学；多模态化；体符号学；计算机符号学；多模态识读能力

2004年，原洛阳外国语大学王铭玉教授的《语言符号学》一书问世，我在序言中肯定了索绪尔明确指出语言学是符号学的一个分支后，接着说了这么一

---

[*] 原载《语言教学与研究》2007年第1期。
[**] 胡壮麟，北京大学资深教授。曾任北京大学外国语学院英语系主任，北京大学澳大利亚研究中心主任，中国高等学校外语专业教学指导委员会委员兼英语组副组长，中国英语教学研究会副会长，国际系统功能语言学学会国际委员会委员。现任中国逻辑学会符号学专业委员会名誉会长，中国功能语言学研究会名誉会长，全国文体学研究会名誉会长，中国英汉语篇分析研究会名誉会长。先后曾任清华大学、北京师范大学等44所大学的双聘教授、客座教授、兼职教授，《外语教学与研究》《中国外语》《当代外语研究》《外语电化教学》等30种刊物和学报的顾问、编委。

段话：

  如今，我们一方面认识到语言是全部符号事实中的一个特殊系统，对语言学的研究推动了对符号学的研究。对符号学的认识加深了我们对语言的认识。另一方面又开拓了我们对其他符号系统的研究。这就是说，符号学有广阔的目标，它的理论旨在探索意义的生成。任何意义，不仅是书面语的意义，诸如视觉、听觉、嗅觉、味觉、触觉，以至抽象的模型、结构、主体意识都应纳入它的视线之内。

本文就以上话题，谈谈自己的认识。

一、从普通符号学到社会符号学

  索绪尔对语言符号学的建立和对普通符号学的展望（Saussure，1974）有其不可磨灭的贡献，但他的有些观点，如关于语言单位和结构是语言系统固有的特性，不受制于外部影响，在语音和意义之间没有必要的联系，意义不是通过与外部现实的关系而是通过该符号与其他符号之间的关系来界定，在符号学研究者中有不同反响（Saussure，1974；Fiske，1982；Beaugrande，1991；Guske，1998）。

  代表英美传统的皮尔斯发展了符号范畴，如图标、索引和语符。他论述的媒介、对象、解释三位一体的三角关系是奥格登和理查兹的语义三角的理论基础。值得注意的是"解释"这个概念的出现，意味着他对人作为解释者，作为主体作用的确认，但由于皮尔斯从哲学上关注逻辑和意义的关系，强调作为个体的人，忽视了作为社会成员的人，因此仍不能摆脱形式主义的研究方法（Martin & Ringham，2000；王铭玉，2004：122）。

  这样，虽然索绪尔曾经观察到"语言是社会事实"，日后对此作出详细解释的却是韩礼德的"语言是社会符号"的理论。即"要在社会语境中解释语言，在此过程中文化本身用符号学术语来说，被解释为一个信息系统"，"人们在他们日常的语言交换过程中，实现社会结构，肯定自己的地位和角色，建立和传递共享的价值系统和知识系统"。这就是说，语言既表达意义，也积极将社会结构和系统符号化。语言的这种双重功能使意义的表达方式多种多样，"从后院的闲言碎语到叙述体小说到史诗般的诗歌"（Halliday，1978）。

由此产生的社会符号学反对把符号作为第一性,反对过分强调用形式主义的方法研究符号系统。社会符号学优先研究的是把指称行为作为实例,并把社会的指称实践作为经常的、可重复的、可识辨的类型。它认为社会有意义的行动构成各种文化(社会符号系统),文化就是相互连接的对社会具有意义的实践系统。我们依赖这种系统使这些实践和其他实践具有意义,不仅仅是通过清晰的信息传递,也通过所有形式的对社会有意义的活动(说话、画图、衣着、烹调、建筑、打架等)。符号系统是对这些实践的抽象(如从言语得到语言符号),这种变化是社会实践的变化(Lemke,2005)。正是这种变化是意义得以产生的过程,即"符号化"(semiosis),这比单纯研究符号间意义关系的系统更为基本,后者只是在产生意义时可资利用的资源潜势。正如 Lemke 所言,社会符号学调查的是特定于某一文化某一社团的符号实践,可以在各种情景语境和文化上有意义活动的语境中产生各种语篇和意义。因此,社会符号学没有必要区分理论符号学和应用符号学,它与话语分析、多媒体分析、教育研究、文化人类学、政治社会学有更紧密的关系。再者,它也回答了索绪尔符号学所难以摆脱的一个悖论:这个理论一方面把语言看作是静态的不变的,另一方面又不得不承认"所指的变化导致概念的变化","思想可能被迫接受符号的物质状态给它提供的特殊方式"。这说明语言结构底层的常规是不固定的,而是受到实际言语的影响(Beaugrande,1991:2-27)。

二、多模态化和多媒体化

在讨论"多模态化"(multimodality)和"多媒体化"(multimediality)之前,有必要澄清一些词义的区别。

首先,本文讨论的 modality 的意义源自 mode(方式/模式/模态/型),它不同于英语语法中的 modality(情态),后者与 modal verb(情态动词)中的 modal(情态的)更为接近,虽然 model 与 mode 在词源上还是有联系的。

其次,我们要区分 mode 和 medium(媒介/媒体)的不同。两者都是历史和文化的产物。模态是可对比和对立的符号系统,媒体是符号分布印迹的物质手段,如产生语篇采用印刷的或手写的手段,说话时发出的声音,身体的动作,或计算机显示器上的光脉冲(Scollon & Levine,2004)。举例说,我们感受客观世界的视觉、听觉、触觉、味觉、嗅觉是不同的感知模式,但眼、耳、手、舌、鼻则是媒体。

再具体说,写文章、唱歌、跳舞是采用符号表达情感的模式。但我们用以写字的纸和墨,歌舞演出时的道具,教室中的黑板和白板,以至扩音器、录音机、电视机、录像机、投射仪、计算机则是媒体。这样,模式是用某种媒体表达信息的特殊方式。媒体是表达信息的物理工具。口语是用声音媒介表达的一种方式,而书面语和面部表情是用光线或图表进行表达的模式。显然,采用某一种媒体仍可以有不同方法表达信息。如采用嘴唇活动或笔录的形式,口语可以由光线/图表的媒介来表达。同理,同样的模式可以用不同媒体表达。在"人—人—系统"的互动中,一种模态可以作为输入模式(从人到系统或其他人)或作为输出模式(从系统到人,或到另一系统),或两者皆可。

  Kress(2001)报道教室中的多模态信息传递有两个理论基础:首先,物质的媒体经过社会长时间的塑造,成为意义产生的资源,可表达不同社团所要求的意义,这就成了模态。所有模态具有表达意义的潜势。非社团成员不能全部懂得这些意义,因为模态和意义具有社会的和文化的特殊性。其次,作为言语的语言模态和作为书面语的语言模态以及其他模态往往是交织在一起的,在信息传递语境下它们同时存在同时操作。这种互动本身就产生意义。使用者经常对表达和信息传递的模态加以改变,以适应社会的信息传递需要,这样,已有的模态被改造,新模态被创造。Kress(2001)认为韩礼德1978年关于信息传递的社会符号学理论推动了多模态表达的研究。

  多模态表达可以分解为同时表达意义的两个或两个以上的单模态(Bernsen,2002)。Holsonova(1999)指出,我们每天在报纸、杂志、广告、招贴画、故事书、教科书、活页文选、百科全书、说明书、计算机界面,甚至在我们相互交往时都离不开多模态。例如,我们谈话时手舞足蹈,有声有色,意味着使用了多模态。我们的国画往往配有诗文和印章也是如此。现在,许多学科都在研究多模态化这个课题,如(社会)符号学、语篇语言学、界面设计、人机对话等。Holsonova把多模态化分析研究的不同方法分为七个视角:① 研究不同模态之间的差异性是强调各模式有各自内在的优劣,因此不同的模态宜用于表达不同的信息类型。② 根据不同模态之间的相似性,重点研究不同模态的相似方面。例如,在分析语言和图画时,采用同样的分析范畴。这种观点认为图画和其他视觉成分与语言一样,也具有符号的语法。③ 根据不同模态之间的相互作用研究各模态是否有主次?是否彼此互补?是否其中一个模态可以加强其他模态提供的信息?是减少其他模态的信息还是增加信息?④ 对不同范态如何可以实现形式化?⑤对不同模态及其相互作用的感知,如有的研究使用眼跟踪器(eye-trackers)和词句协议(verbal protocols)。⑥对会话模态的复制,这方面的研究强调多模态产品的应用不是以感知作为终结。从一个多模态成果获得的信息可以在另一个信递场合重建和讨论。如果在传递过程中信息打包维持原样或发生变化都是值得注意的现象。⑦多模态的互动,包括我们作为个体与他人互动时或采用多模态系统时,使用言语、手势、体语、面部表情,接近或凝视的情景。这时,我们不妨提问:何处何时对这些方法加以整合?这些方式是互补的还是重复的?这些方法是同时出现的,还是有次序的?以上①—④项趋向于研究现有产品的多模态化,⑤—⑦项关注的是这些产品的应用价值。总的来说,在今后研究中,多模态的感知、多模态化的复制和多模态化的互动将受到特别重视。

多媒体符号学的基本原则是所有意义的产生渗透于诸如语言、姿态、描写、动作等可区别的理想的符号资源系统之间,因为意义产生既是符号实践,也是物质过程。每一个物质行为可以就一个以上的符号关系系统构建,如一个书面词即是语言学符号,也是可视的书写符号;一个口语的词的构建也得倚赖非语言的音质;一个图像要按可视的,有时也要按语言学的性质加以理解。因此研究不同符号系统的物质因素和符号学因素如何整合成语篇和林林总总的多媒体产物甚为重要。研究的方法可以先分后合,先分析清楚单个的符号系统,然后将其整合(Lemke,2005)。

模态和媒体的关系归根结底是话语和技术的关系,两者存在着内在的联系。哲学家尼采曾说过,"我们的写作工具对我们的思想也起作用"(Scollon & Levine,2004)。我们今天所谈的语篇分析在许多方面是技术变化的产物。新的传播技术有双重影响。一个影响我们如何采集语料,如笔录和分析语篇资料,另一个更重要的影响是对互动和语篇本身的影响。例如,20世纪60年代后盒式录音机的出现使捕捉瞬息即逝的正在使用的语言成为可能,如今信递技术成就了巴掌大的数字录像机、手机和网上聊天室,杂志已可以通过网络阅读。

Scollon & Levine(2004)认为我们要研究话语和技术的关系以及多模态话语分析,因为:第一,任何话语具有多模态的固有特性。对这个问题的研究可以更全面地了解人类的信息传递。何况新的话语形式不时产生,如互联网和聊天室。教育话语正在从传统的"教师—学生—教科书"的媒介模型转变至更为复杂的形式,有赖于软件设计师,连教师自己也成了这些新话语形式的开发者。第二,这有助于发展话语的新形式。对以互联网为基础或中心的话语的分析将远远超过以互联网为中介的互动过程。如有人利用诸如"屏幕电影"的网络软件处理非常复杂的一系列社会互动过程。第三,为了研究多模式现象的社会活动。利用非常方便的录像材料可以研究各种社会互动过程,在这些过程中,有时讲话很少,但有众多的不时变化的参与者结构和认同,单靠某一模态很难完成。第四,要研究教育性的社会互动过程中的多模态话语分析,因为许多学术性研究人员自己也在教育单位工作,他们进行分析时可不受时间的限制。早期的电影研究只能依赖几分钟长的片段,录像带的资料可达60分钟。现在的技术和软件可对整个学年的种种事件进行比较,能更好地了解一个周期的节奏。第五,多模态语篇分析可应用于分析工作场所的话语,尽管任务、人员结构和日常生活场所有很大不同。员工或同组工作或交接班的社会活动过程是在纷繁复杂的工具、物品和技术条件下进行的,从工作任务简单到垃圾箱、清洁工、废料清理,应有尽有。已有的研究表明,利用录像机和资料提取的新技术发展了新的研究领域,不仅仅是像过去那样分析仅以对话为中心的语类。

三、计算机符号学

采用语符学研究方法的 Andersen 在 1990 年提出计算机符号学的理论。他认为这个理论可以对人机对话的问题获得系统的了解,也可发展对设计计算机系统的初步的指导方针。他对计算机符号学的定义为:"符号学的一个分支,研究基于计算机的符号的特殊性质以及它们在使用中如何作用。"与计算科学通行的方法比较,Andersen 把计算机系统视为在某些语境下为特殊信递功能服务。在这方面,计算机符号学可以支持计算机发展的现行模式,现在主要设计以使用者为导向的界面。一个设计得好的界面应当减低计算机系统的复杂性,不产生新的不透明性,用户能利用这个系统但不必被迫处理与实际工作任务无关的问题。

一般人同意把计算机看作是技术,是工具,是媒体的看法。它与电影、电视、电话、书籍、漫画书、卡通等相同,它是传递信息、会话、请求、娱乐、教育、表达情感等的媒体。但 Andersen et al.(1993)认为计算机不是一般的工具或机器,它是非常灵活的多形态的媒体。它可以同时完成多种媒体的功能,如电子邮件系统、文字处理器、数据库、高级设计工具、涂料箱、计算器、电子书、游戏机等。按照这个观点,计算机基本上是传送者向接受者传递信息的媒体。但我们关注的是为某人代表某事的那些信号。从符号学角度看,基于计算机技术的一些特征值得研究,同时,符号学也成为研究计算机的最理想的科学方法。我们知道,计算机可以描写为根据一套操作规则处理数据,从而生成新的数据。但是所产生的数据是被作为信息阅读的,即根据社会规约被解读为指称某些事物,是被作为符号阅读的。因此,计算机系统也是产生符号的机器,也是符号系统,也是符号技术。正是这样,这应当是符号学关心的中心问题。基于计算机的符号的特征不同于所有其他任何已知符号。因此,有必要对计算机进行符号学研究。

为什么要如此提出这个问题呢?符号学传统上有三个研究领域:一,符号本身,包括不同的符号类型和构建与传递意义的不同方法;二,组织符号的系统的信码,包括信息递送,符号的编码和解码;三,利用符号的文化。为此,Andersen等提出应当:(1)研究基于计算机的符号,结合编程和界面设计讨论因计算机而产生的符号特性;(2)互动媒体的修辞学,处理美学的信码和新的信递媒介的组成,如互动小说和超文本;(3)在文化、历史和有组织的大语境下,分析计算机技术和计算机符号。

由此我们可以看到,人文科学一般着重于把计算机看作物体,很少注意它的表达方面。但Anderson等根据新的视角,考虑到所有三个方面,特别着重计算机的符号表达方面。

相比之下,Kress(2004)更强调人的因素。把计算机作为符号系统进行符号学分析主要指研究计算机系统和人的使用之间的关系。在这个意义上,计算机符号学分析符号的结构和功能、它们在人和计算机之间的信息传递的介入。通过分析人机互动,计算机符号学可为系统设计有规律地发现信递标准。因此计算机科学家也正在日益注意分析信息传递。设计既简单又友善的界面必须考虑硬件和软件的内部制约,也包括人机互动的制约。

四、符 号 资 源

符号系统实际上是符号资源(semiotic resource)系统,通过在可识别的、多半是习惯性的(有时是原创的)方法采用这些资源,人们从而得以进行有意义的活动(Lemke,1993)。这里所谓习惯性的方法指可确认为符号的构造(semiotic formations),是一个社团中的成员同时采用一些符号资源形成的经常的、可重复的、可识别的、有意义的、文化的和历史的特殊类型。如某一时期的文学语类是符号构造。同样,建筑风格、房子类型、宗教仪式、特定节日、饮食、衣着的特定样式,这些构造都可以定义为可行动的有规律的范式,对社会是有意义实践的范式。

根据 Lemke(1993)的介绍,话语构造是就语言资源而说的,社会符号构造则指包括语言在内的其他符号表达的社会意义。如讲话时的姿势、写作时的图形等。特定的语言学的语义或语法资源是语域,如特定的天气预报。除文学语类、非文学语类外,也可有不使用语言的单纯倚赖行动的语类(action genre)。我们自己文化的思想意识将符号资源的概念方面与真实的、自然的、普遍的、不突然变化的、绝对的事物结合起来。因此,符号资源是文化意义的潜势,能独立地将"社会文化"和"自然"结合起来,既可以"使其成为某种结果"(行动),也可以是"告诉人这是什么"(表达、知识)。与我们文化的意识形态不同的是,对符号资源的分析表明,"自然的"如同社会的一样,是"常规的";"真实的"与动作的结果一样,是"文化的"。我们同时进行社会的和自然的活动,实际上这不是两件事,而是一件事。"自然的"具有一个文化所有的特性,对观察者来说是可变的、相对的;就符号学来说,历史的、自然的东西是衍生自文化的事物。

Kress(2001)对此所持的立场是所有的模态(视觉的、姿态的、动作的),像语言一样,在社会使用过程中形成社会资源的模态。这里可以将韩礼德的语言是社会符号的理论扩展至其他模态中,也就是说,所有模态发展成产生意义的互相连接的可供选择的网络。当符号制造者在这些意义网络中进行选择,可视作符号制造者为了表达他在已知语境下想表达的意义所作决策的轨迹。这个轨迹就是符号制造者的兴趣所在(Halliday, 1985; Kress, 1997)。

Thibault(2004)对符号资源的研究比较具体。他从身体动力学的研究区分动态的和静态的:(1)动态的研究指面对面的互动和使用录像机;(2)静态的表达媒体,如文字+图片。传统上对笔录和口语的模态强调语言方面,而把其他资源,如姿势、语音音律、注视、动作等看作是"副语言的",不把这些看作是能与语言同时作用的完整的符号资源。

Baldry(2000)提出对每种符号资源所作的选择同时实现系统功能语言学的三大元功能,并整合其意义。在动态语篇如录像中,过去的问题是如何追踪各阶段的过渡,这要在时间过程中从不同符号资源中作突出哪一模态的选择。现在由于技术的发展这个问题可以处理了,我们可以作复杂的多模态化分析。他所研究的多模态化语类中的互动性符号资源有经济类语篇、动态和静态科学语篇、儿童故事、教育语料库、互联网、CNN 新闻广播、广告、卡通等。这种技术的使用在各种教育语境中也有应用，如超文本讲授诗歌或科技语篇、远程教育中动态编写系统的发展、供非本族语者学习英语的软件、语篇分析和翻译的软件、语言教师在线提取信息、语言分析和语言教学中语料库的使用等。

五、多模态符号的设计

制造语篇和识读语篇的过程都是设计的过程，这个过程是对从书写和书本统治时代沿袭下来的社会和符号的安排。书本和它的页面曾经是写作的场所，写作的逻辑曾经塑造页面的顺序和书本。现在这一局面被新的图像和屏幕超过了。当今占统治地位的媒体是屏幕，不管是游戏机、移动电话、个人电脑或者电视和录像。因此现在屏幕的逻辑正在塑造新的顺序和对屏幕的安排。虽然文字写作可以出现在屏幕上，但它从属于图像的逻辑，如同过去图像可出现于书本上，但从属于文字写作的逻辑。因此图像的逻辑将越来越塑造写作的出现和用途，这一过程已在公众信息传递的事例中出现。过去，作者的形象和写作的方式占统治地位；在新的安排中，设计者和图像的模式占统治地位(Kress, 2004)。

Kress(2004)重视设计者的作用。所有符号资源都具有社会意义，属于特定文化。它们表示意义的潜力被设计者经过思考的动作而被选择。多模态符号(词语、文字、信件、色彩、字体)的复杂信息反映了设计者的兴趣。设计者根据符号特殊的修辞目的，用尽各种招式来劝诱那些有机遇接触该信息的人们。页面/网址的设计者不再是权威性语篇的"作者"，但他是材料的提供者，按照想象中读者的所谓特点进行安排。设计者的力量是将材料集中，加工为访问者可提取的"信息"。安排方式要考虑访问者的兴趣。对访问者来说，"信息是个体选择的材料，经他们转换，成为可以解决有生世界问题的知识"。设计是在一定语境下进行的。在多模态信息传递中，关键是选择和相应的设计。如果表达和塑造信息时有多种方法，有待回答的问题是：就要传递的内容或意义来说，哪一种模态最好？哪一种模态在塑造所传播信息时最能符合设计者的兴趣？设计者的听众或他自己最喜爱哪一种媒体？在选择某个媒体或模态而不是其他时，设计者对自己的定位？所有这些都需要作出抉择，依靠设计者传递信息时对环境的估计，如广告、香水、饮料等。

根据新伦敦小组(New London Group, 2000)的观点，任何制造意义的过程基本上都是设计行为。一般有三个部分：第一，信递行为，我们根据"可资利用的设计"，择取某些符号资源和常规，如话语形式、语类和方言。第二，设计过程，这包括将符号资源转变成自己的声音，将老材料作新用途等。根据这一点，读和听，写和说是进行设计的实例，因为每个人都可利用可资利用的设计来产生意义，根据各自的兴趣和个人经验，将所读到和听到的材料转化成意义。第三，进行"重新设计"：由设计过程产生的资源或重新产生的意义，又可成为一种新的可资利用的设计，具有制造意义潜力的新的资源。这样，设计的观点不仅应用于原创性活动，更应当看作是日常经验的核心部分，因而这是教育过程中应当强调的重要成分(Williamson，2005)。

六、连　　贯

在设计互动中的多模态符号表达时，要考虑每一个模态如何被用来与其他模态一起产生意义。这个过程包括对每个模态的意义功能作进一步的观察和比较，方式是与共现的模态一起审视。Kress(2001)结合课堂的环境谈到三种做法：① 不同符号工具在教室内的作用：教师采用了什么样的课件，老师和学生与这些课件的互动。② 模态彼此之间的关系：通过共现的模态，并在上课过程中对模态的观察，认定模式的重复、再解释和转换。通过对出现情况的比较，认定人们的习惯性为。这些行为在特定时间、特定语境下发生，并有确定的功能。③ 模态之间的表达和信递的矛盾，如说的和做的矛盾。为什么在上课时的某一点上会引入动作？为什么它会促使教师和学生这么做？

应该说，最初教师的言语是突出的模态，它载有信息的中心意义。教师通过言语的方式或视觉的方式确定讨论的问题，决定是否有进行解释的必要。与言语同时出现的意象和动作体现了正在讲授的内容(如血液的连续循环活动和心脏的收缩)。教师的言语，结合他的动作和意象的使用，建立了循环的纲领式解释。

教师的身体，在白板上的图像和模型之间的过渡起到中介的作用。他的身体与图像重叠，他的模型与他的身体重叠。这样，言语、姿势和模态得到充分整合。教师的言语提供解释，他的姿势指明参与者，表示动作，突出言语的内容。模型提供对身体的分析性表达，作为讨论的具体部位以及身体的部分和整体的关系。最后，教科书中的图像提供更为详细的表达，对所有讲解过的内容做视觉的归纳。

不同的符号模态一起活动,通过一系列的语篇特征形成连贯的语篇。教师利用各种模态做相似性和对比性的比较:图像的或实际的,内部的或外部的,观点与实物。通过言语的、视觉的和姿势的描述的重复,在各模态之间实现了连贯。

连贯是由话语的参与者给予的。它具有统一的和有意义的性质。因此,话语分析是给语言片段以统一和意义的特性的问题寻找答案。话语分析就是探索连贯。我们既依靠语言形式(词汇和句法),和语篇的表面衔接,但最终是参与者给语篇以意义和统一。

七、多模态识读

多模态识读(Multiliteracy)指具有能阅读所能接触到的各种媒体和模态的信息,并能循此产生相应的材料,如阅读互联网或互动的多媒体。传统的以读写为主的识读能力在多媒体时代已不够用。其次,教育中的多模态化来自教室中不断增加使用的多种媒体,如图像操作软件、电子音乐、科学模拟、存在于计算机上的虚拟剧场等。多模态化和多元符号学试图给这些信递形式理论化,鉴别各种图像、词语和动作的模态如何互相倚赖,以产生整体意义(Williamson, 2005)。重要的是有时一种模态需要倚赖其他模态来完成信递行为,如没有口述的词语说明,图表会毫无意义;没有模型课件,教师用手做的节奏性动作也就没有意义,因而每一种模态,作为符号资源,对所做的表达都有贡献。学生的任务是将教师的各模式和符号资源转变为理解。

Spiliotopoulos(2005)对多模态识读有更宽广的视野,它指人们能从多种信息传递和信息网络理解各种模态的语篇,能发展批评性思维的技能,能与他人合作并帮助他们发展跨文化意识。已有的定性研究表明,在线互动可协助学生改进他们的写作和批判性思维技能,提高他们的跨文化意识(Spiliotopoulos, 2005; Algren, 2005)。

从现有材料看,多模态识读能力是多层次的。它包括(Andersen, 2005; Johnson, 2005; Joy, 2005; Miranda, 2005):

(1) 参与者能够在信息环境中适当地工作。解决网络环境下出现的常见问题。

(2) 通过使用信息技术,参与者能够检索所寻找的材料,完成与信息技术有关的各项任务,利用技术工具进行阅读和写作各种信息的共生形式(如打印物、图片、照片、录像、音响效果、音乐等),因为这些模态都是在计算机屏幕上用数字方法表达的,而不是传统的纸张。

(3) 批判性地和战略地管理和汇总来自各种数字网络材料库的知识。

(4) 参与者有责任心,受人尊敬,思想开放,能在电子世界中发挥作用,因而能很快并智慧地适应新环境下产生的各种社会问题。

(5) 为特定问题而成立的灵活的在线队伍能利用他们的专业技术互相协作。

(6) 对一个话题能表达综合的知识,采用技术工具,信息性的和劝诱的方法。

(7) 参与者能够对所处社会中信息技术环境(硬件、软件、教育等)如何起重要作用发表自己的意见。

(8) 多模态识读能力包括"非语篇写作",如新的学习方法,学习者能掌握生产技术。不同的技术形式可成为学习过程的工具。

(9) 参与者不仅能识读语篇信息,也有能力解释符号和图像,利用多媒体和其他技术工具如互联网,所有这些使我们能构建意义、学习和与他人互动。

值得注意的是 multiliteracies 这个词,也指多元识读(能力),在全球化的今天,用来描写语言和文化的多样性和对变异的尊重。虽然多元文化概念扩展了对知识的看法,它也加大了能接触不同"识读方法"和不能识读者的鸿沟。这样,识读能力有两层意思,文化识读能力和技术识读能力,后者就是多模态识读能力。

八、多模态化研究的重点

据 Simpson(2003) 报道,在 2003 年一次以多模态化为主题的国际应用语言学研究会上提出如下选题方向:多模态化和新的媒体;在学术和教育情境下的多模态化的应用;多模态化与识读实践;多模态化语料库的建立;多模态化和类型学;多模态化话语分析及其理论问题。

就多模态化话语分析而言,可进一步包括:互联网在话语分析中的作用;社会研究中的多模态话语分析;教育语境下的多模态话语分析;工作场所的多模态话语分析(Levine & Scollon，2004)。

参考文献

王铭玉：《语言符号学》，高等教育出版社 2004 年版。

Algren, Mark (2005), What is Multiliteracy? Multiliteracies for Collaborative Learning Environment. http://veltevens.blok.com/general/home//.

Andersen, P. Bogh (1990), *A Theory of Computer Semiotics: Semiotic Approaches to Construction and Assessment of Computer Systems*. Cambridge University Press, Cambridge.

Andersen, P. Bogh (2005), What is Multiliteracy? Multiliteracies for Collaborative Learning Environment. http://veltevens.blok.com/general/home//.

Andersen, P. Bogh, Berit Holmqvist & Jens, F. Jensen (1993) *The Computer as Medium*. Cambridge.

Baldry, Anthony (2000), *Multimodality and Multimediality in the Distance Learning Age*. Campobasso Palladino.

Beaugrande, Robert de (1991), *Linguistic Theory: The Discourse of Fundamental Works*. Harlow: Longman.

Bernsen, N. O. (2002), Multimodality in Language and Speech Systems — From Theory to Design Support Tool, in B. B. Granstrom, D. House, I. Karlsson (eds.), *Multimodality in Language and Speech Systems*. Dordrecht: Kluwer Academic Publishers.

Fiske, John (1982), *Introduction to Communication Studies*. 2nd edition. London: Routledge.

Guske, Iris (1998), Communication Studies: Communication Codes. To What Extent is Hallidayan "Social Semiotic Theory" Compatible with Saussure's Programme for Sociology? *Zurück zur Startseite*.

Halliday, M. A. K. (1978), *Language as a Social Semiotic*. London: Edward Arnold.

Halliday, M. A. K. (1985), *An Introduction to Functional Grammar*. London: Edward Arnold.

Holsanova, J. (1999), Olika perspektiv på språk, bild och deras samspel. Metodologiska reflexioner, (Different perspectives on multimodality. Methodological considerations) in Inger Haskå & Carin Sandqvist (eds.): *Alla Tiders Språk*. Lundastudier i nordisk språkvetenskap A 55. Lund University Press, Lund.

Johnson, Staci (2005), What is Multiliteracy? Multiliteracies for Collaborative Learning Environment. http://veltevens.blok.com/general/home//.

Joy, Lilia (2005), What is Multiliteracy? Multiliteracies for Collaborative Learning Environment. http://veltevens.blok.com/general/home//.

Kress, G. R. (1997), *Before Writing: Rethinking the Paths to Literacy*. Routledge: London.

Kress, G. R. (2001), Multimodality. A paper presented at the International Literacy Conference, Cape Town, 13-17 November.

Kress, G. R. (2004), Reading Images: Multimodality, Representation and New Media. A paper presented at *Expert Forum for Knowledge Presentation*.

Levine, Philip & Scollon, Ron (2004), *Discourse and Technology: Multimodal Discourse Analysis*. Georgetown University Press. Lemke Online Office.

Lemke, J. L. (1993), Discourse, Dynamics and Social Change, in *Language as Cultural Dynamics*: Special Issue of *Cultural Dynamics* (Halliday, Issue Editor).

Lemke, J. L. (2005), Important Theories for Research Topics on the Website. *J. L. Lemke Online Office*.

Martin, Bronwen & Felizitas Ringham (2000), *Dictionary of Semiotics*. London and New York: Cassell.

Miranda, Nobella (2005), What is Multiliteracy? Multiliteracies for Collaborative Learning Environent. http://veltevens.blok.com/general/home//.

New London Group (2000), A Pedagogy of Multiliteracies: Designing Social Futures, in Bill Cope and Mary Kalantzis.

Saussure, Ferdinand de (1974), *Course in General Linguistics*. Glasgow: Fontana.

Scollon, Ron & Levine, Philip (2004), *Multimodal Discourse Analysis as the Confluence of Discourse and Technology*. Washington DC.: Georgetown

University Press.

Simpson, J. E. B. (2003), *BALL/CUP Seminar on Multimodality and Applied Linguistics*. London, Reading, United Kingdom, 18/July/2003-19/July/2003.

Spiliotopoulos, Vakua (2005), Developing Multiliteracy in Adult ESL Learners Using On-line Forums, *International Journal of the Humanities*.

Thibault, Paul (2004), Body Dynamics and the Multimodal Integration of Meaning across Space-time Scales, A paper presented at the 9th International Pragmatics Conference.

Williamson, Ben (2005), What Are Multimodality, Multisemiotics and Multiliteracies? — A Brief Guide to Some Jargon. *NESTA Futurelab*. Online.

 方法谈：

如何选题并确保选题的理论价值和应用价值？

2004年，我为王铭玉教授的《语言符号学》一书写过序。①正如我在多个场合说过，为他人写序实际上也是自己向每位作者学习的过程。就王铭玉的《语言符号学》，我在序中说过如下的体会：

> 如今，我们一方面认识到语言是全部符号事实中的一个特殊系统，对语言学的研究推动了对符号学的研究。对符号学的认识加深了我们对语言的认识。另一方面又开拓了我们对其他符号系统的研究。这就是说，符号学有广阔的目标，它的理论旨在探索意义的生成。任何意义，不仅是书面语的意义，诸如视觉、听觉、嗅觉、味觉、触觉，以至抽象的模型、结构、主体意识都应纳入它的视线之内。

从上面的摘录中，我对符号学研究已经初步形成一些概念：语言只是符号的一种，语言学隶属于符号学，符号学研究的本质是人们对意义生成和交流的探讨，

---

① 王铭玉：《语言符号学》，高等教育出版社2004年版。

人类表达意义有多种模态,每一种模态又得依赖人体的各个部位或各种物质手段。所有这些,都是人类不同民族、不同社会群体在相互交际过程中逐步形成的共识。正是因为这样的认识启发我在2007年写了《社会符号学研究中的多模态化》一文。坦率地说,我对问题的探索和认识的提高就是这么一步一步走过来的。

王铭玉先生在介绍索绪尔(Saussure)开创的形式主义符号学时,谈到国外其他一些学者的观点,如代表英美传统功的皮尔斯(Peirce)发展了诸如图标、索引和语符等符号范畴,也谈到媒介、对象、解释三位一体的三角关系。由于出现"解释"的词语,意味着对符号做出解释,必然涉及解释者,必然涉及"人"的思维。这是一个进步,但王铭玉接着指出,皮尔斯强调作为个体的人,忽视作为社会成员的人。

正是由于王铭玉先生的启示,促使我联想到导师韩礼德(M. A. K. Halliday)和他倡导的社会符号学理论。语言既表达意义,也积极将社会结构和系统符号化。语言的这种双重功能使意义的表达方式多种多样,"从后院的闲言碎语到叙述体小说到史诗般的诗歌"①。这样,社会有意义的活动构成各种社会符号系统,即各种文化。文化就是相互连接的对社会具有意义的实践系统。

在此基础上,我认识到我们依赖这种系统使这些实践和其他实践具有意义。这比单纯研究符号即意义关系的系统更为基本。也因为这个原因,社会符号学没有必要区分理论符号学和应用符号学。反之,它与话语分析、多媒体分析、教育研究、文化人类学、政治社会学有更紧密的关系。

我进一步注意到社会符号学也突出这样的观点,不同社会不同文化的模态(mode)和媒体(medium)不尽相同,如我们感受客观世界的视觉、听觉、触觉、味觉、嗅觉是不同的感知模式,但眼、耳、手、舌、鼻则是不同的媒体。随着社会和文化的变化和发展,表达思想和意义的模态不时发生变化;至于具体的媒体,如写字的纸和墨,歌舞演出时的道具,教室中的黑板和白板,以至于扩音器、录音机、电视机、录像机、投射仪、计算机变化更大。这些都需要我们密切注意,深入研究。因此,韩礼德1978年关于信息传递的社会符号学理论推动了多模态的表达,即多模态学的研究。

多模态化意味着表达同样的意义可以采用不同模态。中华文化中的"手舞

---

① Halliday, M. A. K. Language as a Social Semiotic. London: Edward Arnold. 1978.

足蹈,有声有色",以及国画中往往配有诗文和印章,都说明国人对多模态学的先知先觉。今天,我们应该进一步关注它的用途。许多学科都在研究多模态化这个课题,如语篇分析、界面设计、人机对话等。在理论上,学术界已把多模态化的分析研究整理为七个视角,即不同模态之间的差异、分析范畴、主次、形式化、感知、复制和互动。

与多模态化相对应的是多媒体化,其基本原则是所有意义的产生渗透于诸如语言、姿态、描写、动作等可区别的理想的符号资源系统之间,因为意义产生既是符号实践,也是物质过程。科学技术的发展已明确告知我们,模态和媒体的关系归根结底是话语和技术的关系,两者存在着内在的联系。它关系到我们对信息或语料的收集,也关系到对话和语篇的生成。这是因为任何话语都具有多模态的固有特性;这方面的研究有助于发展话语的新形式,如互联网、线上会议等。

1990 年,Anderson 提出了计算机符号学的理论。[①]他把计算机符号学定义为:"符号学的一个分支,研究基于计算机的符号的特殊性质以及它们在使用中如何作用。"与计算科学通行的方法比较,Andersen 把计算机系统视为在某些语境下为特殊信递功能服务。这是因为计算机可以同时完成多种媒体的功能,如电子邮件系统、文字处理器、数据库、高级设计工具、涂料箱、计算器、电子书、游戏机等。因此,符号学关注对基于计算机技术的一些特征进行研究,同时符号学也成为研究计算机的最理想的科学方法. 人们难以想象,仅仅三十多年,我们已经进入人工智能 ChatGPT 的时代。这说明计算机符号学研究的重要性。

从计算机符号学的飞速发展让我意识到,这得益于符号资源(semiotic resource)系统的发展。上面提到的社会符号学说明,符号的构造是一个社团中的成员同时采用一些符号资源形成的经常的、可重复的、可识别的、有意义的、文化的和历史的特殊类型。正因为符号资源的丰富积累和运转速度的飞速加快,人类较多的思想意识与"社会文化"和"自然"得以结合起来。这就是说,韩礼德的语言是社会符号的理论已扩展至其他模态中,所有模态发展成产生意义的互相连接的可供选择的网络。由此可见,对每种符号资源所作的选择实际上同时实现系统功能语言学的三大元功能,即概念功能、人际功能和语篇功能。

那么,多模态符号如何进行设计呢?过去主要依赖书写和书本。这一局面

---

① Anderson,P. Bogh. *A Theory of Corpus Semiotics. Semiotics Approaches to Construction and Assessment of Computer Systems*. Cambridge:Cambridge University Press. 1990.

现在已被图像和屏幕超越,尽管文字写作可以出现在屏幕上,它已从属于图像的逻辑。多模态符号(词语、文字、信息、图案、色彩)的选用决定于哪一种模态最为适用?最能表达设计者试图表达的意义?任何制造意义的过程基本上都是设计行为。

在设计互动中的多模态符号表达时,我们必须考虑不同模态之间的"连贯",这才能产生所期待的正确意义。以课堂教学为例,老师在课堂上采用的课件,老师与学生之间对课件的互动,各种模态之间的关系,都涉及多模态教学的效果。

上述多模态化的讨论又将我引向"多模态识读"(Multiliteracy)的概念。它指社会群体应当具有能阅读所接触到的各种媒体和模态所表达的信息和意义,特别是多种模态融合而成的整体意义。由此可见,现代化教育必须考虑多媒体识读能力的培养。它更要求在理解各种模态语篇所表达意义的基础上,能发展批评性思维的技能,能与他人合作并帮助他人发展跨文化意识。因此,多模态识读能力是多层次的,就现有认识,多达九种。

就今后研究的趋向有多个方面,如多模态化和新的媒体,在学术和教育情境下的多模态化的应用,多模态化与识读实践,多模态化语料库的建立,多模态化和类型学,多模态化话语分析及其理论问题。

需要特别关注的是随着人工智能的发展,国内外已掀起对 ChatGPT 的热潮!它不仅要表达意义,而且对意义能进行一定的思考和分析,并进行整理。

韩礼德的语篇连贯标准
——外界的误解与自身的不足*

朱永生**

摘要：语篇的连贯以及如何连贯是话语分析的重大课题，韩礼德较早提出连贯标准。然而，语言学界对他的观点持有不同的看法，本文首先简要介绍韩礼德的连贯标准，然后指出外界的种种误解和韩礼德观点本身的不足，最后对他的连贯标准提出一些修改意见。

关键词：连贯标准；误解；不足

连贯标准的讨论和确立以及它与语篇的识别和解释之间的关系，一直是话语分析的重要课题之一。

如何研究语篇连贯，语言学界有两种方法：一是研究语言本身即语篇所包含的各种衔接手段对连贯所起的作用；二是既注意语言形式本身的使用和变化，又注意情景因素，文化背景和认知能力等非语言因素对语篇连贯的影响与制约。采用前一种方法的代表人物有维多森（Widdowson）、布朗（Brown）和于尔（Yule）等，主张后一种方法的代表人物则有韩礼德（Halliday）、哈桑（Hasan）和但尼什（Danes）等。在国内，有些学者看来正从后一种方法转向前一种方法（如胡壮麟等，1989；张德禄，1993；朱永生，1995、1996）。

就时间而言，较早提出连贯标准的是韩礼德和哈桑。他们在其合著的《英语

---

* 原载《外语教学与研究》1997年第1期。
** 朱永生，复旦大学教授、博士生导师，国际学术刊物 Linguistics and Human Sciences 及《中国外语》等刊物编委、全国高校功能语言学研究会名誉副会长，曾任苏州大学外语系主任、复旦大学外文系主任、复旦大学国际文化交流学院院长、国际系统功能语言学研究会执委会委员、国务院学科评议组成员、全国高校外语教学指导委员会委员、斯德哥尔摩大学孔子学院理事长、教育部汉语国际教育硕士教学指导委员会委员等。研究方向为功能语言学和话语分析。

中的衔接》(1976)一书中,多次围绕衔接的作用谈到语篇的连贯标准。此书出版以后,语言学界对他们的观点作出了不同的反应。赞同者有之,批评者也不乏其人。在批评意见中,有的不无道理,有的则值得推敲。之所以说值得推敲,主要原因是批评者们对韩礼德的观点存在着这样那样的误解。

本文的任务是首先客观介绍韩礼德有关语篇连贯标准的论述,然后试图说明误解所在,分析韩礼德的观点本身有何不足,最后对他的观点提出了几点修改意见。

一、韩礼德有关语篇连贯标准的论述

韩礼德是在论述衔接与语篇相互关系时对语篇连贯提出衡量标准的,他的基本观点体现在《英语中的衔接》一书的几段话中:

(一)衔接概念可由语域(register)概念来补充,因为这两者加在一起能有效地对语篇概念进行界定。语篇是一段在衔接和语域两方面都连贯的话语:它与语境是连贯的,因而在语域方面是前后一致的;它自身是连贯的,因而是衔接的。这两个条件缺一不可,其中任何一条得到满足并不能保证另一条也得到满足(参见 Halliday & Hasan, 1976:23)。

(二)语篇特征(texture)远远超出了衔接的范围。建立各种衔接关系是语篇构筑过程中一个必不可少但不是唯一的组成部分。另外还有两个组成部分:一是句子的语篇结构即句子及其成分是如何根据本身与周围其他句子之间的关系组织起来的;一是语篇的宏观结构,这种结构使话语成为某一类型的语篇,如会话,叙述,诗歌,商业信函(参见 Halliday & Hasan, 1976:234)。

(三)要达到连贯,语篇必须前后衔接,但不仅如此,它还必须按照它所属的语域所允许的范围使用各种衔接手段(参见 Halliday & Hasan, 1976:318)。

从上面的论述可以看出,韩礼德认为语篇连贯必须满足两个条件:一是上下衔接,二是符合语域的要求。所谓上下衔接,就是通过照应(reference)、省略(ellipsis)、替代(substitution)和连接(conjunction)等语法手段与重复(repetition)、同义(synonymy)、上义(hyponymy)和搭配(collocation)等词汇手段把语篇中的不同成分从意义上联系起来。

二、外界的误解

自从韩礼德提出上述观点后,它们得到了许多人的支持与赞赏,也招来了不少人相当尖锐的批评。

应该承认,有些批评意见是确有道理的。但是,在持批评意见的人当中,确实有人对韩礼德的观点存在一定的误解。在笔者看来,只看韩礼德提出的第一条连贯标准,忽略第二条标准,是产生误解的主要原因。

虽然韩礼德不止一次地讲到语域一致对于语篇连贯的重要性,但这一点往往被忽视,结果是创造出这样那样的充满衔接手段但意义不连贯的所谓例证来批驳韩礼德的观点。其中最典型的莫过于安克维斯特(Enkvist,1978:110)提供的例证:

(1) I bought a Ford. The car in which President Wilson rode down the Champs Elysees was black. Black English has been widely discussed. The discussions between the presidents ended last week. A week has seven days. Every day I feed my cat. Cats have four legs. The cat is on the mat. Mat has three letters.

这个例子已被国内外许多学者视为批评韩礼德的有力例证而多次反复引用。的确,这段话里含有大量的衔接手段,但意义毫不连贯。于是,得出的结论是:衔接手段的使用不能保证语篇的连贯。然而,安克维斯特及其支持者们在对韩礼德展开批评时,忘记了两点:第一,韩礼德从一开始就明确指出,衔接不是连贯的唯一手段或标准;第二,韩礼德认为连贯的语篇在语域方面必须是一致的,而在语域方面保持一致的重要条件是整段话语有一个宏观结构,而任何一个宏观结构都必须有一个中心话题。对此,韩礼德(1976)早就说过,"话语不是杂乱无章地从一个话题跳到另一个话题,它总是以给定话题的连贯性和话题展开的可能性有规律地、合理地向前发展"。如果我们把刚刚讲到的这两点都考虑到,就不难看出,例(1)及类似的例子并没有多少说服力。此外,批评者们还忽略了一个问题。这就是人们在使用语言进行交际时,前言后语一般都是相关的,它们是同一个宏观结构中的不同组成部分。像上面这样说一句话就换一个话题的现象,在实际语言使用过程中是极难找到的。

在国外语言学界,产生误解的不仅是安克维斯特,布朗和于尔(1983)在论述应该如何解释语篇时,发表过这样的观点:所谓语篇,就是"受话者和读者视为语篇的话语",在把一段话语或短文作为语篇解释时,受话者和读者"力图使所描写的一系列事件形成一幅连贯的画面,把这些事件联成一体,而不是只看话语中有没有语言上的连接(verbal connections)"。孤立地看,布朗和于尔的这种看法是正确的。但韩礼德并没有要人们只根据语言形式的连接与否来决定一段话语是否算得上是语篇。

三、自身不足

上一节指出了语言学界对韩礼德的观点存在的各种误解以及产生这些误解的根本原因。现在谈问题的另一面。这就是韩礼德提出的语篇连贯标准本身存在的不足。在笔者看来,不足之处主要有如下三个方面。

1. 对连贯的概念缺乏明确的界定

虽然韩礼德对连贯提出了自己的标准,但对什么叫连贯却从未下过明确的定义。他(1976:1)只是说过如下一段含义比较模糊的话:"必定存在语篇特有的、其他地方找不到的某些特征;因此如同语言学描写中常见的那样,我们将论述操本族语者已经'知道'但不知道自己已经知道的现象。"应该说,读了这段话,对什么叫连贯还是不甚了了。

与维多森等人不同,韩礼德是把连贯作为一个常用词而不是一个专门术语使用的,读者对连贯的确切含义只能凭自己的直觉去认识,去体会。这样就难免产生仁者见仁智者见智的现象。以自己的标准去衡量别人的标准,由此产生分歧和误解也就不足为怪了。

2. 对语域一致缺乏足够的论述

韩礼德的确多次讲到语域一致对于语篇连贯的重要性。然而,对于什么叫作语域一致,韩礼德只是三言两语地略过,使人不知道他所说的语域一致是否就是指语篇的宏观结构,还是指句子结构。如果是句子结构,是指句子的内部结构,还是指句子与句子之间的结构。如果是后者,是指主位结构,还是指信息结构,或者其他什么结构。根据笔者的理解,韩礼德所说的语域一致既指宏观结构,又指主位结构和信息结构等微观结构。在笔者看来,韩礼德应该把语域一致这个概念讲得更加清楚一些,说明它到底指什么,包含哪些组成部分,这些组成部分又是如何使语篇上下连贯的。只有这样,才能使人们理解语域一致的真正含义,从而在衡量语篇是否连贯时对语域一致给予足够的重视。

3. 过分强调了衔接的作用

韩礼德以及哈桑(1976,1985)先后多次强调衔接对连贯的重要性,认为衔接是连贯的必备条件之一。然而,语言交际中的许多实例都证明,连贯的语段不一定是衔接的,如维多森(1979)举过的例子:

(2) A: Can you go to Edinburgh tomorrow?
    B: B. E. A. pilots are on strike.

此外,有些语段虽然含有衔接手段,但上下文的连贯仅仅依靠这种衔接手段的使用还是无法建立,如例(3):

(3) A: Does the baby cry at night?
    B: He's two months old.

在这段对话中,代词 he 用来指代上文中的 the baby,从而在两个词项之间建立起相互照应的关系。这个代词的使用,只能说明 AB 两人谈论的是同一个人,即双方知道的那个婴儿,但不能在"婴儿夜间啼哭"和"两个月大"两个命题之间建立意义上的联系,换言之,不能解释这一问一答是否连贯。就这个具体例子而言,连贯的建立必须依靠语言活动参与者调用自己的世界知识来解决。

四、几点修改意见

针对韩礼德连贯标准的不足之处,笔者想提出以下几点修改意见。

1. 明确连贯的真正含义

在讨论连贯标准之前,首先必须确定连贯的定义。

事实上,有些语言学家已经注意到这个问题。van Dijk(1977:93)认为:"连贯是话语的一种语义特征,它依赖的是每个单句的解释与其他句子的解释之间的联系。"Crystal(1987:119)认为,连贯指的是"语篇中所表达的各种概念和关系必须彼此相关,从而使我们能对语篇的深层意义进行合理的推理"。Widdowson(1985:52)在区分衔接和连贯这两个概念时对连贯作了更加明确的界定。他说:"衔接指的是语篇构筑过程中借助各种结构上的运作把不同的命题联系在一起的方式,而连贯指的则是这些命题的言外功能(illocutionary function)以及这些命题如何被用来创造不同类型的话语,如报告性话语、描写性话语和解释性话语等等。如果读者认为话语中按某种顺序出现的命题与他自己能接受的言外功能做到彼此相联,那么他就认为这段话语是连贯的。"

在笔者看来,连贯是一个语义概念,它指的是话语内不同组成部分之间在意义上的联系。这种联系存在于两个不同的层次之中:一是存在于句子与句子之间,更确切地说,是不同句子所含的命题之间;二是存在于话语的真实意图(intention)之间。具体地说,是以下两点:

(i) 话语内不同组成部分所表达的命题之间彼此相关,所谓相关,就是两个或两个以上命题之间有时序、因果、引证或举例等意义上的联系。这里的意义就是话语的本义(meaning)。如例(4)中两个命题之间的递进关系,例(5)中的因果关系:

(4) John is still a bachelor now. He is going to get married next week.

(5) John is still a bachelor now. He is happy and gay.

例(6)不能被接受,原因是两个命题是彼此矛盾,无法共存:

(6) ? John is still a bachelor now. So he is going to get a divorce next week.

需要说明的是,这里所说的命题之间的相关,不仅指相邻的两个句子所含命题的关联,而且指整段话语各个不同命题可以被纳入一个意义的框架。换言之,命题的相关不仅是线性的(linear),而且是整体的(global)。

(ii) 话语内不同组成部分所表达的真正意图彼此相关。所谓真正意图,就是话语的言外之义(illocutionary force),即话语的语用意义(message)。

这个定义如能被接受,便可用来解释为什么语言交际过程中有许多缺乏衔接手段、表面上脱节的话语,在实际上却是前后连贯的,如本文的例(2)及例(7)和例(8):

（7）A：There's the doorbell.

　　B：I'm in the bathroom.

（8）A：What do you think of the play?

　　B：It is a nice theatre.

诸如例(9)这样的语段,应视为不连贯,因为无论是从命题还是言外之义的角度考虑,都无法把上下文联系起来：

（9）John is still a bachelor now. The moon will come out next week.

在笔者看来,话语只要能符合上面任何一条标准,便可视为连贯。当然,同一段话语,尤其是那些表面不连贯的话语,有可能在有些人看来是连贯的,在另一些人看来却是不连贯的,如(10)：

（10）Linus：Do you want to play with me, Violet?

　　　Violet：You're younger than me.

　　　Linus：(puzzled) She didn't answer my question.

这类现象的产生与受话者和讲话者之间的共有知识,受话者的世界知识和认知能力有关。在例(10)中,在 Violet 看来,她的回答与 Linus 的问题之间是连贯的,其言外之义是："我不愿意和比我岁数小的人一起玩,你的岁数比我小,所以我不愿意和你一起玩",或者是"我不喜欢你,不愿意和你一起玩,不过不想明说,于是拿年龄悬殊作为借口搪塞过去"。而作为受话者的 Linus 不知道对方有不愿意和岁数小的人玩这个习惯或不知道对方不喜欢自己这件事,所以无法把对方的回答与自己的问题联系起来。从这个例子可以清楚地看到,共有知识的掌握和及时正确的提取,往往是理解语篇是否连贯的重要保障。

2. 修正衔接与连贯之间的关系

既然不含有衔接手段的话语在意义上有可能是连贯的,语言形式衔接与否就不能像韩礼德那样被视为连贯的必备条件。

在笔者看来,甚至不应该把衔接看作连贯的前提,而应当把它视为语篇连贯可能使用的手段。这就是说,只有语篇在意义上连贯了,才谈得上衔接手段如何促进语篇的产生和解释。这样看问题,并不意味着对韩礼德衔接理论研究的全盘否认。恰恰相反,笔者认为韩礼德的研究成果向人们全面揭示了英语语篇中的不同成分之间是如何通过明晰的语言形式相互联系的。这对于英语语篇连贯方式的研究本身,以及语言教学和翻译等活动,都具有重要的指导意义。在韩礼德之前,没有任何一个语言学家对英语的衔接手段作过如此系统而详尽的描写。

3. 进一步阐明语域一致性的含义及其在语篇中的具体要求

韩礼德和哈桑(1976:22—23)对语域下过明确的定义:"语域是一组意义,是语义模式的组合,这些语义模式通常是根据特定的条件提取的,同时提取的还有用来表达这些意义的词语和结构","语域是由语言特征组成的,这些特征与一组情景特征即话语范围(field)、话语基调(tenor)和话语方式(mode)有特别的联系"。后来,他们(1985:38—39)又进一步指出:"语域是一个语义概念,可定义为若干意义的组合。这些意义与话语范围,话语基调和话语方式等情景因素的组合有着特别的联系。"他们还根据开放的程度把语域分成开放型和封闭型两类,并指出这种区分是相对的,语言中没有绝对开放的语域。

然而,在语域一致这个问题上,韩礼德等人只是强调它对语篇连贯的重要性,至于说它到底指哪些内容,缺少足够的论述。在我们看来,语域一致主要指以下三个方面:

(i) 上下文组织符合该类语篇通常的组织方式,检查的依据是语篇的类型结构;

(ii) 语篇的线性联系即句际之间的语义联系,检查的依据是相邻主位结构之间的变化和新旧信息的分布;

(iii) 语篇的整体联系,检查的依据是通篇有一个能包容语篇内所有小话题(subtopics)的大话题,即能把全篇的内容置于其中的认知框架。

参考文献

Brown, G. & G. Yule (1983), *Discourse Analysis*. Cambridge: Cambridge University Press.

Crystal, D. (1987), *The Cambridge Encyclopedia of Language*. Cambridge: Cambridge University Press.

van Dijk, T. A. (1977), *Text and Context: Explorations in the Semantics and Pragmatics of Discourse*. London: Longman.

Enkvist, N. E. (1978), Coherence, pseudo-coherence, and non-coherence, in

Ostman, J. O., ed., *Cohesion and Semantics*, Abo Akademi Foundation, Abo.

Halliday, M. A. K. & R. Hasan (1976), *Cohesion in English*. London: Longman.

Halliday, M. A. K. & R. Hasan (1985), *Language, Context and Text: A spects of Language as a Socio-Semantic Perspective*. Victoria: Deakin University Press.

Halliday, M. A. K. (1985), *An Introduction to Functional Grammar*. London: Edward Arnold.

Martin, J. R. (1992), *English Text*. Philadelphia: John Benjamins Publishing Company.

Sperber, D. & D. Wilson (1986), *Relevance: Communication and Cognition*. Cambridge: Harvard University Press.

程雨民:《英语使用中的表面不连贯》,《外国语》1986 年第 4 期。

胡壮麟、朱永生、张德禄:《系统功能语法概论》,湖南教育出版社 1989 年版。

胡壮麟:《语篇的衔接与连贯》,上海外语教育出版社 1992 年版。

林纪诚:《试论语篇连贯性的条件》,《现代外语》1988 年第 4 期。

林纪诚:《语义连贯的语用模式》,《外语教学》1989 年第 2 期。

朱永生:《衔接理论的发展与完善》,《外国语》1995 年第 3 期。

朱永生:《语篇连贯的内部条件》,《现代外语》1996 年第 3 期。

 方法谈:

如何从质疑中萌生选题?

一、引言

所有的科学研究都离不开正确的研究方法,语言学也概莫能外。研究方法的具体选择与使用取决于语言学家的语言观及其研究目的。无论是大家名人,还是初入门者,都不可能通过一篇论文来解决语言学的所有问题,只能根据理论意义或实用价值来选择一个具体的研究课题。一旦课题明确之后,方法便成了解决问题的关键。如果自己提不出新的方法,就必须从现有的方法中选最适合自己的一种。例如,理论语言学使用了数理逻辑的方法、应用语言学使用了教育测量和统计的方法,心理语言学使用了心理测量的方法,社会语言学(包括文化语言学)使用了社会学的调查方法,计算语言学使用了计算机的方法,神经语言学使用了神经生理和解剖学的方法,转换生成语言学使用了理性主义的方法,系统功能语言学使用了建构主义的方法,等等(参见桂诗春、宁春岩,1997;刘润清,2002;朱永生,2017)。下面将以本篇论文为例,从为什么要写这篇文章和如何写好这篇文章两个角度,与年轻一代的学者们分享一下当初的想法和做法,希望能以小见大,对大家有所启发。

二、为什么要写这篇文章?

1976年,韩礼德和哈桑合著的 *Cohesion in English* 一书由朗门出版社出版。两位作者认为,任何一个语篇都具有"语篇特征"(texture),而构成这种特征的主要方式便是衔接。他们把英语中的衔接手段大致分为词汇衔接和语法衔接两个大类,其中词汇衔接包括同义关系/反义关系、上下义关系/局部与整体关系、搭配等手段,语法衔接包括照应、替代、省略和替代等手段,并对所有衔接手段进行了前所未有的穷尽性描写,成为语篇语言学发展道路上的一个里程碑。然而,该书出版后不久,便遭到了一些语言学家的质疑,其中最具代表性的是 N. E. Enkvist 和 Widdowson。

Enkvist(1978)的观点是衔接并非语篇连贯的充分条件,例证是:

I bought a Ford. The car in which President Wilson rode down the Champs Elysees was black. Black English has been widely discussed. The discussions between the presidents ended last week. A week has seven days. Every day I feed my cat. Cats have four legs. The cat is on the mat. Mat has three letters.

Widdowson(1979)的观点则是衔接并非语篇连贯的唯一条件,例证是:

A: Can you go to Edinburgh tomorrow?
B: B. E. A. pilots are on strike.

有些读者接受了上面两位学者的观点,由此得出了衔接既不是语篇连贯的充分条件,也不是语篇连贯的唯一条件的结论,从而彻底否定了韩礼德和哈桑的衔接理论的学术价值。这样的情况使我陷入了沉思,这个理论真的一无是处吗?批评者对衔接理论的理解是否全面而正确?衔接理论本身是否做到了尽善尽美,无懈可击?在反复阅读和认真思考之后,我发现上面两个疑惑的答案都是否定的,由此萌生了从外界的误解和自身的不足这两个方面来阐明韩礼德的语篇连贯标准的想法。

三、如何写好这篇文章?

第一步工作是认真看待 Enkvist 和 Widdowson 提出的批评意见,并仔细研读韩礼德和哈桑的相关观点,然后对这些批评意见的正确性进行判断。

第二步工作是指出 Enkvist 和 Widdowson 对衔接理论的误解。针对 Enkvist 的观点,我以韩礼德和哈桑提出的语域(register)一致性即话题统一也是必不可少的语篇特征这个原则为依据,指出 Enkvist 所提供的语料不仅属于非自然生成的自编产物,而且明显违背了语域一致性原则,难以自圆其说;针对 Widdowson 的观点,指出韩礼德和哈桑从来没有说过衔接是语篇连贯的唯一条件,并同时指出,在篇幅较长的语篇内,衔接手段的使用乃是十分常见的现象,从而认为 Widdowson 的批评缺乏足够的理据。

第三步工作是分析了韩礼德和哈桑的衔接理论自身存在的两点不足:一是过分强调了衔接的作用;二是未能对连贯提供明确的界定。

第四步工作是针对外界的误解与衔接理论自身的不足提出了三点建议:① 明确连贯的真正含义;② 修正衔接与连贯的关系;③ 进一步阐明语域一致性的含义及其在语篇中的具体要求。

四、结语

《韩礼德的语篇连贯标准:外界的误解与自身的不足》这篇文章发表后产生了积极的反响,对丰富理论衔接理论发挥了一定的推动作用。之所以如此,是因为该文达到了以下三点要求:① 题目不大,但具有明确的针对性,做到了有的放矢;② 根据课题的需要,使用了对比和甄别的方法找出了批评者与韩礼德之间的分歧所在,做到了言之有据;③ 在揭开外界的误解和分析韩礼德的语篇连贯标准自身不足的基础上,提出了自己的改进建议,做到了言之有物。

参考文献

Enkvist, N. E. Coherence, pseudo-coherence, and non-coherence, in Ostman, J. O. (ed), *Cohesion and Semantics*. Abo: Abo Akademi Foundation, 1978.

Halliday, M. A. K. & R. Hasan. *Cohesion in English*. London: Longman, 1976.

Widdowson, H. G. *Explorations in Applied Linguistics*. Oxford: Oxford University Press, 1979.

桂诗春、宁春岩:《语言学方法论》,外语教学与研究出版社1997年版。

刘润清:《西方语言学流派》,外语教学与研究出版社2002年版。

朱永生:《韩礼德的语篇连贯标准:外界的误解与自身的不足》,《外语教学与研究》1997年第1期,第20—24页。

朱永生:《系统功能语言学札记》,上海外语教育出版社2017年版。

从语言信息结构视角重新认识"把"字句[*]

陆俭明[**]

摘要： 本文首先指出目前"把"字句教学之不足，由此提出从语言信息结构视角重新认识"把"字句的新思路。文章对语言信息结构作了简要介绍，并提出了汉语句子信息结构所遵循的八个准则。接着文章从语言信息结构这一视角分析了表"处置"义的"把"字句，指出从信息传递的角度看，表"处置"义的"把"字句的特点在于：（一）要让"处置者"为话题；（二）要让"处置结果"作为信息聚焦点；（三）运用介词"把"其目的是能自由地将"处置对象"引入句子内，同时表示"处置"的强影响性和说话者的主观认定性，由此凸显"处置结果"。文章最后指出，如果我们能将"把"字句在语言信息结构上与其他句式的差异清楚地告诉外国学生，如果我们能将"把"字句在语言信息传递上的独特性告诉外国学生，这无疑将有助于我们走出"把"字句教学的困境。

关键词： "把"字句；语言信息结构；句子信息结构遵循准则

一、从"把"字句教学一直令人有挫败感说起

"把"字句在现代汉语中是一种很重要的句式。无论在汉语句法研究中还是

---

[*] 原载《语言教学与研究》2016年第1期。本文得到北京大学中国语言学研究中心承担的教育部人文社会科学重点研究项目"现代汉语构式知识库建设及其应用研究"（项目批准号：13JJD740001）经费的资助。

[**] 陆俭明，北京大学中文系教授、博士生导师，现兼任国家语委咨询委员会委员、国家语委语言文字标准审订委员会委员。曾任世界汉语教学学会会长、国际中国语言学学会会长、中国语言学会副会长、北京大学汉语语言学研究中心主任、北京大学文科学术委员会委员、北京大学人文学院学术委员会委员、新加坡教育部课程发展署华文顾问。研究领域涉及现代汉语的本体研究和应用研究及相关理论研究，在学界被誉为20世纪中国现代汉语语法研究八大家之一。

在汉语教学中,"把"字句一直是一个比较受重视的句式。可是,教学实践告诉我们,外国学生在做"把"字句的造句练习时,一般都能造出符合老师所讲的有关"把"字句的语法规则的"把"字句来;但是在实际说话、写作中,老是用不好"把"字句(田靓,2012)。普遍的毛病是,不该用"把"字句的地方用上了"把"字句,而该用"把"字句的地方却又没有用。马真(2008)在《在汉语教学中要重视词语使用的语义背景》一文中就曾举过这样两个留学生的很典型的跟"把"字句相关的偏误句:

> (1) ＊洪水是退了,但是眼前是一片不好的景象:洪水把村舍的房屋冲倒了一大半,把猪、鸡、羊都淹死了,空气里充满了难闻的臭味儿;洪水把成堆的木材也几乎都冲光了,……
>
> (2) ＊玛丽是个勤快的孩子,每天都是她最早起来。等我们起床,早饭已经被她准备好了,屋子也已经被她整理得干干净净。

马真(2008)指出,就一个个小句孤立来看,都符合语法,但是例(1)冒号以后的部分,是要具体描绘洪水过后不好的景象,按说应顺着上文的意思,用表示遭受义的"被"字句,不宜用"把"字句,可是却用了好几个"把"字句,使前后文气很不协调、很不连贯。这个句子宜改为:

> (1′) 洪水是退了,但是眼前是一片不好的景象:村舍的房屋被洪水冲倒了一大半,猪、鸡、羊都被淹死了,空气里充满了难闻的臭味儿;成堆的木材也几乎都被洪水冲光了,……

而例(2)是该用"把"字句而没有用。例(2)的后一句是来具体描述说明玛丽的勤快的,按上下文的意思,这里宜用表示积极处置的"把"字句,不该用"被"字句。该句宜改为:

> (2′) 玛丽是个勤快的孩子,每天都是她最早起来。等我们起床,她已经把早饭准备好了,还把屋子整理得干干净净。

马真(2008)对上面两句的指误与修改非常正确。无论在国内的对外汉语教学中、当今在海外开展的汉语国际教育中,还是在华文教学中,"把"字句对教员、对外国学生来说,一直是有极大挫败感的一种句式。(余文青,2000;李宁、王小珊,2001)应该说"把"字句是学界研究得比较多的一个句式,那么为什么外国学生老是用不好"把"字句呢?问题的症结在哪里呢?不妨先大致了解一下先前乃至目前"把"字句的具体教学内容。

二、目前汉语教学中"把"字句的教学内容

综合各种《现代汉语》教材和汉语教材,到目前为止,汉语教学中所谈论的"把"字句内容,大致如下:

(1) 介绍"把"字句的基本格式:

X 把 Y 怎么样了

甲把乙怎么样了

名词语$_1$+把+名词语$_2$+动词性词语

(2) 介绍"把"字句的语法意义——主要讲"处置"义(如"刘老师把词典放在书架上了""姐姐把我们的衣服都洗干净了")、"致使"义(如"孩子把爷爷哭醒了""那一大盆衣服把姐姐洗得累坏了")、"主观认同"义(如"她把我当作王教授了")、"不如意"义(如"他把钱包丢了")等。

(3) 关于"把"字句的主语(即:X/甲/名词语$_1$)——如果句子表示"处置"义,主语通常是谓语动词所表示的行为动作的施事,常见的是由指人的名词语充任;如果句子表示"致使"义,主语可以是人,也可以是物,也可以是事件。

(4) 关于介词"把"的宾语(即:Y/乙/名词语$_2$)——通常是谓语动词的受事,而且一般要求是有定的、已知的;也可以不限于受事。

(5) 关于"怎么样"部分,也就是"动词性词语"部分——要求是复杂的,最常见的是一个动补结构,而动词有一定限制,特别是不能是不及物动词。

(6) 句子中如果要用到助动词(即能愿动词)或否定词,不能直接放在动词头上,得放在"把"字前边。

此外,在"把"字句研究中,讨论得多的是:① "把"字句表示的语法意义——表处置? 表致使? 表过程? 还是兼表? ② "把"的宾语——一定有定? 可以无定? 可以通指? 是不是次话题? ③ 在汉语教学中还有个"排序"问题——先教哪种"把"字句?

以上大致反映了汉语学界和汉语教学界有关"把"字句的描写性研究成果。

因此,留学生使用"把"字句出现大量偏误,反映了我们以往"把"字句研究与教学的不足。

三、以往"把"字句教学内容之不足

汉语教学对汉语研究来说是"试金石"。汉语教学中出现"把"字句教学的困境,反映了我们先前对"把"字句研究、认识之不足。我认为最主要的一个方面是,没考虑和认识到,表示"处置"义或表示"致使"义或表示"认同"义或表示"不如意"义等,这并非"把"字句的"专利";即不是只有"把"字句才能表示这些语法意义。请看:

【表"处置—位移"义】——下面三个句子都含有这一语法意义:

(3) a. 刘老师把词典放在书架上了。("把"字句)
    b. 刘老师放了本词典在书架上。(复谓句)
    c. 那词典刘老师放在书架上了。(主谓谓语句)

【表"处置—变化"义】——下面四个句子都含有这一语法意义:

(4) a. 姐姐把我们的衣服都洗干净了。("把"字句)
    b. 我们的衣服姐姐都洗干净了。(主谓谓语句)
    c. 我们的衣服姐姐给洗干净了。(带"给"的主谓谓语句)
    d. 我们的衣服都洗干净了。(受事主语句)

【表"致使"义】——下面两个句子都含有这一语法意义:

(5) a. 孩子把爷爷哭醒了。("把"字句)
    b. 孩子哭醒了爷爷。(施事宾语句/使成句)

【表"认同"义】——下面两个句子都含有这一语法意义:

(6) a. 我把他认做我的干儿子。("把"字句)
　　 b. 我认他做我的干儿子。(兼语句/递系句)

【表"不如意"义】——下面两个句子都含有这一语法意义：

(7) a. 我把办公室钥匙落家里了。("把"字句)
　　 b. 办公室钥匙我落家里了。(主谓谓语句)

既然表示"处置"义、表示"致使"义、表示"主观认同"义、表示"不如意"义等并非"把"字句的专利，那么就带来另一个问题："把"字句跟其他句式，诸如主谓谓语句、受事主语句、"给"字句、"被"字句等，在表达上有什么差异？具体体现在哪里？这样的问题，以往好像很少有人去深究。汉语老师当然也就不会给学生讲"把"字句与其他句式之间的差异。这样，外国学生当然就不会了解到底在什么情况下最好用"把"字句，在什么情况下不宜用"把"字句，当然也就不会正确使用"把"字句了。

如何能使"把"字句教学走出困境？汉语学界多有探讨(崔希亮,1995；余文青,2000；李宁、王小珊,2001；赵春利,2006；丁崇明、荣晶,2007；陈满华,2009；施春宏,2010、2011；王占华,2011)。本文拟提出一种新的思路：运用语言信息结构理论来分析。

四、关于语言信息结构理论

本文所说的"语言信息结构"是指用语言作为载体而形成的信息结构。我们知道，语言是一个音义结合的符号系统。而语言的基本功能是传递信息，因此也可以认为语言也是一个信息"编码—解码"的系统。语言，作为一个音义结合的符号系统，有其自身的内在规律；而作为一个信息"编码—解码"系统，也有其自身的内在规律。

对于语言信息结构问题早就有学者注意到了。从信息传递功能着眼来分析句子结构的奠基者，似当推布拉格学派的创建人马泰休斯(Vilém Mathesius, 1882—1945)。根据刘润清(1995)的介绍，马泰休斯一再强调"语言是一个价值系统"，"语言是交际的工具，思维的工具"，因此，"语言研究应以交际需要为出发点","分析语言现象要首先考虑其功能","要以功能为依据"。具体说,"研究语言应从语言功能入手,然后去研究语言形式",因为"说话人先想到要表达什么,然后才去寻找适宜的语言形式"。正是基于这样的认识,马泰修斯于1929年提出了"句子功能透视"(functional sentence perspective,捷克语原文为 aktuální členění větné,也有人译为"句子功能前景"或"句子功能观点")的理论,强调以信息传递这一着眼点来分析话语和文句。具体说,他把一个句子分为三部分:主位(theme)、过渡(transition)和述位(rheme)。主位是"话语的出发点",是"所谈论的对象",是"已知信息";述位是"话语的核心",是"说话人对主位要讲的话,或与主位有关的话",也是说话者要传递给听话人的主要信息;"过渡"是属于"非主位的但又负载最小交际能力的成分"。例如:

(8) He has fallen ill.(他病了。)
　　 主位　过渡　述位

句中的 He 是主位,是所谈论的对象;ill 是述位,是话语的核心;has fallen 是过渡,是负载最小交际能力的成分。新崛起的功能学派就普遍接受了布拉格学派的句子功能前景理论和"主位""述位"的概念,只是把"过渡"归入了述位,认为最基本的信息结构是"主位—述位"(Halliday, 1985)。通常所说的"话题—说明"结构(亦称"话题—陈述"结构)是"主位—述位"结构中的一种。即:

(9) He has fallen ill.(他病了。)
　　 主位　　述位
　　 话题　　说明

在国内,早在20世纪40年代,我国学者就有新旧信息的意识。吕叔湘先生在《从主语、宾语的分别谈国语句子的分析》一文中谈到主语、宾语和施事、受事位置关系时说道:

由"熟"而及"生"是我们说话的一般的趋势。这不完全是为了听者的便利,说话的人心里也是已知的先浮现(也可以说是由上文遗留下来),新知的跟着来。大多数句子都是施事者是已知的部分,所施事是新知的部分,例如

"大鱼吃小鱼,小鱼吃虾米,虾米拱起背",说到第二句"小鱼"已见于上文,"吃虾米"是新添的部分,到了第三句,"虾米"又成了已知的部分,"拱起背"是新添的部分(吕叔湘,1946/1990)。

吕先生这段话里关于新旧信息的意识十分明显。遗憾的是,吕先生后来没有再从这个视角去分析汉语语法现象,更没有能将这种意识深化为理论。

20世纪80年代以来,国内外对语言信息结构的关注与讨论开始多起来了。国外如韩礼德(Michael A. K. Halliday)、Knud Lambrecht、Mary Dalrymlpe、Irina Nikolaeva、狄克(Simon C. Dik)、海曼(John Haiman)、克拉克和汉威兰德(Clark & Haviland)、切夫(Wallace Chafe)、普林斯(Alan Prince)、霍珀(Paul J. Hopper)等,都讨论过语言传递信息的问题,其中韩礼德谈论得比较多。在国内,如张斌(文炼,1984)、陆俭明(1987)、陆丙甫(1993)、张伯江和方梅(1996)、沈家煊(1998)、袁毓林(1998)、徐列炯和刘丹青(1998、2003)、萧国政(2001)、温锁林(1999)、张伯江(2005)、方梅(2005)、刘丹青(2005、2008)以及曹逢甫(1995、2005)、邓守信(2011)等,都谈论过语言信息结构。但总起来说,多偏向于理论探讨,而从语言信息结构的视角来研究、解释汉语语法现象还注意得不够,更未见有人系统谈论汉语信息结构的内在规律。

在语言这个音义结合的符号系统中,其音义结合的符号,按大小可区分为:语素、词、词组、句子、句群、段落、篇章。语言信息结构只跟句子、句群、段落、篇章这些语言动态单位(吕叔湘,1979)相对应,因此一般将语言信息结构分为句(子)信息结构和篇章信息结构。跟句法关系密切的当然是句(子)信息结构。

关于句(子)信息结构,有一点首先需要明了,那就是句子所传递的信息跟句子所表示的意义不是一码事。例如"你有钱吗?"这一问句,就句子所表示的意义来说,该问话表示问话人询问听话人有没有钱。可是它所传递的信息可以因说话环境的不同而不同——在有的上下文语境中,是传递"问话人要向听话人借钱"的信息;在有的上下文语境中,是向听话人传递"如果你没有钱,我可以借些给你"的信息;而在有的语境中,譬如在黑夜有人跑上来突然这样问你,这可能意味着要打劫⋯⋯可见,句子的意义是句子所传递的信息的基础,而句子所传递的信息一方面取决于句子的意义,另一方面取决于句子所处的语境。打个不一定恰当的比喻,句子的意义如同光源,它光芒四射,任何一根光线,遇上某个语境,就呈现并传递某种信息。

句(子)信息结构的关注点是:
(1) 以什么为话题?有无标记?
(2) 以什么为焦点?有无标记?
(3) 是已知信息还是未知信息?
(4) 已知信息量的大小或未知信息量的大小。
(5) 是前景信息,还是背景信息?
(6) 信息结构会遵循什么样的准则?

现在我们就根据上述关注点,来探讨一下汉语句(子)信息结构遵循的一些准则。

五、汉语句(子)信息结构遵循的准则

根据我的观察与分析,汉语句子信息结构似需遵循以下一些准则:

准则一: 作为一个句(子)信息结构,必定含已知信息与未知信息;二者一般形成"话题—陈述(评论)"信息结构。例如:

(10) 张三　　　　去上海了。
　　 话题　　　　陈述(评论)
　　 已知信息　　未知信息

准则二: 在句(子)信息结构中,已知信息成分可以省去,但未知信息成分不能省去。例如:

(11) 老师:好哇,你考上浙江大学了!萧云考上哪个大学啦?
　　 王平:∅[萧云]考上北京大学了。　("萧云"属于旧信息,省去了)

准则三: 在句(子)信息结构中,未知信息单元一般位于已知信息单元之后成为信息结构的常规焦点,如果位于已知信息单元之前,必须有标记。例如:

(12) ′萧云昨天在王府井花两千元买了件大衣。
　　 萧云′昨天在王府井花两千元买了件大衣。

　　　　萧云昨天在'王府井花两千元买了件大衣。
　　　　萧云昨天在王府井花'两千元买了件大衣。
(13)　是萧云昨天在王府井花两千元买了件大衣。
　　　　萧云是昨天在王府井花两千元买了件大衣。
　　　　萧云昨天是在王府井花两千元买了件大衣。
　　　　萧云昨天在王府井是花两千元买了件大衣。
　　　　萧云昨天在王府井花两千元是买了件大衣。

例(12)作为新信息成分的标记是重音(这里用"'"表示),例(13)作为新信息成分的标记是"是"。易位形式也可以视为标记。例如:

(14) 问:你喝点儿什么?　　答:啤酒吧,我就。
(15) 快出来吧,你们!
(16) 到家了吧,他大概。

这三句都是易位句,易位成分之前的成分是新信息。

准则四:在句(子)信息结构中,核心动词后如果出现多个信息单元,信息未知程度高的居于信息未知程度低的之后。例如:

(17) a. 我教了小红三回。　　b. *我教了三回小红。
(18) a. 我给了那个人一条鱼。　　b. *我给了一个人那条鱼。

准则五:核心动词前如果出现多个信息单元,作话题的信息单元之外,其余信息单元,已知信息量大的居于已知信息量小的之前。例如:

(19) a. 汪萍昨天在那超市买了一件上装。
　　　b. *汪萍在超市昨天买了一件上装。
　　　c. 昨天汪萍在超市买了一件上装。
　　　d. *昨天在超市汪萍买了一件上装。
　　　e. 在超市汪萍昨天买了一件上装。
　　　f. *在超市昨天汪萍买了一件上装。

句中动词前有三个信息单元:"汪萍""昨天""超市",都可以作话题。"汪萍"是专有名词,"昨天"的对比项只是"今天"一个,而"超市"的对比项不止一个,因此从信息量的已知程度来说,三者信息量的已知程度显然是:汪萍>昨天>超市。这样,说话者一旦选定其中某一个为话题,那么按照准则五,例(19)的 a、c、e 三句能接受,而 b、d、f 三句不能接受,就很好理解了。

准则六:在句(子)信息结构中,背景信息居于前景信息之前。

在篇章信息结构中有两个重要的概念:前景信息和背景信息。"一个叙事语篇中,总有一些语句它们所传达的信息是事件的主线或主干,这种构成事件主线的信息称作'前景信息'。前景信息用来直接描述事件的进展,回答'发生了什么?'这样的问题。另一些语句它们所表达的信息是围绕事件的主干进行铺排、衬托或评价,传达非连续的信息(如事件的场景、相关因素等等),这种信息称作背景信息。背景信息用来回答'为什么'或'怎么样'发生等问题。"(方梅,2005)这里要提醒大家注意的是,前景信息和背景信息并不只在篇章信息结构中存在,在句信息结构中也存在。例如:

(20)(打电话)你下了课来一下。　(21)(打电话)下了课你来一下。

无论是例(20)还是例(21),其中的"下了课"都属于背景信息。再如:

(22)他明天骑车去天津。　　　(23)她去天津买自行车。

这两句里都有表事件的"去天津",但它在例(22)里属于前景信息,在例(23)里属于背景信息。有的句子,孤立看,不成句,站不住。例如:

(24)﹡我吃勺园7号楼餐厅。[对比:我吃食堂]

但加进一定的背景信息,就可以说了:

(24′) a. 勺园二号楼食堂的饭不好吃,我现在吃勺园七号楼餐厅了。
　　　b. 以前我偶尔在勺园七号楼餐厅吃,我现在每餐(天)都吃勺园七号楼餐厅。(转引自萧国政,2001)

从上面所举的例子可知,背景信息可在句内,也可能在上文。

准则七: 说话者所传递的新信息一定要大于听话者对该新信息所拥有的信息量。① 例如:

(25) 我很冷。　　　(26) 他很冷。　　　(27) *你很冷。

"冷"是属于"感受"性质的形容词。例(25)(26)能说,因为符合准则七;例(27)不能说,因为不符合准则七。

准则八: 问句答话的信息焦点与问话的疑问点在句中位置相一致。例如:

(28) 问:<u>谁</u>告诉你的?　　答:<u>姐姐</u>告诉我的。
(29) 问:你想吃<u>什么</u>?　　答:我想吃<u>饺子</u>。
(30) 问:你<u>什么时候</u>回去?　答:我<u>明天</u>回去。

再看下面的对话:

(31) 问:你刚才喝什么了?　答:a. 我刚才喝了杯<u>咖啡</u>。
　　　　　　　　　　　　　　b. *<u>咖啡</u>我刚才喝了。

例(31)a 答话可取,b 答话让人感到答非所问,原因就在于 b 句答话违反了准则八。

语言信息结构理论对句法现象的解释能力有多大,现在还不好说,还需深入研究之后才能有所认识。限于篇幅,下面只举一个实例——表"让步"的"X是X(了)"小句句式。

"X是X(了)"是让步转折复句中居前的那个小句。例如:

(32) a. 那衣服漂亮,买吧。　　b. <u>漂亮是漂亮</u>,就是太贵了。
(33) a. 小芳这孩子真聪明。　　b. <u>聪明是聪明</u>,就是太贪玩儿了。

---

① 参看朱敏(2012)。她从"陈述句的信息流向"角度概括出了三种不同人称在陈述语气中受限程度的排序:第二人称>第一人称>第三人称。

(34) a. 那文章看了吗? b. 看是看了,但我没有看懂。
(35) a. 昨天去庙会玩儿了吧? b. 去是去了,可是到那儿一看人太多,我就回来了。

学界都认为,前面的小句"X是X(了)"表示"让步/容让"。那"X是X(了)"小句为什么能"表示让步/容让"的意思?过去百思不得其解。现在语言信息结构理论为我们提供了解释的理据——那"X是X(了)"小句里边,前面那个X(如各例中的"漂亮""聪明""看"和"去")是承接上一句[如例(32)的"那衣服漂亮,买吧";余者类推]而来的,实际是一个话题,它表示的是旧信息。按语言信息结构理论,既然"X"作了话题,后面的陈述中应提供新信息,可是"是X"所提供的并不是新信息,只是重复了话题所说的内容。从信息传递的角度说,这等于是"在原地踏步";而"在原地踏步"意味着"让步/容让"(此例是张伯江先生所提供的)。

六、从语言信息结构的视角重新认识汉语"把"字句的特点

从语言信息结构的视角认识"把"字句在信息传递上的特点,陆俭明(2015)的《消极修辞有开拓的空间》中谈到了一些。考虑到有些读者,特别是广大汉语教师未必能看到,有些内容恕我在这里不避重复。

现在我们就从语言信息结构的视角来比较一下"把"字句跟其他句式的异同,由此认识"把"字句在信息传递上的特点。这里仅就表"处置"义的"把"字句跟其他也能表"处置"义的句式进行比较,不过这种比较以及所获得的结论大体也适用于表其他语法意义的"把"字句。

在具体比较之前,先简单说一下表"处置"义的句子。根据"构式—语块"句法分析法,表"处置"义的句子由四个语义块构成。就"把"字句来说,这四个语义块是:

	处置者	(把)处置对象	处置方式	处置结果
(36)	刘老师	[把]词典	放	在书架上了。
(37)	姐姐	[把]我们的衣服	都洗	干净了。

需要注意的是,处置方式与处置结果,有时可以融合在一起。例如:

(38) a. 弟弟把我的杯子打了。
　　 b. 昨天换下来的衣服姐姐都洗了。

这里只说出了处置方式"打"/"洗",处置结果隐含其中。

下面是都能表示"处置"义(程度有不同)而分别属于不同句式的句子:

(39) a. 姐姐洗干净了所有的衣服。
　　 b. 所有的衣服姐姐都洗干净了。
　　 c. 所有的衣服都给姐姐洗干净了。
　　 d. 所有的衣服都被姐姐洗干净了。
　　 e. 所有的衣服都洗干净了。
　　 f. 姐姐把所有的衣服都洗干净了。

上面六个句子都不同程度地表示"处置"义,但分属于不同的句法格式。它们表示的基本意义是一样的:"所有的衣服都洗干净了。是谁洗干净的?是姐姐洗干净的。"(其中只是 e 句未指明是谁洗干净的)。可是它们在表达上,也就是它们所具体传递的信息,是各有区别的。区别在哪里呢?

a 句是"主—谓—宾"句,或者说"主—动—宾"句。这种句子格式是以"姐姐"为话题,以"所有的衣服"为信息聚焦点。a 句只是客观陈述"姐姐洗干净了所有的衣服"这一事实,凸显"'姐姐'洗干净的是'所有的衣服'而不是别的什么东西"这一层意思。

b 句是主谓谓语句。也是陈述客观事实,但跟 a 句不一样,b 句以"所有的衣服"作为话题,以"洗干净了"或"姐姐洗干净了"作为信息聚焦点,凸显所有的衣服"洗干净了"这一层意思。

c 句是"给"字句。就话题与信息聚焦点看,与 b 句一样,但 c 句用了介词"给",信息结构的性质跟 b 句不完全一样了,除了陈述事实外,施动者"姐姐"通过介词"给"的引介,更清楚地指明洗干净衣服的是"姐姐"而不是别人,即要凸显处置者"姐姐"。

d 句是"被"字句。就话题与信息焦点看,与 b、c 句一样,但 d 句用了介词"被",信息结构的性质跟 b 句、c 句也就不一样了,增添了不如意的"遭受"之义,具体说含有"姐姐洗干净所有的衣服,这并非说话者的意愿"之意。

e 句是受事主语句。e 句跟前面的 b、c、d 句,特别跟 b 句有相同之处——都以"所有的衣服"为话题,以"洗干净了"为信息聚焦点;但 e 句跟 b、c、d 句又有不同——不关心"是谁洗干净的"问题,也不含有主观色彩,只是客观陈述"所有的衣服都洗干净了"这一事实。

f 句就是我们所关注的"把"字句。从信息传递的角度说,f 句跟 a 句相比较,虽然都以"姐姐"为话题,但是 a 句以"所有的衣服"为句子的信息聚焦点,而 f 句则以"洗干净了"为句子的信息聚焦点;跟 b、c、d、e 句相比较,虽然都以"洗干净了"为信息聚焦点,但是 b、c、d、e 句都以"所有的衣服"为话题,而 f 句则以"姐姐"为话题。

从上可知,从语言信息结构的视角看,"把"字句在信息传递上跟 a、b、c、d、e 句式都有差异,有其自身特点,即以谓语动词的施事即处置者为话题,要以"处置及其结果"为信息聚焦点。

按常规,话题得居于句首,信息聚焦点得居于句尾。可这样一来,有个问题:那处置的对象,即谓语动词的受事,如果也必须在句子中出现,那么该放在什么位置上?拿"姐姐洗衣服"这样一件事来说,"洗"的结果通常是"衣服"由脏变干净;现在如果要将"姐姐"作为话题,要将处置及其结果"洗干净"作为信息聚焦点,那么"衣服",也就是处置对象,如果也要在句中出现,该放在什么位置上?实际只容许一个位置,那就是"话题与信息聚焦点之间"这一位置,说成:

(40) 姐姐　衣服　洗干净了。

"姐姐衣服洗干净了"只能分析为①:

(40′) 姐姐　衣服　洗干净了。
　　　 主　　　谓　　　　
　　　　　　 主　　 谓　　

可是像例(40)这种主谓谓语句,它要受到多方面条件的限制。

---

① 似乎也能分析为"姐姐衣服|洗干净了"(主谓关系),但不允许这样分析。为什么?因为上文已经交代要让处置者"姐姐"作话题。如果将"衣服"先与"姐姐"捆绑成偏正结构,那么这个句子信息结构的话题立即转移了,就变成"衣服"了,不能再是"姐姐"了。因此,对于例(40)我们只能将它分析为主谓谓语句。

条件限制一：这类主谓谓语句，在语义上其小主语"衣服"只能被理解为是大主语"姐姐"的领有物（有的句子，大主语与小主语之间是隶属关系），即"姐姐"领有"衣服"。类似的主谓谓语句都是如此，请看下列各例主谓谓语句：

(41) a. 姐姐衣服洗干净了。
　　 b. 老张眼镜打破了。
　　 c. 小明苹果吃完了。
　　 d. 汪萍咖啡已经喝完了。
　　 e. 王教授试卷已经批改完了。
　　 ……

各句的"姐姐"与"衣服"、"老张"与"眼镜"、"小明"与"苹果"、"汪萍"与"咖啡"、"王教授"与"试卷"都分别暗含着所属关系。① 这就意味着如果"姐姐"所洗的不是自己的衣服，而是别人的衣服，就不能采用这种主谓谓语句式。语言事实告诉我们，情况确实如此。例如：

(42) a. 姐姐衣服洗干净了。
　　 b. *姐姐弟弟的衣服都洗干净了。
　　 c. *姐姐大家的衣服都洗干净了。
　　 d. *姐姐老王的衣服洗干净了。

例(42)b—d 句不能说，有没有可能是因为"衣服"带上了"名词语+的"的定语的缘故？语言事实告诉我们，并不是因为这样。请看：

(43) 姐姐棉布的衣服洗干净了。

这里虽然"衣服"也带有"名词语+的"的定语，但照样可以说，因为它可以理解为那"棉布的衣服"是"姐姐的"，即因为"姐姐"与"棉布的衣服"之间有领属关系。可是这样一来，必然要提出一个问题：如果处置者所处置的对象不是自己

---

① "王教授"与"试卷"的所属关系可以理解为"归王教授批改的试卷"。

所领有的事物,而又必须在句子中出现,那该怎么办?

条件限制二:处置对象作为小主语,在长度上要受到限制。也就是说,即使处置对象"衣服"是"姐姐"自己的,也要求"表示处置对象的那个成分"在长度上要比较短,如果长了,句子就不容易接受。请看:

(44) a. 姐姐<u>衣服</u>洗干净了。
　　 b. 姐姐<u>棉布的衣服</u>洗干净了。
　　 c. *姐姐<u>棉布的、脏得不像话的衣服</u>洗干净了。
　　 d. *姐姐<u>全是油腻脏得不像话的棉布衣服</u>洗干净了。

根据我们的问询调查,例(44)c、d 句不被接受。下文例(45)b、c、d 句也不被接受。

(45) a. 弟弟<u>杯子</u>打破了。
　　 b. ?弟弟<u>最漂亮的杯子</u>打破了。
　　 c. *弟弟<u>最漂亮的用来喝咖啡的那两个杯子</u>打破了。
　　 d. *弟弟<u>最漂亮的镶有金边的用来喝咖啡的那两个杯子</u>打破了。

条件限制三:那处置对象不能由人称代词或指人的名词充任。譬如我们不能说"*我他/邹刚调走了",只能说"我把他/邹刚调走了"。

那么假如处置对象非得置于话题与信息聚焦点之间,而又得克服上述的条件限制,是否有别的办法呢?有,其中常用的一个办法就是用"把"一类介词来引介处置对象。请看①:

(44′) a. 姐姐把<u>衣服</u>洗干净了。

---

① 克服那限制条件的另一种办法,那就是话题后停顿(包括带上某个语气词)。例如:
　(i) a. 姐姐(呀/呢),脏得不像话的衣服都洗干净了。
　　　 b. 姐姐(呀/呢),全是油腻脏得不像话的衣服都洗干净了。
　　　 c. 姐姐(呀/呢),全是油腻脏得不像话的棉布衣服都洗干净了。
　(ii) a. 弟弟(呀/呢),很漂亮的杯子打破了。
　　　 b. 弟弟(呀/呢),很漂亮的用来喝咖啡的杯子打破了。
　　　 c. 弟弟(呀/呢),很漂亮的用来喝咖啡的那两个杯子打破了。

b. 姐姐把大家的衣服洗干净了。

　　c. 姐姐把棉布的、脏得不像话的衣服洗干净了。

　　d. 姐姐把大家的全是油腻脏得不像话的棉布衣服洗干净了。

(45′) a. 弟弟把杯子打破了。

　　b. 弟弟把最漂亮的杯子打破了。

　　c. 弟弟把最漂亮的用来喝咖啡的那两个杯子打破了。

　　d. 弟弟把最漂亮的镶有金边的用来喝咖啡的那两个杯子打破了。

(46) a. 我们把邹刚调来了。

　　b. 我们把那坏蛋赶走了。

这就是说,介词"把"的作用可以自由地将处置对象引入句内——不论那处置对象与话题所指之间是否存在所属关系,也不论那处置对象有多长,也不论那处置对象是否由人称代词或指人名词充任。

至此,我们基本可以了解我们为什么要使用介词"把"——为了要让施事,即处置者作话题,要让处置结果成为信息聚焦点,而且又得让处置对象进入句子,于是就采用"把"字句式。

然而,"把"字句的表达作用还不限于此,它还能凸显处置的结果,那是因为"把"字句具有"强影响性"(张伯江,2000)和"处置的主观认定性"(沈家煊,2002)。"把"字句有凸显处置结果的特殊表达作用,这从下面四组例子中看得更清楚:

(47) a. 去年张三骗了李四,李四给骗惨了,这我哪能不记得?

（"主—动—宾"句）

　　b. 去年张三骗了李四,李四没有受骗,这我哪能不记得?

（"主—动—宾"句）

(48) a. 去年张三把李四骗了,李四给骗惨了,这我哪能不记得?

（"把"字句）

　　b. *去年张三把李四骗了,李四没有受骗,这我哪能不记得?

（"把"字句）

(49) a. 张三用力砸了那铁锁,门当然就给砸开了。（"主—动—宾"句）

　　b. 张三用力砸了那铁锁,可是门没给砸开。　（"主—动—宾"句）

(50) a. 张三用力把那铁锁砸了,门当然就给砸开了。("把"字句)
　　 b. ＊张三用力把那铁锁砸了,可是门没给砸开。("把"字句)

先对比例(47)与例(48)。例(47)前一小句采用"主—动—宾"句式,只是客观陈述了张三对李四实施了欺骗行为这一事实,至于李四是否受骗,小句本身并未明确说明;只因为这样,所以在那小句后面,既可以接上"李四给骗惨了"这一小句,也可以接上"而李四没有受骗"这一小句。可是例(48)采用"把"字句,则就凸显了李四受了骗这一结果,所以后面可以接上"李四给骗惨了"这一小句,可是就不能再接上"而李四没有受骗"这一小句了。

再对比例(49)与例(50)。例(49)前一小句采用"主—动—宾"句式,只是客观陈述了"张三用力砸了那铁锁"这一事实,至于门是否被砸开,那小句本身并未明确说明;只因为这样,所以在那小句后面,既可以接上"门当然就给砸开了"这一小句,也可以接上"可是门没给砸开"这一小句。可是例(50)采用"把"字句,则就凸显了张三砸开了门这一结果,所以后面可以接上"门当然就给砸开了"这一小句,可是就不能再接上"可是门没给砸开"这样的小句了。

至此,我们大致可以看出,从语言信息结构的角度看,表示"处置"义的"把"字句存在三个明显的特点:一是要让"处置者"为话题;二是要让"处置结果"作为信息聚焦点;三是运用介词"把",以便能自由地将"处置对象"引入句子内,同时表示"处置"的强影响性和说话者的主观认定性,由此凸显"处置结果"。

上文曾引用了马真(2008)所举的两个与"把"字句相关的偏误句,即第一部分里的例(1),而且认为马真(2008)对那两个偏误句的指误与修改非常正确。但是,人们还是要追问:为什么例(1)用了"被"字句就能使前后文气协调、连贯了呢?她没深究。其实从语言信息结构的视角看,特别是从篇章信息结构看,例(1)上文是说"眼前是一片不好的景象",下文是来具体描述洪水过后那"不好的景象"的,这就不能让"洪水"来作话题,而应让遭受洪水之害的事物来作话题。采用"被"字句,不仅可以让遭受洪水之害的事物来作话题,更增强了遭受不幸的意味。

上面我们从语言信息结构的视角重点分析了表示"处置"义的"把"字句,其分析思路也适用于其他"把"字句。

如果我们将"把"字句在语言信息结构上与其他句式的差异和"把"字句在语言信息传递上的独特性清清楚楚地告诉外国学生,无疑将有助于我们走出"把"

字句教学的困境。笔者虽不敢说外国学生就不会错用"把"字句了,但肯定会使他们大大减少"把"字句使用不当的偏误。

七、余 论

最后再说两小点:

其一,对于语言信息结构,前人和时贤论著中已有所讨论,但尚缺乏系统的思考,语言信息结构是尚待探究的问题,起码下面这些问题值得探究:

问题之一:语言信息结构与语言结构之间到底是什么关系?

问题之二:句子信息结构到底是一个什么样的结构?

问题之三:句子信息结构具体该如何分析?

问题之四:如何确定某个信息单元信息量的大小?

问题之五:句子信息结构是否具有二重性?[①]

问题之六:在句子信息结构中到底可分析出多少种焦点?

问题之七:在句子信息结构中到底可分析出多少种话题?

问题之八:话题是否可以成为新信息? 如果可以,这样的语言信息结构又该如何分析?

其二,上面所谈的有关从语言信息结构角度分析"把"字句的内容,我们不能照搬到课堂上就这样讲给外国学生。而要将上述内容转化为教学内容,而且得用深入浅出、通俗易懂的教学语言来给学生讲解。至于具体怎么讲,我们将另文讨论,也期盼对此有兴趣的汉语教师来设计一下,为大家提供一个教学参考方案。

参考文献

曹逢甫:《主题在汉语中的功能研究——迈向语段分析的第一步》,谢天蔚译,语文出版社1995年版。

曹逢甫:《汉语的句子与子句结构》,王静译,北京语言大学出版社2005

[①] 句子信息结构二重性,是萧国政(2001)的观点。他认为,任何句子信息结构都具有二重性,即一个完整的句子至少具备二重信息结构;即使句子表面只显示一重信息,但必定隐含着另一重信息。例如,"鸟飞",不成话;"鸟飞了""鸟在飞",成话。为什么? 因为"鸟飞"只有一重信息,所以不成话;而"鸟飞了""鸟在飞",有二重信息——前者"鸟飞"而且"飞了",后者"鸟飞"而且"正在飞",所以成话,站得住。有时表面看只一个词,但也含二重信息,如:"滚!"(=你滚,别站在这里!)

年版。

陈满华:《构式语法理论对二语教学的启示》,《语言教学与研究》2009年第4期。

崔希亮:《"把"字句的若干句法语义问题》,《世界汉语教学》1995年第3期。

邓守信:《汉语信息结构与教学》,2011年8月23日在北京语言大学所作的报告。

丁崇明、荣晶:《汉语第二语言学习者应学的"把"字句及其变换》,《语言文字应用》2007年第6期。

方梅:《篇章语法与汉语研究》,载刘丹青主编《语言学前沿与汉语研究》,上海教育出版社2005年版。

李宁、王小珊:《"把"字句的语用功能调查》,《汉语学习》2001年第1期。

刘丹青:《话题理论与汉语句法研究》,载沈阳、冯胜利主编《当代语言学理论和汉语研究》,商务印书馆2008年版。

刘丹青:《语言学前沿与汉语研究》,上海教育出版社2005年版。

刘润清:《西方语言学流派》,外语教学与研究出版社1995年版。

陆丙甫:《核心推导语法》,上海教育出版社1993年版。

陆俭明:《试论句子意义的组成》,《语言研究论丛》(第四辑),南开大学出版社1987年版。

陆俭明:《消极修辞有开拓的空间》,《当代修辞学》2015年第1期。

吕叔湘:《从主语、宾语的分别谈国语句子的分析》,收入《吕叔湘文集》(第二卷),商务印书馆1990年版。

吕叔湘:《汉语语法分析问题》,商务印书馆1979年版。

马真:《在汉语教学中要重视词语使用的语义背景》,载蔡建国主编:《中华文化传播:任务与方法》,上海人民出版社2008年版。

沈家煊:《语用法的语法化》,《福建外语》1998年第2期。

沈家煊:《如何处置"处置式"?——论把字句的主观性》,《中国语文》2002年第5期。

施春宏:《从句式群看"把"字句及其相关句式的语法意义》,《世界汉语教学》2010年第3期。

施春宏:《面向第二语言教学汉语构式研究的基本状况和研究取向》,《语言教学与研究》2011年第6期。

田　靓：《汉语作为外语/第二语言教学的"把"字句研究》，北京大学博士学位论文，2012年。

王占华：《"把"字句的项与成句和使用动因——一个基于二语教学的"把"字句解析模式》，《世界汉语教学》2011年第3期。

温锁林：《汉语句子的信息安排及其句法后果——以复动句为例》，载邢福义主编：《汉语法特点面面观》，北京语言文化大学出版社1999年版。

文　炼：《关于句子的意义和内容》，《语文研究》1984年第1期。

萧国政：《句子信息结构与汉语语法实体成活》，《世界汉语教学》2001年第4期。

徐烈炯、刘丹青：《话题的结构与功能》，上海教育出版社1998年版。

徐烈炯、刘丹青主编：《话题与焦点新论》，上海教育出版社2003年版。

余文青：《留学生使用"把"字句的调查报告》，《汉语学习》2000年第5期。

袁毓林：《语言信息的编码和生物信息的编码之比较》，《当代语言学》1998年第2期。

张伯江：《论"把"字句的句式语义》，《语言研究》2000年第1期。

张伯江：《功能语法与汉语研究》，载刘丹青主编：《语言学前沿与汉语研究》，上海教育出版社2005年版。

张伯江、方　梅：《汉语功能语法研究》，江西教育出版社1996年版。

赵春利：《基础阶段"把"字句的教学设计》，《语言文字应用》2006年第6期。

朱　敏：《汉语人称与语气选择性研究》，世界图书出版公司2012年版。

Halliday, M. A. K. (1985), *An Introduction to Functional Grammar*. 外语教学与研究出版社2000年版。

 方法谈：

老问题如何才能出新意？

"把"字句是学界讨论最多的问题之一。引发我重新讨论"把"字句的原因是，在汉语二语教学中"把"字句教学屡屡让"教"和"学"双方都有很大的挫败感——老师花了很大力气教，学生花了很大力气学，可是总不能获得理想的教学效果。

马真(2008)一文中就曾举过这样一个留学生的很典型的使用"把"字句的偏

误句：

> (1) *洪水是退了,但是眼前是一片不好的景象：洪水把村舍的房屋冲倒了一大半,把猪、鸡、羊都淹死了,空气里充满了难闻的臭味儿；洪水把成堆的木材也几乎都冲光了,……

马真(2008)指出,就一个个小句孤立来看,都合语法,但是例(1)冒号以后的部分,是要具体描绘洪水过后的不好景象,按说应顺着上文的意思,用表示遭受义的"被"字句,不宜用"把"字句,可是却用了好几个"把"字句,使前后文气很不协调、很不连贯。这个句子宜改为：

> (1′) 洪水是退了,但是眼前是一片不好的景象：村舍的房屋被洪水冲倒了一大半,猪、鸡、羊都被淹死了,空气里充满了难闻的臭味儿；成堆的木材也几乎都被洪水冲光了,……

马真(2008)对上面这个偏误句的评说与修改,非常正确。从例(1)看,应该说这一偏误句的作者汉语水平相当好了,可是为什么还用不好"把"字句？汉语二语教学对汉语研究来说,可以说是"试金石"。汉语教学中出现"把"字句教学的困境,反映了我们先前对"把"字句研究、认识之不足。这就引发我去思考与研究。

对于"把"字句,我们常说它主要表示五种语法意义：其一,表示"处置—位移"义,如："刘老师把词典放在了书架上"；其二,表示"处置—变化"义,如："姐姐把我们的衣服都洗干净了"；其三,表示"致使"义,如："孩子把爷爷哭醒了"；其四,表示"认同"义,如"我把他认做我的干儿子"；其五,表示"不如意"义,如"我把办公室钥匙落家里了"。既然对"把"字句已分了类,每一类"把"字句所表示的语法意义也已研究清楚了,那为什么外国学生使用"把"字句会出现偏误呢？

经多方思考,我发现上述每一种语法意义都并非"把"字句"专属"。上述任何一种语法意义,其他句式也都能表示。

【表"处置—位移"义】——下面三个句子都含有这一语法意义：
(2) a. 刘老师把词典放在书架上了。【"把"字句】
　　b. 刘老师放了本词典在书架上。【复谓句】

c. 那词典刘老师放在书架上了。【主谓谓语句】

【表"处置—变化"义】——下面三个句子都含有这一语法意义：

(3) a. 姐姐把我们的衣服都洗干净了。【"把"字句】

　　b. 我们的衣服姐姐都洗干净了。【主谓谓语句】

　　c. 我们的衣服姐姐给洗干净了。【带"给"的主谓谓语句】

　　d. 我们的衣服都洗干净了。【受事主语句】

【表"致使"义】——下面三个句子都含有这一语法意义：

(4) a. 孩子把爷爷哭醒了。【"把"字句】

　　b. 孩子哭醒了爷爷。【施事宾语句/使成句】

【表"认同"义】——下面三个句子都含有这一语法意义：

(5) a. 我把他认做我的干儿子。【"把"字句】

　　b. 我认他做我的干儿子。【兼语句/递系句】

【表"不如意"义】——下面三个句子都含有这一语法意义：

(6) a. 我把办公室钥匙落家里了。【"把"字句】

　　b. 办公室钥匙我落家里了。【主谓谓语句】

　　我们知道，母语为汉语的中国人运用"把"字句，不是根据书上说的条条，而是凭从小积聚的丰富的语感；外国学生对汉语没什么语感，使用"把"字句只是凭汉语老师告诉他们的条条。上面说，"把"字句所表示的各种语法意义，别的句式也能表示，这说明在汉语二语教学中给学生讲授"把"字句，不能光是给"把"字句分类，分别说明每类"把"字句所表示的意义就了事；还必须告诉他们，在什么语言环境下适宜使用"把"字句，在什么语言环境下不宜使用"把"字句。

　　那么具体该运用什么样的语言学理论来说清楚"把"字句跟其他句式在表达上的异同呢？根据我的研究与认识，认为应该运用"语言信息结构"理论。那几年我潜心思考研究语言信息结构，《从语言信息结构视角重新认识"把"字句》就是在这样的思考研究下撰写成文的，而该文也正是我有关语言信息结构研究的一个研究成果。

　　《从语言信息结构视角重新认识"把"字句》共分七节——

(一) 从"把"字句教学一直令人有挫败感说起；

(二) 目前汉语教学中"把"字句的教学内容；

（三）以往"把"字句教学内容之不足；

（四）关于语言信息结构理论；

（五）汉语句子信息结构遵循的准则；

（六）从语言信息结构的视角重新认识汉语"把"字句的特点；

（七）余论。

每一节的标题已清楚显示各节的内容，不必再加以导读。

我推荐《从语言信息结构视角重新认识"把"字句》一文，一方面希望让大家了解，对语言研究中的老问题"还可以出新意"，即还可以进一步挖掘并从新的视角加以开发；另一方面也希望引起大家对语言信息结构的关注，更希望对语言信息结构问题有兴趣的年轻学者投入语言信息结构的研究中来。

渥太华依托式课程教学及其启示*

俞理明　韩建侠**

摘要：本文介绍渥太华大学双语教学模式及其成功的经验，主张我国的大学双语教学要克服"潮流化"和"保守性"的倾向，把双语教学建立在科研的基础上，为大学英语教学改革闯出一条新路子。

关键词：双语教学；依托式教学；大学英语

一、引　言

国内的大学双语教学刚刚起步，一些学校虽然已经开始了双语教学的试验和探索，积累了一定经验，但据笔者观察，目前高校的双语教学没有很好地建立在科研的基础上，还存在不少问题。比如，如何有效地在大学进行双语教学？对进入双语教学班的学生的目标语是否要有一定要求？双语教学成功的标志是什么？国内学术杂志上关于这些问题的讨论尚不多见。笔者之一曾于2002年5月到渥太华大学考察了该校的双语教学，深受启发，认为我国高校可以参照渥太华大学依托课程内容的语言教学（Content-based language instruction）模式，解决语言和学科分离问题。

---

　*　原载《外语教学与研究（外国语文双月刊）》2003年第6期。本文考察的资助来自加拿大政府的"中国学者加拿大研究特别奖"（Special Award for Canadian Studies for Chinese Scholars）。

　**　俞理明，上海交通大学外国语学院教授，博士生导师。历任中国英汉语比较研究会教育语言学专业委员会会长、名誉会长，中国语言教育研究会副会长，中国英语教学研究会二语习得专业委员会理事；中国教育研究学会外语教学专业委员会学术委员，全国双语教育实验学校理事会副理事长等。在国际和国内重要杂志发表论文数十篇，完成专著、译著和各种教材十多部。除语言教育领域的研究外，还致力于中—加文化、教育和学术交流，2002年获加拿大政府颁发的加拿大研究特别奖。

　韩建侠，枣庄学院外国语学院教授，研究方向为外语教学、二语习得。

二、渥太华大学的双语教学模式

加拿大学者出于其特殊国情的需要,对双语教学模式的探讨已有近40年的历史。他们首创的"浸入式语言教学"(immersion language teaching)模式被誉为"在加拿大教学史上开展研究最深入、最广泛、最细致的一个项目"(Fortier,1990)。"浸入式"教学开始于20世纪60年代,其方法是让二语学习者像习得母语一样习得二语,对象是幼儿园到初中年龄段的儿童和少年(Stern,1978a,1978b)。从1982年开始,以渥太华大学为代表的加拿大部分高等院校开始探索在成年人群体,即在高等教育中开展双语教学的路子,他们运用"浸入式"教学的成功经验,一反传统的第二语言/外语教学的方法,把第二语言/外语教学渗透到学科教学的课堂中。这一做法称为"依托课程内容的语言教学法"(以下简称"依托式教学")。

渥太华大学的双语教学主要可以分为两个阶段:封闭式教学(sheltered content instruction)和附加式教学(adjunct language instruction)(Brinton et al.,1989)。

开始于1982年的封闭式教学,由于和"浸入式"教学方法有相似之处,也被称为"后后期浸入式教学"(late,late immersion)(Krashen,1984)。所谓"封闭"是指参加双语班的学生和普通班的学生分开,单独地"封闭"在一起学习有关大学课程。最初的封闭式教学模式是由渥太华大学第二语言学院和心理学院于1982年冬共同创建的,教学内容是用英语(适用于ESL学习者)或法语(适用于FSL学习者)讲授《心理学概论》。凡顺利通过第一学期课程、二语达到中等或以上水平、并对此项目感兴趣的学生都可以报名参加。该课程由心理学教师用学生学习的二语讲授,教学大纲、教材以及考试内容与普通班(即未参加双语项目的班级)完全一致。语言教师同时参与整个教学过程,每次用大约20分钟的时间帮助学生复习或预习语言材料,使其掌握语言的应用,并在课余时间随时帮助学生解决所遇到的语言问题。

一个学期的教学实验取得了令人满意的成绩。研究结果表明,在学期末,实验班的学生学科课程学得和普通班一样好;二语水平有很大的提高,其语言水平的提高程度不亚于参加传统的二语课程班的学生;不同的是,前者在二语使用上比后者更有自信心(Edwards et al.,1984)。渥太华大学的研究者把这归功于含有大量可理解输入的封闭式双语教学环境,学生对目标语的广泛接触,以及学生焦虑感最大限度地降低。

1983年,渥太华大学的研究者又重复了该项实验;1984年双语课程扩大到两个学期。这期间,为 FSL 学生开设了《加拿大史》的双语课程,一年以后为 ESL 学生也开设了相应的课程。Haupt man 等(1988)对此进行了为期三年的研究,其研究结果与第一次实验的结果一致,即双语班的学生在学科水平、语言水平和语言运用上都取得了很大的进步,成绩不亚于普通班。

1985 年,由于财政预算等因素的限制,封闭式教学转为附加式教学。所谓附加式教学,指的是不再把所有的二语学习者"封闭"起来,而是让他们和本族语学生一起上相关的课程,但他们同时进行每周 90 分钟语言课程的学习。附加的语言课程不仅可以给学生提供语言支持,使他们能顺利完成学科课程,而且给他们提供了使用二语的"真实"场景(Burger et al.,1984)。Ready 和 Wesche(1992)对五个 FSL 和两个 ESL 课程班进行了评估式研究,证实了附加式教学和封闭式教学一样,实现了获得学科知识和提高语言能力的"双丰收"。北美和澳大利亚等地大学进行的以学科为基础的第二语言或外语教学模式同样支持并推广了这些研究结果(Brinton et al.,1989;Wesche,1993)。

推行依托式教学,从本质上说,就是通过学科学习来带动英语学习。Stryker 和 Leaver(1997)认为这种教学法的成功主要有三方面的原因:以学科内容为核心;使用真实的语言及语言材料;在课堂教学中注重学生的语言、认知和情感等因素。

三、依托式教学对我国大学英语教学的启示

在大学英语教学中,我们一向过于重视英语基本功,认为只有把语言基本功打好了,才能学好学科专业英语。李丽生(2002:39)指出,我国大学英语教学的一个误区是"我们目前推行的四、六级考试过于强调普通英语水平的测试"。她认为,只有把公共英语的基础打好才能搞好专业英语教学的做法"在某种程度上制约了我国大学英语的发展"。因此,"尽快改革目前的这种教学模式,提高专业英语教学的比重,用专业学科知识的学习带动英语学习,以英语提升专业水平"(李丽生,2002:39),是我们大学英语教学改革的当务之急。笔者认为,渥太华大学依托式教学的成功为我国大学英语教学的改革提供了借鉴的样式。依托式教学的成功经验告诉我们,在一定条件下,可以通过学科学习来提高英语水平,这对我国建立新的教学模式有很大的启示。

1. 在科研的基础上开展双语教学

我国高校目前进行双语教学时,对双语教学的合理性及其胜过传统课堂的

优越性很少进行认真的理论探讨,对双语教学班的教学效果也很少有人像渥太华大学那样去反复进行论证。

此外,在渥太华大学的依托式教学模式里,教师和学习者百分之百地使用目标语进行教学,而我国高校确实有百分之百使用英语授课的"双语班",但更多的是英汉夹杂的"双语班",如广东教育厅要求教师逐渐使用英文加中文的双语教学方式(刘刚,2002)。Jiang(2002)在对上海某高校双语教学的调查研究中发现,双语课堂中汉语的比例大约占60%,英语占40%。渥太华大学的依托式教学效果已为实验所证实,而我们混杂型"双语班"的有效性究竟如何?能否取得与渥太华大学同样效果?只有经过细致的科学调查,才能对这些问题作出回答。

目前采用英汉夹杂的"双语班"是一个不得已而为之的权宜之计,但目标一定要明确,即经过几年努力,我们的双语课堂百分之百地使用目标语进行教学。目前流行一种说法,双语教学就是在课堂上交替使用本族语和目标语这两种语言,如果我们不对这种"望文生义"式的双语教学的定义加以纠正,而把交替使用母语和目标语称为双语教学的话,那就会满足于现状,妨碍我们创建百分之百地使用目标语的双语教学模式。

2. 学生的外语水平

我国目前对双语教学的探索实行英语和汉语相结合的运作方式,其主要原因可能是考虑到学生的实际外语水平不高,无法适应完全使用英语授课的方式。而渥太华大学双语教学的实验证明,通过相应的二语水平考试并达到中等水平的学生绝大部分能够理解所学的课程内容,用二语完成作业,通过课程考试和语言考试(Edwards et al., 1984; Burger & Doherty, 1991)。笔者认为,我国的双语教学顺利实施的前提条件之一也应该是学生具有相应的英语水平,如果我们的大学生能够达到渥太华大学进入双语教学的英语水平线,那么学生就具备了"用专业学科知识的学习来带动英语学习"的语言基本功。

3. 真实的语言环境

双语教学的另一个要求是真实的语言环境。许多开设双语课程的学校使用英文原版教材就是为了符合这一要求。经过加工的语言材料往往缺乏必要的冗余信息,不能给学生提供真实的语言场景,因此无法使学生从有效的暗示中抓住问题的精髓,这也许是目前双语教学效果不明显的一个潜在原因。只有课程内容和真实的语言场景相结合才可以培养学生运用语境处理未知信息的能力,进而提高其外语水平。由此可见,100%真实的语言环境才是进行双语教学的必要条件之一,我国的双语教学应该向这个方向迈进。

4. 教师的培养

要培养出专业/外语类复合型人才,首先教师必须是专业/外语类复合型人才;要进行双语教学,教师应具有用外语上课的能力(吕良环,2001)。而目前普遍存在的情况是语言教师不了解学科课程内容,而学科教师往往过不了语言关。对合格教师的培养和培训也是我们应该亟待解决的问题。

5. 学科教师和语言教师相结合

渥太华大学的经验告诉我们,学科教师和语言教师紧密结合,是成功进行双语教学的有力保证。因而我国的双语教学也可以借鉴渥太华大学的模式,在对学科教师进行语言培训的同时,鼓励语言教师走进学科教师的双语课堂,帮助学生解决学科课程中遇到的语言问题。同时,我们也可让大学英语教师开设英美文化、历史地理等课程,把语言教学融入文化知识的传授。

参考文献

Brinton, D. M., M. A. Snow & M. B. Wesche (1989), *Content-based Second Language Instruction*. Heinle & Heinle Publishers.

Burger, S., M. Chrétien, M. Gingras, P. Haupt man & M. Migneron. Le role du professeur de langue dans un cours de matière académique en langue seconde. *La Revue Canadienne des Langues Vivantes* 41/2: 397 - 402.

Burger, S. & J. Doherty (1991), Sheltered instruction for young adult immigrants. TESL Ontario Conference.

Edwards, H., M. Wesche, S. Krashen, R. Clément, B. Kruidenier (1984), Second-language acquisition through subject-matter learning: A study of sheltered psychology classes at the University of Ottawa. *The Canadian Modern Language Review*. pp. 41 - 42.

Fortier, d'Lberville (1990), *Commissioner of Official Languages Annual Reports* 1989, 1990.

Hauptman, P., M. Wesche, & D. Ready (1988), Second language acquisition through subject-matter learning: A follow-up study at the University of Ottawa. *Language Learning* 38/3: 433 - 475.

Jiang, Q. H. (2002), A transition — EAP is needed from EGP to bilingual instruction. Unpublished MA thesis. Shanghai Jiaotong University.

Krashen, S. D. (1984), Immersion: Why it works and what it has taught us[J]. *Language and Society* 12: 61–64.

Ready, D. & M. Wesche (1992), An evaluation of the University of Ottawa's sheltered program: Language teaching strategies that work. In R. Courchêne, J. Glidden, J. St. John & C. Thérien (eds.). Comprehension-based Second Language Teaching/L'enseignement des langues secondes axésur la comprehension. Ottawa: Ottawa Press. pp.389–405.

Stern, H. H. (1978a), Bilingual schooling and foreign language education: Some implications of Canadian experiments in French immersion. *Alatis*. pp.165–188.

Stern, H. H. (1978b), French immersion in Canada: Achievements and directions. *Canadian Modern Language Review* 34: 836–854.

Stryker, S. B. & B. L. Leaver. (1997), *Content-based Instruction in Foreign Language Education*. Washington, D. C.: Georgetown University Press.

Wesche, M. B. (1993), Disciplined-based approaches to language study: Research issues and outcomes. In M. Krueger & F. Ryan (eds.). *Language and Content: Discipline-and Content-Based Approaches to Language Study*. Lexington, MA: D. C. Heath. pp.57–59.

李丽生：《SCLT 教学模式及其对我国大学英语教学改革的启示》，《外语界》2002 年第 4 期。

刘　刚：《关于双语教学的几点思考》，《四川行政学院学报》2002 年第 2 期。

吕良环：《谈双语教学与双语教师的在职英语培训》，《全球教育展望》2001 年第 12 期。

方法谈：

如何从实践中找到值得研究的问题？

以理论为导向的应用语言学沿用的是将语言学理论单向地应用于实践的研究范式的"单行道"，这种研究思维导致了理论与实践互动联系的忽略。而教育语言学并不是单纯的语言学在教育领域的"应用",而是以语言和教育中的现实问题为研究导向,强调研究、理论、政策与实践四位一体(Spolsky,1978;Hornberger,2001)。

实践出真知,好的外语教育的文章来自外语教育的具体实践。我想以"我的高校英汉双语教学研究之路"作为话题,具体说明是如何从大学英语教学实践里找到"在我国高校外语教学语境下如何进行双语教学"这一值得研究问题的。

一、在教学实践中探索高校英汉双语教学研究

1. 实践中找出研究课题

我国加入WTO后,需要大量既精通专业知识又具有高水平外语能力的专业人才,对于"哑巴英语"和"聋子英语"现象,人们再也无法容忍,一场大规模的大学英语教学改革就此拉开帷幕。2001年,教育部开始鼓励开展针对大学本科专业学习的双语教学,与此同时,我和外语教学界一些同仁开始探索运用双语教学理念来改进我国大学英语教学的路子。我那时正好获得加拿大政府颁发的"中国学者加拿大特别研究奖"(Special Award for Canadian Studies for Chinese Scholars),奔赴加拿大对该国的浸入式双语教育进行为期五周的考察。

加拿大出于其特殊国情的需要,他们首创的"浸入式"教学模式被誉为"在加拿大教学史上开展研究最深入、最广泛、最细致的一个项目"(Fortier,1990)。从1982年开始,以渥太华大学为代表的加拿大一些高等院校开始探索在二(外)语课堂里,一反传统的听说读写译的训练,是把二(外)语教学渗透到学科教学的课堂中,他们称之为"依托课程内容的语言教学"(content-based language instruction),简称CBI(依托式)。CBI和传统的二语(外语)教学最根本区别就是前者不像后者把语言学习作为教学目标,而是在学习学科知识的过程中,提高学习者的二语(外语)能力。渥太华CBI教学模式经过多年反复实验,其研究结果表明,依托式语言班的学生在学科水平、语言水平和语言运用上都取得了很大的进步,实现了学科知识的获得和语言能力的提高的"双丰收"(Edwards, Wesche, Krashen, Clément, & Kruidenier:1984; Hauptman, Wesche, & Ready, 1988; Wesche, 1993)。

但在当时,国内学界对双语教学尚缺乏足够的认识,出现了两种错误倾向:一种情况是因为国内没有现成的经验可以借鉴和现成的理论可以参考,就裹足不前;另一种情况则截然相反,不分时机、不看条件盲目进行双语教学。我认为

借鉴渥太华大学依托式双语教学的成功经验，可以避免这两种错误倾向。为了把这依托式教学理念引进到我国高校外语教学实践中去，我设立了"渥太华依托式教学课程和我国双语教学的开展"这样一个课题。那么我是如何做好这一课题的呢？

2. 研究和政策、实践、理论紧密联系

前面说过，教育语言学主张研究、理论、政策、实践四位一体（Hornberger, 2001），这一原则始终贯彻在我的课题整个过程之中。从政策层面上来讲，需要吃透教育部（2001）号文件精神和教育部1999年颁布的《大学英语教学大纲》（修订本），以及其他一系列文件。这些文件对我国大学外语教学如何更好适应我国加入WTO后的人才需要给出了一系列明确指示，这就是我的课题的决心和信心所在。

除了吃透政策外，还需要彻底搞清楚双语教育的理论。加拿大著名学者卡敏斯（J. Cummins）明确表示：集他一生双语教育研究的经验，"第二语言作为媒介的教学能够提高第二语言水平而且不会影响学生的第一语言水平或学科知识的掌握"（Cummins, 2009: iv）。卡敏斯这一论断的理论根据就是他制作的"共同的潜在能力理论模型"（Common Underlying Proficiency Model，简称CUP，Cummins, 1984；Cummins & Swain, 1986），该理论模型用冰山来比喻双语者的两种语言，从露出水平面的冰山顶部来看，这两种语言好像是彼此分离的两座冰山，然后，在水平面下是一个共同的冰山根部。两种语言表面看似不同，双语者操控的却是同一个中心处理系统。卡敏斯这一理论模式被加拿大几十年双语教育实践反复证实，同时又反过来指导着加拿大双语教育的实践。

卡敏斯从心理学角度论证双语教学的可行性，现在再从二（外）语教学理论角度来看依托式教学的优势。从性质上来说，CBI是一种交际性的语言教学方法，是一种在交际语言教学原则的基础上发展而成的交际教学路径（Stryker & Leaver, 1997）。Richards和Rodgers（2001）指出，这种把学科内容和语言教学密切联系的教学手段可以弥补学生在语言能力和语言实际应用能力之间存在差异的有效方法，它与传统的外语教学方法最大的不同之处就是，"通过学习题材（subject matter），而不是单纯学习语言来获得语言能力"。总之，CBI的教学理念是：重在通过语言进行学习（learning through language），而不仅仅是学习语言（learning language），这也叫内容驱动（content-driven），而传统的通过听说读写训练学习语言的方法叫语言驱动（language-driven）。

最后,这一课题成为发表在《外语教学与研究》的文章《渥太华大学依托式课程教学及其启示》(俞理明、韩建侠,2003),课题的落脚点正如文章写道:"……本文简要介绍了渥太华大学的双语教学模式,并且提出自己的一些看法,希望我国的大学双语教学既要克服潮流化,又要避免保守性的倾向,把双语教学搞好,为大学英语改革创出一条新路子。"

二、研究无止境

本课题虽然完成,但笔者的"高校英汉双语教学研究之路"才刚刚开始。课题只是在理论上说明渥太华大学依托式教学理念对我国大学英(外)语教学改革有借鉴意义,还没有实证研究来证明。于是,我们开始探索在我国高校大学英语教学背景下的CBI的效果。研究取得和渥太华大学相同的结果:一个学期下来,和对照组相比,实验组表现出更强的学习英语的愿望和更高的阅读水平和语言综合使用能力,除此之外,实验组学生还系统地学到了美国文明发展历史的知识(袁平华、俞理明,2008)。

此外,教育部(2001)文件的重心是专业课的双语教学,这种双语教学后来称为英语作为媒体的教学(English Medium Instruction,简称EMI)。在CBI模式里,在学习开始前不需要学习者的英语达到能应付课程内容的熟练程度。EMI则不同,学生的英语水平必须达到不会损害他们专业知识学习。也就是说,要有效开展双语教学,学生的英语水平要达到一定的阈限(Threshold Level)(Cummins,1984)。那么怎样确定我国大学生进入双语教学的阈限? 一个新课题由此而生。我们发现渥太华大学二语学院研制了二语水平考试,规定只有达到中等水平或以上的学生才能进入CBI课程。于是,我们做了一个我国大学四、六级考试和渥太华大学二语水平测试的相关研究。我们的研究发现如果大学英语四级考试中取得优秀的成绩或通过大学英语六级考试的,就达到渥太华大学的中等或者中等以上的水平,这样的学生可以通过英语这一弱势语言获取学科知识,同时提高其弱势语言的水平(韩建侠、俞理明,2007)。

为了证实上面的结论,我们又开展了一个新的课题。上海交大/密歇根大学联合学院是全英语授课的,他们的英语四级考试达到了优秀。我们的研究问题是:这样的学生的学科成绩是否会受到损害? 我们把他们和交大用汉语进行教学的常规教学组的学生作对比。研究结果表明,两组学生在学科成绩(以化学为例)上不存在显著性差异,但从英语能力来说,实验组优于对照组(俞理明、韩建侠,2011)。我们的一系列实证研究说明,学生的认知能力和学业既可以通过单语渠道,也可以通过得到充分发展的双语渠道得到充实,这个意思用我们学界通俗的话来表达就是"1+1>2"。

随着时间的推移,CBI 教学理念不仅在大学英语课堂上,也不仅在专业学习的双语教学中普及,我国外语界还有研究者把 CBI 教学理念推行到英语专业的教学改革之中,并且取得一定的成效。大连外国语大学常俊跃教授和他的同事们开始在英语专业探索使用 CBI 教学模式(常俊跃等,2008;常俊跃、董海楠,2008;常俊跃、赵永青,2010),进而运用到英语专业整体课程体系的改革(常俊跃等,2013;常俊跃,2014)。常俊跃教授还在把 CBI 教学理念运用到我国外国语院校外语专业的教学实践过程中,制作出"内容语言融合"(Content and Language Integrated Learning)的理论模式,并在此基础上开创出区域和国别研究,现在这已经成为外国语言文学专业的五大学科领域之一。

三、余论

现在回过头来看,当年我把课题定名为"渥太华依托式教学课程和我国双语教学的开展"是欠妥的。这是因为"双语教学"既可以指为大学英语教学服务的 CBI,也可以指为专业教学搭建平台的 EMI,既然我的课题研究对象是前者,不是后者,因此,课题更为恰当的名称应当是"渥太华依托式教学课程和我国大学英语教学的开展"。当时我所以对此缺乏足够的认识的一个非常重要原因是渥太华大学依托式课程本身兼有 CBI 和 EMI 的特征。中、加二国的社会、文化存在巨大差异,我们不可能原封不动照搬渥太华依托式教学模式,不对 CBI 和 EMI 作区分,甚至相提并论,这在渥太华大学似乎问题不大,但在我国大学英语教学的语境里,是行不通的。课题无论是名称还是在具体的文章里,笼统提"双语教学",会引起我国学界对这个概念的误解。

世纪之交以来,多轮次、大规模的大学英语教改告诉我们,传统的听说读写训练的语言驱动教学路子事倍功半,是高校外语教学低效费时的根源;而走内容驱动的教学路子则能取得事半功倍的效果(俞理明、韩建侠,2012)。而专业课的双语教学,正如中国科学院院士、同济大学教授汪品先所说那样:"已经成为我国当前的主流趋势。"(汪品先,2015)20 年左右的高校教学实践无可辩驳证明 21 世纪初教育部在高校推行的双语教学是一个意义重大、影响深远的明智的举措。

文章行将结束,我想自我调侃一下。如果说世纪之初我所做的那个课题内容和名称因为名实不副而难以交差,那么多亏这些年的坚持实践,这一课题到现在可以交差了。

参考文献

Spolsky, B. (1978), *Educational Linguistics: An Introduction*. Rowley, MA: Newbury House.

Hornberger, N. H. (2001), Educational linguistics as a field: A view from Penn's program on the occasion of its 25th anniversary. *Working Papers in Educational Linguistics* 17(1-2): 1-26.

教育部:《关于加强高等院校本科教学工作提高教学质量的若干意见》,2001年。

Fortier, d'Lberville (1990), Commissioner of Official Languages Annual Reports 1989, 1990.

Edwards, H., M. Wesche, S. Krashen, R. Clément. & B. Kruidenier (1984), Second-language acquisition through subject-matter learning: A study of sheltered psychology classes at the University of Ottawa, *The Canadian Modern Language Review* 41(2): 268-282.

Hauptman, P., M. Wesche & D. Ready (1988), Second language acquisition through subject-matter learning: A follow-up study at the University of Ottawa, *Language Learning* 38(3): 433-475.

Wesche M. B. (1993), Disciplined-based approaches to language study: Research issues and outcomes. In M. Krueger & F. Ryan (eds), *Language and Content: Discipline-and Content-Based Approaches to Language Study*, Lexington, MA: D. C. Heath. pp.57-59.

俞理明、韩建侠:《渥太华大学依托式课程教学及其启示》,载《外语教学与研究》2003年第6期,第465—469页。

《大学英语教学大纲》,上海外语教育出版社1999年版。

Cummins, J. (2009), Preface, In Liming. Yu, E. Yeoman & J. Han (eds.), *Bilingual Education: The Implications of the Canadian Immersion Education to the Bilingual Instruction in Chinese Universities*, iii-vii Beijing: Foreign Language Teaching and Research Press.

Cummins, J. (1984), *Bilingualism and Special Education: Issues in Assessment and Pedagogy*, Clevedon, UK: Multilingual Matters.

Cummins, J. & M. Swain (1986), *Bilingualism in Education: Aspects of Theory, Research and Practice*, London and New York: Longman.

Stryker, S. B. & B. L. Leaver (1997), *Content-based Instruction in Foreign Language Education*, Washington D.C.: Georgetown University Press.

Richards, J. & T. Rodgers (2001), *Approaches and Methods in Language Teaching* (2nd edition), Cambridge: Cambridge University Press.

袁平华、俞理明:《以内容为依托的大学外语教学模式研究》,《外语教学与研究》2008年第1期,第59—64页。

韩建侠、俞理明:《高校进行双语教学学生所具备的英语水平》,《现代外语》2007年第1期,第65—72页。

俞理明、韩建侠:《初始英语水平对全英语双语教学效果的影响》,《中国外语》2011年第3期,第59—66页。

常俊跃、赵秀艳、李莉莉:《英语专业低年级阶段系统开展内容依托教学的可行性探索》,《外语与外语教学》2008年第12期,第24—30页。

常俊跃、董海楠:《英语专业基础阶段内容依托教学问题的实证研究》,《外语与外语教学》2008年第5期,第11—20页。

常俊跃、赵永青:《学生视角下的英语专业基础阶段"内容·语言"融合的课程体系》,《外语与外语教学》2010年第1期,第13—17页。

常俊跃、赵永青、赵秀艳:《关于我国高校英语专业培养目标、培养要求和核心课程的思考》,《外语教学与研究》2013年第6期,第933—940页。

常俊跃:《英语专业内容依托课程体系改革的影响及启示》,《解放军外国语学院学报》2014年第5期,第23—31页。

俞理明、韩建侠:《内容驱动还是语言驱动——对我国高校大学英语教学的一点思考》,《外语与外语教学》2012年第3期,第1—4页。

汪品先:《一场"去中国化"运动是不是正在中国悄悄掀起?》,《文汇报》,2015年2月27日。

论生态话语和行为分析的假定和原则*

黄国文**

摘要： 在生态话语和行为分析过程中，决定某一话语是属于有益性话语、破坏性话语还是中性话语的主要标准是由分析者的生态观决定的。本文基于儒家传统，提出一个基本假定（"以人为本"）和三条原则（良知原则、亲近原则、制约原则）来指导生态话语和行为分析。本文认为，这个假定和原则是中国语境中和谐话语分析的核心要素。

关键词： 生态观；以人为本；良知原则；亲近原则；制约原则

一、引　言

生态语言学研究的是语言与生态问题，大多数研究都与"生态危机"有关（包括气候变化、环境污染、物种丧失等等）。对于生态问题，一般都赞成绿水青山，蓝天白云；但是，在具体实践中，不同人往往就有不同的看法。比如说，工业化所带来的污染问题，在发达国家过上好日子的人希望去工业化，而生活在贫困地区或生活条件差的人则希望工业化，期待科学技术提高生活水平。

对很多人来说，生态语言学基本上属于批评语言学，但它的研究范围比批评语言学更广，是探讨怎样保护地球和环境等问题。对于不利于生态平衡、物种多

---

* 原载《外语教学与研究（外国语文双月刊）》2017年第6期。

** 黄国文，教育部国家级人才特聘教授，广东省优秀社会科学家，华南农业大学外国语学院教授、博士生导师。现任国际生态语言学学会（IEA）中国地区代表，中国英汉语比较研究会副会长，中国英汉语比较研究会英汉语篇分析专业委员会主任，广东外国语学会会长。担任CSSCI来源期刊《中国外语》主编，M. A. K. Halliday Library Functional Linguistics Series 语言学丛书（Springer）联合主编，国际期刊 *Journal of World Languages*（de Gruyter）联合编辑；曾任国际期刊 *Functional Linguistics*（Springer）期刊联合主编。

样性的社会实践,要批评、反对、抵制;对于有利于生态的社会实践,则要推崇、鼓励。英国生态语言学研究者Stibbe(2015)根据话语的性质区分了三种类型:有益性话语(beneficial discourse)、破坏性话语(destructive discourse)、中性话语(ambivalent discourse)。判断话语类型的标准是研究者的意识形态、伦理准则、价值观、生态哲学。

本文的目的是探讨生态话语和行为分析中的一个基本假定和三条原则;这个假定是"以人为本"(the assumption of people-orientedness);三条原则是:良知原则(the principle of conscience)、亲近原则(the principle of proximity)、制约原则(the principle of regulation)。以人为本的假定和三条原则可用于指导我们的社会实践,指导我们的生态话语和行为分析及生态语言学研究。

二、生态哲学观

关于人的哲学观、价值观、伦理观等问题,可以从人类、历史、宗教、社会、经济、教育等方面讨论。生态语言学研究者的生态哲学观是由他们的世界观、哲学观、价值观、伦理准则影响和决定的。据Stibbe(2015:11)说,他与丹麦的资深生态语言学研究者Jorgen C. Bang讨论了生态语言学问题,Bang认为,生态语言学的基础是为当地和全球文化做贡献,其中合作、分享、民主对话、和平和非暴力、生活各层面的平等以及生态可持续性都是生态语言学的根本特点和首要价值观。Bang这里所说的隐含着一种明显的世界观和价值观。

Naess(1995:8)使用"生态观"(ecosophy; ecological philosophy)来描述某些生态哲学原则。他认为,生态观指生态和谐观,其规范性显而易见,包含标准、法则、前提、价值取向和相关状态假设。一个人生态观的形成受很多因素影响,主要是由他所处的环境(包括生长的地方、生活的条件、受教育的程度、所接触人的范围、对历史、地理乃至人类发展史的了解以及自己的价值观、伦理准则等等)和他的经历等因素影响后形成的。有人认为要以生态为中心(ecocentric),有人认为要以人类为中心(anthropocentric),有人对生态问题抱悲观主义态度,有人则抱乐观主义态度。生长在同一个环境下并接受几乎同样教育的两个人,也可能采取完全不同的生态观。

Stibbe(2015:13—14)概述了生态观,并认为生态观复杂深奥,一个人的生态观随着其所接触的新观点及发现的新证据而获得的新体验在不断变化和不断演化。要概述一种普世的生态观非常困难,一个人的生态哲学观可能是不断变化的。

Stibbe(同上)提出了自己所认同的生态哲学观,并用一个英语单词"Living!"(生活!)来概述。他所提出的生态观包括了七个要素:重视生活(valuing living)、福祉(wellbeing)、现在和未来(now and the future)、关怀(care)、环境极限(environmental limits)、社会公正(social justice)和适应性(resilience)。他对这些要素做了比较详细的说明。这七个要素没有"重要—次要"之分,也没有先后顺序,因此是同等重要。认真研究这些要素,我们发现它们的重要性可以区分,且应该有顺序。

首先,最重要的是"重视生活";只有重视生活、热爱生活,才能明白生命的意义,才能爱护自己,关心他人。接着是"福祉",就是要活得有质量,活得开心,这样生活才是幸福的。要活得有质量、开心,就不能只考虑当下,还要考虑未来,这就是"现在和未来"这个要素的内容;我们今天好好活着,也要考虑明天的日子,还要想着子孙后代能幸福生活。我们要幸福的生活,就要有吃的东西来满足我们,因此就会杀鸡宰牛来提高生活质量,这其实是人类为了自己的生存和福祉而伤害其他生命。对此,要有同情心和感恩之心,对杀害动物要感到遗憾,要认识到人类对其他物种的影响和伤害,要尽量把伤害最小化,通过爱护、保护生态来"反哺"供养着我们的生态系统,这就是"关怀"。因为我们要活得有质量,伤害其他动物和植物是不可避免的,但我们要时刻意识到"环境极限"问题,不能过度消耗自然资源,不能严重破坏生态系统,不能浪费资源,尽力减少自然的消耗量。在我们幸福生活的时候,要想到地球上还有很多人缺乏生存或维持幸福生活所需的资源。我们过度的消费或浪费,是以剥夺别人幸福生活为代价的,这就是"社会公正"要考虑的问题。要想人人幸福地生活,地球上的各种资源就需要由富到贫进行重新分配。由于人类对生活水平的要求越来越高,这就势必对生态造成越来越多的破坏,这也是工业社会发展所带来的必然结果;因此,我们要适应环境变化,提高适应环境变化的能力,重视生活中的"适应性"问题,并寻求新的社会生活方式。

从 Stibbe(2015)所说的生态哲学观七个要素看,我们认为,出发点还是以人类为中心,首先是要重视人的生活("重视生活"),而且要过得好("福祉"),然后既考虑现在也考虑未来("现在和未来"),也关心别人("关怀""社会公正"),最终是要认识到地球所能提供给人类的资源是有限的("环境极限"),因此必须提高对环境的"适应性"能力。

三、儒家生态观——以人为本

很多关于儒家生态思想的论著(Zhou，2017；Zhou & Huang，2017；蒙培元，2004；乔清举，2013)都用"天人合一""以天地万物为一体""天地以生物为心"等思想来概括生态观。就社会实践而言，人类是追求美好生活的，无论过去、现在还是将来(狩猎文明时代、农业文明时代、工业文明时代、生态文明时代、物种文明时代)，人类都会利用自然资源来提高自己的生活质量。因此，吃鱼吃肉来提高生活的质量是常见的，不可避免的。

《论语·述而篇》中有"子钓而不纲，弋不射宿"的记载，说的是孔子用鱼竿钓鱼而不用渔网捕鱼，用弋射的方式获取猎物，但从不射取休息中的鸟兽。"钓而不纲"隐含的是不贪，"弋不射宿"隐含的是不乘危，所以一般都认为前者是赞扬孔子的"智"，后者是赞扬孔子的"仁"。《论语·乡党篇》有这样的记载："厩焚。子退朝，曰：'伤人乎？'不问马。"马棚失火，孔子退朝赶回来问："有人受伤了吗？"而不是问伤着马没有。孔子生活的春秋时期，马应该比仆人或养马的人要珍贵，但马棚失火以后，孔子先问人，而没有问马的情况，这是为什么？也许可以从下面王阳明的话语中找到答案。

王阳明是明代思想大家，被称为是儒家精神的复活者。其《传习录·钱德洪录》(鸿雁，2013：349—350)中有这么一段记载：

问"大人与物同体，如何《大学》又说个厚薄？"

先生曰："惟是道理自有厚薄。比如身是一体，把手足捍头目，岂是偏要薄手足？其道理合如此。禽兽与草木同是爱的，把草木去养禽兽，又忍得？人与禽兽同是爱的，宰禽兽以养亲，与供祭祀，燕宾客，心又忍得？至亲与路人同是爱的，如箪食豆羹，得则生，不得则死，不能两全，宁救至亲，不救路人，心又忍得？这是道理合该如此。及至吾身与至亲，更不得分别彼此厚薄。盖以仁民爱物皆从此出，此处可忍，更无所不忍矣。《大学》所谓厚薄，是良知上自然的条理，不可逾越，此便谓之义；顺这个条理，便谓之礼；知此条理，便谓之智；终始是这条理，便谓之信。"

在这一段回答里,王阳明说得非常清楚:我们对禽兽和草木一样有爱,但我们用草木去饲养禽兽;我们对人和禽兽一样有爱,但我们宰杀禽兽以奉养亲人、祭祀祖先、招待客人;我们对至亲和路人一样有爱,但如果只有一箪食一豆羹,人吃了便能活命,不吃便会死,但我们又不可能同时拯救两个人,遇到这种情况,我们只能放弃路人而去救至亲。王阳明认为,《大学》上所说的厚薄,是良知上自然而有秩序的,不可逾越,这就称为义,遵循这个秩序(条理),就称为礼;明白这个秩序(条理)就称为智;自始至终坚持这个秩序(条理)就称为信。

按照张学智(2004:31)的观点,王阳明是"主张在万物一体境界的观照下合理地取用万物"的。无论是禽兽与草木之间,还是宰禽兽以养亲之间或至亲与路人之间,不能两全,该取舍时就得取舍,这就是道理,也是良知上自然的条理,不可逾越。因此,"王阳明的万物一体境界是爱万物和合理取用万物的统一。人是自然界的一个成员,人从他所在的环境中取得生活资料以维持自身的生存和发展是至为合理的要求,实际上人类几千年来一直将此视为天经地义,没有人会怀疑人从自然界取得生活资料的合法性"(同上)。

无论是几百年前王阳明所说的,还是现在Stibbe(2015)所说的,观点其实一致,即人类应当最小限度地影响、采用和破坏其他物种,要有节制、有限制地取用自然资源,尽量保持生态的平衡;这也是生态环境伦理学所研究的问题。但是,人类首先考虑的是自己的生活。

荀子在《王制》篇中说:"水火有气而无生,草木有生而无知,禽兽有知而无义;人有气、有生、有知,亦且有义,故最为天下贵也。"这里说的是,水火有气却没有生命,草木有生命却没有知觉,禽兽有知觉却不讲道义;人有气、有生命、有知觉,而且讲究道义,所以人是天下最为贵重的。人之所以最为贵重,是因为人会思维,有意识,有语言,能结合成社会群体,群体中有等级名分;人有了道义,确定了名分,就能沟通协调、团结一致、和谐相处;群体强大了,就能战胜外物。

虽然我们信奉"天人合一""以天地万物为一体""人以天地生物之心为心"等传统的生态思想,认为动物、植物等都有生命,都要得到爱护、保护。但在人与动物的选择上,首先选择的是人,这在古今中外都是这样的。这就是我们所讲的"以人为本"的理念。

"以人为本"是春秋时期齐国名相管仲提出来的:"夫霸王之所始也,以人为本。本理则国固,本乱则国危。"(见《管子》商务印书馆"万有文库"版本,1936年版,第二册第8页)说的是霸王的事业之所以有良好的开端,是因为以人民为根本。这个本理顺了国家才能巩固,这个本乱了国家就会危亡。管仲所说的"以人为本",就是以人民为本。新中国成立后,"以人为本"也成为坚持全心全意为人民服务的根本宗旨和科学发展观的核心。因此,我们认为,进行生态话语和行为分析,首先就要接受"以人为本"这个基本假定。

四、三条原则

本文遵循儒家思想,认为人与其他生命形式(包括动物、植物等)的主要不同是"性善",人是天下第一宝贵的;做人必须有道义、有良知,这是人与其他物种的主要区别之一;我们的世界观、价值观、伦理观、生态观中的要素有重要与次要之分,也有先后顺序之分。因此,我们的假定是"以人为本"。从生态哲学来看,有三条原则可以指导我们的生态话语和行为分析与生态语言学研究:良知原则、亲近原则、制约原则。下面我们通过一些例子来讨论这三条原则。

1. 良知原则

"良知"这一概念来源于《孟子》,但王阳明给了自己的理解和阐释,赋予它更多的内涵,其中最主要的是,良知是对性体的自觉,是道德判断的主体。"致良知"是阳明学说的核心内容,是他的宇宙论和道德论,也是其修养论。《传习录》中多次谈到"良知"。他说:"良知者心之本体"(《传习录·答陆原静书》,见鸿雁,2013:274),又说:"知是心之本体,心自然会知。见父自然知孝,见兄自然知弟,见孺子入井自然知恻隐。此便是良知,不假外求"(《传习录·徐爱录》,见鸿雁,2013:177)。根据王阳明的观点,心自然会感知,因为知是心的本体,心是一切知识和体验的起源,包括道德意识,道德原则与规范,孝悌忠信、仁义礼智和伦理准则都起源于心,对周围一切的反应和一切行为也是起源于心。见到父亲自然就会有孝敬之心,见到兄长自然会尊敬,见到小孩落井恻隐之心就会自然产生。这就是良知,全凭本心,不需从心外的其他地方求得。因此,"心之本体即是天理"(《传习录·答欧阳崇一》,见鸿雁,2013:289),天理显现于心,具体表现为对事物价值判断和态度,因此"良知"成为衡量一切是非善恶的内在标准。

在对待生态系统中的物种,我们的良知原则主要是指生态良知。"生态良知是由于人类逐渐意识到人与自然之间的生存论意义上的关联而产生的一种关爱、保护自然的自然、自觉、自愿的'善'的观念"(王天孜,2005:1)。

下面我们看一个关于男子虐杀鹦鹉的例子:

网传男子虐杀鹦鹉将其淹死拔毛　疑因鹦鹉咬人

近日网络流传一段虐杀鹦鹉的视频,视频中男子拿着一只鹦鹉,鹦鹉不时发出凄厉的叫声,而后男子把整只鹦鹉浸到水盆中。"看看还会叫吗,死的,杀好了,一万多块钱,会咬人要它干什么。"而后的视频中的鹦鹉已经被拔光了毛。

据报道,这是发生在我国云南省的一个事件,这则消息于2016年1月4日在多个网站出现,有些网站还链接了该男子虐杀鹦鹉的视频。从报道上看,鹦鹉被残酷地杀死,虐杀鹦鹉的男子还用嚣张的话语来表达他的态度。黄国文、陈旸(2016)曾用这个例子来比较不同的报道所传达的信息。这篇报道只突出了残忍杀死鹦鹉的事实,但没有提到虐杀鹦鹉的男子所应该受到的谴责或惩罚,也没有对此事件作出任何评论。很明显,对这件事,报道人是抱着局外人的心态"看热闹",客观地陈述事实,没有表达自己的伦理准则和价值判断,标题中用"疑因鹦鹉咬人"来给读者传递"男人虐杀鹦鹉是因为鹦鹉咬人"这样的信息,为残杀鹦鹉的行为找原因。

从良知原则看,报道中的男子没有关爱、保护动物的自然、自觉、自愿的"善"的观念,从他的话语中可以看出,这是一个"暴发户"的行为,表现了"我是有钱人,我可以任性,我想杀就杀"的心态。这也反映了目前中国一些"土豪"的所思所想、所作所为。写报道的人也没有遵循良知原则,对这种事情采取的是"事不关己"和"看热闹"的态度,应该表达的价值判断没有表达,或者说报道表达了作者冷漠的心理和良知的缺失。

良知是判断一切善恶是非的标准,离开良知,我们就无法判断是非、辨别善恶,正如王阳明所说的,"凡所谓善恶之机,真妄之辩者,舍吾心之良知,亦将何所致其体察乎?"(《传习录·答顾东桥书》,见鸿雁,2013:253)。我们如果舍弃心中的良知,对于善恶的原因、真假的区别就无法去体察了。很多学者都已经指出,良知对构建和谐社会有重要意义。

2. 亲近原则

就儒家生态观而言,研究者都会说,儒家思想追求自然和谐和人与自然的和谐,天人合一,天地以生物为心。但正如郑家栋(2003:11)所说,"儒家思想的核心或曰本质特征并不在于一般的追求自然和谐,而在于谋求自然和谐与差等秩序的统一","'和谐'中本来就包含了'差等'";"'差等'之对于儒家是更为本质的东西",这种"差等"观念导致儒家认同和接受现实的伦常法规和等级秩序。因此,自然中的各种生命形式(自己、至亲、朋友、路人、飞禽、鸟兽、草木、山川,等等)都被理解为一个由近及远、从亲到疏的序列。

很多儒学研究者都研究人与自然的关系,因此很多人都会讨论儒学与生态问题(蒙培元,2004;乔清举,2013)。杜维明(2003:7)明确指出,"王阳明说人和人之间的关系,人和动物的关系,人和植物的关系,人和山川的关系,都是一体的。但是这个'体'是绝对要分殊的。而人的本身,对于亲人的关系,对于路人的关系,也有分。分并不表示没有共同体的观念,而是怎样把多元性、多样性和'一体'配合起来的问题"。杜维明说的多元性、多样性和"一体"配合起来,其实也是等级秩序问题。

人与地球上其他生命形式的关系是有亲疏之分的。从以人为本的基本假定看,每个人都是首先以"我"为中心的;在对待其他生命形式时,就是从"我"的亲疏关系开始的。与其他生命形式的亲疏关系可以从不同的维度定义:地理的、空间的、时间的、认知的、感情的、知识结构的,等等。例如,一个人在接触狗(包括读有关狗的书、文章和观看有关电影、视频和照片等)或养狗之前,天下所有的狗对他来说都是一样的,但是,他如果养狗,就会慢慢地喜欢或不喜欢某一类狗;同一类狗,他养了多年的那只肯定要比市场上或公园里的那类狗要亲近。同样地,一个人到陌生的地方,开始同所有人都不是亲近的,但通过跟人接触,慢慢就可以按照与自己的亲疏关系把周围的人分出三六九等。这就是我们讲的亲近原则。

这里举个例子说明。据《孟子·梁惠王上》记载,齐宣王(战国时齐国国王田辟疆)与孟子谈论用仁德统一天下的道理时,有这样的情节:孟子说到他听说过这样一件事:一天齐宣王坐在堂上,有个人牵着牛从堂下经过,大王见了,问:"把牛牵到哪里去?"那人回答说:"要用它祭钟。"大王说:"放了它!我不忍心看它惊惧哆嗦的样子,像这么毫无罪过就被拉去杀掉。"那人问:"那么就不要祭钟了吗?"大王说:"怎么可以不要呢?用羊替代它!"齐宣王说用羊替代牛,不是因为牛比羊大(而吝啬地)不舍得,而是不忍心,因为他看到了牛惊惧哆嗦的样子。孟子评论说:这种做法就是仁德的表现方式,因为当时大王看到了牛而没有看到羊。君子对于禽兽,看到它们活蹦欢跳的,就不忍心看见它们死去;听到它们哀叫悲鸣,就不忍心再吃它们的肉。

根据这个故事我们可以提出一条生态哲学中的"有序"(亲近)原则:当某一

物种(动物、植物)与你有关联时,你会对它有感觉、有感情,对发生在它身上的事情有反应。这就是我们所说的亲近原则。假设当时齐宣王看到的动物不是牛,而是羊,他可能就会提出用牛来替代羊。同样,上面讲到的王阳明说到的当只有一箪食时,要给的是至亲的人而不是陌生的路人,也是这个道理。

3. 制约原则

人作为有思维、有思想、有语言的物种,与其他动物的最大不同是有意念,有理性,讲究道义,有等级制度,有社会组织,有行为规则。这里讲的"制约",有三个层次:一是个人的良知和修养给自己的制约,二是社团的"乡规民约"的制约,三是社会、机构的法制制约。一个人、一个社区、一个社会、一个国家是否足够文明、是否有生态意识,可以从规则的制定和执行来衡量。从国家、各级政府立规上说,首先要把人当人来看待,这就是我们前面所说的"以人为本"的假定,第二是所制定的规则要有可操作性,权力必须公平、规范、有约束力和被约束的限制。个人的规则要服从于社区的规则,社区的规则要服从于社会、机构的法制制约,这样才有可能达到社会安定、人与人和人与自然的和谐相处。

举个例子。2017年1月29日发生了一起老虎咬人的事件:一个普通的打工者想去参观宁波雅戈尔动物园,因为不想花钱买门票便做出了逃票的决定,翻墙进了动物园。进去后被一只300多斤的西伯利亚虎(东北虎)咬死,动物园人员用鞭炮驱赶老虎,但那只老虎没有走开。最终老虎被宁波市公安局特警队员用枪击毙。人终于被紧急送进医院,但已经无法救活了。这个事件的结局是老虎死了,人也死了。这无疑是个悲剧,公众对此事的议论存在着完全不同的意见,出现了"挺虎派"和"挺人派"的对立。据有关资料称,西伯利亚虎是珍贵动物,至2015年初统计,世界上仅存不足500头,被列入《世界自然保护联盟》(IUCN)2011年濒危物种红色名录。

这件事的起因是逃票的人没有遵守规则,导致自己丧失生命。如果按照制约原则,那会赞成"挺虎派"的观点;但是作为政府有关部门,首先是遵守"以人为本"的假定,即使是在判断到人的生命已经十分危险或已经死亡的情况下,为了抓紧时间抢救人,决定击毙老虎,以便能把人送去医院抢救。无论公众怎样表达自己的观点和不同意见,政府有关部门把老虎击毙的行为是根据以人为本的理念做出的。虽然西伯利亚虎是珍贵保护动物,虽然这个悲剧是由于人违反规则造成的,虽然当时把人救出后也不一定能救活,但是,把老虎击毙是正确的决定,因为我们无论怎样强调保护动物(哪怕是濒危物种),人的生命是最可贵的。这就反映了我们提出的生态哲学中的以人为本的理念。

再举一例。在中国,"养狗"传统上是为自己服务的,即为用而养的,如看门、防盗等。由于经济发展和受国外文化的影响,有些城市人也养狗(犬)作为宠物来陪伴自己,有些人甚至把自己养的犬当作亲人来对待。但是,城市里养犬也给社区带来一些问题,遛犬时不及时清理粪便、不牵犬绳和犬吠扰民等不文明养犬行为时有发生,市民向有关管理部门投诉的情况越来越多。因此,不同层级的政府机构都先后出台了有关"养犬管理条例",对养犬不登记、不续期、携犬外出不牵犬绳等违规养犬行为提出整治办法;但是,这几类突出的不文明养犬行为还是无法杜绝。养犬人没有规约自己,"乡规民约"也无法制约这些行为,所以最后只能由政府有关部门来处理。例如,据《羊城晚报》(2017年8月14日,A6)报道,从8月份起,广州开展最严养犬执法整治专项行动。《羊城晚报》报道的标题是"养犬不登记 遛狗不牵绳 查!"。有关部门除了按照有关条例来处罚外,还是希望养犬人能自觉遵守政府规定和道德行为规范,为自己的爱犬申领犬牌,定期注射狂犬疫苗,同时做到遛犬牵犬绳、拾粪便,不干扰他人,自觉规范养犬行为,做一名有责任心的养犬人。

从上面两个例子可以看出,制约原则在生态话语和行为分析中非常重要;在大多数情况下,来自三个方面(个人、社团、国家)的制约都是必要的,它们相得益彰、互相作用,一个人的良知和修养会制约自己的行为,一个追求平和的社团(社区)是有"乡规民约"来制约大家的行为的,一个文明的社会是有法制、机制来制约和管理自己的。

4. 三条原则的配合

上面提出的三条原则相辅相成,提出这些原则也是试图给"和谐话语分析"(Harmonious Discourse Analysis)(见黄国文,2016;赵蕊华、黄国文,2017)提供一些分析视角和指引。何时采用何条原则,要视问题的性质而定。在很多情况下,三条原则常常是一起工作的。例如,上文列举的宁波雅戈尔动物园老虎咬人事件,以人为本的假定和三条原则都用得上。公安局特警队员到来时明知救活那个人的机会已经没有或几乎没有,但还是要及早把人送去医院,因此只能把老虎击毙,这是根据以人为本(人最重要)的假定来做决定的。从感觉、感情、良知看,人要比老虎可贵、重要,这是遵守良知原则。从我们的社会、政府和人类来说,跟人的关系肯定比跟老虎的要更加亲近。但是,从制约原则看,该男子的行为违反了规定(参观动物园是必须购票的),但由于有了"以人为本"的假定,这条原则就被违反了。必须指出的是,如果我们只强调以人为本、良知和亲情(亲近),容忍违背"制约原则",那就常常要以扰乱社会秩序为代价。

五、结　语

从文献上看,从事生态哲学研究的学者都会说,人是自然界的产物,也是自然界的一部分,人不能任意凌驾于自然界之上,不能随意控制、征服、改造自然。但是,在社会实践中,以人类为中心,通过改造自然来提高生活水平的例子处处可见。因此,才需要一代一代对生态友好的人的努力,唤起大众的生态良知,保护自然,保护环境,就是保护我们自己,也是保护我们的子孙后代。

在对待生态问题上,虽然很多学者都批评人类中心主义,有些人甚至提倡不繁衍后代,即"人类自愿灭绝运动"(Voluntary Human Extinction Movement)。但是,在社会实践中,人类中心主义是无法消除的。本文通过引用儒家的关于人是天下最为贵重的理念,认为我们现在的生态哲学观中还是要以人为本;当然,这个假定是基于人要有良知的理念;同时,在人类社会中,亲疏关系也是永远存在的;但是,只有良知和亲情是不够的,应该也有制约。因此,我们认为,在进行生态话语和行为分析中,应该有"以人为本"的基本假定和三条原则(即良知原则、亲近原则、制约原则)来作为生态话语和行为分析的指导思想。

参考文献

Naess, A. (1995), The shallow and the long range, deep ecology movement. In A. Drengson & Y. Inoue (eds.). *The Deep Ecology Movement: An Introductory Anthology*. Berkeley: North Atlantic Books. 3–10.

Stibbe, A. (2015), *Ecolinguistics: Language, Ecology and the Stories We Live by*. London: Routledge.

Zhou, W. J. (2017), Ecolinguistics: Toward a new harmony. *Language Sciences* 62: 124–138.

Zhou, W. J. & G. W. Huang (2017), Chinese ecological discourse: A Confucian-Daoist inquiry. *Journal of Multicultural Discourses* 12: 264–281.

杜维明:《儒家人文精神与生态》,《中国哲学史》2003 年第 1 期,第 6—8 页。

鸿雁编:《王阳明全书》,云南人民出版社 2013 年版。

黄国文：《外语教学与研究的生态化取向》，《中国外语》2016年第5期，第1、9—13页。

黄国文、陈旸：《生态哲学与话语的生态分析》，《外国语文》2016年第6期，第55—61页。

蒙培元：《人与自然——中国哲学生态观》，人民出版社2004年版。

乔清举：《儒家生态思想通论》，北京大学出版社2013年版。

王天孜：《论生态良知》，硕士学位论文，2005年。

张学智：《从人生境界到生态意识——王阳明"良知上自然的条理"论析》，《天津社会科学》2004年第6期，第29—35页。

赵蕊华、黄国文：《生态语言学研究与和谐话语分析——黄国文教授访谈》，《当代外语研究》2017年第4期，第8—12页。

郑家栋：《自然和谐与差等秩序》，《中国哲学史》2003年第1期，第11—12页。

方法谈：

如何进行语言学的本土化研究？

语言学是研究语言的科学，语言学理论是没有国界的，就像物理学和化学的理论；像"物理""化学"这样的学科，我们是不说"英国物理学""英国化学"的，当然，我们也不说"中国物理学"和"中国化学"。那么，为什么我们常常看到"英语语言学"或"English Linguistics"和"中国语言学"或"Chinese Linguistics"呢？其实，"英语语言学"这类说法指的是把英语这种语言当作个别语言研究的学科分支。研究人类语言普遍规律的语言学（即普通语言学或理论语言学）是没有国界的，它要探讨的是人类语言的共性和一般的规律，为了达到这样的研究目的，就需要对人类的各种语言单独进行研究（如对英语的研究、对汉语的研究），单独对于个别语言的研究就形成了语言类型学研究，最终就能找到人类语言的共性和普遍规律。因此，在语言学研究领域，就有"普通语言学"与"个别语言学"（particular linguistics）和"理论语言学"与"应用语言学"之分。这样看来，语言学理论研究（普通语言学、理论语言学）没有国界；但语言研究者有自己的国家和不同的价值取向，因此有不同的家国情怀。但是，个别语言学和应用语言学研究者就有国界之分。比如说,中国的应用语言学研究者在中国大地研究中国人学习英语是正常的,但如果他们在中国大地研究英国人学习英语就比较少见。

关于生态语言学的学科属性,我们(黄国文、赵蕊华,2019)曾做过比较详细的讨论。简单地说,生态语言学是语言学的分支学科,跟社会语言学一样,属于广义的应用语言学;这样看来,生态语言学研究是有国界之分的,生态语言学研究者也就都有国家归属感,有和其他国家的研究者不同的价值取向的,在对待同一个学术问题上常常会有不同的观点。例如,对于"气候变化"这类问题,不同国家的研究者会有不同的看法。对于世界上存在的生态问题,大多数是与"政治"有关的。

既然关于生态语言学的研究是取决于研究者的家国情怀和价值取向,那作为中国的研究者,就必须考虑研究的本土化问题。具体地说,首先就是要采用中国人的视角、解决中国的问题。因此,在阅读国外学者撰写的学术论著时,就要看看他们的生态哲学观与我们的是否是一致的、相近的或者是相反的。如果与我们的是一致的,并能解决我们中国的问题,那就可以采用或借鉴,如果是相近的,就可以加以修正或改造,如果是相反的,就要抵制、批评,甚至批判。说到底,提倡或追求学术本土化,就是要立足本土,坚持问题导向,聚焦问题,最终解决我们自己的问题。

我们(如黄国文,2016、2018;黄国文、赵蕊华,2019、2021;Huang & Zhao,2021;赵蕊华、黄国文,2017、2021)多次从不同角度对"和谐话语分析"(Harmonious Discourse Analysis)的各个方面进行论述。简单地说,它的哲学根源是中国儒家的生态哲学。在"论生态话语和行为分析的假定和原则"中,我提出了生态话语和行为分析中的一个假定,就是"以人为本"。这个假定的提出是因为我们信奉"天人合一""以天地为万物一体""人以天地生物之心为心"等传统的中国生态哲学思想,在保护自然、保护环境等方面,"人"的责任最大,人也是最聪明、最重要的,所以在处理人与自然和谐共生过程中,人起的作用是最大的。因此,在人与动物的选择上,首先选择的应该是人,这点在古今中外都是这样的。这个"以人为本"理念就是根据中国生态哲学思想提出来的。

在"以人为本"的假定下,我们遵循的是儒家的生态哲学思想,认为人与其他生命形式(包括动物、植物等)的主要不同在于"性善",作为正常的人,首先必须要有道义,有良知,要性善,这是人作为最聪明的动物的特点,也是人与其他物种的主要区别之一;基于这样的事实,我们提出了三条原则,用于指导我们的生态话语分析和生态语言学研究:良知原则;亲近原则;制约原则。

良知原则的核心是"良知",这一概念来源于《孟子》,但王阳明(见鸿雁,2013)赋予它更多的内涵,对它作了更深刻的阐释:良知是对性体的自觉,良知是道德判断的主体。在处理语言与生态问题时,人对其他生命体的影响是巨大的;在对待生态系统中的其他生命形式,良知原则主要是指生态良知。具体地说,生态良知的提出,"是由于人类逐渐意识到人与自然之间的生存论意义上的关联而产生的一种关爱、保护自然的自然、自觉、自愿的'善'的观念"(王天孜,2005:1)。

亲近原则是基于我们所认同的生态哲学观提出的。根据儒家生态观,我们追求的是生态系统中的和谐,是自然和谐和人与自然以及人与人之间的和谐,就是要达到天人合一、天地以生物为心。郑家栋(2003:11)认为,"儒家思想的核心或曰本质特征并不在于一般的追求自然和谐,而在于谋求自然和谐与差等秩序的统一",郑家栋特别指出,"'和谐'中本来就包含了'差等'";而"'差等'之对于儒家是更为本质的东西"。这种"差等"观念在儒家学说中非常重要,因为它导致儒家思想接收者认同和接受现实的伦常法规和等级秩序。这样的儒家思想使我们认识到自然中的各种生命形式(自己、至亲、朋友、路人、飞禽、鸟兽、草木、江河、山川等)是一个由近及远、从亲到疏的系列。亲近原则就是基于这样的思想而提出的。

制约原则的提出是基于这样的事实,每个人都生活在一定的社会环境中;不同的社会结构有相同、相似或不同的制约方式。人有思维、有思想、有语言,人与其他动物的最大不同是:人"性善",人有意念,有知觉,讲究道义伦理,社会结构有等级制度,有社会组织,有行为规则;人无论生活在哪个社会(国家、地区)或哪种环境,都受到制约。制约有不同的层次:个人的、群体的、社会的、国家的、国际的。制约可以是个人的良知、修养、教育等给自己的制约,也可以是群体、社团(社区)的"乡规民约"方面的制约,还可以是社会、机构的法制制约,当然还可以是国际组织所约定的制约。一个人、一个群体、一个社区、一个社会、一个国家乃至国际上绝大多数国家是否文明、是否有生态意识,完全可以从规则的制定和执行来评判。

无论是以人为本的假定,还是良知原则、亲近原则和制约原则的提出,都是基于我们生活的环境、我们的生活经历和我们所持有的"三观"(世界观、人生观、价值观)和生态哲学观。从这个角度说,和谐话语分析框架的提出,就是学术本土化追求的一种努力和尝试。

　　语言与生态的关系问题是一个跨学科的问题，不同学科、不同国家、不同民族的学者都很关心这个问题，并根据自己的三观和生态哲学观去判断、去解释、去分析问题和解决问题。中国作为一个大国，中国的大国崛起，就要求中国的学者要有大国人的担当和责任，要解决中国的问题，要为全球的问题提出中国的方案，要构建人类命运共同体。由于我们提出的和谐话语分析是具有中国本土化的特点，所以国外的学者给予高度的重视。例如，Stibbe（2023：265）对和谐话语分析的评论是：

> More recently, in China, scholars have developed Harmonious Discourse Analysis (Huang, 2018; Huang and Zhao, 2019). This approach is unique because it is strongly rooted in traditional Chinese philosophies of harmony, particularly the three Confucian principles of conscience, proximity and regulation (Huang, 2017: 880). Huang and Zhao (2021: 16) describe how in Harmonious Discourse Analysis, "by examining language-related ecological problems in discourse, we aim to present the various relations of humans with other ecological participants and to promote harmonious relations via language". The importance of Harmonious Discourse Analysis is that it provides an example of ecolinguistics travelling across the world and being reinvented in line with the culture, philosophy and ecology of the place it has arrived in.

Stibbe 在上述这段话中，有两句话特别说到和谐话语分析的中国本土化特点："和谐话语分析方法是独特的，因为它深深植根于中国传统的和谐哲学，特别是儒家的良心、亲近和规范三原则"；因此，"和谐话语分析的重要性在于，它提供了一个生态语言学在世界各地实践的例子，并根据它所到达的地方的文化、哲学和生态进行改造"。

　　美国学者 Poole（2022：10）也做出了与 Stibbe（2023：265）相似的关于和谐话语分析中国本土化特点的评论：

> Chinese ecolinguists have forwarded an approach to ecolinguistics

titled Harmonious Discourse Analysis (Huang & Zhao, 2021). Harmonious Discourse Analysis integrates the theoretical framework of systemic functional linguistics with traditional Chinese philosophy in order to develop a context-sensitive, locally informed framework for application in non-Western settings.

这里说的"和谐话语分析将系统功能语言学的理论框架与中国传统哲学相结合,以建立一个对语境敏感的、了解本土情况的框架,来适用于非西方环境"明显表示,和谐话语分析一方面将系统功能语言学与中国传统哲学思想结合起来,另一方面,该分析方法从中国语境出发,研究本土问题,这种研究有别于西方学者的研究。

学术研究既可以重视人类的共性问题,也可以聚焦本土问题。做普通语言学研究,就是关注人类语言的规律和普遍特征;做个别语言学研究,就是关注个别语言的特点;这两类研究是互补的、互相依赖的,缺一不可:做普通语言学研究,离开个别语言学研究就是无源之水;做个别语言学研究,没有考虑语言的普遍特性,没有语言学理论指导,所得出的结论就没有普适意义,只见树木,不见森林。

参考文献

Huang, Guowen & Zhao, Ruihua: Harmonious discourse analysis: approaching peoples' problems in a Chinese context. *Language Sciences*, 85 (2021) 101365, https://doi.org/10.1016/j.langsci.2021.101365.

Poole, R. (2022), *Corpus-assisted Ecolinguistics*, London: Bloomsbury.

Stibbe, A. (2023), *Ecolinguistics: Language, Ecology and the Stories We Live by* (2nd edn)清华大学出版社。

鸿雁主编:《王阳明全书》,云南人民出版社 2013 年版。

黄国文:《外语教学与研究的生态化取向》,《中国外语》2016 年第 5 期,第 1、9—13 页。

黄国文:《论生态话语和行为分析的假定和原则》,《外语教学与研究》2017 年第 6 期,第 880—889 页。

黄国文:《从生态批评话语分析到和谐话语分析》,《中国外语》2018 年第 4

期,第 39—46 页。

黄国文、赵蕊华:《什么是生态语言学》,上海外语教育出版社 2019 年版。

黄国文、赵蕊华:《功能话语研究新发展》,清华大学出版社 2021 年版。

王天孜:《论生态良知》,硕士学位论文,2005 年。

赵蕊华、黄国文:《生态语言学研究与和谐话语分析——黄国文教授访谈》,《当代外语研究》2017 年第 4 期,第 8—12 页。

赵蕊华、黄国文:《和谐话语分析框架及其应用》,《外语教学与研究》2021 年第 1 期,第 42—53 页。

郑家栋:《自然和谐与差等秩序》,《中国哲学史》2003 年第 1 期,第 11—12 页。

关于外国语言学研究的几点思考*

潘文国**

摘要：本文思考了外国语言学研究的三个问题：(1) 外国语言学研究的最终目标。从对"两张皮"现象的重新分析出发，认为外国语言学研究的最终目标应该为中国的语言建设服务；(2) 外语研究的创新性。从分析什么不是创新着手，提出外语研究的创新必须具有本土意识、问题意识和理论意识；(3) 外语研究要顶天立地、眼高手低。认为外语研究既要瞄准国内外学术研究的前沿，注重理论创新，又要关注眼前切实需要解决的问题，特别是外语教学和翻译。文章还特别强调打好语言基本功特别是提高母语水平对从事外语研究的重要性。

关键词：语言学研究；创新；理论与实践

一、外国语言学研究的最终目标

1. 再论"两张皮"问题

中国的语言学界可以划分为中国语言学和外国语言学两大版块，连学科都有"语言学及应用语言学"与"外国语言学及应用语言学"之分，尽管学界从理论上不以为然，但这却是一个不争的事实。搞外语的与搞中文的互不往来，在各自召开的学术会议上很难见到另一方的身影。这在全世界是个非常独特的现象。20世纪80年代初，吕叔湘等(1987)就已大声疾呼要消除"两张皮"的现

---

* 原载《外语与外语教学》2007年第4期。

** 潘文国，华东师范大学终身教授，博士生导师，中国英汉语比较研究会名誉会长。第二届许国璋外国语言研究奖、首届英华学术/翻译奖特等奖获得者。在汉英对比研究、汉语字本位理论、汉语等韵理论、汉语构词法史、中外命名艺术、西方翻译理论、翻译理论与实践、哲学语言学、对外汉语学、中国文化对外传播等方面均具重要影响。

象,21世纪初还召开过两次专题的学术讨论会,但情况似乎没有什么根本上的改观。这究竟是什么原因呢?原来我们以为这是因为中国搞汉语的人的外语差,搞外语的中文差。但这一二十年来中国大学生的外语水平大有提高,许多人还出过国门,接触过外国的语言学,但"两张皮"的情况依然。可见,外语差已不是造成"两张皮"的根本原因。那么,根本原因在哪里呢?看来我们还需要从更深的层面进行考察。这就是从这个现象的独特性入手。上面说过,"两张皮"是中国的语言研究所特有的现象,在别的国家几乎不可能见到。我们很难想象,比方说在英国、美国或者法国、俄国,英语语言学、法语语言学或者俄语语言学会同一般语言学研究造成"两张皮"现象。从"独特性"着眼,我认为造成"两张皮"的原因至少有以下两个:一个是从中文方面看,中国语言及其文字在世界语言中太特殊了,本身需要研究的东西太多了,以至于许多人终身沉浸其中,还只能研究其中的一小部分甚至只是一个角落,如文字学、训诂学或者语法学什么的,一旦进入其中就很难跳出来,外面的东西再好似乎也很难用上;另一个是从外语方面看,国外的语言理论层出不穷,日新月异,令人几乎应接不暇,一位研究者花费若干年精力,能弄通一两家已经不容易了,何况外国理论还在翻新,稍不留神就又"落后"了,只好拼命再学。而这些理论无一不是在西方语言基础上形成的,由于西方语言与汉语的巨大差异,根本不知道如何用到汉语上,结果只好停留在就外国语言学论外国语言学,以外国理论解释外国语言了事。至多只是偶尔举几个汉语例子,不过是为了证明外国理论的"普适性"。而从根本上来说,是始终游离在中国语言学外面的。更有人进而认为,学习外国语言学只要能解释外语问题就可以了,连中文例子都不必举。那就是更自觉地坚持"两张皮"的立场了。因而,如果这两个问题不解决,"两张皮"现象就不可能从根本上得到消除。而解决这两个问题,就不仅仅是学好外语、学好中文这样浅层次的问题,而是一个更深的理论问题。因为说到底,这两个问题其实是一个问题,就是必须找到一个中国语言学与外国语言学之间的好的接口。这样,从中国语言学方面看,就会感到有一种需要,认识到中国语言文字再特殊,作为世界语言大家庭的一员,它与世界语言总有着共通之处,要真正"攻"好中国语言学这块"玉",必须借助外国语言学这块"石";而从外国语言学这头来看,就要找到一个落脚点,弄清外国语言学研究的根本目标是要解决中国的语言问题。

2. 外国语言学研究最终必须为中国的语言建设服务

说外国语言学研究的最终目标必须为中国的语言建设服务,很多人恐怕不以为然，认为这只是搞中文研究的人的任务，搞外语嘛，只好学好外语就行了：外国语言理论能不能指导中文我们不用管，只要能帮助我们学好外语就行了。对此我们不敢苟同。当然，一般的学外语、教外语的人这么说这么想，我们也无可厚非；但是，如果把外语教学、外国语言研究当作一件事业，我们就必须思考这些问题：第一，我们诚然是在学外语，但是，我们是在真空里学外语吗？我们是在把母语忘得一干二净的基础上来学外语的吗？作为中国人，我们学习外语（例如英语），与英美人学习他们的母语，以及说其他语言的人学习英语，难道是一模一样的吗？这里面有些什么相同或不同的规律？会导致什么相同或不同的方法？难道不需要研究或不值得研究吗？如果我们能够通过研究，找到多快好省的方法，我们还会坚持"少慢差费"的方法吗？第二，在中国的外语教学，说到底是对中国人的外语教学。外国的语言理论产生了外国的语言教学法，例如传统语言学产生了语法翻译法、结构主义产生了句型替代法、功能主义产生了情景法等，这些方法在国外的环境下，产生了大小不等的功效，也暴露出大小不等的不足之处。但这些理论和方法能否用于中国的背景、汉语的环境，外国人却不会告诉我们现成的答案，需要通过我们自己的研究和实践。外国的语言理论和语言教学理论如果不结合中国人学习外语的实际，可以说毫无用处；而要结合这一实际，不了解汉语、不研究汉语、不懂得汉语学习规律和外语学习规律的异同，那是不能想象的。第三，研究外国语言学到底为了什么？有人说，就是为了研究外国语言学本身；有人说，是为了与国际语言学研究接轨；有人说，是为了研究人类普遍的语言，等等，不一而足。但从这些答案里，笔者看不出要排斥汉语的道理。试问：同样研究外国语言学，中国人的长处和短处在哪里？还不是凭你懂得一点外国人不懂或不怎么懂的汉语？如果没有你自己不放在眼里的汉语这个"特长"去跟外国人比拼搞"外国语言学"，那你可能什么都不是；再有，人类普遍的语言学难道可以少得了汉语？适用于全人类的语言理论难道可以不包括汉语中的事实和规律？如果真的认为我们所研究的外国语言学是普适于人类全部语言的普通语言学，就更必须要有汉语的参与，而这一任务更多地落在"外国语言学"（如果把它理解为"普通语言学"的话）研究者身上。因此，研究汉语甚至可以说是"外国语言学"研究者天然的使命。第四，中国的语言研究者有个非常好的传统，从马建忠到赵元任，从王力到吕叔湘，他们学习、研究外国语言学，其最终目标无一不是为了建立、发展中国自身的语言学。这一优良传统不应该到我们这一代终结。尤其是在当前的情况下，在经过了百年的屈辱之后，中国正在重新崛起,中国语言学也要重新崛起,作为中国的语言学者,不论是研究"中国语言学"的,还是研究"外国语言学"的,都应在这伟大的事业中承担起自己应尽的历史责任。

二、外语研究的创新性

我国明确提出,到 2020 年,中国要建成创新型的国家。"创新"一下子成了当代中国最热门的话题之一,在学术界尤其如此。在这样的形势下,外语界怎么办?外语研究,或者说外国语言学研究,应该怎样走创新之路?我想从正反两方面来谈谈对这个问题的看法。

1. 什么不是创新?

首先必须明白,创新研究必须立足在本学科的基础上,外语研究的创新必须要与"外国语言学"有关。我们当然无法"创造"一个"外国语言学"的理论,但我们所做的却不能离开"外国语言学"这一背景。由于有了"外国语言学"这一前提,因此外语研究的创新就会表现出与其他学科的不同之处。我们最好先来了解一下什么不是外语研究的"创新",也许这样有助于我们理解和探讨什么是"创新"。

第一,纯粹的介绍不是创新。20 世纪 70 年代以来的西方,特别是美国的语言理论可谓层出不穷,中国学者如果有机会出国,时时会感到种种新潮的冲击,出于急于让国内的同行共享这一愉悦常会产生一种想将这些新理论介绍进国内的冲动。这诚然是为国内所欢迎的,国内一些学术刊物也非常喜欢这类稿件,一般来说比较容易被接受。但我们必须明白一点,尽管这类文章的录用率很高,但纯粹的介绍却不是创新。请注意这里的"纯粹"二字,所谓"纯粹"的介绍就是以叙述的笔调一五一十地介绍一种新理论或新观点,完全不掺杂介绍者自己的观点和意见。在一种新理论引进之初,这种介绍是必要的,但毕竟是"原始"的。过了这一阶段人们就会不满足于这种介绍,而要求有介绍者对这种理论的主观评价。这时就会出现不"纯粹"的介绍,亦即伴随主观评述的介绍。这就要求介绍者必须深入了解被介绍的东西甚至作专门的研究,其结果,上乘的介绍者可以写出专门的论著(如姚小平先生之介绍洪堡特),次一等的能写出专门的研究文章(或以"前言"、或以"导读"的形式出现)。像这种非"纯粹"的介绍就可以看作是创新研究的一种,更是值得我们提倡的。

第二,外国理论加中国例子不是创新。由于国内的舆论强调引进外国理论

"必须结合中国的实际",有的引进者生怕别人指责他不结合汉语实际,因此在介绍外国理论时常常刻意地强调这一点,或是把原来是外语的例子生硬地译成汉语(说"生硬地",倒不是因为他译不出通顺的汉语,而是为了保留原书要解释的某一理论或观点),或是仿照外语例子生造几个汉语例子(说"生造",同样是因为要"说明"原著想说明的那些理论或观点)。这种情况可以说是大量的,例如为了说明汉语的"时态",生造出很多疙里疙瘩的句子等。本来,语言理论是要能说明语言事实的,但在这样的"介绍"甚或"研究"里,却是以语言事实去迁就理论。这种研究当然不是创新。

第三,"解释"别人的理论不是创新。这些年来,要说语言学研究中有什么词最受青睐的话,"解释"就是一个。有人还提出语言研究三阶段论,说什么传统语法阶段是"规定性的",结构主义阶段是"描写性的",生成语言学开始到现在是"解释性的","解释"是语言研究的最高原则。姑不论这种"三阶段"的说法本身有没有道理(依我看,这种"三阶段"说根本不能成立,"规定"并非一无是处,即使在今天,"教学语法"还必须是规定性的。"描写"和"解释"更不是互相对立、有他没我的,硬要将它们与某种理论捆绑在一起,只能说是别有用心),就算"解释"是语言研究的"最高原则",也不能成为某些人坚持外语研究只能是用外国理论来"解释"汉语(或者换个说法,是用汉语来验证外国理论)作借口。因为西方"解释"说的提出者同时也是演绎法的积极主张者,他们认为"真正的"科学研究不能用归纳法,而必须用演绎法(这里我们同样先不去讨论"归纳法"和"演绎法"应不应分开、能不能分开)。而演绎法实际就是一个"假设-推理"的过程。因而他们的研究常常先假设一个理论,然后用语言事实加以验证;如果发现有误,便修正假设,再加以验证,如此循环,使理论不断趋于完善。应该说,这不失为一种卓有成效的研究方法(但不是唯一的方法),近几十年来,西方的很多新理论都是这么创造出来的。这种方法受到中国一些人的追捧,也是可以理解的。但是,一些跟在西方理论后面鼓吹要用"解释"方法来研究汉语的人,我们却不能认同他们的研究是"创新"。为什么?因为运用"解释"亦即演绎方法的前提是自己提出假设,西方的学者都是这么做的,因而他们的研究无疑是创新。而中国的追随者自己没有理论,用的是别人的"假设",因而他们的工作只剩下了"验证"。这样的研究,永远出不了创新的成果。

2. 外语研究的创新

那么,什么是外语的创新性研究呢?其实,从上面讲的"不是创新"的反面,我们就很容易得出以下三点正面的结论。

第一,要有本土意识。这是从第一个"不是"推导出来的。

外国语言学是产生在外国的,有其产生的背景、土壤,还有各自的针对对象和适用范围,在中国研究外国语言学,可以说肯定不是为了外国语言学本身,而且由于上述背景等条件的先天不足,这样的研究肯定不能超越外国的同行,也无法达到"赶上和超过"西方先进水平的目标。在中国研究外国语言学,不能脱离"在中国"这个最重要的前提。因此,任何想要取得突破性、创造性的外国语言学研究成果,必须以与中国和汉语的实际相结合为前提,而最有可能出成果的必然是与中国或汉语相关的领域,例如对比研究、翻译研究以及以中国人为对象的英语教学研究,等等。事实上,国内外语界已经意识到了这个问题,近20年来的研究可说是大量地转向了这些领域,即便以介绍国外新理论为宗旨的文章也很少脱离中国需要的"纯粹"介绍。一些表面上看来没有涉及中文或中国的研究,实际上也常常隐含了为中国语言建设服务的考虑。我们把这个叫作本土意识。这个方向是正确的而且必须坚持。

第二,要有问题意识。这是从第二个"不是"推导出来的。

这是上一个认识的深入。意识到要结合中国和汉语的实际这只是外语创新研究的第一步,第二步还要进一步认识到什么是真正的"结合"而不是"粘合",更不是"迎合"。吕叔湘(1986)早就说过:"外国的理论在那儿翻新,咱们也就跟着转。这不是坏事,问题是不论什么理论都得结合汉语的实际,可是'结合'二字谈何容易,机械地搬用乃至削足适履的事情不是没有发生过。"事实上,不光是外语界,整个中国语言学界20世纪以来的研究中存在的最大问题就是食洋不化,照搬照套,"机械地搬用乃至削足适履的事情"不光是"发生过",而且可说贯串了整个世纪。当前我们提倡语言学、包括外国语言学的创新研究可说主要就是针对这个情况来的。那么,怎么防止这一情况呢?我认为在于提倡问题意识。前面我们说到外国理论加汉语例子的过程中造出许多"疙里疙瘩"句子的情况,其实这里就已经隐含了创新的可能:如果要造出不通或不顺的句子才能说明某种外国理论,这一事实本身就说明这种理论在解释汉语时有不足之处,或者是我们对理论的理解不深不切,或是还没有找到外国理论和汉语之间的切合点,或是这一外国理论根本不适合于汉语。总之,被迫造出不通不顺的句子就是"问题",从"问题"出发深入思考,我们就有可能产生突破性的见解!由于"问题"常常是在套用外国理论生造汉语句子的过程中产生的,我们还可以"逆向思维"一下,如果不要生造,就使用地道的汉语句子,看外国理论能否适用,这样也许能得到更大的启发。这就是我(1997:1)主张的"换一种眼光"。

第三,要有理论意识。这是从第三个"不是"推导出来的。

前面我们提到,"解释"不是唯一的研究方法,主要是针对现在有人对"解释"的过度吹捧,同时我们也不认为"归纳"和"演绎"是可以分割开来、只取一端的研究方法。成功的研究,都应该是"归纳"和"演绎"方法的结合,但相对来说,作为创新研究,演绎法更应该得到重视。正确的研究方法应该是:通过收集归纳部分事实,经过提炼,提出假设,再到更多的事实中去进行论证,推导出更具一般性的道理;如果发现事实与假设相矛盾,则修改假设,再进行论证;如此反复,使研究不断深入。可以看出,在这样的研究过程中,"创新"的关键在于"假设",假设得到验证则成为理论,假设得到证伪也具有理论上的价值。目前国内一些"解释"论者的最大问题在于缺少自己的"假设",他是把外国人的假设作为假设,而致力于在汉语中证实或者证伪。由于外国人的理论假设并不是从汉语的事实中提炼出来的,因此在汉语中无论得到了证实或证伪都带有一定的偶然性,并不能证明该理论的正确性。因此这类研究不论对于外国语言学也好,对于中国语言学也好,都不能说是创新的研究。之所以会把这样的研究看作就是理论研究,是因为他们从根本上缺乏理论意识,缺乏自主创新精神,还是骨子里的崇洋媚外思想。要真正做到外语研究的创新,必须立足于我们自己发现的事实,例如中国人学习外语的事实、外语和中文对同一现象表达不同的事实,来提炼出自己的假设和理论。

三、外语研究要顶天立地、"眼高手低"

1. 外语研究要顶天立地

"顶天立地"的概念是时任教育部部长周济于2006年11月在高校服务地方发展工作会议上提出来的,他(2006)指出:"不少科研项目'两头够不上':上不着天,与科学前沿发展水平相距甚远;下不着地,与社会的实际需求关系不大。很多论文只是简单重复的跟风研究,没水平,也没有现实意义。"而今后的发展,"应该坚持'顶天立地'的方向。所谓'顶天',就是要高度重视现代科学和技术前沿的研究,围绕国家战略需求,不断创造国内外高水平成果;所谓'立地',就是要高度重视面向国民经济和社会发展主战场,切实解决发展实践中大量的科技问题"。这样的现象,在外语界同样存在。我们现在的科学研究可说也处在"上不着天,下不着地"的状态,既没有原创性的重大成果,对实际问题的解决又重视不够。因此,今后外语科研的发展方向,同样应坚持"顶天立地"四个字。外语科研的"顶天",就是要瞄准国际语言科学研究的前沿,结合中国的需要和汉语的实际,拿出原创性、能够立足于世界语言学之林的成果来。这方面最可能取得突破的是两个领域:一个是立足汉语的普通语言学研究,这可以成为对世界语言学研究的重要补充和完善;另一个是结合汉语的翻译学理论研究。由于汉语汉字与世界大多数语言文字之间的重大差异,建立在汉外互译基础上的翻译理论肯定会对现有的翻译理论产生重大的影响,中国学者在这方面可说大有可为。外语科研的"立地",则是眼睛向下,做一些切切实实的工作。这方面最重要的也是两个领域:一个是中国的外语教学。以英语而言,现在中国拥有全世界最多的学习英语的人口,学过英语的人数已经超过了英、美两国的总人口,但效率之低也令人瞠目结舌,据调查95%的人学的英语根本派不了用处。造成这一结果的原因很多,英语教学本身也可以从中找找原因,其中一定有很多值得研究的课题。如果我们能走出一条使中国人多快好省地学好外语的途径,这对中国经济和社会发展的影响可能不会亚于一项重大的科技发明创造;另一个领域是翻译。1998年以前,中国学者对翻译理论的重视不够,人们讨论的常是翻译有没有理论、要不要理论之类。21世纪以来,翻译理论研究得到了前所未有的重视,特别是大量的西方翻译理论介绍和引进、一大批翻译方向博士生的培养,使翻译理论研究出现了一个少见的高潮。但一个倾向掩盖着另一个倾向。我们发现,一方面是翻译理论研究得到了重视,另一方面是社会上翻译质量的低下依然如故。我们似乎没有找到一个翻译理论指导翻译实践的有效途径,在这种情况下,热闹非凡的翻译理论研究也许会有流于空谈的危险。因此,再一次强调翻译研究者眼睛向下,对在关注翻译理论的同时更关注一下如何切实提高中外互译的质量是有必要的。

2. 外语研究要"眼高手低"

这是对从事科研工作者的一个很基本的要求,我们希望特别提出来提醒年轻的研究者,特别是硕博士们的注意。"眼高"就是眼界要高,要瞄准国内外的学术前沿,要有创立新学说、新理论的勇气;"手低"就是要踏踏实实,一步一个脚印,从最基础的研究做起。"眼高"包括不迷信权威、不崇拜洋人,但如果"眼高"不能伴之以"手低",就会变成妄自尊大,反而成为人们的笑柄。"手低",最重要的是打好基本功,对于外语研究者来说,首先要提高英语特别是汉语的水平,这是从事任何与语言相关的研究的最重要条件。说来令人难以置信,在从事汉外对比研究时,人们常常感到没有把握的不是外语,而是我们的母语——汉语;在从事翻译实践的时候(不管是中译外,还是外译中),出问题的更多的是在汉语上(中译外是理解问题,外译中是表达问题)。20 世纪中国人的汉语水平每况愈下,外语专业学生尤其明显。这其中有很多问题值得总结,包括语言理论和语言教学理论。当前外语界的总体理论研究水平不高,可能与中文水平不高大有关系。新一代的学者对此一定要有清醒的认识和足够的重视。

参考文献

吕叔湘:《序》,载龚千炎:《中国语法学史稿》,语文出版社 1987 年版。

潘文国:《换一种眼光何如?——关于汉英对比研究的宏观思考》,《外语研究》1997 年第 1 期。

周　济:《在高校服务地方发展工作会议和高等学校为社会主义新农村建设服务座谈会上的讲话》,引自《中国网》,http://www.china.com.cn/education/txt/2006-12/06/content-7462202.htm,2006 年 12 月 6 日。

方法谈:

如何反思西方语言学理论对中国语言现象的解释力?

这篇文章的写作有两个背景,大背景和小背景。大背景是 21 世纪初,国务院学位办刚刚批准设立"外国语言学及应用语言学"硕博士点,作为"外国语言文学"一级学科下的一个二级学科,外语界对此既欢欣鼓舞又有些迷茫,因为在此之前在"中国语言文学"一级学科下已经有了个"语言学及应用语言学"二级学科。两个二级学科的名称只差两个字,两者之间有什么区别和联系?外国语言学及应用语言学这个学科究竟应该怎样定性?如何开展研究?在此情况下,学界进行了热烈的讨论,举行了几次学术会议,一些杂志也推出了相关专栏。本文开始是在某次研讨会上的主题发言,经整理后作为一篇专栏文章发表。小背景则是我本人那几年正在华东师大和上海交大先后为"语言学及应用语言学"专业以及"外国语言学及应用语言学"专业的博士生开设一门名为"语言哲学"的通设课,在这过程中我提出了"哲学语言学"的命题,提倡对语言及语言学的各种概念进行哲学性的思考。有关"语言学"的问题也是思考的内容之一。大背景决定了写这篇文章的必要性,小背景则决定了我写这篇文章的独特切入点。

由于同时为中文和外语两个专业开设这门课程,因此我对"中国语言学"和"外国语言学"的思考与只在一个领域从事研究的人可能有些不同。我认为对中国的学者来说,这两者本来就是一回事。时代已经到了21世纪,研究"中国语言学"的,再也不能关起门来只搞自己的一套,何况经过20世纪的洗礼,所谓"现代中国语言学"早已有了浓厚的西化色彩,其深入和发展不得不关注国外语言学的动态与发展;同样,研究"外国语言学"的也不能假装自己生活在外国,不食中国的人间烟火,一味沉浸在外语中无法自拔。因此与其强调二者之"别",我更关注二者之"合",特别是如何"殊途"而"同归",站在中国人的立场看,这个"归"不能不是中国,不能不是中国社会和中国语言自身发展的需要。2004年《中国外语》创刊,邀请了一些学者题词祝贺,我写的是"中国人学外语,学外语为中国"12个字,这实际体现了自己当时对"外国语言学"这门学科的根本思考和基本立场,也是这些年来所有研究的基本出发点。这篇文章也是如此。

这篇文章分三个部分:"外国语言学研究的最终目标""外语研究的创新性"和"外语研究要顶天立地、'眼高手低'"。从表面上看,三者似乎不甚关联,实际上却是一篇哲学语言学的论文,分别从本体论、方法论、认识论和价值论角度对"外国语言学"这个对象作了剖析。常有人问学术论文如何才能写得深刻,写得既有理论价值又有实际意义?我想从哲学的角度,也就是上述几个维度切入是一个很值得推荐的选择。

"外国语言学研究的最终目标"一节实际是对"外国语言学"作为一门学科的本体论思考,这门学科究竟应该如何定性?设立这个学科的宗旨是什么?根本目标是什么?这是一个需要思索并取得共识的重要问题。定性可以从对象自身着手,但也不妨从外围着手,特别是从与其相关的其他事物着手。解决"外国语言学"的定性问题当然可以从"语言学""外国"等含义着手,但更好的办法也许是抬高一个层次,从其与其最相关的"中国语言学"的关系出发。因此我特别以当时外语界广为关注的"两张皮"现象作为抓手切入。这一现象当然有其历史和现实的原因,但毕竟是不正常、不合理的。"中国语言学"和"外国语言学"的提法不应促其分,而应促其合。说到底,语言学只有一个,不应有中外之分。之所以分成"中""外",只是出于分工与侧重的需要。两者的关系是"合则两利,分则两伤"。对中国学者来说,虽则有分工与侧重的不同,而其最终的目标应该是一致的,就是为了发展中国自身的学术。中国语言学是"借外以知中",外国语言学是"研外以达中"。对于生活在中国的研究者来说,为外国语言学而研究外国语言学的道路是既没必要,也走不通的。

如果说第一节是对"外国语言学"的学科性质的认定,第二节则是对"外国语言学研究"方法论的认定。我把方法论的问题集中在"创新"这个词上。任何学科的研究都要求"创新",创新是学科的生命线,没有创新,学术研究就毫无价值。"外国语言学"学科当然也是如此。那么,外国语言学研究如何创新?我在这里用了个"欲进先退"的策略,先退一步,谈什么"不是"创新,从而纠正了一些常见的误解,堵死了某些想当然的"研究"之路。所谓"就外国语言学而研究外国语言学"者,常见的方法是三条:一是单纯的引进介绍;二是在介绍中插入几个汉语例子;三是就外国理论进行推论阐释,甚至偶引中国古人以为证。我认为这些都不能算"创新",因为它不能达到上面所说的"外国语言学"学科的根本目标,促进中文的研究,解决中国的问题。这一方法论与本体论是不匹配的。在此基础上,我针锋相对地提出了三条"外国语言学"研究"创新"的方法论原则:第一,本土意识。引进和介绍以服务中国语言建设为标的,以解决中国问题为前提;第二,问题意识。从中国和汉语的现实问题出发,从国外语言理论和实践中寻找有价值的东西以为参照;也可从外国理论与中文现象龃龉的事实出发,发现和修正外国理论中的问题;第三,理论意识。语言学只有一个,语言学理论从本质上来说应该也只有一个。但事实是现在有很多家的"普通"语言学理论。这只能说明,这些形形色色的"普通语言学"理论,其实未必真正"普通",只不过是各家从自己理解的事实出发,作出的推理和阐释而已;而他们所坚信并引为基本依据的事实,往往出自对自身母语的观察,当然也会加上一些从熟悉的外语和从各种途径了解到的一些别的语言的某些事实。对本族语的理解越深刻,对自己提出的"普通"语言学理论也就越自信。中国的"外国语言学"者都以研究"普通语言学"为己任,但真正能丰富并充实普通语言学理论大厦的,也只有从自身语言也就是汉语中观察到的事实并从而建立的理论。这三条原则,哪一条都离不开中国和中国语言,因此真正在中国有创新价值的普通语言学理论,必然是外国语言学与中国语言学结合的产物。

相对于前两节的思辨性,文章的第三节可能更具可操作性。它包括两个部分,分别谈在中国从事"外国语言学"最有可能取得突破的几个领域和对研究者本身的素质要求。"上天入地"是比方,"眼高手底"也是比方。"上天"指理论领域,"立足汉语的普通语言学研究"和"结合汉语的翻译理论"是中国学者最有可能取得突破性进展的领域;"入地"指应用领域,寻找最适合中国人的外语教学路子以及切实提高中外互译质量是当今对"外国语言学者"的社会关切和期望所在,也是学科的价值所在。"眼高"同时须"手低"是对研究者素质的要求,"上天入地"是目标,"眼高手低"是基础,没有基础,目标就是空话。"手低"就是中外两种语言特别是中文的基本功。这是当前外语学者和研究者的短项,不是喊喊口号就能解决的。强调外语学者和研究者的中文能力也是我几十年来的关切,这篇文章里谈的虽然不不多,但绝不是可有可无的。

　　从总体来看,这篇文章的写作有四个方面可供借鉴:第一,对热点问题的关注,问题来自实践和社会的关切;第二,高屋建瓴的视野,不就事论事,而找一个更高的观察点,从而更能纵观全局;第三,辩证的思路,尤其在讲"创新"的问题上,先不谈何谓"创新",却先谈"什么不是创新",从反面导向正面的结论,立论就更坚实;第四,抓大而不放小。既关注理论的阐述,也关注实践和应用的方面。归根到底,理论是为实践服务的,理论最终也要接受实践的检验。

> 第二部分　专精覃思，审思明辨

认知语言学中的语境：定义与功能[*]

魏在江[**]

摘要：语境是语言学中最重要、最复杂的概念之一。从认知语言学的基本观点、基本主张来看，认知语言学不可能回避语境的研究，语境在认知语言学中占据相当重要的地位。本文从原型范畴、隐喻转喻、构式语义等方面论述语境在认知语言学中的地位和作用，揭示认知语言学必须重视语境的重要性的道理。

关键词：认知语言学；语境；定义；功能

一、引　　言

语境是语言学中最重要、最复杂的概念之一，多年来，语言学家为语境的研究做出了可贵的探索，取得了丰硕的成果。Alexander Bergs and Gabriele Diewald（2009）认为，语法与话语中的语境这一概念似乎是最重要、谈得最多的，可能也是最不明白的概念之一。语境问题是非常困难、非常棘手的（slippery）、非常不稳定的（volatile）。van Dijk（2009）认为，对语境的研究不能脱离社会和认知。可是，在George Lakoff 的 *Women Fire and Dangerous Thing*（1987）、George Lakoff & Mark Johnson 的 *Philosophy in the Flesh*（1999）和

---

[*]　原载《外国语》2016 年第 4 期。
[**]　魏在江，广东外语外贸大学英文学院教授，博士生导师。中美富布莱特高级访问学者，曾在美国俄勒冈大学（The University of Oregon）访学，师从著名哲学家 Mark Johnson 学习语言哲学、认知语言学。主要研究方向为：认知语言学、对比语言学、语用学、语篇分析等。2015 年 3 月受聘广东外语外贸大学"云山杰出学者"。现为华夏文化促进会体认语言学专业委员会副会长、中国英汉语比较研究会认知语言学专业委员会常务理事、中国语用学研究会常务理事等。

John Taylor 的 *Cognitive Grammar*（2002）三部影响巨大的著作的 subject index 中,没有见到 context 的词条。*Cognitive Linguistics in Action*（2011）一书收录了原型语境、认知语法的语境、语用语境、概念隐喻理论及概念整合的社会和文化语境四个方面的论文,但该书的主题索引（subject index）也没有收录 context 这一词条。认知语言学家似乎避免使用语境这一术语,对语境没有给予明确的定义,对语境的功能没有明确的论述,态度似乎比较模糊。笔者 2015 年 5 月 5 日通过电子邮件问及 Mark Johnson 教授这一问题时,他说:"你问了一个非常难的问题（You have raised a very difficult question）。"因此有必要对认知语言学的语境研究加以关注,本文拟从原型范畴、隐喻转喻、构式语义等方面就这一问题作一讨论,论述语境在认知语言学中的地位和作用,揭示认知语言学必须重视语境的重要性的道理。

二、语境研究的历史回顾

我们知道,语境这一概念最早是由波兰的人类学家马林诺夫斯基在 20 世纪 20 年代提出来的,他首先把语境分为情景语境和文化语境,并对这两种语境的构成成分加以分析和细化,这可以说是语境研究的发轫之作,也是对语言学研究的重要贡献。

Wardraugh(1976)把语境分为了八种：物理语境、心理语境、个人语境、功能语境、社会语境、发展语境、生物语境、历史语境。Halliday(1985/2004,2008)发展了功能语言学中的语境思想,提出了语域（register）的概念,并把语域分为语式、语场、语旨。Sperber & Wilson(1986)的关联理论提出了认知语境的概念,认为人类的认知的取向就是思维的优化,人们以最小的认知加工努力取得最大的认知效果,这就是关联理论中的最佳关联,人类认知就是在认知语境中寻求最佳关联,语境是变项,不是给定的,而是选择的,这就与传统的语境观有很大的不同,传统观点认为语境是常项,是事先给定的。Verschueren(1999)提出了动态关系语境观,指语境与语言结构之间的动态关系,亦即语境的广泛性和动态性。van Dijk(2009)提出了社会认知语境观,认为语境会因人而异,是存在于人们各自头脑中的心理模型,是关于交际环境的心理建构,把交际事件的社会、文化等客观存在和个人认知方面的因素结合起来,使社会、情景和话语相互关联,力图将语境研究完善成一套跨学科的、自成体系的理论。John Benjiamins Publishing

Company 于 2011 年和 2012 年先后推出 Context and Contexts 和 What Is a Context? 两本论文集，论述了语境研究的语言学方法以及所面临的挑战。

国内学者也非常关注语境的研究。裴文(2000)论述了言辞语境、副言辞语境和文化语境三种语境，其专著名为《现代英语语境学》。周明强(2005：1)也认为有必要建立语境学。朱永生(2005：1—2)认为，不同的语言学家对语境有不同的分类，而每种分类基本上都是两分法，如情景语境与文化语境、局部语境与整体语境、可能语境与真实语境、强式语境与弱式语境、静态语境与动态语境、显性语境与隐性语境、物质语境与社会语境等。谢应光(2009)认为，认知语法理论是语法研究回归语境化的典型，在认知语法中，语境因素经过概念化、抽象化和语法化为语法体系奠定了基本框架。陈香兰、申丹(2011)论述了转喻与语境的关系，"What's X doing Y?"构式是否存在转喻思维实际上取决于语境条件：说话者知道发生的事情，说话目的不是获得信息，而是表达不满、担忧以及想请求受话者采取行动。何自然(2012：202)论述了语境和转喻词语的识别问题，认为转喻的使用和理解离不开语境。王建华(2012)把语境分为言内语境、言伴语境和言外语境，并结合语言教学论述了语境的作用。

三、认知语言学对语境的有关论述

近年来，我们欣喜地看到，认知语言学的论著中对语境的论述明显多起来了。2011 年 7 月 11—16 日首次在西安外国语大学承办的第 11 届国际认知语言学大会，主题为：语言、认知、语境(Language, Cognition, Context)，这表明认知语言学开始明确地重视语境的重要作用了。认知语言学在过去 30 年中，经历了三个发展阶段：第一阶段是初创期；第二阶段到 20 世纪 90 年代中期，集中于认知语义学的基本概念：原型、辐射网络、概念隐喻、意象图式以及 Langacker 和 Talmy 基于识解及使用语法的各个方面；第三阶段，见证了语境类型的扩大，出版的著作大多数都是探讨词汇、用法、社会语境等方面。这里我们首先看看认知语言学家有关语境的论述。

Langacker(1987：401—405)在《认知语法基础(Ⅰ)：理论前提》一书中的一章是：Categories and Context。他说："所有的语言单位都是语境依赖的(All Linguistic units are context-dependent)。"Langacker 把语境分为如下三类：系统语境：语言单位在图式网络整体代表一种语言语法的位置；情景语境：引起特殊用例事件的语用语境;句法语境(syntagmatic context):复杂表达法的构成中语言单位的结合(pertaining)。从狭义方面看,语境只包括即时的、短暂临时的(transient)环境,即一个用法事件发生的环境。从广义方面看,它包括静态的、共有的知识。Langacker(1997)后来曾专门写了一篇论文,题目就叫"认知语义学的语境基础",说明语言意义的概念观为什么和在多大程度上能够以语境概念为基础。

Andrea Tyler(2008)认为,语言是在语境中使用的观点是认知语言学和语篇分析两个分支的中心观点,懂得一门语言就是懂得语言是怎样使用的。Dirk Geeraerts(2010)认为,认知语言学与语境的关系主要体现在以下三个方面:① 作为再语境化的认知语言学:认知语言学对语境的四个成分——意义、词汇、语篇和使用、社会语境给予了特别的关注,认知语言学把意义置于语法建构机制的中心地位;② 语境中的认知语言学:认知语言学理论和方法多元化不会局限在语言学的范围之内,事实上,它已经延伸到认知科学的其他领域了;③ 认知科学内的认知语言学:在过去的十年中,认知语言学已经发展成为理论语言学与描写语言学中最具有活力、最具有吸引力(attractive)的框架了,是什么使认知语言学如此具有魅力、如此具有活力、如此具有吸引力呢?这是因为认知语言学作为一种科学范式,不是一个人的事业,而是一个语言共同体。各种认知流派之所以能聚集在一起,是因为它们都展示了语言研究再语境化的各种方法。Vyvyan Evans 和 Melanie Green(2015:112—113)认为,一个话语或用法事件中的语境对于认知解释非常关键,一个词被使用的语境对于词的意义有重要影响。在认知语言学家看来,交际总是发生在一定的语境中,语言为社会交际的属性所影响,不可避免地要受到人类认知的影响。语言是人类认知的一部分,不是一个自足的独立的系统,语言被认为是不仅受语言内部因素的影响,而且在更大的程度上是由外部因素所决定的,外部因素包括一般人类认知能力以及社会的多元化、文化群落、话语类型和交际模式等。这是认知语言学共同的基本主张,也是认知研究中不可忽视语境因素的重要理据和基本动因。

四、认知语言学对语境的定义

20世纪语言学理论的发展特点是一系列去语境化和再语境化运动。语法的去语境化产生的后果导致了自足的语法模式和不同形式与语境的分离,主要影响是:① 通过从语言到能力的基本转变,语言学从语言作为社会语码的社会语境中分离开来;② 通过聚焦于语义的生物遗传方面的研究,语言学从认知语境中分离开来;③ 通过聚焦于形式规则系统,语言学和实际语言运用的情景语境分离开来。20世纪80年代以来,认知语言学采用基于用法的语法研究模式,研究实际语言的使用,基本特点就是再语境化趋势(drift),把语法和语境方面更加紧密地联系起来了。在当代语言学语境研究方面,认知语言学的语法再语境化研究占据了独特的地位。认知语言学的再语境化研究不仅能够帮助决定语言学语境的外部地位,而且对语言学框架的内部发展有很明显的重要作用。换句话说,再语境化是一种共同的黏合剂,把认知语言学各个分支黏合在一起。

语言的意义、词汇、语用、社会语境和语法的联系越来越密切了。很显然,人们注意到了语言的功能交际属性、语言的社会属性,语言被看成一种交际互动的方式。认知语言学是一种成功:从最初相对边缘化的地位到今天已经发展成为目前语言学中的主流之一。搜索"生成语言学"和"认知语法",就会惊奇地发现,在学术产出和影响方面,认知语言学已经超过生成语言学了(文旭,2014)。认知语言学的中心概念都是关于意义的,意义是动态的,绝非自足的;意义是基于用法和使用的,在本质上是视角化的。语言的定义和基本特征不仅仅是单纯的认知,而且也包括社会的、文化的情景认知。文化模型同样在认知活动中起到重要的作用,基于语言使用的方法重视语言之间、语言内部的变异研究,实际语言使用中的变异是由社会语言等因素决定的,构式的形成也与社会因素密切相关。下面是Dirk Geeraerts(2010)的认知语言学的语境特征图,试图揭示基于用法的语境的认知特征:

图1表明,认知语言学把四个关键语境因素:社会代码、行为、意义及词汇与语法研究的互动关系再次引入到语法研究之中,表明了把语境和构式、构式语法进行整合的可能性。语境既包括语言内部因素,如一个给定成分的句法或者语篇的环境,也包括语言外部因素,如时间、地点、参与者和方式等。需要强调的是,与大多数语用学和社会语言学的语境研究方法不同,认知语言学的语境概念不聚焦于具体言语中的言语事件,而是关注言语描写的认知表征,它不是孤立的心智经验,而是与储存在长时记忆中相关知识有关,让人立刻产生联想:一是有关范畴的特殊语境知识;二是当前语境可以唤起与之相关的长时记忆中的其他

语境。认知语言学中,原型、语义网络、概念隐喻、转喻、概念整合、理想化认知模型、框架以及所有识解机制都是语义概念,这些语义概念包括语义学的语境化观点,顺应了语言研究的再语境化趋势。基于这样的认识,本文将认知语言学中的语境定义为:语境是一种基于身体体验并通过范畴、概念、意象图式等识解出来的一种心智现象。

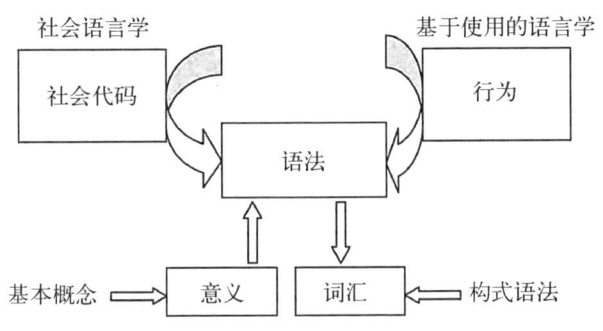

图 1　认知语言学的语境引入

上面的定义表明,认知语言学中的语境因素既包括常规的语境中的要素,如时间、地点、人物、场景等,也有自己独特的术语和独特的内涵,主要包括现实、体验、图式、范畴、概念(隐喻、转喻)等多种术语,它们共同构成认知语言学的语境成分。Langacker(1987:147)强调了心智概念的重要性。van Dijk(2009:24)否认语境的客观性,批判了传统的语境定义中重客观轻主观的倾向,强调从社会认知的视角对语境展开跨学科研究,尤其强调心理学的作用,突出认知的基础。我们认为,对于认知语言学来说,很重要的一点就是语境的概念应该被认为是一种心智现象。可以预言,认知语言学再语境化将为认知科学的整合发展做出自己的贡献。

五、认知语言学中语境的功能:案例分析

从认知语言学的基本观点、基本主张来看,认知语言学不可能回避语境的研究,可以肯定地说,语境在认知语言学中占据相当重要的地位。这一点我们已经从认知语言学的代表性人物和代表性著作中得到证实。下面我们拟通过两个案例分析,从原型范畴、隐喻转喻、构式语义等方面来论证语境在认知语言学中的功能。

1. 原型范畴

语言交际是一个演绎推理的过程,在这个过程中,交际者将新信息(话语,包括伴随话语的其他信息)放置于语境之中组合处理,从而得出结论(意义)。由于人们的阅历知识及所处外部环境不同,认知能力也就不可能一样,各自所建立的原型范畴也就有所差异,因此而产生的认知环境(cognitive environment)也就有所不同。在交际中说话者可以使许多假设显映,但听话者要对哪一个假设进行处理,取决于这些假设对听话者认知环境的影响。Ungerer & Schmid(2008:50)以"on the beach"为例,形象地说明了认知语境与认知模型之间的关系。

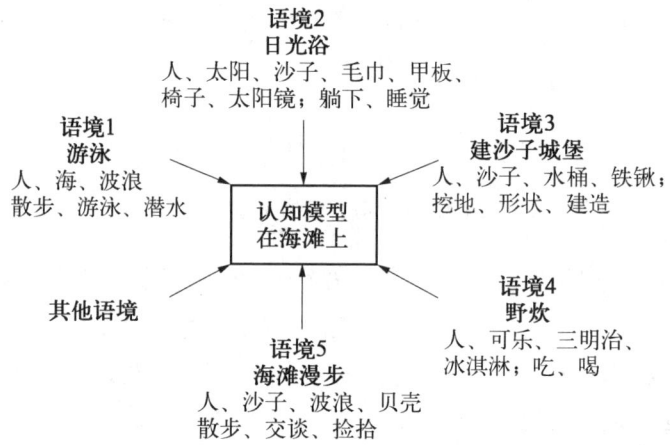

图 2 认知模型——在海滩上(F. Ungerer & H. J. Schmid, 2008:50)

在图 2 中,范畴:人、海、沙子和其他因素发生在各种语境中,形成了"在海滩上"这个认知模型。因此,人、海、沙子的认知模式与认知模式"在海滩上"紧密相关,这些认知模式结合起来就形成了网络。从图 2 中我们可以清楚地看出认知语境是动态的、多样的和变化的。此例中许多范畴如 PEOPLE, SEA, SAND 和别的范畴不断地在各种语境中发生关联,从而组成了这样一个模型 ON THE BEACH。有关人、海和沙子的认知模型与在海滩上的模型有着十分密切的关系。在每一个范畴的行为中,我们多多少少有意识地参考了已经贮存在大脑中的一个或多个认知模式,即使我们面对不熟悉的事物或情景时,我们都会尽力唤起相似的经历,并很快形成一个认知模式。如图 2 中"其他语境"所示,认知模式是开放的,是很难穷尽性地加以描写的,具有选择性;认知模式本身不是孤立的认知实体,而是互相作用、相互关联的。语言范畴是动态的、语境敏感的、富有弹性的。很显然,我们绝不可能回避认知模式的影响,也不可能离开它们而认知。

2. 隐喻和转喻

语境的作用在隐喻的理解方面是不言而喻的。James Martin(2006)认为,过去20年中,心理语言学的研究结果表明,语境对隐喻语言的理解有很强的影响。各种实验有关隐喻认知处理的语境效果既不是实验室里假想的事实,也不是特殊目的隐喻认知处理机制的假想事实。实验室里观察到的效果反映了各种语境中隐喻语言一致共现的模式。Michiel Leezenberg(2001)论述了隐喻与语境的关系,他举了这么一个例子:

(1) a. Anchorage is a cold city.
    b. No, last summer, people were fainting because of the heat.
    c. No, last summer, I went there and met friendly people everywhere.
(Leezenberg, 2001:178)

从 b 可以得知,a 句中的 cold 意思是寒冷的,是基本意义,而从 c 中得知 a 中 cold 的意思是"冷淡的,不热情的",则为隐喻意义。这说明隐喻意义的产生和理解,必须依赖于语境,这里的语境实际上是上下文语境。根据认知语义学的研究,意义都可用场境来进行分析,场境的组成部分之间以及组成部分与整个场境之间都具有转喻关系(metonymic relations)。Panther 和 Thornburg(1999:337)提出了一个事态场境(State of Affairs Scenario),事态包括状态、事件、过程和行为,当然也包括我们所关注的言语行为。Panther 与 Thornburg 把认知与语用结合在一起,提出了言语行为转喻的概念,通过这种转喻,一种以言行事被用来代替另外一种以言行事,言外转喻与语境的关系非常紧密。

3. 构式语义

构式语法认为,语言和语言知识是由语言结构各个层面的规约化的象征形式—意义匹配关系组成的:词汇、形态、句法甚至音系、语篇等。构式的意义和功能经常被要求具有非组合性,构式并不孤立存在,而是通过所谓的一串关系和家族相似性形成一个结构(structural inventory),构式集语义、语用、语篇特征于一体。构式语法中语境被用来帮助分析构式的意义和语用方面的特征,语境形成构式语义的一部分,构式也可以提供语境信息,说话人认为有必要对听话人提供话语的相关信息。Goldberg(1995)说得更直白,构式语法不在语义和语用之间做严格的区分,连同语义信息一起,包括焦点成分、话题化和语域等信息都在构式中得以体现出来。

(2) 少一点兰博,多一点基辛格。(参考消息,2012.10.11 第14版 海外视角)

这个例子中的构式为"少一点+N,多一点+N",构式整个意义是一种比较意义:少一点不好的事情,多一点好的东西,其中"兰博""基辛格"属于指称转喻,分别指称不同特点的事物、人。"兰博"是美国影星史泰龙所饰演的好勇斗狠的越战退伍军人。美国外交需要多一些像基辛格那样深思熟虑的人,而少一些只会充满敌意、好斗的兰博式人物。有评论说,美国未来必须采取具建设性和互益性的外交政策,唯有如此,才能使太平洋不致波涛汹涌、怒海覆舟。如果没有相关语境背景知识,很难理解这两个词的意思。这里的语境不是上下文语境,而是言外语境了。语言的使用总是离不开语境的,不同语境影响到对转喻语言的选择与理解。王初明(2015)认为,构式的使用不仅受制于构式语境,而且还须与说话的情境匹配,以保证使用得体并在语法上可以接受。构式之间的交互和构式与情境的交互必然服从于人使用语言的交际意图,是交际意图撬动各类语境因素与语言结构之间的交互,离开了人的交际意图,构式之间、构式与情境之间便无从关联,也就无语境效应可言。可见,语境因素在转喻的理解方面、构式的生成与理解方面的作用是不言而喻的。结合认知语言学对语境的论述和前人对语境的研究,以及语境在认知语言学中的作用,我们在此总结出一个认知语言学中的语境模型图,见图3。

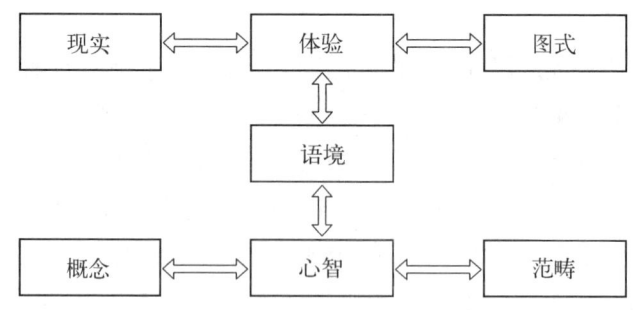

图3 认知语言学的语境模型

图3说明,在认知语言学看来,语境因素不仅仅是传统的一些要素,更重要的是,语境是一种心智现象。认知语言学中,语境通过概念、范畴、图式等方式体现了认知识解,体现了现实与体验的互动,既有客观因素,更有人的主观认知。Goldberg(1995)指出,构式语法拒绝语义学和语用学之间严格的界限,有关焦点成分、话题化和语域的信息在有关语义信息的构式里呈现出来。构式语法建立在重现经验的基础上,在语言使用的经验基础之上研究语义和认知,把语言看成是概念和构式的网络,认为语言不是在词项加规则的基础上建立起来的。构式的研究离不开语境因素。

以上就语境在认知语言学中的作用进行了案例分析,论证了语境在认知语言学研究中的不可忽视的功能。在未来的日子里,认知语言学本身需要进一步完善(朱永生,2005:158)。认知语言学需要在更宽更大的认知语境中进行研究:关注作为语法基础的语言使用,关注基于体验的语法构式和词汇研究,关注语言的社会语境研究等。

六、结 束 语

什么是语境,它包括哪些因素,其他几家语言学派如语用学、功能语言学、社会语言学等对此都作出了自己的回答,给出了明确的定义,尽管他们的回答不一定很完善或很完美。我们认为,认知语言学也必须正视语境这一概念,给出自己的定义,进一步明确语境在认知研究中不可忽视的地位。本文从原型范畴、隐喻转喻、构式语义等方面论述了语境在认知语言学中的地位和作用,尝试性地从认知语言学角度给出语境的定义,结合案例对认知语言学中语境的功能进行了论述,揭示了认知语言学必须重视语境概念阐释的重要性。

参考文献

Bergs, Alexander & Gabriele Diewald. Constructions and context: When a construction constructs the context//Bergs, Alexander & Gabriele Diewald. *Contexts and Constructions*. Amterdam: John Benjamins Publishing House, 2009. 43-62.

Evans, Vyvyan & Melanie Green. *Cognitive Linguistics: An Introduction*. Edinburgh: Edinburgh University Press, 2006. /Beijing: World Book Publishing

Company, 2015.

Fetzer, Anita & Etsuko Oish. *Context and Contexts*. Amsterdam//Philadelphia: John Benjamins Publishing Company, 2011.

Finkbeiner, Rita, Meibauer, Jörg & Petra B. Schumacher. *What is a Context?*. Amsterdam/Philadelphia: John Benjamins Publishing Company, 2012.

Friedrich, Ungerer & Hans-Jorg Schmid. *An Introduction to Cognitive Linguistics* (second edition). Beijing: Foreign Language Teaching & Research Press, 2008.

Geeraerts, Dirk. Recontextualizing Grammar: Underlying trends in thirty years of Cognitive Linguistics//Tabakowska, Elzbieta, Choinski, Michal & Lukasz Wiraszka. *Cognitive Linguistics in Action: From Theory to Application and Back*. Berlin /New York: De Gruyter Mouton, 2010. 71-102.

Goldberg, Adele. *Construction: A Construction Grammar Approach to Argument Structure*. Chicago: Chicago University Press, 1995.

Halliday, M. A. K & C. Mattiessen. *An Introduction to Functional Grammar*. Beijing: Foreign Language Teaching & Research Press, 2008.

Lakoff, George & Mark Johnson. *Philosophy in the Flesh: The Embodied Mind and Its Challenge to Western Thought*. New York: Basic Books, 1999.

Langacker, R. W. *Foundations of Cognitive Grammar, Volume I: Theoretical Prerequisities*. Stanford: Standford University Press, 1987.

Langacker, R. W. The contextual basis of cognitive semantics//Nuyts, J. & E. Pederson. *Language and Conceptualization*. Cambridge: Cambridge University Press. 1997. 229-252.

Langacker, R. W. *Cognitive Grammar: An Introduction*. Stanford: Stanford University Press, 2008.

Leezenberg, Michiel. *Contexts of Metaphor*. Amsterdam: Elsevier Science Ltd, 2001.

Martin, James. A Corpus-based analysis of context effect on metaphor comprehension//Stefanowitsch, Anatol & Stefan TH. Gries. *Corpus-Based Approaches to Metaphors and Metonymy*. Berlin & New York: Mouton de

Gruyter, 2006. 216–236.

Panther, K. & L. Thornburg. *Metonymy in Language and Thought*. Amsterdam: John Benjamins Publishing House, 1999.

Panther, K. & L. Thornburg. *Grammar in Metaphor and Metonymy*. Amsterdam: John Benjamins Publishing House, 2009.

Sperber, Dan & Deirdre Wilson. *Relevance: Communication and Cognition* (2nd ed.). Oxford: Blackwell, 1995.

Taylor, John. R. *Cognitive Grammar*. Oxford: Oxford University Press, 2002.

Tyle, Andrear. Introduction//Tyler, Andrea, Kim, Yiyoung & Mari Takada. *Language in the Context of Use (Discourse and Cognitive Approaches to Language)*. Berlin / New York: Mouton de Gruyter 2009. 1–25.

van Dijk, Teun. *Discourse and Context: A Socio-cognitive Approach*. Cambridge: Cambridge University Press, 2008.

Verschueren, J. *Understanding Pragmatics*. Beijing: Foreign Language Teaching and Research Press, 2001.

Wardraugh, Ronald. *The Context of Language*. Rowley, Massachusetts: Newbury House Publishers, 1976.

陈香兰、申丹:《转喻与语境:"What's X doing Y?"构式转喻思维的限制性因素》,《外语教学与研究》2010年第2期,第104—108页。

何自然:《语用学探索》,暨南大学出版社2012年版。

裴 文:《现代英语语境学》,安徽大学出版社2000年版。

王初明:《构式和构式语境与第二语言学习》,《现代外语》2015年第3期,第357—365页。

王建华、周明强、盛爱萍:《现代汉语语境研究》,浙江大学出版社2002年版。

文 旭:《语言的认知基础》,科学出版社2014年版。

谢应光:《语境因素在认知语法理论构建中的作用》,《外国语文》2009年第3期,第54—59页。

周明强:《现代汉语实用语境学》,浙江大学出版社2005年版。

朱永生:《语境动态研究》,北京大学出版社2005年版。

方法谈：

如何厘清文献综述的述与评？

学术研究中，文献综述是必不可少的环节，是科研的"基本功"。课题申报、科研论文、硕博士学位论文写作，都需要文献评述。文献综述既要"综"，也要"述"，"综"是综合分析整理，是基础，"述"是对文献的观点和结论进行叙述和评论，是提升。本部分将针对学术论文写作中的文献综述如何写这一问题进行讲解，结合案例进行分析说明。

一、什么是文献综述

文献综述简称综述，又称文献回顾，文献分析，是对某一领域，某一专业或某一方面的课题、问题或研究专题搜集大量相关资料，然后通过阅读、分析、归纳、整理当前课题、问题或研究专题的最新进展、学术见解或建议，对其做出综合性介绍和阐述的一种学术论文。劳伦斯·马奇和布伦达·麦克伊沃在《怎样做文献综述——六步走向成功》（上海教育出版社，2020）中，提出了文献综述的六步模型，将文献综述的过程分为六步：选择主题、文献搜索、展开论证、文献研究、文献批评和综述撰写。

文献综述由两部分构成：对已有文献的检索和整理；对搜集来文献的阅读、归纳、整合与升华。文献综述顾名思义由"综"和"述"组成。"综"即综合，要求对文献资料进行综合分析、归纳整理，使材料更精练明确，更有逻辑层次；"述"即评述，要求对综合整理后的文献进行比较专门、全面、深入、系统的论述。一篇好的文献综述，应有完整的文献资料搜集和整理，应该有概括、分析和评价，能够发现问题，发现问题，分析问题并解决问题，以问题为导向，层层推进，找到创新思路。朱光潜曾经说过，什么是创造，就是平常的旧材料之不平常的新综合。写综述是科研的基本功，很多时候人们往往忽略这方面的问题，认为文献综述很容易写，这其实是一种误区。

二、文献综述的特点

综合性：综述要"纵横交错"，点线面体结合，既要以某一专题的发展为纵线,反映当前课题的进展,又要从国内到国外,进行横的比较,因而需要占有大量素材,经过综合分析、归纳整理、消化鉴别,使材料更精练、更明确、更有层次和更有逻辑,进而把握研究对象的发展规律,预测发展趋势。

评述性:透过现象看到本质,专门地、全面地、深入地、系统地论述某一方面的问题,对所综述的内容进行综合、分析、评价,反映作者的观点和见解,并与综述的内容构成整体。综述不仅仅需要描写该问题研究的历史,而且也要搜集最新资料,厘清学术发展的脉络,获取最新动向。

三、文献综述的意义

(1) 理顺学术史,进入学术前沿。学术研究需要把握问题的来龙去脉,了解事物的正反两面,联系新知和旧知,清晰地回顾和交代学术发展的历史,回应别人的研究,说明自己研究的价值。没有参考别人,没有吸收已有的学术成果,就不会在别人的基础上有所发展和超越。

(2) 有助于发现问题,找到研究方向和研究角度。问题往往是从综述出来,发现问题是科学研究的第一步。梳理学术演进的脉络、传统、流变,明确研究对象的最新进步和成果,争论及分歧的焦点,发展趋势,明确研究的方向。

(3) 有助于划清知识产权界限,是学术规范的必然性要求。学术研究必须明示前人已经取得的成绩,引出自己的问题,推陈出新。对已有研究成果综述,划清知识产权界限,区别他人成果与自己原创,这也是保护自己的学术创新的需要。

四、写综述的注意事项

文献综述的基本写作思路可分为三块:① 归纳与分类。对所选文献的研究重点、研究手段及研究结论先进行归纳;② 概括与评价。分析评价这些文献研究所作出的贡献影响、优点与不足;③ 整合与提升。整合回顾,提出改进的方向与进步研究的切入点。也就是说,第一先摆事实:把语言事实摆出来;发现问题,找到事实与事实之间的关联。第二再讲道理:用理论分析问题,由小见大。从事实到理论,从理论到事实。初学者可以适当模仿、借用、套用,为我所用。学习前辈的治学精神和治学方法。从不会到会,是一个厚积薄发的过程。

写文献综述可以采用"填充法",简而言之就是画导图、列框架、不断细化内容。具体如下:一个主题:即确定论文选题,围绕这个选题查找、阅读、挖掘文献信息。一个导图：围绕论文选题，在阅读文献的基础上，列一个文献综述的大纲，再按照大纲一步步把内容填充进去。一般说来，文献综述需要引用：① 该话题的第一篇文章：本领域的开山之作。② 里程碑式文章：文章达到一个高峰，或者突出的进展，是要引用的。文献必须是全面的，尽量完整收集该主题的所有文献，重要的文献不能缺失。文献必须是权威的、有代表性的。同时，引用文献要忠于文献内容，不能篡改文献内容；不能把自己的观点凌驾于文献资料之上；不能只根据摘要就加以引用。与自己的研究相矛盾或不一致的研究必须引用。

一般而言，一篇文献综述中"综"与"述"的比例以 7∶3 为宜。在"述"的时候一定要有原创性观点，不能只是简单地对已有文献进行描述性统计式的评论，要在综述的基础上提出新的命题或模型。首先，提出问题，寻找研究的空白之处，思考所探讨的研究领域有哪些未被关注的问题，哪些研究问题还有局限；再次，分析问题，如在搜集数据方面有哪些不足，或者研究结果是否存在不恰当的陈述、观点等；最后，解决问题，在已有研究存在的争议方面，逐渐上升为研究主题，提出新的研究思路，揭示文献综述和将要进行的研究有怎样的关联。针对已有文献的整体评价，提出自己的理论视角或研究方法，明确解决问题的路径与方案。

如何规避重复率过高：文献综述≠文献综抄。如果完全引用原文，就会导致重复率高的结果，需要用自己的话重新表述，进行分类，尽可能减少原文的引用。这就需要花费大量的时间精力进行文献阅读和分析，提炼升华。在做文献综述时，头脑时刻要清醒：我要解决什么问题，人家是怎么解决问题的，说的有没有道理。同时，缩小范围，不要做"大题目"，要做"小题目"。以本文为例：

论文首先指出，语境是语言学中最重要的概念之一，也是最复杂的概念之一，多年来，语言学家为语境的研究做出了可贵的探索，取得了丰硕的成果。Bergs and Diewald（2009）认为，语法与话语中的语境这一概念似乎是最重要、谈得最多的，可能也是最不明白的概念之一。语境问题是非常困难、非常棘手的（slippery）、非常不稳定的（volatile）。

再次，论文就语境研究进行历史回顾：大致按照时间顺序，先国外后国内进行回顾，其中包括关联理论的语境观、功能语言学的语境观等。我们知道，语境这一概念最早是由波兰的人类学家马林诺夫斯基在 20 世纪 20 年代提出来的，他首先把语境分为情景语境和文化语境，并对这两种语境的构成成分加以分析和细化，这可以说是语境研究的发轫之作，也是对语言学研究的重要贡献。国内学者也非常关注语境的研究,如裴文(2000)、周明强(2005:1)认为有必要建立语境学,以及朱永生(2005:1—2)、谢应光(2009)、陈香兰和申丹(2011)、何自然(2012:202)、王建华(2012)等关于语境研究的观点。

最后,论文专门讨论认知语言学对语境的有关论述。近年来,我们欣喜地看到,认知语言学的论著中对语境的论述明显多起来了,2011年7月11—16日首次在西安外国语大学承办的第11届国际认知语言学大会的主题就是:语言、认知、语境(Language, Cognition, Context),这表明认知语言学开始明确地重视语境的重要作用了。论文列举了Langacker(1987:401—405)和Dirk Geeraerts(2010)有关语境的观点。论文将认知语言学中的语境定义为:语境是一种基于身体体验并通过范畴、概念、意象图式等识解出来的一种心智现象,强调从认知语言学的基本观点、基本主张来看,认知语言学不可能回避语境的研究,可以肯定地说,语境在认知语言学中占据相当重要的地位。论文通过两个案例分析,从原型范畴、隐喻转喻、构式语义等方面来论证语境在认知语言学中的功能。

总之,文献综述并不容易写好,需要我们认真重视,不可掉以轻心。学术研究要求爬到巨人的肩膀上,站得高看得远,才能取法乎上。撰写文献综述需要关注研究主题的确定、系统地搜索和筛选文献、深入分析和评价文献、逻辑清晰的结构和表达、引用和格式规范以及总结和提出未来研究方向。一篇好的文献综述既高屋建瓴,又脚踏实地;既探赜索隐,又醍醐灌顶。学术研究工作是一项既传承又必须创新的工作,需要熟练掌握本专业领域的理论演进轨迹和学术渊源,搞清楚学术发展脉络和传承关系。文献综述非常重要!

也论汉语词重音*

张吉生**

摘要：关于汉语是否有词重音一直有两种相反的声音。本文依据Hyman(2014)对词重音的定义,从超音段功能类型视角,从汉语轻声现象、音步与韵律词的关系和韵律音步与诗律音步的区别三个方面,对主张汉语有词重音的依据一一进行分析。文章认为,汉语轻声现象不足以证明词重音的存在,汉语没有音系音步,连读变调域是韵律词,诗律音步与韵律音步不是同一概念。因此,没有足够证据证明汉语有词重音。

关键词：词重音；超音段功能类型；音步

一、引　言

关于汉语(本文专指普通话)有没有词重音(word stress 或 lexical stress)一直有很多争论,有人(如 Chao,1942/2006；王力,1979；厉为民,1981；Duanmu,1993,2004；端木三,2016；冯胜利,1998,2016 等)认为汉语有词重音,有人(如高名凯、石安石,1963；林焘、王理嘉,1997；张洪明,2014；周韧,2017；张吉生,2020 等)认为汉语没有词重音。由此带出一系列问题,如：汉语有没有音步？如汉语有音步,是左重还是右重？一个语言的韵律层级可否没有音步？声调语

---

* 原载《中国语文》2021年第1期。本文初稿内容分别宣读于北京外国语大学"许国璋讲坛"特邀演讲(2017年11月)、上海大学文学院特邀演讲(2018年10月)、第12届东亚理论语言学国际研讨会应邀嘉宾演讲(2019年7月,澳门大学)。

** 张吉生,华东师范大学外语学院英语系教授(退休),上海大学文学院兼职教授；研究方向为：生成音系学、汉语音系、手语音系。在 Lingua、Journal of Chinese Linguistics、《中国语文》《当代语言学》《外国语》《语言科学》等国内外期刊发表论文 60 余篇,为牛津大学的《牛津语言学研究百科全书》(Oxford Research Encyclopaedia of Linguistics)撰写《汉语音节结构》("Chinese Syllable Structure")。

言是否也可以同时是重音语言？等等。

纵观半个多世纪来的相关研究,主张汉语有词重音的主要三大理由是:第一,汉语有轻声,轻声不重读,因此汉语(双音节)词有轻重之分,表现为左重;第二,汉语有些词的左重或右重有语义区别性,这就是词重音;第三,汉语肯定有音步,音步必分左重或右重,所以汉语有词重音。本文将依据 Hyman(2014)对词重音的定义,从超音段功能类型视角分析汉语实际语料,解析汉语是否有词重音,回答上述问题。

二、什么是词重音

所谓重音是指一个音高或音强或时长的突显形式落在某个音节上,一个承载重音的音节叫重读音节。反之,一个不承载重音的音节叫非重读音节。词重音是相对于非重读音节存在的。英语和其他日耳曼语重音运用上的差别远远多于世界上其他大部分语言(Ladefoged,2005:238)。重音语言的特点是一个形态词必须有一个也最多只有一个音节具有最高的节律突显,这种重音也叫词重音。有人认为词重音具有普遍性,只是重音的表现形式不同(参看 Goedemans & van der Hulst,2009:239—241)。如这观点成立,就没有必要讨论汉语有没有词重音了。当然也有许多学者(如 Newman,1947;Schiering et al.,2010)认为,确有一些语言没有词重音,包括一些非洲声调语言,也有非声调语言。Hyman(2014:56—61)认为,之所以有上述分歧,有的是纯个人原因,因为有的人听得到轻重,有的人听不到。但主要是不同的理论问题,即对词重音没有统一认识。Hyman(1977,1978,1981,1985,2014)对词重音做了许多专门研究。基于大量跨语言语料的分析,他提出词重音有以下特征:

(1) Hyman(2014:61)的词重音特征:
    a. 必要性:　　每个词必须有主重音。
    b. 唯一性:　　每个词只有一个主重音。
    c. 规则性:　　主重音的位置有规可循。
    d. 自主性:　　词重音规则不牵涉语法信息。
    e. 词界性:　　词重音规则基于词界。
    f. 边沿性:　　词重音应该靠近词界(或左或右)。

g. 非莫拉性： 词重音跟音节长短(重量)无关。
h. 排他性： 重音或有或无,没有次重音。
i. 听感性： 词重音有语音特征(能够听出来)。

上述词重音特征是一种跨语言的普遍现象,并非任何一种重音语言都必须同时具备上述特征。Hyman(2014)认为,在上述9个词重音特征中,(a)(b)(f)是必须的,其他特征因不同语言类型而异。另外,衡量一种语言是否是重音语言,要看该语言常用词的主体结构,如不能因为英语个别功能词没有重音(如the,a等)就否定英语符合重音语言的特征,并主要考察双音节以上(包括双音节)的词,单音节不能作为依据,因为英语所有单音节实义词都重读,没有轻重区别,汉语所有独立载调音节的字也都重读。

重音语言有固定重音型(fixed stress,如拉丁语)和自由重音型(free stress,如俄语);还有重量敏感性(quantity-sensitive,如阿拉伯语)和重量不敏感性(quantity-insensitive,如Pintupi语①)。自由重音型语言的词重音就很难用规则预测;重量敏感性语言的词重音与音节的重量有关,即重读(stressed)音节一定是重(heavy)音节。要回答汉语有没有词重音这个问题,首先要搞清楚什么是词重音。世界上有重音语言,如拉丁语、英语和俄语等,也有非重音语言,如法语、匈牙利语和芬兰语等(Hyman,2014:78)。

在汉语有没有词重音的讨论中,另一个问题是混淆了词重音与节律重音(metrical stress)的区别。根据Hayes(1995),节律重音主要构建句子的韵律节奏,节律重音模式有节奏地组织句子层级结构。简言之,词重音是线性的,是词库内的;节律重音是非线性的,是词库外的。词重音和节律重音可表达如下(以英语 Doctors use penicillin 一句为例):

图1展示了英语句子 Doctors use penicillin 的节律重音模式及与词重音的关系,其中底层的加号"+"表示词库内的词重音或次重音,减号"-"表示非重音;(s)表示重读,(w)表示弱读。

节律重音是有层级结构的,从下往上,从小到大,一层一层建构节律重音单位,每个结构单位只有一个主重音。一个词库内的重读音节在一个大的节律单位可以不重读,如重读音节 use 在 use penicillin 的"V+N"结构中不重读;句中

---

① 一种西澳大利亚语土著语(参看 Hansen 和 Hansen,1969)。

主语 doctors 在词库内第一个音节重读,但在主谓结构中,相对于谓语,主语 doctors 不重读(除非是焦点)。因此,节律重音与词重音的另一个区别是前者与语法或句法结构有关,后者与语法或句法结构无关[见(1d)]。如端木三(1999)所言的辅重结构就是一种节律重音模式。如英语的 French wine("A+N"定中结构),主重音在 French;drink wine("V+N"动宾结构)的主重音是 wine。节律重音也称韵律重音或韵律突显(prosodic prominent),具有普遍性,因此汉语当然有节律重音。汉语双音节动宾结构是右重(Chao,1942/2006),如"纳税""陪客";定中结构是左重,如"公事""蓝天"等。但词重音与语法或句法结构无关,如英语 doctor 一词,无论作主语、定语或宾语,第一个音节[dɒk]永远是该词的重读音节。因此,Hyman(2014:64)指出,讨论重音(stress-accent)问题,要区别词重音与短语重音的不同。当我们搞清楚什么是词重音后,我们再讨论汉语是否有词重音。

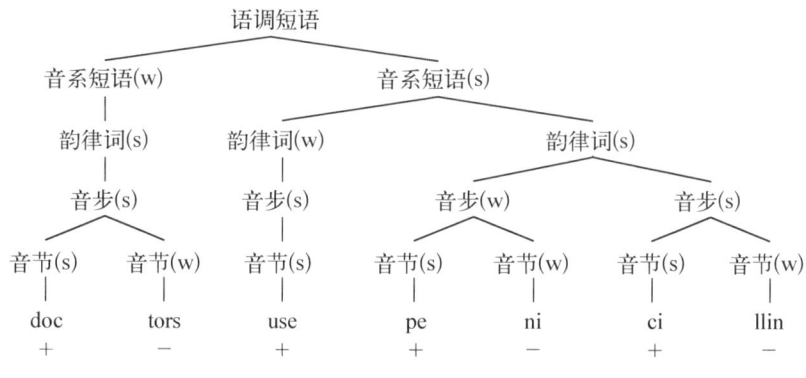

图 1　词重音与节律重音

三、超音段特征的功能类型

词重音的实现在不同语言中有不同方式,但不外乎音高、音强和时长这三种形式,其中音高是最基本的。Levi(2005)指出,许多语言主要依据基频识别重读音节。无论是音高、音强,还是时长,或三者的结合,重音是超音段特征。超音段特征在语言中的音位功能主要有三种形式:重音(stress)、音高重音(pitch accent)和声调(tone)。无论表现哪一种功能,超音段特征都可以用 H(高)和 L(低)来表征。H 可指重音语言的重音,音高重音的高音调,或声调语言的高调值;L 可指重音语言的非重读音节,音高重音语言的低音调,或声调语言的低调值。如表达一个三音节词,其 H 和 L 的音高特征模式一共有八种可能:H.L.L、L.H.L、L.L.H、H.H.L、L.H.H、H.L.H、L.L.L、H.H.H。

在重音语言(如英语)、音高重音语言(如日语)和声调语言(如汉语)这三种不同类型语言中,其词汇音高有不同的结构模型。以一个三音节词为例,其音高结构可举例如下。

(2) 不同类型语言三音节音高模型举例

　　a. 英语(重音语言):

　　　H.L.L:possible /ˈpɒsəbl/ "可能的"

　　　L.H.L:beginner /bɪˈɡɪnə/ "新手"

　　　L.L.H:engineer /endʒɪˈnɪə/ "工程师"

　　　*L.L.L、*H.H.L、*H.H.H、*L.H.H、*H.L.H

　　b. 日语(音高重音语言):

　　　H.L.L:せかい[se ka i] "世界"

　　　L.H.H:さくら[sa ku ra] "樱花"

　　　L.H.L:さとう[sa to u] "砂糖"

　　　*H.H.H、*H.H.L、*L.L.L、*L.L.H、*H.L.H①

　　c. 汉语(声调语言)②:

　　　H.L.L:hua⁵⁵ yu²¹⁴ san²¹⁴ "花雨伞"

　　　H.L.H:duo⁵⁵ yu²¹⁴ tian⁵⁵ "多雨天"

　　　L.L.H:lao²¹⁴ jiu²¹⁴ gang⁵⁵ "老酒缸"

　　　L.H.L:wu²¹⁴ xiang⁵⁵ bing²¹⁴ "五香饼"

　　　L.L.L:zhi²¹⁴ yu²¹⁴ san²¹⁴ "纸雨伞"

　　　H.H.L:sheng⁵⁵ jiang⁵⁵ fen²¹⁴ "生姜粉"

　　　H.H.H:san⁵⁵ qing⁵⁵ shan⁵⁵ "三清山"

　　　L.H.H:jing²¹⁴ gang⁵⁵ shan⁵⁵ "井冈山"

语料(2)说明:

---

① 一般认为日语没有 H.L.H 音调模型,音调下降后不会再上升。但也有人认为日语有些方言及对外来语的音译有 H.L.H 模型(参看久保博雅,2019)。

② 汉语阴平(55)、阳平(35)、上声(214)、去声(51)四个声调有不同形式的音系赋值,最常见的音系赋值分别是 H、LH、L、HL(参看 Yip,2002:180)。

(i) 在重音语言中,一个三音节词只有三种结构,H.L.L、L.H.L 和 L.L.H,三个音节只能有一个 H,也必须有一个 H,即必须满足(1a)(1b)。

(ii) 在音高重音语言中,一个三音节词的第一二两个音节必须是曲折调(即 H.L 或 L.H)。

(iii) 在声调语言中,一个三音节词的声调调值可以是任何一种形式,因为一个音节一个声调代表一个语素,其间的关系是任意的。三种不同语言的音高特征结构说明了音高这一超音段特征在不同语言中的不同功能具有不同的类型学特征,这种类型学特征可表示如表1。

表1 音高功能的类型学特征

	H.L.L	L.H.L	L.L.H	H.H.L	L.H.H	H.L.H	L.L.L	H.H.H
重音语言	√	√	√	×	×	×	×	×
音高重音	√	√	×	×	√	×/√	×	×
声调语言	√	√	√	√	√	√	√	√

表1说明,音高特征在不同类型语言中的表现及其功能具有类型学的区别。这种不同类型的音高模式受到相关制约条件的制约。制约英语音高模式是 *Lapse 和 CULMINATIVE 两个制约条件,定义如下。

(3) *Lapse(Elenbaas & Kager,1999:282)
每一个弱节奏必须与强节奏或词界相邻。

(4) CULMINATIVE(简称 CUL,根据 Hyman,2014:61)
一个词最多只有一个主重音。

制约条件(3)规定语言中不能出现*LLL 音高模式;制约条件(4)不允许一个三音节词有*L.H.H、*H.H.L、*H.L.H、*H.H.H 这样的音高模式。制约日语音高模式主要是 OCP(Initial),其定义如下:

(5) OCP (Initial)
词首两个音节的音高必须曲折(或 H.L,或 L.H)。

根据制约条件(5)，日语任何一个合法词的第一、二两个音节只能是 H.L 或 L.H，不允许 * H.H 或 * L.L（如 2b 所示）。汉语每个字都有单字调，多字复合词音高模式不受上述制约条件的制约。比较三种不同类型的语言，重音语言音高模型受限最多，其次是音高重音语言，声调语言最自由。显然，在声调语言中一些常见的音高模式在重音语言中是不合法的。这是否说明重音语言不能有声调，或声调语言不能有重音。但答案是重音语言可以有声调，或声调语言也可以有重音。如日耳曼语①的瑞典语同时有声调。瑞典语有两个声调：分别叫"锐音"（acute accent）和"钝音"（grave accent）。② 瑞典语的这两个不同音高模式（pitch pattern）有词汇区别意义，如下所示。③

(6)　　　　实际词　　　　　　锐音　　　　钝音
　　　vâken　　↔　　vǎken　　冰窟窿　　醒着
　　　slûtet　　↔　　slǔtet　　最后　　　关闭
　　　skâllen　↔　　skǎllen　 树皮　　　颅骨
　　　êgen　　 ↔　　ěgen　　 拥有　　　奇怪的

瑞典语的这两种音高模式只出现在重读音节，因此虽然瑞典语既有重音又有声调，但它不会违反制约条件 CUL 和 * Lapse。

再譬如声调语 Saramaccan 语④也有词重音，如下所示（语料来自 Good，2004：16）。⑤

(7) a. ˈsákásɑ　　卧室　　　ˈbćkúsu　　盒子
　　　 ˈsíkísi　　　六　　　　miˈnísíti　　部长
　　b. siˈkífi　　　写　　　　mɑˈníni　　礼貌
　　　 ɑfoˈkáti　　律师　　　mɔˈfínɑ　　贫乏的
　　c. ˈmɔkisá　　挤压　　　ɑˈlukutú　 酸枣

----

① 日耳曼语都有词重音。
② "锐音"和"钝音"在不同语言有不同表现。瑞典语的锐音是一个升降调形(ˆ)。钝音则有两个音峰，表现为升降升调形(ˇ)（根据 http://www.glottopedia.org/index.php/Swedish_Phonology#Tone_Accents）。
③ 语料来自 http://www.glottopedia.org/index.php/Swedish_Phonology#Tone_Accents。
④ 这是一种大西洋克里奥尔语。
⑤ 语料(7)中，元音上的"ˊ"表示高平调，元音上没有标记表示低平调，音节前"ˈ"表示重音符号。

Good(2004)的研究发现,Saramaccan 语的词重音是音步划分的标记,Saramaccan 语音步是扬抑格,最佳音步是双音节,双莫拉①单音节也可以成为音步,重读音节主要以音强和时长来实现,重读高调音节的音高更高。词重音往往在最左边的高调音节上,以声调为"高高低"音节结尾的词为例,重音在第一个高调音节上[如(7a)],最后一个低调音节成为节律外音节(即不被音步分解)。尽管最后两个音节的"高低"是最佳扬抑格音步,但"(高)(高低)"的音步组合违反了*Clash 制约条件。② Good(2004)认为,尽管 Saramaccan 语既有声调又有重音,但重音的分配不会违反重音语言必须遵守的*Clash 制约条件。Saramaccan 语的词重音也完全符合 Hyman(2014)指出的词重音特征[如(1)所示]。

重音语言和声调语言是不同的语言类型,有不同的音高表现模式。但如果一种声调语言又同时有词重音,也一定不能违反重音语言必须遵守的音系制约条件。

四、提出汉语词重音的主要理由

如上所提,汉语是否有词重音有不同的观点。主张汉语有词重音的理由主要有三个方面:轻声、轻重区别词义和音步结构。这一小节我们将根据汉语实际语料——分析汉语这三个方面与词重音的关系。

1. 轻声与轻重音节的关系

主张汉语有词重音立场的主要依据之一是汉语有轻声(如厉为民,1981;端木三,1999;Duanmu,2004;冯胜利,2016 等)。他们认为汉语轻声音节是非重读音节,非重读相对于重读,这就意味着汉语有重音。汉语轻声主要有下列四种形式。③

(8)　　拼音　　声调　　例词　　　拼音　　　声调　　例词
　a.　　baba　　51.$_0$　　爸爸　　yeye　　　35.$_0$　　爷爷
　　　　tingting　55.$_0$　听听　　kankan　　51.$_0$　　看看

---

① 莫拉(mora)是音节重量单位,一般 CVC 和 CVV 音节是双莫拉,CV 音节是单莫拉。
② *Clash(Kager,1999:165):两个重读音节不能相邻出现(*H.H)。所有重音语言都不能违反此制约条件。
③ 此处采用拼音;下标"$_0$"表示轻声,即没有声调。

b.	jiaozi	214.0	饺子	tizi	55.0	梯子
	zhentou	214.0	枕头	mutou	51.0	木头
c.	shenqi	35.0	神气	shangliang	55.0	商量
	zhangfu	51.0	丈夫	doufu	51.0	豆腐
d.	dongxi	55.55	东西(方向)	dongxi	55.0	东西(物品)
	didao	51.51	地道(隧道)	didao	51.0	地道(纯)

例(8)是汉语四种轻声音节现象,a 类是叠音词,汉语双音节叠音词(包括称谓、动词等)的第二个音节往往是轻声。b 类是后缀,汉语有不少后缀,如"头""子""儿"等往往读轻声。c 类汉语中有一些高频使用的双音节复合词(包括并列、偏正、述补、述宾、联合、递续等)的第二个音节读轻声。d 类汉语中有些词的音节轻声与否有词汇区别意义。根据类似例(8)语料,厉为民(1981)等认为汉语与英语、俄语等印欧语言一样,具有词重音。他们认为轻声只出现在右音节,因此汉语是左重结构。冯胜利(2016)在《北京话是一个重音语言》提出的主张也主要基于上述例子。一般而言,如果一个语言中构成词的音节有重读与非重读之分,那么,我们基本可以说这个语言有词重音,或这是重音语言。

张洪明(2014)认为,汉语中像例(8)这种现象,不是非重读音节,而是轻声,轻声本质上是一种声调现象。Duanmu(1993)则认为,轻声是因为音节不重读,所以没了声调。而 Yip(1980:57,84)认为汉语是声调决定重音,而不是重音决定声调。其实,关键问题是汉语如例(8)这种轻声现象是否普遍。根据 Yin(1989)的统计,[T.0]形式只占全部汉语双音节词的 14%,即 86%的双音节词没有非重读音节现象。万学仁、熊杰(2011)统计了 2008 版的《现代汉语常用词表》①的 56 008 个词(主要是双音词),其中轻声(包括单音节虚词,如"着""了""的"等)2 043 个,只占 3.6%。显然,轻声现象在现代汉语词汇中所占比率很小,无论如何,我们无法根据如此小比率的轻声现象来判定汉语有词重音,就如我们不能根据英语有一些单音节功能词无重音来判定英语不是重

---

① 《现代汉语常用词表》由国家语言文字工作委员会于 1997 年批准立项,课题组主要基于 10 多本汉语词典,用山西大学和清华大学计算机中心所储存的语料进行词汇覆盖率检测,最后进行人工干预,于 2007 年完成,2008 年由商务印书馆出版。该词表所收录的常用词是指以汉语为母语中等水平的人,在社会语文生活中经常见到和使用的,通用、稳定、频率较高的普通话单音节和双音节词。

音语言。

无论轻声占汉语词汇是14%,还是3.6%,绝大多数汉语双音节词汇是[T.T]形式,即没有轻声。那么汉语[T.T]双音节词有轻重吗?Shen等(2013:45—58)专门对汉语双音节词的声学特征进行了分析,没有发现[T.T]双音节词有左重或右重的突显音节模式。邓丹(2010:62—80)通过对2 239个双音节词(不包括轻声)的声学分析,发现有41.7%的双音节词前后音节等重,58.3%的双音节词中有些前重,有些后重,其中的差异与不同声调调型有紧密关系。王韫佳等(2003:734—742)对汉语的韵律词重音做了感知心理实验,他们的实验发现汉语语流中的韵律词有H.L、H.H和L.H三种模式,主要与声调有关。根据Hyman(2014:61)提出的词重音九个特点,见(1),一个词只有一个重音,但汉语有约86%的双音节词没有轻声,即两个音节都重读。① 也有不少实验语音分析发现,汉语孤立双音节或三音节词通常表现为右重,主要是时长延长,音高主要还是受声调调值和调型的影响(如林茂灿等1984;颜景助、林茂灿,1988等)。但这种右重不是词重音的标记,而是词界突显的标记。显然,上述这些现象都不符合重音语言的重音分配原则。上述分析与周韧(2017:540)的论点一致,即"汉语不是一种重音语言,这在当代实验语音学界几乎可以说已经成为一种共识"。

关于词重音的重量突显问题,还有一种观点认为重音可以是一种抽象概念,不一定要具备语音的听感性。如端木三(2016:61)认为:"感觉明显不明显,跟重音有无,并不完全是一回事。很多东西人们并不一定能直接感觉到。"学界普遍认为,重读音节一定有某种语音的突显,或音高,或时长,或音强(Fry,1955,1958;van der Hulst,2014:7)。重音语言母语者都能准确听辨出词重音(Fry,1958)。我们不能说汉语有词重音,只是我们听不出来。这也不符合Hyman提出的重音特征(1i)。

2. 汉语中轻重区别词语的现象

上面讲到汉语双音节词有前重也有后重,有些与声调类型有关,如"开水"(55.214)表现为前重,"水车"(214.55)是后重。但汉语中还有另一种现象,有一些双音节词,两个词的音系结构一样,它们音同字不同(即义不同),但语音实现时会产生前后音节不同的重音,如(9)所示。

---

① Duanmu(1993:7)也认为,载调(full tone)音节都重读。

(9) 双音节词不同重音的区别性功能①

	例词	声调	强弱	内部结构		例词	声调	强弱	内部结构
a.	散步	51.51	W.S	（动＋名）	b.	攻击	55.55	W.S	（联合）
	散布	51.51	S.W	（状＋动）		公鸡	55.55	S.W	（定中）
c.	攻势	55.51	W.S	（动＋名）	d.	陪客	35.51	W.S	（动宾）
	公事	55.51	S.W	（定中）		陪客	35.51	S.W	（定中）

上述双音节词在使用中确实有轻重区别。显然，例(9)中的四对词各自的轻重区别与声调无关。冯胜利(2016：451)也用例(9)这些语言现象来证明汉语是重音语言。但是，仔细观察例(9)可以发现，凡定中结构总是左重，动宾结构总是右重。Chao(1942/2006：347—348)认为这种重音现象与词的内部结构有关，动宾结构是抑扬格。Hyman(2014：61)认为，词重音与语法结构无关。与语法或句法结构有关的重音是词库外的节律重音，如图1所示。词重音是在词库内的词汇信息，而节律重音是词库外的韵律信息。Selkirk(1984)认为句法与音系之间有一种匹配关系，如一个 XP 结构的中心词 X 往往不重读，即重读不落在中心词。这也称辅重结构(Duanmu, 2012：89—114)。不少人认为例(9)是汉语有词重音的有力证据。但实际上，汉语的词与词组没有明显界线，有些复合词的内部保留着词组的特征，词组又经常可以当词用。如(9d)的动宾"陪客"是右重，定中"陪客"是左重。这种重音由词内的语法关系决定，是词库外的节律重音遗留的痕迹，不是词库内生成的词重音。当然，汉语复合词的这种由内部结构引起的轻重区别不是很普遍，因为汉语本没有词重音，不像英语那种重音语言，复合词与短语的重音明显不同（如 ˈdark room"(洗照片的)暗室"，dark ˈroom"黑暗的房间"）。另外，汉语复合词与短语没明显区别，如"理发"既可以是复合动词，也可以是动宾短语。因此，例(9)现象不能用来证明汉语有词重音。

3. 汉语韵律重音与音步

主张汉语有词重音的另一理由是音步结构的需要。当我们在讨论重音时，通常会提到音步——语言中的一个韵律结构单位。根据 Nespor 和 Vogel (2007：16)，人类语言韵律层级包含如下结构单位：

---

① 例(9)中的强弱，W 表示弱读音节，S 表示重读音节。

(10) 韵律层级(从大到小)
　　韵律话语(Phonological Utterance)　　U
　　语调短语(Intonational Phrase)　　I
　　音系短语(Phonological Phrase)　　φ
　　黏附组(Clitic Group)　　C
　　韵律词(Prosodic Word)　　ω
　　音步(Foot)　　Σ
　　音节(Syllable)　　σ

音步是大于音节,小于韵律词的韵律结构单位。音步是决定重读音节和非重读音节位置的辖域(Nespor & Vogel,2007:83),即音步一定与重音有关。Kager(2007:200—201)基于已有研究(如 Hayes,1985,1987,1995;McCarthy & Prince,1986;Prince,1990),把人类语言韵律结构中的音步类型归纳为以下两类三种:

(11) 音步类型
　　(i) a. 重量不敏感性拍音节扬抑格(quantity-insensitive syllabic trochee)
　　　　b. 重量敏感性拍莫拉扬抑格(quantity-sensitive moraic trochee)
　　(ii) 重量敏感性抑扬格(quantity-sensitive iambic)

所谓扬抑格音步或抑扬格音步,就是重音的分配是左重还是右重。汉语有没有词重音这个问题涉及汉语有没有音步。许多人认为音步是人类语言必有的自然结构。有一种观点称严格阶层假说(Strict Layer Hypothesis),其基本概念如下:

(12) 严格阶层假说(Trask,1996:337—338)
　　韵律层级模式中的一种假说,要求一个给定的层级上的所有材料必须受上一个更高层级节点的统辖。

严格阶层假说表明了两个原则:(i) 韵律结构中的任何一个层级都受上一

层级节点的统辖,一个高节点韵律层级只能统辖下一个节点的韵律层级,不能跨层级统辖;(ii) 一个韵律层级的节点不能统辖相同层级,如一个韵律词不能统辖另一个韵律词。但该假说受到了许多语言事实的挑战,许多研究(如 Hyman et al., 1987:87—108;Tanaka, 1990:1—38)证明有些语言一个层级可以统辖相同韵律层级,有些语言没有黏附组这一韵律层级,有不少语言落单的音节不在音步域内(Hayes, 1981)。早在 20 世纪 60 年代,Abercrombie(1967)指出,"对于没有词重音(stress accent)或有音节节拍的语言来说,音步概念是否有用现在还不清楚"(参看 Trask, 1996:147)。张洪明(2014:303—327)就认为汉语没有词重音,不需要用音步来规范重音的分配。汉语从本质上讲还是单音节语言,即一个音节一个语素(一个字),绝大多数音节(除轻声)都重读,因此汉语有强烈的音节节拍感。汉语是声调语言,汉语双音节词允许 H.H 或 L.L 这种音步所不允许的结构。因此,正如 Prince(1983)所言,音步不见得是韵律层级中的必需层级单位。上海话就是最不需要音步的语言之一。上海话连读变调域是韵律词,举例如下:

(13) 上海话连读变调(根据许宝华等,1981、1982、1983)①

	例词	单字调		变调
a.	春分	HL.HL	→	H.L
b.	扳搓头	HL.HL.LH	→	H.M.L
c.	修坏脱	HL.LH.H	→	H.M.L
d.	小家败气	MH.HL.LH.MH	→	M.H.M.L
e.	水淋溚沛	MH.LH.H.MH	→	M.H.M.L
f.	清水大闸蟹	HL.MH.LH.LH.MH	→	H.M.M.M.L
g.	像煞有介事	LH.H.MH.MH.LH	→	M.H.M.M.L

根据(13),上海话连读变调基本是两种模式:(i) 二、三字组变调基本是整个变调域调型是第一个音节调型的扩展;(ii) 四、五字组变调基本是第三个音节开始是个低平调。在上海话音系分析中音步不起作用。

---

① 根据许宝华等(1981:145),上海话 5 个声调调值为:阴平[53] HL、阴去[34] MH、阳去[13] LH、阴入[55] Hq 和阳入[12] LMq。此处的音系赋值根据 Chen(2000:306)。

认为汉语韵律结构一定有音步的主要有三个理由：第一，生活中的很多词语都是自然音步；第二，音步是汉语连读变调域；第三，汉语诗律有音步。

冯胜利(1998：41)认为汉语韵律结构一定有音步，因为汉语很多独立词语结构都是自然音步，如"巴西""古巴""加拿大""墨西哥""工农兵"都是自然音步。冯胜利(2016：455)把汉语自然音步结构规定为"小不减二，大不过三"。我们认为产生所谓自然音步的感觉主要因素有二：(i)汉语中的大量自然音步其实是韵律词，可以独立运用，因此影响深刻；(ii)受现代汉语双音节化的影响。张洪明(2014：324)认为："双音节化不等同于音步化。音步化是节律化，两个相关的音节有二元化的节律凸显对比。双音节化是指汉语词的负载单位由原来一个音节为主，变成了两个音节为主。"音步在韵律层级中不是独立自由单位。Nespor和Vogel(2007：109)指出，在韵律结构中，只有韵律词才与语法词同构。因此，汉语中上述所谓的"自然音步"实际上都是韵律词，或汉语中基本没有一个韵律词有两个"自然音步"。曹剑芬(2001：117)认为，汉语的"韵律词也就是音步"。如果一个语言中的音步就是韵律词，音步就没有存在的意义。

王洪君(2000)认为，有些音步是韵律词，有些音步不是韵律词。根据王洪君(2000：531)的分析，汉语韵律结构中音步和韵律词的关系可举例如下。

(14) 例词　　　　　音节　　　音步　　　韵律词

例词	音节	音步	韵律词
雨伞	2	1	1
买纸	2	1	1
雨伞厂	3	1	1
保险锁	3	1	1
小雨伞	3	2	2
买雨伞	3	2	2
干干净净	4	2	1
取长补短	4	2	1

为什么在王洪君(2000)的分析中，"保险锁"是一个音步，而"小雨伞"是两个音步？因为常速下的"保险锁"上声变调为[35.35.214]，即三字一个变调域；而"小雨伞"的上声变调是[214.35.214]，即只有"雨伞"是变调域。王洪君认为，最普遍的音步是双音节，韵律词就是语法词，音步是连读变调域。汉语四字成语是

一个词,基本都是 2+2 结构,在慢语速时中间可以有停顿。因此很容易被认作是一个韵律词中的两个音步。确实,大多数情况下,一个语法词往往就是一个韵律词。但韵律词的域在语流中不是固定的,通常语速慢时韵律词的域比语速快时韵律词的域要小。不少语言学家(如 Booij,1983)认为,韵律词的域有三种可能:比语法词大,比语法词小,与语法词同域。如"Budapest"(布达佩斯)一个语法词分两个韵律词:[Buda]ω[pest]ω,因为匈牙利语有韵律词内[±后位性]和谐特征一致的要求。其实,例(14)中的"小雨伞"和"买雨伞"语速快时都是一个韵律词,因为快语速的连读变调都可以是[35.35.214],即连读变调域是韵律词,不是音步,因为音步域不会因语速快慢而改变。快时读"干干净净"中间没有停顿,当然是一个韵律词。但慢语速读"干干-净净"时中间有停顿,此时的"干干"加"净净"还是一个韵律词吗?如快速的"小米老酒"的上声变调可以是[35.35.35.214],即一个语法词就是一个韵律词。但慢速时的连读变调是[35.214.35.214],即两个韵律词。因此,汉语上声变调域是韵律词,不是音步。

端木三(2016:57)还认为,如汉语没有音步,汉语诗歌节奏如何表现。许多人把音系(韵律)结构中的音步与诗律中的音步混为一谈。根据 Trask(1996:147),音步有两种:一种是诗歌中的基本节奏单位,另一种是音系学中的基本节奏单位。

我们认为,韵律音步与诗律音步不是同一种结构,理由有二:

第一,根据(11),韵律音步只有两种类型:抑扬格和扬抑格。但诗歌格律音步类型可有以下七种(参看 Cummings,2006):

(15) 诗歌格律音步类型

音步名称	重音模式	音节数
a. 抑扬(iamb)	弱+强	2
b. 扬抑(trochee)	强+弱	2
c. 扬扬(spondee)	强+强	2
d. 抑抑扬(anapaest)	弱+弱+强	3
e. 扬抑抑(dactyl)	强+弱+弱	3
f. 抑扬抑(amphibrach)	弱+强+弱	3
g. 抑抑(pyrrhic)	弱+弱	2

当然,就某一种语言的诗歌节律会采用不同的音步结构。但是,像有些诗歌中的"扬扬格"或"抑抑格"音步在音系结构中是不允许的。

第二,音系音步是词库内重音分配的辖域,如英语 metricality 一词有两个音步,无论这个词在句中作什么句法成分,音步结构永远不会改变。但诗律音步是因美学的需要而人为编制的。拿莎士比亚的十四行诗为例,其格律往往是五音步抑扬格(iambic pentametre),例如:

(16) 英语五步诗歌格律①
S   W/W S   /W S/W S/W   S
Shall I com-pare thee to a sum-mer's day?
W   S   /W   S/W   S   /W   S/W S
Thou art more love-ly and more tem-perate.
W   S   /W   S/W   S/W   S/W   S
Rough winds do shake the dar-ling buds of May…

众所周知,英语的音系(韵律)音步是扬抑格,但莎士比亚的十四行诗通常是抑扬格。诗歌中的五步抑扬格是诗人打破词界人为建构的。显然,韵律音步与诗律音步完全不是同一回事。汉语的严格诗律是由声调的平仄搭配建构的。张洪明(2014:315)认为,"这里由平仄音节交替构成的音步是汉语诗律学意义上的音步,但此音步(诗律学)非彼音步(语言学)"。总之,无论汉语诗歌格律是否用音步,与汉语音系结构有无音步没有关系。

五、结　　语

本文根据 Hyman(2014)对词重音的界定,从超音段特征的功能类型视角,分析了不同语言重音、音高重音和声调的不同表现形式和类型特征。文章通过跨语言的语料分析,阐述了重音语言、音高重音语言和声调语言的区别,归纳出这三种不同类型语言三音节词的音高表现模式:重音语言不能违反 CUL 和

---

① 该诗句的重音划分摘自 Gussenhoven 和 Jacobs(2011:216)。词中的连字符号是本文作者所加,表示跨音步界。

*Lapse 的音系制约条件；音高重音语言不能违反 OCP(initial)制约条件；声调语言不受音高模式制约条件的限制，即可违反 CUL、*Lapse 和 OCP(initial)。

本文认为，汉语没有严格意义上的词重音：第一，汉语的轻声现象在汉语词汇中的比率很小，不足以证明汉语是左重结构；第二，汉语有一小部分词可以通过左重和右重来区别词义，但这种左重与右重的区别往往与词内的语法结构有关，属于词库外的节律重音的遗留，不是词库内的词重音；第三，根据汉语实际语料，汉语所谓的自然音步都是韵律词，汉语上声变调域是韵律词，不是音步；第四，音系音步与诗律音步不是同一个音步概念，汉语有无诗律音步与汉语有无音系音步没有关系。因此，汉语绝大多数双音节或多音节词的结构不具备 Hyman(2014)提出的词重音特征，汉语只是声调语言，没有严格意义上的词重音。本文的分析支持张洪明(2014：323)的观点，作为声调语言，汉语在词层面没有结构性的范畴化、系统化的轻重音。

参考文献

曹剑芬：《汉语韵律切分的语音学和语言学线索》，《新世纪的现代语音学——第五届全国现代语音学学术会议论文集》，清华大学出版社 2001 年版。

邓　丹：《汉语韵律词研究》，北京大学出版社 2010 年版。

端木三：《重音理论和汉语的词长选择》，《中国语文》1999 年第 4 期。

端木三：《音步和重音》，北京语言大学出版社 2016 年版。

冯胜利：《论汉语的"自然音步"》，《中国语文》1998 年第 1 期。

冯胜利：《北京话是一个重音语言》，《语言科学》2016 年第 5 期。

高名凯、石安石：《语言学概论》，中华书局 1963 年版。

久保博雅：《愛媛県松山市睦月島方言における重起伏調アクセント》，《論叢国語教育学》2019 年第 15 期。

厉为民：《试论轻声和重音》，《中国语文》1981 年第 1 期。

林茂灿、颜景助、孙国华：《北京话两字组正常重音的初步实验》，《方言》1984 年第 1 期。

林　焘、王理嘉：《语音学教程》，北京大学出版社 1997 年版。

万学仁、熊　杰：《谈谈〈现代汉语常用词表〉中的轻声词语》，《内江师范学院学报》2011 年第 5 期。

王洪君：《汉语的韵律词与韵律短语》，《中国语文》2000 年第 6 期。

王　力：《汉语诗律学》，上海教育出版社 1979 年版。

王韫佳、初　敏、贺　琳：《汉语语句重音的分类和分布的初步实验研究》，《心理学报》2003 年第 6 期。

许宝华、赛珍珠、钱乃荣：《新派上海方言的连读变调》，《方言》1981 年第 2 期。

许宝华、赛珍珠、钱乃荣：《新派上海方言的连读变调（二）》，《方言》1982 年第 2 期。

许宝华、赛珍珠、钱乃荣：《新派上海方言的连读变调（三）》，《方言》1983 年第 3 期。

颜景助、林茂灿：《北京话三字组重音的声学表现》，《方言》1988 年第 3 期。

张洪明：《韵律音系学与汉语韵律研究中的若干问题》，《当代语言学》2014 年第 3 期。

张吉生：《英汉音系对比研究》，外语教育与研究出版社 2020 年版。

张吉生：《也论汉语词重音》，《中国语文》2021 年第 1 期，第 43—55 页。

周　韧：《汉语韵律语法研究中的轻重象似、松紧象似和多少象似》，《中国语文》2017 年第 5 期。

Abercrombie, David (1967), *Elements of General Phonetics*. Edinburgh: Edinburgh University Press.

Anfara, Vincent A. & Norma T. Mertz (2006), *Theoretical Frameworks in Qualitative Research*. California: SAGE Publications.

Booij, Geert (1983), Principles and parameters in prosodic phonology. *Linguistics* 21: 249–280.

Chao, Yuen Ren (1942/2006), Iambic rhythm and verb-object construction in Chinese. In *Linguistic Essays by Yuenren Chao*, 347–349. Beijing: The Commercial Press.

Chen, Matthew Y. (2000), *Tone Sandhi: Patterns across Chinese Dialects*. Cambridge: Cambridge University Press.

Cummings, Michael J. (2006), Metre in poetry and verse: A study guide. http://www.shakespearestudyguide.com/meter.html.

Duanmu, San (1993), Rime length, stress, and association domains. *Journal of East Asian Linguistics* 2(2): 1–44.

Duanmu, San (2004), Left-headed feet and phrasal stress in Chinese. *Cahiers de Linguistique Asie Orientale* 33(1): 65-103.

Duanmu, San (2012), Word-length preferences in Chinese: A corpus study. *Journal of East Asian Linguistics* 21(1): 89-114.

Elenbaas, Nine and René Kager (1999), Ternary rhythm and the lapse constraint. *Phonology* 16: 273-329.

Emike, Acheoah John (2015), The pragma-crafting theory: A proposed theoretical framework for pragmatic analysis. *American Research Journal of English and Literature* (2): 21-32.

Fry, Dennis Butler (1955), Duration and intensity as physical correlates of linguistic stress. *Journal of the Acoustical Society of America* 27: 765-768.

Fry, Dennis Butler (1958), Experiments in the perception of stress. *Language and Speech* 1: 120-152.

Goedemans, Rob and Harry van der Hulst (2009), StressTyp: A database for word accentual patterns in the world's languages. In Martin Everaert, Simon Musgrave and Alexis Dimitriadis (eds.), *The Use of Databases in Cross-Linguistic Studies*, 235-282. New York/Berlin: Mouton de Gruyter.

Good, Jeff (2004), Tone and accent in Saramaccan: Charting a deep split in the phonology of a language. *Lingua* 114: 575-619.

Gussenhoven, Carlos and Haike Jacobs (2011), *Understanding Phonology*. London: Routledge.

Hansen, Kenneth C. and Lesley E. Hansen (1969), Pintupi phonology. *Oceanic Linguistics* 8: 157-170.

Hayes, Bruce (1981), *A Metrical Theory of Stress Rules*. Doctoral dissertation, MIT.

Hayes, Bruce (1985), Iambic and trochaic rhythm in stress rules. In Mary Niepokuj, Mary VanClay, Vassiliki Nikiforidou and Deborah Feder (eds.), *Proceedings of the Eleventh Meeting of the Berkeley Linguistic Society*, 429-446. Berkeley: Berkeley Linguistic Society.

Hayes, Bruce (1987), A revised parametric metrical theory. In Joyce McDonough and Bernadette Plunket (eds.), *Proceedings of NELS 17*, 274-289. GLSA, University of Massachusetts at Amherst.

Hayes, Bruce (1995), *Metrical Stress Theory: Principles and Case Studies*. Chicago: University of Chicago Press.

Hyman, Larry M. (1977), On the nature of linguistic stress. In Larry M. Hyman (ed.), *Studies in Stress and Accent*, 37-82. Los Angeles: University of Southern California.

Hyman, Larry M. (1978), Tone and/or accent. In Donna Jo Napoli (ed.), *Elements of Tone, Stress and Intonation*, 1-20. Washington, DC: Georgetown University Press.

Hyman, Larry M. (1981), Tonal accent in Somali. *Studies in African Linguistics* 12: 169-203.

Hyman, Larry M. (1985), *A Theory of Phonological Weight*. Dordrecht: Foris Publications.

Hyman, Larry M. (2014), Do all languages have word accent? In Harry van der Hulst (ed.), *Word Stress: Theoretical and Typological Issues*, 56-82. Cambridge: Cambridge University Press.

Hyman, Larry M., Francis Katamba and Livingstone Walusimbi (1987), Luganda and the Strict Layer Hypothesis. *Phonology Yearbook* 4: 87-108.

Kager, René (1999), *Optimality Theory*. Cambridge: Cambridge University Press.

Kager, René (2007), Feet and metrical stress. In Paul de Lacy (ed.), *The Cambridge Handbook of Phonology*, 195-227. Cambridge: Cambridge University Press.

Kawulich, Barbara (2009), The role of theory in research. In Mark Garner, Claire Wagner, Barbara Kawulich (eds.), *Teaching Research Methods in the Social Sciences*. pp.88-99. Routledge.

Ladefoged, Peter (2005), *A Course in Phonetics*. Belmont: Wadsworth Publishing Company.

Levi, Susannah V. (2005), Acoustic correlates of lexical accent in Turkish.

Journal of the International Phonetic Association 35: 73 - 97.

McCarthy, John J. and Alan Prince (1986), *Prosodic Morphology, Rutgers Technical Report TR - 32*. New Brunswick: Rutgers University Center for Cognitive Science.

Nespor, Marina and Irene Vogel (1986/2007), *Prosodic Phonology*. Dordrecht: Foris Publications.

Newman, Stanley (1947), Bella Coola I: Phonology. *International Journal of American Linguistics* 13(3): 129 - 134.

Prince, Alan (1983), Relating to the grid. *Linguistic Inquiry* 14(1): 19 - 100.

Prince, Alan (1990), Quantitative consequences of rhythmic organization. In Michael Ziolkowski, Manuela Noske and Karen Deaton (eds.), *Parasession on the Syllable in Phonetics and Phonology*, 355 - 398. Chicago: Chicago Linguistic Society.

Schiering, Ren, Balthasar Bickel and Kristine A. Hildebrandt (2010), The prosodic word is not universal, but emergent. *Journal of Linguistics* 46: 657 - 709.

Selkirk, Elisabeth O. (1984), *Phonology and Syntax: The Relation between Sound and Structure*. Boston, MA: MIT Press.

Shen, Weilin, Jacqueline Vaissière and Frédéric Isel (2013), Acoustic correlates of contrastive stress in compound words versus verbal phrase in Mandarin Chinese. *Computational Linguistics and Chinese Language Processing* 18(3): 45 - 58.

Tanaka, Shin-ichi (1990), Intrasyllabic boundaries: A violation of Strict Layer Hypothesis. *Tsukuba English Studies* 9: 1 - 38.

Trask, Larry (1996), *A Dictionary of Phonetics and Phonology*. London: Routledge.

van der Hulst, Harry (2014), The study of word accent and stress: Past, present, and future. In Harry van der Hulst (ed.), *Word Stress: Theoretical and Typological Issues*, 3 - 55. Cambridge: Cambridge University Press.

Wise, Alyssa Friend & David Williamson Shaffer (2015), *Journal of Learning Analysis*. (2): 5 - 13.

Yin, Yun-Mei (1989), *Phonological Aspects of Word Formation in Mandarin Chinese*. Doctoral dissertation, University of Texas.

Yip, Moria (1980), *The Tonal Phonology of Chinese*. Doctoral dissertation, MIT. Published in 1990, New York: Garland Publishing.

Yip, Moria (2002), *Tone*. Cambridge: Cambridge University Press.

 方法谈：

如何在理论框架下展开论证、提升思辨素养？

此文属于理论语言学的定性研究。语言学研究，无论是定量研究还是定性研究，都必须有一个好的理论框架。语言学研究的理论框架是指在研究语言现象时所采用的一种理论体系，包括概念、理论假设、研究方法和技术等方面的内容，它提供了研究者进行研究的指导和范式（Anfara & Mertz, 2006；Kawulich, 2009；Wise & Shaffer, 2015）。理论框架是语言学研究的基础和前提，它为研究问题的确立提供基础，通过理论框架，可以确定研究的目的和问题，确定研究的范围和深度，为研究提供方向（Emike, 2015）。在语言学研究中，理论框架与研究问题有着最紧密的关系，两者相互依赖又相互影响，好的研究问题促使你发现和掌握好的理论框架，好的理论框架帮助你确立好的研究问题，并指导你解决问题。

文章作者基于查阅了大量有关汉语词重音的论述和研究，深入全面系统地阅读了有关词重音的理论和相关论述，根据掌握的知识和语感对汉语有词重音的观点提出质疑。为了阐明汉语没有词重音，文章根据相关理论，建立起一个以词重音概念为核心的超音段功能类型理论框架。以这个理论框架为依据，重新梳理了持汉语有词重音观点的多种理由，进而展开对汉语是否有词重音的论证。论证突显在三个方面。

第一是概念。理论语言学研究，核心概念必须清晰准确。关于汉语是否有词重音的核心概念是词重音。词重音的定义一定要出自权威，要有理有据，清晰明确。不少持汉语有词重音的作者，开篇先问汉语有重音吗，明显混淆了语言中重音和词重音两个不同的概念。人类所有语言都有重音；但有些语言有词重音，有些语言没有词重音（Hyman, 2014：56）。"词重音"，顾名思义就是词汇层面的重音,即词库内信息。作者根据权威观点对词重音的定义(Hyman,2014:61)和词库以外的重音形式,提出词库内重音和词库外重音的外延概念。显然,许多持汉语有词重音观点提出所谓汉语词重音现象都属于词库外重音,包括说话的强弱节奏、双音节复合词或短语与语法结构有关的轻重音节,如动宾结构重宾语,定中结构重定语等,这些都属于词库外重音。可见,明确概念十分重要。有许多错误分析,都是概念不清,甚至错误概念引起。有些研究就是由于混淆了不同的概念,拿符合概念A的例句或现象来说明概念B。甚至有些研究,没有依据,没有分析,自己凭空提出一个概念,根据自己的定义收集"证据",得出错误的结论。

概念是理论框架的核心,论证必须围绕着概念展开,去伪存真,得出的结论必须支持这个核心概念,并得到概念的验证。

第二是逻辑。一个好的针对性强的理论前沿的理论框架能指导你的论证由浅入深,有理有据,由表及里地展开,其中的关键是逻辑。所谓逻辑就是事情的因果规律。首先理论框架内的核心概念与相关理论要有逻辑关系。譬如词重音与超音段特征功能类型的逻辑关系。词重音表达的主要形式是音高(pitch),音高作为超音段特征的词汇功能主要有三个:重音(stress)、声调(tone)和音高重音(pitch accent)。论证汉语是否有词重音,就要厘清重音语言、声调语言和音高重音语言之间的类型学区别。这里主要涉及一个逻辑问题,即重音与声调的关系。无论你提出问题还是分析问题,要有清晰的逻辑理据。世界上关于重音与声调的关系有四种语言,有重音没声调、有声调没重音、既没重音也没声调、既有重音又有声调(Hyman,2006:237)。但重音语言有个戒律,两个重读音节不能相邻出现,跨语言语料证明四种类型中的任何一种语言,都不会违反这一戒律。

在学术论证中,支持和反对某个观点的人都会利用逻辑这个武器为自己的观点辩护。譬如,一种主张汉语有词重音的观点提出,汉语有音步,有音步就有词重音,这就是逻辑。因为音步是分配词重音的辖域,一个音步内必有轻重音节区分。如果你简单直接承认汉语当然有音步,你就前功尽弃,最后只能放弃你的观点。但当你查阅相关文献后,你发现并非所有语言都有音步(Abercrombie,1967;Prince,1983),不是所有语言都需要音步[如上海话就不需要音步(张吉生,2021)]。你必须有严谨的逻辑去证明汉语实际没有音系音步。否则,你的论证不能达到预设的目的。

学术研究,逻辑很重要,研究者必须有清晰的逻辑思维,较强的逻辑分析能力。逻辑混乱,分析得出的结论会不堪一击。

第三是方法。语言学研究十分讲究研究方法,定量研究有定量研究的方法,定性有定性的方法。此文是定性研究。定性研究的方法主要靠逻辑分析和逻辑推理,如上所述。分析和推理必须依据理论,根据事实(语料),对要证伪的观点、内容、理由逐条分析。持汉语有词重音的观点一共有三条理由:轻声、轻重音节的双音节词、音步。对这三条要逐条解析,以事实说话,任何分析不能不顾语言事实,违背实际语料。分析和推理更不能强词夺理,无中生有。只有以正确理论为依据,以实际语料为证据,有理有据地分析推理才能以理服人,论证才站得住脚。

此文能在《中国语文》发表得益于它在一个好的理论框架下确立了一个有价值的研究问题,采取了科学的分析方法,提供了逻辑严密的分析过程,得出了以理服人的研究结果。当然,此文的研究结论并非绝对真理,关键是得出研究结论的论证必须建立在有理论依据,符合语言事实,经得起逻辑推理的基础,这样的论证才是科学的,这样的研究才有价值。

总而言之,理论框架对语言学研究,尤其是理论语言学研究有何等重要。任何一项有价值的研究都需要有一个有价值的研究问题。好的理论框架首先能帮助你确立一个好的研究问题。笔者认为,如何提出一个有价值的问题,需要有一种高屋建瓴,令你茅塞顿开的理论启发你、引导你。解决问题更需要有针对性强的权威理论为框架,在理论框架的指导下,分析严谨,旁征博引,逻辑推理,你的论证才站得住脚,你的结论才有说服力。

有的研究生写论文没有理论框架,直接提出问题,分析问题,得出结论,看似也是在研究。但没有理论框架指导下提出的问题,可能这个问题并不成立,或问题提法不对;没有理论框架指导下的分析,不可能做到系统分析,或者分析不到位,甚至错误分析。有的研究生写论文,尤其是学位论文提出的理论框架与实际分析无关,看起来高大上的理论框架只是个摆设,它并没有真正指导你的研究分析,这种论文的质量可想而知。有些论文提出的问题不错,有一定的研究价值,但理论框架不对,结果引导出不恰当的分析,得出错误结论。

如何为你要开展的语言学研究选择好的理论框架,要考虑到以下三要素:

(1) 研究问题的特点。不同的研究问题需要采用不同的理论框架,因此需要针对具体的研究问题,选择不同的理论框架。

(2) 研究目的和范围。研究目的和范围不同,所需的理论框架也不同。

(3) 已有研究的成果。任何研究都需要对已有研究的成果进行评估和分析，了解已有研究的优点和不足，从而选择合适的理论框架。

一个好的针对性强的理论框架确定后，要进一步细化研究问题，根据研究问题建构研究假设，在理论框架指导下，采用合适、科学方法收集语料分析数据，展开严谨的论证，得出的结论必须经得起语料或数据的验证，必须符合理论指导下的逻辑推理。从问题思考，到理论框架选择，在理论框架下展开论证，通过分析得出结论的整个过程就是思辨素养培养和发展的过程。

职业英语能力构念的实证研究*

曾用强**

摘要：职业英语能力与英语语言能力的构念不同。近二十年随着职业英语教育快速发展,学生的职业英语应用能力日益引发重视,完整、科学、系统地界定职业英语能力构念显得十分必要和重要。本研究通过问卷调查法实证探讨了职业英语能力构念,建立了职业英语技能结构。职业英语能力构念研究对职业英语教学、职业英语能力培养、职业英语能力等级考试研发等具有积极的指导意义。

关键词：职业能力;英语能力;职业英语技能构念;职业英语教育

一、引　言

中国英语能力等级量表(以下简称"量表")的颁布为我国英语教学、学习、测评提供了一个统一的标准参照框架,起到"车同轨、量同衡"的作用(刘建达,2015a,2015b;林蕙青,2016;曾用强,2017)。但是,量表主要是从语言活动、语言知识、语言技能、语言策略等语言系统本身定义英语能力的构念,没有考虑实际工作岗位所需的英语应用能力。比如,量表界定的翻译能力与职场实际翻译能力含有不完全相同的内涵;不少学生在校英语考试成绩理想,在工作岗位上英

---

* 原载《外语界》2020年第2期。本研究是2019年度职业院校外语教育教学研究重大课题"职业英语教育质量评价体系的建设"(编号FLE0001)的阶段性成果。

** 曾用强,二级教授,广东省外语艺术职业学院校长,广东外语外贸大学博士生导师。现为教育部高职院校外语教学指导委员会副主任委员、广东省高职院校外语教学指导委员会主任委员、教育部高考内容改革专家委员会委员、全国英语教育研究会副会长。从事语言测试、计算语言学及远程英语教育的教学与科研工作;主持或参与过多项国家级和省部级的科研项目,其中包括《中国英语能力等级量表编制》《高等职业院校应用英语专业教学标准》和《职业英语教育质量测评体系的建设》等。

语运用表达能力不能令人满意的现象时有发生。从中可知,英语语言能力与职业英语能力的构念定义存有差异。

"职业教育与普通教育是两种不同教育类型,具有同等重要地位",这是2019年颁布的《国务院关于印发国家职业教育改革实施方案的通知》对职业教育提出的改革设想。职业英语教育注重实用性,所学即所用,强调语言能力与职业技能的融合。随着各行业的国际化程度日益提升,使用英语的场合越来越多,我国职业英语教育进入前所未有的发展机遇期。然而,职业英语教育在发展进程中也面临着诸多关键问题,尤其是定位问题:如何定位职业教育中的职业英语,以区别于普通教育中的学科英语(或学术英语),体现职业教育的类型和特点?我国学界迄今尚无完整、科学、系统的职业英语能力构念定义。本研究将对职业英语能力的构念开展实证探究。

二、职业英语能力的构念

探讨职业英语能力构念之前,有必要先了解职业能力(vocational competence)的构念定义。关于职业能力,目前还未形成一个公认的概念。学者和专家从不同角度对职业能力进行了界定。孟广平(2000)、严雪怡(2007)认为,职业能力有广义和狭义之分,狭义的职业能力指某种岗位的工作能力,广义的职业能力指某类职业群的共同基础能力。邓泽民等(2002)从性质定义、条件定义、结构定义和过程定义四个角度出发,比较分析不同领域职业能力的界定,把职业能力概括为:个体在特定职业活动或情景中通过类比迁移与整合所学知识、技能和态度形成的一定职业任务的完成能力。陈宇(2003)认为,职业能力可以结构化,主要包括"职业特定技能""行业通用技能""核心技能"三个层次。"职业特定技能"是国家职业分类大典划分的技能范围;"行业通用技能"是特征和属性相同或者相近职业群所体现出来的共性的技能;"核心技能"是人们在职业生涯甚至日常生活中必需的、体现于具体职业活动的最基本的技能,具有普遍的适用性和广泛的可迁移性。徐国庆(2005)指出,职业能力是一种"联系",在知识和工作任务的要素之间形成联系的过程就是职业能力形成的过程。吴晓义(2006)指出,职业能力是指包含知识、技能、态度和个性心理特征的职业活动能力。杨黎明(2011)认为,职业能力是指某一职业所需的专业能力和非专业能力的总和,是个体当前就业和终身发展所需的能力。

国际上不少机构和组织编制了各类职业能力框架。比如,"欧洲职业资格框架"(European Qualifications Framework)包括知识(knowledge)、技能(skills)、责任与自主(responsibility and autonomy)。苏格兰学分与职业资格框架(Scottish Credit and Qualifications Framework)则从五个方面分12级(从入门1级到博士12级)描述职业能力。

不同学派的职业能力定义存在差异。心理学派认为职业能力是直接影响职业活动效率和确保职业活动顺利进行的个体心理特征;能力学派指出职业能力是完成特定职业任务所需的知识、技能、态度和经验;结构学派认为职业能力是综合职业能力,包括完成职业活动所需的身心素质、职业道德、创业精神以及技能等;过程学派提出职业能力的形成和发展必须借助特定的职业活动或模拟职业情景,通过已有知识和技能的类比迁移,使相关的一般能力得到特殊的发展和整合,形成较为稳定的综合能力(Billett et al., 2014;Mulder, 2014)。综上所述,笔者认为职业能力是个体对获得的知识、经验、技能和态度在特定的职业活动或情景中进行类比迁移与整合而形成的完成一定职业任务的能力。

职业能力构念的基本要素和层次为职业英语能力构念界定提供了参考依据。职业英语能力的基本要素包括行业能力、英语能力和社会能力,每个要素又由通用知识与技能、特定知识与技能两个层次构成,具体如图1所示。当前我国职业英语教育的人才培养方案正是基于职业英语能力结构制定。

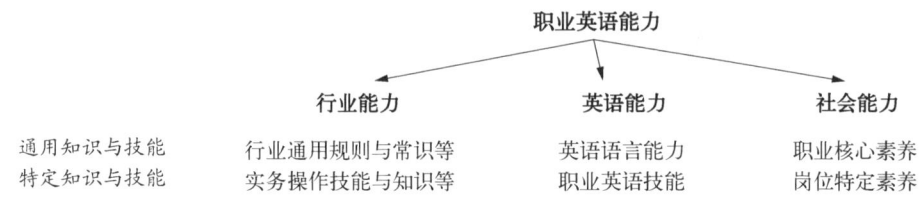

图1 职业英语能力结构

图1中,作为职业英语能力最重要的能力要素,英语能力包括英语语言能力和职业英语技能两方面。英语语言能力是英语能力的基础组成部分,对此量表已经给出定义。职业英语技能是职业岗位相关的实际英语应用能力,是英语能力的核心组成部分。因此,职业英语能力构念研究着重围绕职业英语技能展开。

三、研 究 方 法

职业英语技能的内涵不同于英语语言能力,是应用英语语言知识和技能完成岗位任务的能力。科学界定职业英语技能的结构具有重要作用,有助于制定人才培养方案、设计教学方案与实施能力评价、招聘行业人才等。我们主要采用问卷调查法,调查分析全国范围内职业院校毕业生不同职业岗位的英语使用情况,以此建构职业英语技能。

1. 问卷设计

调查问卷涵盖所学专业、从事的行业、具体工作岗位,并要求按以下示例尽可能详细地描述工作岗位上使用英语的情况:

(1)平时经常通过邮件回复客户关于产品的咨询,包括产品特征、价格以及售后服务等。

(2)在广交会上向国际客户介绍公司的产品,与对方谈判产品交易的相关事项,包括价格、数量、交货标准等。

2. 调查对象

调查对象为不同工作岗位的高职毕业生。问卷通过微信平台向毕业生发放,共收回1 452份有效问卷,采集到4 679条描述语。

3. 数据分析

问卷收回后,我们采用内容分析法对问卷中的岗位英语描述进行归类与分析。分析之前,我们基于岗位任务的基本要素,建立了一套文本编码体系,包含场合、形式、任务、内容和对象五项基本要素(见表1)。

表1 问卷文本编码体系

要素	编码	示例
场合	CH	交易会、平时等
形式	XS	口头、笔头、邮件、社交软件等
任务	RW	咨询、谈判、回复等
内容	NR	产品信息、单证、协议、数据等
对象	DX	客户、经理等

基于编码体系的标注分析主要从受访者的描述语中,提炼出英语使用的场合、形式、任务等职业英语技能的基本构成要素,比如:

<u>平时</u>经常通过<u>邮件</u> <u>回复</u> <u>客户</u> 关于产品的咨询,包括产品特征、价格以及
CH   XS RW DX   NR

售后服务等。

基本要素提取之后,再经过二次归类整理,凝练信息采集、信息处理和信息沟通等三个维度,最终基于这3个维度建立职业英语技能的结构。

四、研究结果

1. 描述性统计结果

问卷数据的描述性统计结果显示,高职毕业生从事的行业范围较广,岗位类型多样,毕业生从事的主要行业和岗位具体如表2所示。从行业来看,毕业生在外贸、教育和培训、电商、销售和零售、物流行业的从业率位于前五。从岗位来看,业务员、销售员、教师和培训员、行政助理和文员、跟单员的从业率位于前五。

表2 行业与岗位的统计结果

变量	变量值	频数
行业	外贸	350
	教育、培训	253
	(跨境)电商	191
	销售、零售	113
	物流	91
岗位	业务员	317
	销售员(市场推广)	308
	教师、培训员	221
	行政助理、文员	201
	跟单员	172

表3的专业及其英语使用频率统计结果表明,高职英语专业不常用和不用英语的比例仅为6.4%,非英语专业不常用和不用英语的比例为10.3%,毕业生在工作岗位上使用英语的频率较高。

表 3　专业及其英语使用频率的统计结果

	经常使用	比较常用	一 般	不常用	不 用	合 计
英语专业	293(20.2%)	249(17.1%)	186(12.8%)	65(4.5%)	28(1.9%)	821(56.5%)
非英语专业	148(10.2%)	165(11.4%)	168(11.6%)	89(6.1%)	61(4.2%)	631(43.5%)
合 计	441(30.4%)	414(28.5%)	354(24.4%)	154(10.6%)	89(6.1%)	1 452(100%)

结合高职毕业生从事的行业和岗位、专业及其英语使用频率的调查结果来看,大部分毕业生在工作岗位上需要使用英语,但是他们用不用英语、常不常用英语、怎么用英语,不是取决于在校时所学的专业或所学的是"专业英语"还是"公共英语",而是由工作岗位所决定。在校学习时的英语水平与实际岗位上的英语应用能力之间存在关联,但两者没有必然的因果关系。比如,学生在学校英语考试中的"阅读理解"分数很高,但毕业后在实际工作岗位上并不一定能够通过"阅读"理解公司所需的资源。学生在学校表现的是"reading for comprehension"能力,在岗位上则需具备"reading for information"能力。这也在一定程度上表明,职业英语技能与英语语言能力具有不同的构念。

2. 编码信息统计结果

参照编码体系,我们对通过问卷采集得到的 4 679 条岗位任务描述语进行标注,主要分析英语使用的场合、形式、任务和内容 4 类编码的统计结果。①

使用英语场合的频数统计结果表明,职场中使用英语的场合很多,大体可以归纳为五类:① 日常场合,如接待、平时交流等;② 业务场合,如产品宣传、销售等;③ 展会场合,如广交会、产品推介会等;④ 会议场合,如研讨会、员工培训等;⑤ 往来场合,如出国参观、考察等(见表 4)。

表 4　使用英语场合的频数

场 合	频 数	百分比
日常(接待、客服、平时交流等)	2 452	52.4
业务(产品或企业宣传、销售等)	1 562	33.4

---

① 任务和内容已经包含关于"对象"编码的信息,因此编码信息统计分析不再专门讨论"对象"编码。

续 表

场合	频数	百分比
展会(广交会、进博会、产品推介会等)	440	9.4
会议(研讨会、员工培训等)	150	3.2
往来(出国参观、考察等)	75	1.6
合计	4 679	100

从表5使用英语方式的频数统计结果可以看出,职场英语使用一般可以分为口头和书面两种方式。除了使用频率最高的面对面交流方式,邮件、社交软件或平台等交流媒介和工具也得到较多应用。

表5 使用英语方式的频数

方式	频数	百分比
面对面	1 820	38.9
邮件	1 259	26.9
书面	566	12.1
社交软件或平台	524	11.2
电话	229	4.9
其他	281	6.0
合计	4 679	100

表6提炼所得的岗位任务类目多样,其中查阅、记录、整理类任务频数最大,交流、交谈类任务频数居于其次,谈判、翻译以及编写任务等相对较少,这可能与高职毕业生的英语能力水平相关。

表6 岗位英语任务的频数

任务	频数	百分比
查阅、记录、整理、咨询、回复(信息)	1 416	30.3
交流、交谈、接待	1 007	21.5
介绍、描述、推介(产品等)	876	18.7

续表

任务	频数	百分比
授课（讲解）	424	9.1
谈判	299	6.4
翻译	165	3.5
撰（编）写	151	3.2
其他	341	7.3
合计	4 679	100

我们对岗位任务进行二次整理，进一步凝练和归类岗位任务。根据任务类型，岗位任务可以分为信息（资讯）获取、信息（资讯）整理、信息（思想）沟通与交流等。根据交流媒介，岗位任务包含笔头任务（如记录、整理）和口头任务（如交谈、接待），并且很多任务既是书面的，又是口头的（如咨询、推介）。根据互动性，岗位任务可以分为单向任务（如咨询、授课）和互动任务（如交谈、谈判）。根据任务目标，岗位任务包含传递、咨询、说服和反驳四类，比如交谈是互相传递信息，推介是说服对方接受推销产品。在实际职场中，一个岗位任务的描述通常包含媒介、互动性和目标等要素，比如谈判是与客户互动的口头说服，询盘是单向的书面或口头咨询等。

表 7 英语任务内容的频数统计结果表明，应用文撰写频数最大，产品信息、市场信息描写与提供的频数分别位居第二、三位，公司文件准备和客户信息收集更新依次居后，单证、单据整理等相对较少。

表 7 英语任务内容的频数

内容	频数	百分比
应用文（文件、报告、说明书、邀请函等）	885	18.9
产品信息（名称、规格、价格、特征、功能、技术参数等）	706	15.1
市场信息（订单、发货信息、统计报表、财务报表等）	690	14.7
公司文件（客户投诉报告、会议记录、市场调研报告、公司宣传文案等）	652	14.0
客户信息	636	13.6
单证、单据、合同、协议等	572	12.2
其他	538	11.5
合计	4 679	100

综合表 4—7 的数据分析，我们根据岗位任务的结构层次和类型对任务内容进行细分。按照结构层次，任务内容可以分为公司、客户、产品和业务四个层次；按照类型，任务内容可以分为文书资料、数据、信息、思想和情感态度五类。

简言之，任何公司或企业的中心任务都是建立客户（或服务对象）与产品之间的经济关联，例如贸易公司向客户推销产品，旅游公司吸引游客参观景点。这种关联引发多方面的业务活动，比如公司发布产品信息、举办展会、与客户谈判合同条款、解决客户投诉等。业务活动开展需要处理各种文书资料、数据、信息、思想、情感态度等。因此，职场的工作任务就是建立公司、客户、产品和业务之间的各种关联。

五、职业英语技能结构及其应用

通过分析岗位英语使用的场合、形式、任务、内容等方面，我们可以把职业英语技能解读为：基于特定的工作任务目标，获取、处理必需的信息后完成信息交流的能力。具体而言，英语技能的基本元素包括语言信息获取、语言信息处理、语言沟通与交流，这些元素又建立在典型的职场活动之上。职业英语技能结构具体如图 2 所示。

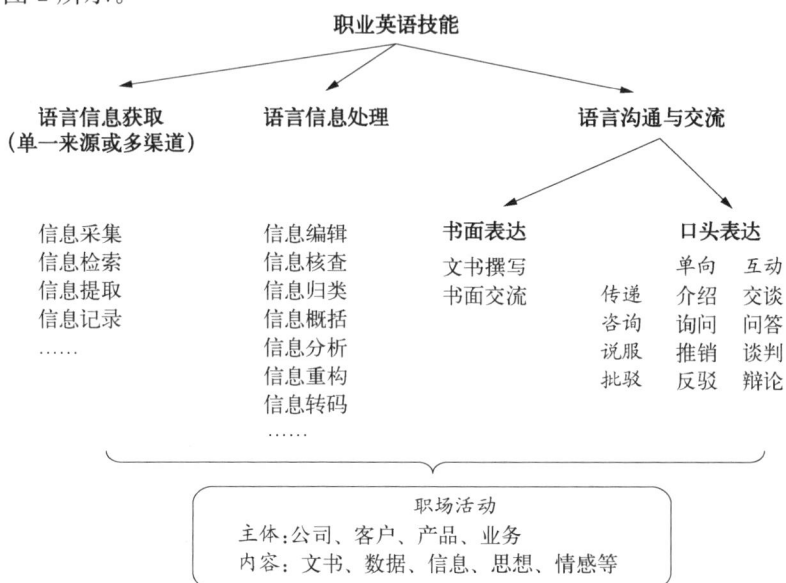

图 2　职业英语技能结构

语言信息获取主要涉及：① 信息来源，从哪里获取信息，如单一来源或多渠道；② 信息媒介，如何获取信息，如听、读、看；③ 信息形式，获取怎样的信息，如文本、音频、视频、图表等。语言信息获取具体表现为信息检索、信息记录等形式。

语言信息处理包括信息编辑、信息核查、信息归类、信息概括、信息分析、信息重构和信息转码等。

语言沟通与交流涉及：① 交流方式，包括书面和口头；② 交流对象，包括上级、下级、平级等；③ 交流目标，包括传递、咨询、说服、批驳等；④ 交际互动，包括单向和双向（互动）；⑤ 交流内容，包括公司、客户或产品的数据、信息、思想、情感等。

职业英语教学中，语言能力培养是基础，职业技能训练是目标（Gessler，2017）。学习英语终究是为了应用英语。职业英语技能构念厘清了英语在职场中的主要应用，包括从信息获取、信息处理到信息沟通与交流。这些英语应用除了涉及听说读写等语言技能外，还需借助综合的社会能力。比如，商务谈判需要应用英语的听说读写技能，还需具备基本的谈判礼仪和灵活应变能力等。

系统、科学的职业英语技能构念定义具有广泛的应用价值，首要的是编制职业英语技能等级描述语。例如，我们可以基于图2职业英语技能结构编写职业英语技能的"能做"描述语：

能通过采访或咨询客户，收集国际客户的信息资料，并对相关资料进行归档。

能用英语撰写标准的传真、邮件、信函等商务或公务文件，信息准确，格式正确。

参加展会时，能为国际客户解读公司产品，包括图表或图示的信息。

在国际商务会议中，能就商品的质量、价格及其他相关问题与客户进行面对面谈判。

职业英语技能构念及其等级描述语也能用于指导职业英语教育的教材编写、教学任务设计、职业技能等级考试开发以及职业倾向诊断等不同方面。

六、结　束　语

本研究通过问卷调查实证探讨了职业英语能力构念，重点聚焦其核心组成部分职业英语技能结构。职业英语能力构念和涵盖语言信息获取、语言信息处理、语言信息沟通与交流三个维度的职业英语技能结构能对职业英语教育的教、学、测、评等方面起到积极的指导作用。基于职业英语能力构念设计的"职业英语能力等级测试"(Vocational English Test System,VETS)已经发布,"职业英语教学资源库"正在建设之中。职业英语能力构念的理论和实践应用研究将积极推动我国职业英语教育健康、科学、稳定发展。

参考文献

Billett S, Harteis C & Gruber H (eds.). *International Handbook of Research in Professional and Practice-based Learning* [C]. Dordrecht: Springer, 2014.

Gessler M. Areas of learning: The shift towards work and competence orientation within the school-based vocational education in the German dual apprenticeship system[A]. In Mulder M (ed.). *Competence-based Vocational and Professional Education*[C]. Cham: Springer, 2017. 695-717.

Mulder M. Conceptions of professional competence [A]. In Billett S, Harteis C & Gruber H (eds.). *International Handbook of Research in Professional and Practice-based Learning*[C]. Dordrecht: Springer, 2014. 107-137.

陈宇:《职业能力以及核心技能》,《职业技术教育》2003年第33期,第26页。

邓泽民、陈庆合、刘文卿:《职业能力的概念、特征及其形成规律的研究》,《煤炭高等教育》2002年第2期,第104—107页。

林蕙青:《建立国家外语测评体系 提升国民语言能力》,《中国考试》2016年第12期,第3—4页。

刘建达:《我国英语能力等级量表研制的基本思路》,《中国考试》2015年第1期,第7—11,15页。

刘建达:《基于标准的外语评价探索》,《外语教学与研究》2015年第3期,第417—425页。

孟广平:《能力·能力本位教育与职业技术教育课程开发》,《职业技术教育》2000年第12期,第32—33页。

吴晓义:《"情境—达标"式职业能力开发模式研究》,东北师范大学博士学位论文,2006 年。

徐国庆:《解读职业能力》,《职教论坛》2005 年第 36 期,第 1 页。

严雪怡:《教育分类、能力本位与广义的职业能力培养——纪念孟广平同志逝世两周年》,《职业技术教育》2007 年第 7 期,第 11—13 页。

杨黎明:《关于学生职业能力的发展》,《职教论坛》2011 年第 3 期,第 4—15 页。

曾用强:《中国英语能力等级量表的"阅读量表"制定原则和方法》,《外语界》2017 年第 5 期,第 2—11 页。

 方法谈:

研究方案如何体现研究目的?

任何一项研究首先需要明确研究目的。只有清晰的研究目的,才会有合理的研究方案。研究方案必须体现研究目的。那么研究方案如何体现研究目的?首先,我们需要搞清楚研究目的和研究方案的基本概念。研究目的就是提出一个研究问题,并寻找问题的解决路径,比如关于语言某一现象的研究,研究目的可能是论述相关理论的重要观点,或验证某一重要的假设,或建构自己的理论模型等。

所以定义研究目的首先是提出一个研究问题,而研究问题的核心又是确定研究变量,一项研究可能只涉及一个变量,也可能涉及多个变量,即,关于变量之间的关系研究,包括差异性或关联性。概括起来,研究目的一般从两个层面定义:其一是变量及变量关系,其二是变量的处理方式,如本页表 1 所示:

表 1 研究目的的定义

	单一变量	多 变 量	
		差 异 性	关 联 性
论 述	✓	✓	✓
验 证		✓	✓
建 构	✓	✓	✓

任何一项研究都可以在表1中找到它的位置。当研究目的确定之后,就要开始研究方案的设计。研究方案是体现研究目的的每个研究环节的总和。研究目的确定了研究变量以及如何建立变量之间的关系,那么研究方案就是通过特定的研究方法把研究变量转换成变量值,即,研究数据,并对数据进行分析,得出符合研究目的的研究结论。所以研究变量是连接研究目的和研究方案的核心元素,如本页图1所示:

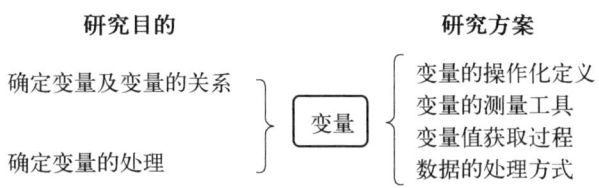

图 1　研究目的与研究方案的关系

研究方案体现研究目的的基本步骤包括:① 对变量进行操作化定义;② 选择或开发信度、效度高的测量工具;③ 研究设计,即,选择具有代表性受试,应用测量工具通过特定的流程获取变量的值,即,研究数据;④ 采用科学的方法处理这些数据。表2概括了常见的研究方法(获取变量值的方法)、数据类型及数据分析方法:

表 2　常见的研究方法、数据类型及数据分析方法

研究方法	数据类型	数据分析方法
(心理、语言……)测试	数值	统计分析
量表	数值、文本	统计分析、内容分析
问卷	数值、文本	统计分析、内容分析
文献	文本	
日志	文本	
访谈	文本	内容分析
有声思维	文本	
语料库	文本	
田野调查	文本	
仪器设备等	数值	统计分析
……		

下面我们以《职业英语能力构念的实证研究》为例,解释研究方案如何体现研究目的。该项研究的目的是建构职业英语技能的结构。职业英语能力是本研究中由多个层面组成的单一变量。研究方案就是围绕该变量展开设计的。

研究变量的操作化定义。变量的操作化定义通常需要一定理论(或模型)作为支撑。本研究综合了国内外职业能力的理论模型,结合我国职业英语的特征,定义了三维度、两层次的职业英语能力的结构:职业英语能力包括行业能力、英语能力和社会能力三个维度,每个维度又由两个层次构成:通用知识或技能、特定知识或技能,如本书第 139 页图 1 所示:

是基于操作化定义,为变量选择信、效度高的测量工具。由于本研究只是聚焦在职业英语技能这个维度,我们选择了调查问卷作为获取变量值的测量工具。所有的测量工具都需要经过信、效度验证。通常情况下,我们都会选择已经经过信度、效度验证的测量工具,以此来获取变量的值。

受试的选择以及变量值的获取过程是研究方案中的重要环节。受试选择的基本原则就是代表性和覆盖面。本研究的调查包括全国范围内职业院校毕业生不同岗位的英语使用情况。调查对象为已经在各个不同岗位上工作的往届的高职毕业生。我们通过微信平台向毕业生推送调查问卷。

数据回收后,最重要的环节就是数据分析。由于本研究的数据以文本为主,我们采用内容分析法,对问卷中的岗位英语描述进行归类与分析。在分析之前首先需要建立一套文本编码体系。我们基于岗位任务的基本要素,定义了文本的编码体系,包括以下五项基本要素,见本书第 140 页表 1。

我们基于编码体系的标注分析,目的是从受访者的描述语中提炼出构成职业英语技能的最基本要素,比如,英语使用场合、形式、任务和内容等,然后再对这些基本要素进行二次归类整理,凝练了信息采集、信息处理和信息沟通等三个维度,最终基于这三个维度建构职业英语技能的结构组成。基于以上的分析,职业英语技能结构可以归纳如本书第 145 页图 2。

以上就是本研究方案所包含的主要环节,研究结论体现研究目的:建构职业英语技能的结构。研究变量从确定到变量值的获取,是研究方案体现研究目的的过程。同一研究变量可以有不一样的操作化定义,也可能使用不一样的测量工具,所以同一研究目的,可以有不一样的研究方案。

How does Consecutive Interpreting Training Influence Working Memory: A Longitudinal Study of Potential Links between the Two

Yanping Dong, Yuhua Liu and Rendong Cai

Abstract: With an intention to contribute to the issue of how language experience may influence working memory (WM), we focused on consecutive interpreting (CI), analyzed its potential links with WM functions and tested these links in a longitudinal experiment, trying to answer the specific question of how CI training may influence WM. Two comparable groups of Chinese learners of English received either CI or general second language (L2) training for one semester, and were tested before and after the training with the tasks of n-back (non-verbal updating), L2 listening span, and letter running span (verbal spans). CI performance was tested in the posttest. The results showed that (1) updating efficiency in both the pretest and posttest predicted CI performance, and CI training enhanced updating efficiency while general L2 training did not;

---

* 原载 *Frontiers in Psychology*, June 2018, Volume 9。

** 董燕萍,浙江大学外国语学院心理语言学教授,国家高层次人才项目特聘教授,中国英汉语比较研究会心理语言学专业委员会会长。研究主要围绕语言能力和认知能力的发展或衰退而进行,多数成果为双语(尤其是口译加工)的心理语言学研究。

刘玉花,博士,华南农业大学心理语言学副教授,研究专长为双语认知及翻译心理。

蔡任栋,博士,广东外语外贸大学心理语言学副教授、硕士生导师。研究兴趣主要包括口译心理加工过程、双语加工与发展中的个体差异因素等。

(2) the relationship between verbal spans and CI performance was weaker (i.e., only pretest L2 listening span correlated with CI performance and predicted CI performance with marginal significance), and CI training did not make a unique contribution to these spans (i.e., no group differences). The results indicated an "interpreter advantage" in updating, which was probably due to that updating was more central in the CI task than WM spans. Theoretically, we believe that updating and CI are closely related because they share the same underlying mechanism, or more specifically updating and the recalling process in the CI task share the same attentional control process, a unique link between updating and the CI task. Methodological implications are discussed.

Keywords: interpreter advantage, interpreting training, consecutive interpreting, working memory, attentional control

INTRODUCTION

Working memory (WM) is considered part of the most basic executive functions that are essential to higher level cognitive processing, including language processing (e.g., Baddeley, 2003; Diamond, 2013). The relationship of the other direction, i.e., how cognitive experience such as language learning influences executive functions, is still not clear and is currently a hot topic of research (e.g., Green et al., 2014), with the issue of "bilingual advantage" as a typical example in the language domain. In our point of view, the assumption for this line of research is that the executive functions that are most essential to a certain kind of cognitive processing (e.g., bilingual processing) tend to be most influenced by corresponding cognitive experience (e.g., bilingual experience). However, the results are quite mixed, and one of the problems is that *higher-level cognitive processing (e.g., language processing) is complex in terms of its involvement of or "correspondence" with executive functions*, which, for convenience's sake, the present paper refers to as *this problem of complexity*. Take bilingual processing as an example. It is believed that when compared with monolingual processing, the executive function of inhibitory control is most essential to bilingual processing because it has been found that the bilingual's two languages are non-selectively activated, and the bilingual has to inhibit the language not needed at the moment (e. g., Green, 1998). And yet, the concept of bilingualism is complex in the sense that there are different kinds of bilingualism involving different degrees of language switching and bilingual activation (e. g., Valian, 2015; Xie and Dong, 2017), which may partly explain the inconsistent findings regarding the issue of bilingual advantage in inhibitory control (see Paap et al., 2015, for example).

The same problem of complexity exists in the issue of an "interpreter advantage" in WM. This issue has been investigated for about two decades, but no unanimous conclusion has been reached. Like bilingualism, there are different types of interpreting, but the distinction between consecutive interpreting (CI) and simultaneous interpreting (SI) is universally recognized (e.g., Liang et al., 2017) and is probably relevant to the function of WM. Few studies on the advantage issue have tried to make this distinction, and yet we believe this distinction is beneficial to reducing the influence of the complexity problem and to making further substantial progress on the interpreter advantage issue. The present study, therefore, focused on CI training (most basic and most common type of interpreting training), and tried to find out and then test its unique links with WM functions (when compared with general L2 training), hoping to answer *the research question of how CI training may influence* WM. This exploration may help identify the specific role of WM in the task of CI beyond its role in general language processing, and it may shed light on the issue of how language experience may affect WM and other executive functions.

Interpreting Training/Experience and WM Advantage

Interpreting is one of the most difficult language tasks and its performance relies heavily on WM. The important role of WM in interpreting was not only recognized by Keiser (1965) half a century ago and in theoretical formulations such as the process models (Cowan, 1988; Mizuno, 2005), but also supported by a series of empirical studies (Padilla et al., 1995; Christoffels et al., 2003, 2006; Liu et al., 2004; Köpke and Nespoulous, 2006; Signorelli et al., 2012; Tzou et al., 2012; Timarova et al., 2014; Morales et al., 2015). However, as far as we know, the relationship between WM and interpreting is still ambiguous and controversial.

To investigate how interpreting training may influence WM (e.g., the interpreter advantage issue), previous research often compares how expert interpreters and novice interpreters (or non-interpreters) perform in WM tasks. The findings are mixed. For example, in the complex span task of listening (which is similar to the classical reading span task of WM), novice interpreters performed significantly better than both control groups in Köpke and Nespoulous (2006), but there were no group differences among professional interpreters, advanced and beginning student interpreters in Liu et al. (2004). With a comprehensive review, Dong and Cai (2015) found that the lack of consistent evidence for an interpreter advantage in WM may be attributed to several weaknesses in some previous studies, such as insufficient sample size, lack of participant control group, lack of control for factors such as age and language proficiency. Take the first factor as an example. The participant sample size was rather small in some of the studies (e.g., 10 in Padilla et al., 1995; 11 in Liu et al., 2004; 12 in Chincotta and Underwood, 1998; less than 13 in Signorelli et al., 2012), which may lead to insufficient statistical power. Brysbaert and Stevens (2018) recommended that a properly powered reaction time experiment with repeated measures has at least 1600 observations for each condition, e.g., 40 participants and 40 stimuli for each condition.① Apart from these weaknesses, another limitation is the fact that most previous studies have adopted a cross-sectional design. The

---

① This is consistent with Rouder's Rule of Thumb, i.e., if one runs with-subject designs in cognition and perception, one often gets high-powered experiments with 20 – 30 participants so long as they run about 100 trials per condition (http://jeffrouder.blogspot.be/2017/09/the-justification-of-sample-size.html).

presence of some weaknesses such as age is inherent in a cross-sectional design study because professional interpreters are generally older than novice or student interpreters. Also, a cross-sectional design cannot clarify the causation of an interpreter WM advantage. The possibility is that some personal traits, such as good WM skills, may have led the interpreter to select that particular career. In a word, more research is needed to clarify the relationship between WM and the task of interpreting or the experience of interpreting training.

The Present Research

Previous research has made invaluable contributions, and to push the research frontier forward, the present research adopted two main measures when trying to answer the question of how CI training influences WM functions: (1) focusing on CI training and comparing it with general L2 learning experience (as control); (2) using a longitudinal design with a sufficient sample size that was well controlled in relevant background characteristics (e.g., age, intelligence, social economic status, and language learning history). These measures were intended to ensure that any WM differences between the two groups after the treatments could be attributed to the differences between the treatments.

Theoretically, the embedded-processes model proposed by Cowan (1988, 1995) is most relevant to the present study. The critical idea is that human memory is a single storage system composed of elements at various levels of activation. This system can be conceived as long-term memory (LTM), in which some elements are above the threshold of activation. These activated elements, thought to be in short-term memory (STM), are outside of conscious awareness but nevertheless affect online processing such as semantic priming. Some elements in STM fall into *the focus of attention* (*FOA*) and are in a hyper-activated state, and therefore have to be maintained or manipulated with conscious effort. According to Cowan (1995: 100), "... WM is based on that activated information along with central executive processes," i.e., WM is composed of the FOA and the central executive. Based on Cowan's (1988) model, Mizuno (2005) proposed his enlarged embedded-processes model for interpreting, adding the two processes of language comprehension and production at the two sides of the original model, and emphasizing the interaction between the memory system and the language system during the process of interpreting (see **Figure 1**).

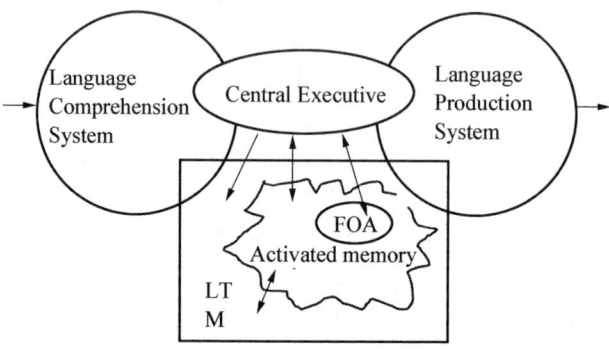

Figure 1　The process model of working memory (WM) and interpreting by Mizuno (2005, p.744).

This conceptualization of WM from the perspective of embedded processes explains well not only the dynamics of the memory system, but also the difference between CI and general L2 training in terms of WM. In a CI task, the interpreter listens to a stretch of source language input, and then recalls as accurately as possible in another language what has been conveyed in the input. In general L2 training, the learner comprehends and produces but does not have to recall the messages heard. In other words, although both the consecutive interpreter and the general L2 learner have to focus on a segment of message they are listening to or they are producing, the consecutive interpreter has to recall from the beginning of a stretch of input. Using the terms in Cowan's (1988) model, for the interpreter to recall, the Central Executive turns attention to (i.e., reactivate) the stretch of input which has already passed FOA, and the content in FOA is being updated. Although the FOA has to be constantly updated for both the interpreter and the general L2 learner to perform well in any genuine language task, interpreting or recalling as accurately as possible in another language is certainly more demanding in terms of accuracy and response time (RT) when compared with the general L2 tasks of listening, reading, speaking, and writing. In a general L2 conversation, for example, listening comprehension is important, but the conversation partner could ask for clarification if he or she does not get the message, and it is often good enough to get the gist. On the other hand, the situation is apparently more demanding for the interpreter. *We thus hypothesized that the updating function of WM was closely related to CI performance, and CI training could help enhance updating.* In addition, interpreters may process the source language input in a parallel way, i.e., their processing of the source language may be influenced by the target language (e.g., Dong and Lin, 2013), suggesting that interpreters may have a more efficient way processing the source language so that they can recall details better and perform better in tasks of verbal WM spans. Furthermore, Ecker et al. (2010) found that WM capacity was a strong predictor of WM updating, suggesting that WM spans and WM updating are closely related. *Our second hypothesis was thus that verbal WM spans were related to CI performance, and CI training could help enhance verbal WM spans.*

To test the two hypotheses, the present study employed three WM tasks: a visuo-spatial n-back task, a L2 listening span task, and a letter running span task. Although we were fully aware that no task is pure (e.g., Valian, 2015), and the connection between a WM task and the function that the task is supposed to measure may be controversial, we tried our best to overcome potential limitations and be as specific and as accurate as possible while following most studies in the literature. *The visuo-spatial n-back task* asks participants to identify whether the current square on the computer screen is in the same location with the square presented n trials back. "The n-back task is often assumed to measure updating, with subjects actively updating the current contents of a limited portion of temporary memory" (Redick and Lindsey, 2013: 1111). Apparently, the n-back task matches well with the recall task in CI, although the former seems simpler and is a non-linguistic task. Using different versions of the n-back task (e.g., visuo-spatial or letter), three previous studies (Timarova et al., 2014; Morales et al., 2015; Dong and Liu, 2016) have found some relationship between interpreting training and updating ability. *The listening span task* is a complex verbal span task[①] that requires participants to process aurally presented sentences and remember the last word of each sentence. This task has been used in the literature to test interpreters' advantage, but the findings were mixed (Liu et al., 2004; Köpke and Nespoulous, 2006). As for *the letter running task*, we do not yet find any research using this task to explore the issue of WM in interpreting. The task requests participants to recall the last n letters from a series of presentation of $m + n$ items, and it is believed that a fast version of the task (fast presentation of the letters) measures "the capacity of the FOA" (Lilienthal et al., 2012: 135) or scope of attention (Bunting et al., 2006), including attention control, its scope, and effortful retrieval (Broadway and Engle, 2010). It seems that consecutive interpreters have to do the same, controlling their attention and keeping their focus (which could be large in scope and effortful in retrieval). The latter two tasks were intended to test the second hypothesis, with the letter running task not so verbal as the listening span task.

It seems that WM tasks are rarely independent of each other, and as to empirical evidence for how exactly the three WM measures (n-back, listening, and letter running span tasks) relate to each other, there are only a few relevant

---

① There are other ways to test verbal WM spans: L1/L2 reading/listening/speaking span tasks. Many studies have indicated that these spans are closely related to each other. In addition, Cai and Dong (2012) found that three factors were in play in these spans (together with non-verbal digit and spatial spans), and their influences are hierarchical with different distinguishing power, from relatively strong (information type: verbal or non-verbal), to medium (encoding modality: listening, reading, or speaking), to relatively weak (encoding language: L1 or L2). To be more specific, two findings were relevant to the present study: (1) three pairs of spans were most closely clustered: L1/L2 listening spans; L1/L2 reading spans; L1/L2 speaking spans. (2) Listening and reading spans clustered on the next scale point, which then clustered with speaking spans. Since the verbal spans closely correlate with each other, since the listening span closely clusters with the classical reading span (Daneman and Carpenter, 1980), and since the L2 listening span has been tested in the literature of interpreters' WM advantage, we decided to choose the L2 listening span as an appropriate measure of verbal spans. Future studies are encouraged to include complex WM tasks in the L1, such as L1 listening span.

findings. Briefly, Redick and Lindsey (2013) found that n-back task performance weakly correlated with complex spans (reading span), and Broadway and Engle (2010) found that the running span significantly correlated with complex spans (reading or operation spans). The relationship between n-back task performance and the running span has been discussed in the difference between active and passive input processing in the running span task. If a person processes input actively, he prepares responses (probably by rehearsing and grouping targets) in advance of a trial in a test; if a person processes input passively, he waits to prepare responses until the time of the trial, i. e., when the input presentation has been completed. It is argued that active input processing in running memory span reflects WM updating in the form of rehearsal and grouping (e.g., Morris and Jones, 1990; Conway et al., 2005; Friedman et al., 2006). On the other hand, passive input processing measures the number of items extracted from sensory memory into the FOA (Cowan et al., 2005), reflecting the size of FOA. Empirical evidence found that ONLY a slow presentation of the letters (e.g., 2000 ms) appeared to allow updating and rehearsal processes (Bunting et al., 2006). In addition, Broadway and Engle (2010: 569) argued that "unless explicit instructions to rehearsals are given and enforced, it should not be assumed that participants engage in WM updating in running memory span". Following this line of evidence, the present study used a fast presentation rate (500 ms) for the running span task, and we believe it mainly measures the sizes of FOA.

To sum up, although a neat one-to-one mapping relationship between WM tasks and WM functions is rare (if not impossible), the present study followed most studies in the literature (e.g., Morales et al., 2015; Dong and Liu, 2016) and used the n-back task to test our first hypothesis that the updating function of WM is closely related to CI performance, and CI training enhances updating. Similarly, we used the listening span task and a fast version of the letter running span task to test our second hypothesis that verbal WM spans are closely related to CI performance, and CI training enhances verbal WM spans. To increase data reliability and validity, we adopted a more-controlled design, and to reduce the influence of the complexity problem in interpreting training, we focused on CI and compared it with general L2 learning.

MATERIALS AND METHODS

Participants

Two groups of young adult Chinese learners of English (93 in total, mean age=19.72 years, SD=0.79) were recruited at a university in China, and they received, respectively, two critical courses: general L2 training (EGP: English for General Purposes, 43 participants) and CI training (50 participants). All participants were non-English majors, and prior to the pretest, they had received no interpreting training. The two courses were optional but regular and registered courses in the university, and students were granted credits officially for the course they selected. The course of EGP was mainly an introduction to English culture and communication, with half class time spent on lecturing and the other half on student discussions (altogether 32 h of class time). Teachers and students were required to speak in English in the classroom. For the course of CI (mainly from L2 English to L1 Chinese), one third of the class time was spent on lecturing (e.g., illustrating interpreting strategies that mainly relates to effective source language comprehension, effective memory, and effective transmission) and two thirds on practice (altogether 32 h of class time). Apart from the 32 h of class time in each critical course, the two groups of participants did not differ either in their after-class practice (about 40 h in each course as indicated by data collected after the posttest). The two instructors for the two courses had been teaching their respective course for many years. Furthermore, the two courses were comparable in class size (50 students for each class).

Apart from the two critical courses, the participant groups were comparable in their trainings in other courses in the experimental semester. First, each group spent 32 h of class time (plus 56 after-class practice) in the course of "Comprehensive English" which includes trainings of basic skills of listening, speaking, reading, writing, and translation. Second, each group spent 256 h of class time in courses not related to language training (English).

Procedure and Tasks

All participants were tested twice (pretest and posttest), respectively, at the beginning and end of an academic semester of 16 weeks. All participants took the pretest in the following order: a questionnaire, the L2 listening span task, the letter running span task, a cloze test, the n-back task, and an IQ test; and the posttest in the following order: a questionnaire, the three WM tasks, and CI test.

An English cloze test (Bachman, 1985) was used to test L2 proficiency (30 points in total), [①] while Raven's Advanced Progressive Matrices Set (Raven et al., 1977) to collect participants' IQ (72 points in total). The composite questionnaire in the pretest was used to collect information about participants' self-rated L2 proficiency, age, and parental education (Marian et al., 2007), and the questionnaire in the posttest was used to collect information about participants' self-rated L2 proficiency and courses they took in the experimental semester. There were altogether 40 points in self-rated L2 proficiency, i.e., overall score of listening, speaking, reading, and writing, respectively, on a 10-point Likert scale. Father or mother education varied between 1 and 6, with 1 – 6, respectively, representing one's highest diploma in primary school, middle school, high school, college (2-year professional training), university (4-year university education), and graduate

---

[①] In a cloze test, participants are required to fill in blanks in a passage with words appropriate for the context. In the following example, the answers for the two blanks are *kinds*, *types* or *examples* for the first, and *to* for the second.

The science of automatic control depends on certain common principles by which an organism, machine, or system regulates itself. Many historical developments up to the present day have helped to identify these principles.

For hundreds of years there were many (1) _____ of automatic control systems, but no connections were recognized among them. A very early example was a device on windmills designed (2) _____ keep their sails facing into the wind ...

education.

Three tasks were used to test participants' WM: the visuo-spatial 2-back task, the L2 listening span task, and the letter running span task.

Visuo-Spatial 2-Back Task

Adapted from Soveri et al. (2011), the visuo-spatial 2-back version of the n-back task was used to measure participants' updating function. After the instructions, a blue square was presented in one of 25 possible locations on the screen. Participants were asked to determine whether the location of the current square matched the location of the square before the previous one (2-back). There were altogether 42 2-back trials (28 non-target and 14 target trials). Each square remained on the screen for 500 ms and participants had to respond within 3 000 ms. Participants were required to respond as quickly as possible without sacrificing accuracy. As indicators of participants' updating ability, both RT and accuracy rate were computed.

L2 Listening Span Task

Adapted from Cai et al. (2015), the task consisted of 60 English sentences, each of which contained 8 – 12 words. Half of the 60 sentences did not make sense (e.g., "You've got to be more delicious about your future"). The non-sense version was created by simply replacing one or two words (e.g., "optimistic" with "delicious") from an otherwise normal sentence. This way of creating the material followed the practice by Unsworth et al. (2009) (also see McVay and Kane, 2012; Redick et al., 2012, for examples). Participants were asked to listen through earphones to sentences auditorily presented and to remember the last word of each sentence. After hearing each sentence, participants were asked to make a judgment of the acceptability of the sentence by pressing one of the two keys. Sentences were presented in sets, and after the acceptability judgment of the last sentence in each set, participants heard an auditory cue (a "Ding" sound) and began to recall the last word of each sentence presented. No constraints were imposed on the order of recall except that participants should not begin with the last word of the last sentence in each set.① The set size (number of sentences) varied from two to six, with three trials in each set size. The presentation order of set size was randomly arranged for each participant. L2 listening span was the number of words correctly recalled (maximum score=60).

Letter Running Span Task

Adapted from Broadway and Engle (2010), the task asked participants to recall the last n letters (targets) in the order of presentation from a list of $m+n$ letters (inputs). There were a total of four sets of unrelated letters, with three lists of letters in each set. The number of letters to be recalled varied across sets (from 3 to 6) and was randomly ordered. Within each set, the input length was varied across lists, ranging from 3 to 8 letters. Each set began with instructions informing participants the number of last letters to be recalled, followed by the presentation of three lists of letters. Each list began with a fixation ("+") for 500 ms, followed by visually presented letters one after another. Each letter was displayed for 300 ms and the interval between two letters was 200 ms. At the end of each list, participants recalled the letters they remembered by choosing among 12 letters displayed on the screen. A strict serial recall was required. No time constraint was set for recall. Before the experimental sequence, participants completed a practice set of four lists of unrelated letters, with the target length of two letters. Letter running span was the cumulative number of letters correctly recalled in lists where more letters were shown than were to be recalled ($m>0$).

---

① Researchers interested in the relationship between WM and interpreting frequently adopted free recall in reading and listening span tasks (e.g., Padilla, 1995; Christoffels et al., 2006; Signorelli, 2008). There are two motivations for this: (a) The very first developers of the reading span task accepted free recall themselves as they said "Because the test proved so difficult, the subject was given credit for any set for which he recalled all sentence final words, irrespective of the order of recall" (Daneman and Carpenter, 1980, p. 458); (b) Köpke and Signorelli (2012) argued that randomly determined order constraints were not very likely to be relevant to interpreting because word order in interpreting was determined by syntactic and semantic factors. Therefore, in spite of the popularity of serial recall for such WM tasks in experimental psychology, we adopted free recall for the listening span task in the present study so that we can compare our results with those of relevant previous studies. However, we do encourage further studies adopting serial recall, especially studies comparing free recall and serial recall.

English – Chinese CI Test

At the end of the experimental semester, the CI group received an English – Chinese (E - C) CI test, in which participants were required to orally translate an English speech into Chinese. The test material is an approximately 6-min long coherent speech recorded by a native English speaker at an average rate of 143 words per minute. The speech was divided into segments, with each segment consisting of two to three sentences. Participants listened to each segment at a time, at the end of which a sound signal would indicate the time to start interpreting. The duration allowed for interpreting a segment was 1.5 times the duration of the segment itself. Another sound would then indicate the time to stop, and after a brief interval, a new segment was presented. Participants were allowed to take notes and refer back to these notes when they interpreted. Participants' oral responses were recorded for scoring later. The CI materials (including the way of segmentation) had been used to assess students from the same population for many times before the present study, and both the students and teachers considered the materials appropriate for their CI assessment in terms of difficulty level, speed, and topic familiarity. Besides, no complaints about materials were made by our participants after the test. As for the scoring of participants' interpreting products, we followed the criteria used before, which included information (accuracy and completeness, 70%) and target language (grammar and appropriateness, 30%).

RESULTS

Data Trimming

Data from two participants (in the interpreting group) were excluded from further data analyses because of their abnormal performance in the IQ test (below 55 out of a total of 72, meaning "retarded" according to Raven et al., 1977). As described above, participants' listening and letter running spans were, respectively, measured by the number of words or letters correctly recalled. Two measures were collected for the 2-back task: accuracy rate and RT. For n-back RT data, data from erroneous responses and those with RT less than 200 ms were discarded. Then outlier responses deviating by more than three SDs from the mean RTs for each participant were eliminated. Altogether less than 5% of extreme data (less than 200 ms, and outliers of three SDs from the mean) was affected (for the control group: pretest, 1.92%; posttest, 1.37%; for the interpreting group: pretest, 1.14%; posttest, 2.19%).

Statistical Analyses

For clarity, the results of the statistical analyses are reported in two sections, answering two questions: How do CI training and general L2 training differ in their influences on WM? Are the updating and verbal span functions of WM related to CI performance?

How Do CI Training and General L2 Training Differ in Their Influences on WM?

To find out whether there were any group differences in the training effect, an analysis was conducted with Participant Group (CI group vs. control group) as the between-subject factor and Test Phase (pretest and posttest) as the within-subject factor. But before this analysis, we conducted a group comparison on the pretest measures to examine whether the two participant groups were comparable on the relevant factors that may influence WM performance or development. The result of this group comparison is shown in **Table 1**.

Table 1 Pretest group means (with SD) and comparisons of participants' background characteristics and working memory (WM) task performances.

	Control ($n=43$)	Interpreting ($n=48$)	df	t-value	p-value
Background characteristics					
Interpreting	No	No			
Tested L2 proficiency	13.79(3.55)	12.97 (3.61)	89	1.077	0.284
Self-rated L2 proficiency	19.67(4.60)	20.10(5.74)	89	−0.391	0.697

	Control ($n=43$)	Interpreting ($n=48$)	df	t-value	p-value continued
Age*	19.86(0.88)	19.58(0.71)	89	1.652	0.102
AoA*	9.02(2.44)	9.29 (2.28)	89	−0.541	0.590
Father education*	2.39(0.69)	2.75(1.26)	89	−1.632	0.106
Mother education*	1.97(1.01)	2.16(1.21)	89	−0.808	0.421
Intelligence	67.51(2.43)	66.56(3.25)	89	1.561	0.122
WM task performances					
L2 listening span	26.20(7.01)	26.10(5.49)	89	0.080	0.936
Letter running span	23.60(4.18)	22.38 (5.30)	89	1.218	0.226
2-back: RT	843.06(273.11)	870.92(265.92)	89	−0.493	0.623
2-back: accuracy*	0.85(0.095)	0.84 (0.087)	89	0.477	0.634

* *Data for these variables were not normally distributed, and therefore Mann–Whitney tests were conducted, resulting in the same patterns as shown by independent t-test. For Age: $U=844.00$, $Z=-1.65$, $p=0.098$; for AoA: $U=986.50$, $Z=-0.37$, $p=0.713$; for Father education: $U=910.50$, $Z=-1.02$, $p=0.306$; For Mother education: $U=952.00$, $Z=-0.67$, $p=0.506$; For 2-back accuracy: $U=955.00$, $Z=-0.61$, $p=0.540$.*

The results of the comparisons, as revealed in **Table 1**, yielded no significant group differences in any of the indices of WM capacity or in L2 proficiency. *Since students selected their courses out of their own will, the null group differences suggest that students of interpreting did not choose the CI course because of some preexisting advantage in WM.*

Table 2 presents participants' posttest performance, and their gains from pretest to posttest, together with the group difference in each gain. The gains seem to indicate that the CI group tended to make more progress than the general L2 group in each of the four WM indices. However, a significant group difference was found only in updating RT (2-back RT) ($p=0.025$) but not in the other three indices, which can also be shown by the effect size. According to a rough interpretation of the effect size values (Cohen, 1992), the group difference of updating RT (2-back RT) in gains from the pretest to the posttest was medium in effect size ($d=0.48$), while that of letter running span was small ($d=-0.22$), and those of L2 listening span and updating accuracy were between small and medium ($d=-0.35, -0.31$).

Table 2 Posttest group means (with SD) in WM, their gains from pretest to posttest, and the group difference in each gain.

	Control group ($n=43$)		Interpreting group ($n=48$)		Group difference in each gain		
	Posttest mean	Gain	Posttest mean	Gain	t-value	p-value	Effect size d
L2 listening span	27.97 (7.68)	1.77 (5.37)	29.75 (6.29)	3.65 (5.49)	−1.645	0.103	−0.35
Letter running span	23.27 (5.19)	−0.33 (5.44)	23.20 (4.99)	0.82 (4.96)	−1.062	0.291	−0.22
2-back: RT	841.74 (261.17)	−1.32 (225.44)	766.15 (217.20)	−104.77 (206.17)	2.287	0.025	0.48
2-back: accuracy	0.88 (0.087)	0.03 (0.072)	0.90 (0.069)	0.06 (0.076)	−1.450	0.151	−0.31
CI performance			85.40 (6.21)				

Analysis of variance (ANOVA) was further conducted to find out how each group progressed in each index of data. **Table 3** shows the result of ANOVA (SPSS Statistics Version 19), with Participant Group as the between-subject factor (CI group, control group) and Test Phase as the within-subject factor (pretest, posttest) (see **Table 1** for pretest performance and **Table 2** for posttest performance).

Table 3 Summary of Participant Group×Test Phase analyses for each task index of the WM tasks.

	Main effect of phase			Main effect of group			Interaction effect		
	$F(1, 89)$	p	η_p^2	$F(1, 89)$	p	η_p^2	$F(1, 89)$	p	η_p^2
L2 listening span	22.486	0.000	0.202	0.431	0.513	0.005	2.707	0.103	0.030
Letter running span	0.216	0.643	0.002	0.540	0.464	0.006	1.127	0.291	0.013
2-back: RT	5.497	0.021	0.058	0.243	0.623	0.003	5.228	0.025	0.055
2-back: accuracy	31.816	0.000	0.263	0.019	0.890	0.000	2.101	0.151	0.023

	Simple effect (of progress) for participant groups	
	Control	Interpreting
2-back: RT	$p=0.968, r=0.006$	$p=0.001, r=0.457$

As can be seen in **Table 3**①, the main effect of Test Phase (pretest vs. posttest) was significant in L2 listening span and the two indices of the 2-back task, reflecting a general training or practice effect. No main effect of Group was found in any index of the three WM tasks. The interaction effect was significant only in 2-back RT ($p=0.025$, $\eta_p^2=0.055$). *The simple effect analysis showed that the interpreting group made a significant progress in 2-back RT ($p=0.001$, $r=0.457$), while the control did not make any progress ($p=0.968$, $r=0.006$).*②

Are the Updating and Verbal Span Functions of WM Related to CI Performance?

We first conducted correlation analyses and the results are summarized in **Table 4**. As shown in **Table 4**, among the pretest WM indices, 2-back RT and listening span significantly correlated with CI performance, while for the posttest WM indices, only 2-back RT significantly correlated with CI performance.

Table 4 Correlations between CI performance and pretest or posttest WM

	2-back RT		2-back ACC		Letter span		Listening span	
	Pre-	Post-	Pre-	Post-	Pre-	Post-	Pre-	Post-
CI	−0.377**	−0.294*	0.091	−0.218	0.017	0.111	0.301*	0.197

**, * *Correlation significant, respectively, at the 0.01, 0.05 level (2-tailed).*

---

① We did not intend to collect RT data for the two span tasks because most previous research on the topic did not collect RT for WM spans. And yet, we "unintentionally" recorded participants' RTs for the listening span task, i.e., the time it took each participant to judge if each presented sentence made sense or not. An analysis of these RT data indicated that the main effect of Participant Group ($p=0.342$, $\eta_p^2=0.010$) or that of Testing Phase ($p=0.107$, $\eta_p^2=0.029$) or their interaction ($p=0.949$, $\eta_p^2<0.001$) was not significant. Future studies are encouraged to collect and analyze RT data for WM span tasks.

② We had deleted two participants' data because of their abnormal performance in the IQ test. However, the results were more or less the same if these data had been included. With all participants' data included, the interaction effect was not significant in L2 listening span ($p=0.139$, $\eta_p^2=0.024$), letter running span ($p=0.318$, $\eta_p^2=0.011$), and 2-back accuracy rate ($p=0.083$, $\eta_p^2=0.033$), but significant in 2-back RT ($p=0.023$, $\eta_p^2=0.056$), with the interpreting group making a significant progress ($p=0.001$, $r=0.457$) while the control group did not ($p=0.968$, $r=0.006$).

Since both pretest 2-back RT and listening span significantly correlated with CI performance ($p=0.008$ and $p=0.038$, respectively), we further conducted a hierarchical multiple regression analysis to see whether both factors significantly predicted CI performance in the posttest (two predictors: pretest 2-back RT and listening span; one dependent variable: posttest CI performance). As seen in **Table 5**, pretest 2-back RT significantly predicted CI performance ($p<=0.012$), while this prediction was only marginally significant for L2 listening span ($0.05<p<0.10$). The result of marginal significance for L2 listening span may seem strange because the correlation was significant (see **Table 4**), and the two pretest indexes of 2-back RT and L2 listening span did not correlate with each other for the interpreting group ($r=0.023$, $p=0.541$), showing the absence of multicollinearity. And yet, with the two variables entering the same regression model, the significance value did change (see **Table 5**). Since the correlation coefficient of 0.301 for L2 listening span was not very large ($p=0.038$), it is understandable that the prediction was only marginally significant.

Table 5 Summary of hierarchical multiple regression analysis on the predictive effects of pretest WM (ID: independent variables) on CI performance (DV: dependent variable).

	DV	Block	IV	ΔR^2	ΔF	Δp	Beta
1	CI	1	2-back RT	0.142	7.436	0.009	−0.377
		2	Listening span	0.053	2.916	0.095	0.232
2	CI	1	Listening span	0.069	3.323	0.075	0.262
		2	2-back RT	0.126	6.909	0.012	−0.357

In short, among the three WM functions we have tested, only updating in the pretest significantly predicted CI performance in the posttest, and in the posttest, only updating significantly correlated with CI performance. Pretest L2 listening span correlated CI performance, but when entering the same regression model with updating, the prediction effect was only marginally significant.

DISCUSSION

With an intention to contribute to the issue of how language experience influences executive functions, the present study tried to reduce the problem of complexity in language experience, and focused on CI training and its effects on WM. With an analysis of the distinctive features of CI compared with general L2 learning in terms of WM requirements or involvement, we hypothesized that: (1) the updating function of WM was closely related to CI performance, and CI training could help enhance updating, (2) verbal WM spans may correlate with CI, and CI training may help enhance verbal WM spans. To increase the reliability of experimental data, we adopted a longitudinal design with a sufficient sample size and with participant groups that were controlled in their background characteristics (e.g., age, intelligence, social economic status, and language learning history). There were three main results: (1) Among all the WM indexes, only pretest and posttest n-back RT and pretest L2 listening span correlated with posttest CI performance; when both pretest n-back RT and pretest L2 listening span entered the same regression model, n-back RT significantly predicted posttest CI performance while this prediction was only marginally significant for L2 listening span. (2) For the index of n-back RT, the two participant groups differed significantly, with the interpreting group making a significant progress in the posttest, and the control group making no progress, while for the index of n-back accuracy, both groups improved equally significantly in the posttest. (3) For the two indices of WM spans, the two groups did not differ from each other, with both groups having improved significantly in L2 listening span in the posttest and neither group getting improved in the letter running span. In a word, our first hypothesis has been verified, and our second hypothesis was only weakly and partly supported.

The Two Hypotheses on WM and CI

In our point of view, the most important finding for the present study is the relationship between updating and CI: updating efficiency (here specifically referring to updating speed based on a relatively high accuracy) predicted CI performance (see **Table 5**)①, and CI training enhanced updating efficiency (while general L2 training did not, see **Table 3**). Our analysis of the CI task in Section "Introduction" tried to explain this finding: recalling source language information in the target language is more demanding in terms of accuracy and speed when compared to listening and speaking in general L2 learning, and the process of recalling seems to match well with the process of updating as tested in the n-back task. For the prediction part of this finding (**Table 5**), we did not find similar reports in the literature, but we did replicate this prediction result in our later studies (with participants of higher L2 proficiency receiving much more CI training; manuscripts being prepared). The closest case in the literature was reported by Timarova et al. (2014) who found that professional interpreters of higher accuracy rates in a letter 2-back task performed better in the interpretation of numbers. For the enhancement part of this finding (**Table 3**), two previous studies reported similar results. Morales et al. (2015) reported better updating ability from simultaneous interpreters (SIs) when compared to general bilinguals. Dong and Liu (2016) found that CI training significantly enhanced updating ability, while the two control groups of written translation or general L2 training made only marginal or no progress. When comparing findings from the literature, we have to pay attention to the fact that professional interpreter or SIs are consecutive interpreters at the same time, but the other way around is not necessarily true.

The second hypothesis concerning the relationship between verbal WM spans and interpreting training was only weakly and partly supported. The

---

① As to why the correlation with CI performance was better in the pretest than in the posttest in the present study, it was probably related to the high negative correlation between pretest 2-back RT and 2-back RT gain (from pretest to posttest): $r = -0.530$, $p < 0.001$. In other words, participants with relatively low pretest updating ability tended to improve more in the posttest, and participants with relatively high updating ability had less room to improve.

pretest L2 listening span correlated with CI performance[①], but when it entered the same regression model with the index of updating RT, the prediction effect was only marginally significant. In addition, there was a tendency for the interpreting group to make more progress in the posttest in both verbal span indices (a stronger tendency for L2 listening span than for letter running span, see **Table 2**), but that tendency was not significant (**Table 3**). These results are not good enough for us to make claims about the presence or absence of an interpreter advantage in WM spans. They could be reflections of the elusive nature of an interpreter advantage in complex verbal spans (generally verbal reading and listening spans) in the literature (e.g., advantage in Köpke and Nespoulous, 2006; Zhang, 2008; but no such advantage in Liu et al., 2004). With more training or with higher L2 proficiency, the relationship between CI performance and L2 listening span at least could be stronger, but more research is certainly needed to verify this hypothesis.

What we wish to emphasize is a potential connection between the two parts of the results for each hypothesis. (1) Results for Hypothesis One: updating efficiency predicted CI performance, and CI training enhanced updating efficiency (while general L2 training did not); (2) Results for Hypothesis Two: verbal WM spans did not significantly predict CI performance (i.e., only pretest L2 listening span correlated with CI performance and predicted CI performance with marginal significance), and CI training did not make a unique contribution to these spans. Briefly speaking, the reason for the second part probably lies in the first part. That is, the reason why one semester's CI training brought participants an "interpreter advantage" in updating (but not in verbal spans) is probably that updating (but not verbal spans) is closely connected with the CI task, and therefore updating or a

---

[①] The reason for why L2 listening span correlated significantly with CI performance in the pretest but not in the posttest is probably the same as explained in Footnote 7. That is, participants with relatively low pretest L2 listening span tended to improve more in the posttest, and participants with relatively high L2 listening span had less room to improve, as shown in the negative correlation between pretest L2 listening span and its gain in the posttest: $r=-0.290$, $p=0.005$.

process parallel to updating (but not verbal spans) is trained in CI training. This process in CI is recalling information in the CI task. We may apply this line of thought to similar issues investigating how cognitive experience influences executive functions. Take the issue of "bilingual advantage" as an example. Experimental results for the bilingual advantage issue are quite mixed, most probably because inhibitory control is not more needed in some cases of bilingual experience than in monolingual experience, and therefore no inhibitory control advantage exists in such cases. Further research in this issue, therefore, may have to investigate the nature of bilingualism in terms of its involvement of executive functions when compared with monolingualism. For the present study, we may claim that CI involves updating more than it involves verbal WM spans. Whether this claim is true or false for similar cases of CI (e.g., CI by participants of higher L2 proficiency receiving more CI training) or for the relevant case of SI requires further research. More research of this line would fill blank patches in the dynamic picture for the relationship between interpreting and WM, which would then provide at least implications for the research on the relationship between cognitive experience and executive functions, and on the nature of cognitive experience itself.

Based on our theoretical analysis and experimental data, we believe that *updating and the recalling process in the CI task share the same attentional control process*. As analyzed in Section "Introduction," the consecutive interpreter listens to a stretch of source language input, and then recalls as accurately as possible in the target language within a very short time. The Central Executive has to direct its attention backward to update information that has passed the FOA. This process is the same as the process in the n-back task in which the participant has to recall (or make judgments about) the stimulus that are n trials back. In other words, this updating attentional control process has been repeatedly exercised in CI training, leading to an interpreter advantage in updating.

Methodological Issues

The experimental results in the present study also touched some methodological issues. The first one concerns the result that the L2 listening span was significantly enhanced in both groups while the letter running span did not improve in either group. This contrast is most probably a result of encoding more meaningful and less meaningful materials in the two tasks. Specifically, there are two possible reasons. First, the L2 listening span improved in both groups because both groups received language training in the pretest-posttest interval, while it may be too difficult for the language trainings to produce any effect on the letter running span in a short time. Second, since the materials of sentences in the L2 listening span task were meaningful, or more meaningful than the letters in the letter running span task, the meaningfulness may have produced more practice effect from the pretest itself, and may have benefited more from the trainings after the pretest. However, we believe that this difference between the two tasks did not affect much the major conclusions in the present study, because the design with a control group in the present study must have alleviated potential influences.

The second methodological issue concerns experimental control in the research on interpreter advantage. Although the problem of lack of control exists in the research on bilingual advantage, it seems more serious in the literature of research on interpreting, most probably because interpreters, especially simultaneous or professional interpreters, are not easily available. Nevertheless, rigid control is essential to valid conclusions no matter how hard it is to find matched groups of participants. Apart from what we have discussed about sample size in Section "Introduction," participants need to be controlled in their *age*. Professional interpreters are generally older than students of interpreting, but WM capacity declines as a function of age (e.g., Charlton et al., 2010; Caplan et al., 2011). That could explain the finding that, in Signorelli et al. (2012), younger interpreters (mean age: 34.5) performed better than older interpreters (mean age: 56.2) in non-word repetition and cued recall tasks. Even among our participants that did not differ much from each other in age (19.86 years old with an SD of 0.88 for the control group), "age" negatively correlated with pretest letter running span ($r =$

-0.255, $p=0.015$) and posttest L2 listening span ($r=-0.267$, $p=0.010$). The second factor that needs to be controlled is *L2 proficiency*, which has been found to play a role in WM capacity (e.g., Service et al., 2002). This role was evidenced by Tzou et al. (2012), where participants with higher L2 proficiency showed larger WM capacity than those with lower L2 proficiency. This relationship was supported by many pieces of evidence in the present study. For example, "tested L2 proficiency" correlated with pretest 2-back RT ($r=0.237$, $p=0.024$) and pretest L2 listening span ($r=0.274$, $p=0.009$). Besides these two factors, other factors like intelligence, socioeconomic status (SES) may also contribute to the differences and need to be controlled. For example, a significant unique variance in fluid intelligence was associated with WM (e.g., Shelton et al., 2010), and SES was found to explain a significant portion of the variance in cognitive achievement including WM (e.g., Noble et al., 2007). The present study found a marginally significant correlation between father education and L2 listening span ($r=0.199$, $p=0.058$).

Conducting longitudinal studies may help in experimental control, but there must be a control group matched with the experimental group in relevant background characteristics. Without the control group, the present study would have reached the probably wrong conclusion that interpreting training significantly enhanced L2 listening span (see the significant "main effect of testing phase" in **Table 3**). With the control group, we cannot reach that conclusion because of the null "interaction effect" in **Table 3**. This null effect indicates that the significant gain in L2 listening span in the posttest could be a result of the mixed effects of repeated testing (i.e., pretest and posttest), general L2 training or even exposure, and genuine influence of interpreting training. There are similar cases in the literature. For example, Zhang (2008) conducted a longitudinal study with three groups of participants: beginning interpreting trainees, advanced interpreting trainees, and professional interpreters (their age means were 23.4, 23.6, and 32.3, respectively), and comparing each group's pretest and posttest scores (paired t-test), found that the beginning trainees' reading span and advanced trainees' coordinating ability were significantly improved by the 6 months' experience of interpreting. Macnamara and Conway (2014) tested twice a group of 21 bimodal bilinguals with 2 years in between when participants received SI between American Sign Language (ASL) and English, and found that interpreting training enhanced the WM component processes of coordination and transformation (as tested by backward digit span and letter-number sequencing), but not processes of storage and processing (as tested by reading span and operation span).

In addition, conclusions on "advantage" research depend on how the supposedly advantageous group and a control group differ in the first place. If we had recruited a control group that did not receive the 32 (class) hours of general L2 training (but well matched otherwise) during the experimental semester, the interaction effect of L2 listening span between Participant Group and Testing Phase in **Table 3** may have reached significance, which may then lead to results similar to those for n-back RT (i.e., "L2 listening span was significantly enhanced by interpreting training"). Our conclusion about the question of how interpreting training influences WM, therefore, is based on a comparison between interpreting training and general L2 training, i.e., the additive effect of interpreting training above general L2 training.

The present study may help resolve controversies on the letter running task. For this purpose, we ran a correlation analysis on the four indices of WM, the results of which are listed in **Table 6**. On the one hand, there was no significant correlation between the two indices of the n-back task and the index of letter running in either the pretest or posttest, suggesting that the letter running task cannot be taken as a measurement of updating as suggested in some previous studies (e.g., Morris and Jones, 1990; Conway et al., 2005; Friedman et al., 2006). Since Bunting et al. (2006) found that only a slow pace of presentation of the letters (e.g., 2000 ms) appeared to allow updating and rehearsal processes to take place, the insignificant correlation between the two tasks is expected because the lapse between letters in the present research was normal or shorter, i.e., 500 ms. On the other hand, the two span tasks (L2 listening span and letter running span) correlated with each other in the posttest, which is consistent with what Broadway and Engle (2010) may have suggested since they found that the running span significantly correlated with the complex spans of reading (and listening and reading spans correlated with each other, see Cai and Dong, 2012). Taking all the three tasks into consideration, the correlations between them (Table 6) further specify the idea that the letter running span is more closely related to the verbal span of L2 listening than to updating ability measured in the n-back task.

Table 6 Correlations between WM indices in the pre- and post-tests (Pearson correlation, 2-tailed, 91 participants).

	2-back RT		2-back ACC		Letter span	
	Pre-	Post-	Pre-	Post-	Pre-	Post-
2-back ACC	0.185	0.308**				
Letter span	0.113	0.140	−0.001	0.003		
Listening span	−0.105	0.028	0.102	0.131	0.129	0.333**

** $0.001 < p < 0.05$.

To sum up, the most critical finding for the present study is that both parts of our first hypothesis about updating were fully supported while neither part of our second hypothesis about verbal WM spans was (i.e., only pretest L2 listening span correlated with CI performance and predicted CI performance with marginal significance). This suggests that updating efficiency (even when measured by a non-verbal version of the n-back task as in the present study) is more central to the CI task than WM size, at least for beginning student interpreters like ours, and is therefore more exercised in CI training, leading to an interpreter advantage in updating efficiency. The underlying mechanism is that updating and the recalling process in CI share the same attentional control process.

ETHICS STATEMENT

The present study was exempt from this requirement because we did not interfere with the classes that the participants received. We only collected cognitive data at the beginning and end of the semester, and all participants gave written informed consent for data collection in accordance with the Declaration of Helsinki.

AUTHOR CONTRIBUTIONS

YD had the idea and design, and wrote 90% of the paper. YL managed the experiments, analyzed the data, and helped with the writing. RC designed part of WM tasks and helped with the writing.

FUNDING

The research was supported by a grant (15AYY002) to the YD from the National Social Science Foundation of China.

REFERENCES

Bachman, L. F. (1985). Performance on cloze tests with fixed-ratio and rational deletions. *TESOL Q.* 19, 535–556. doi: 10.2307/3586277

Baddeley, A. (2003). Working memory and language: an overview. *J. Commun. Disord.* 36, 189–208. doi: 10.1016/S0021-9924(03)00019-4

Broadway, J. M., and Engle, R. W. (2010). Validating running memory span: measurement of working memory capacity and links with fluid intelligence. *Behav. Res. Methods* 42, 563–570. doi: 10.3758/BRM.42.2.563

Brysbaert, M., and Stevens, M. (2018). Power analysis and effect size in mixed effects models: a tutorial. *J. Cogn.* 1: 9. doi: 10.5334/joc.10

Bunting, M., Cowan, N., and Saults, J. S. (2006). How does running memory span work? *Q. J. Exp. Psychol.* 59, 1691–1700. doi: 10.1080/17470210600848402

Cai, R., and Dong, Y. (2012). Effects of information type, encoding modality, and encoding language on working memory span: evidence for the hierarchical view (In Chinese). *Foreign Lang. Teach. Res.* 44, 376–388.

Cai, R., Dong, Y., Zhao, N., and Lin, J. (2015). Factors contributing to individual differences in the development of consecutive interpreting competence for beginning student interpreters. *Interpret. Transl. Train.* 9, 104–120. doi: 10.1080/1750399X.2015.1016279

Caplan, D., DeDe, G., Waters, G. S., Michaud, J., and Tripodis, Y. (2011). Effects of age, speed of processing, and working memory on comprehension of sentences with relative clauses. *Psychol. Aging* 26, 439–450. doi: 10.1037/a0021837

Charlton, R. A., Schiavone, F., Barrick, T. R., Morris, R. G., and Markus, H. S. (2010). Diffusion tensor imaging detects age related white matter change over a 2 year follow-up which is associated with working memory decline. *J. Neurol. Neurosurg. Psychiatry* 81, 13–19. doi: 10.1136/jnnp.2008.167288

Chincotta, D., and Underwood, G. (1998). Simultaneous interpreters and the effect of concurrent articulation on immediate memory: A bilingual digit span study. *Interpreting* 3, 1–20. doi: 10.1075/intp.3.1.01chi

Christoffels, I. K., de Groot, A. M. B., and Kroll, J. F. (2006). Memory and language skills in simultaneous interpreters: The role of expertise and language proficiency. *J. Mem. Lang.* 54, 324–345. doi: 10.1016/j.jml.2005.12.004

Christoffels, I. K., de Groot, A. M. B., and Waldorp, L. J. (2003). Basic skills in a complex task: a graphical model relating memory and lexical retrieval to simultaneous interpreting. *Biling. Lang. Cogn.* 6, 201–211. doi: 10.1017/S1366728903001135

Cohen, J. (1992). A power primer. *Psychol. Bull.* 112, 155–159. doi: 10.1037/0033-2909.112.1.155

Conway, A. R., Kane, M. J., Bunting, M. F., Hambrick, D. Z., Wilhelm, O., and Engle, R. W. (2005). Working memory span tasks: a methodological review and user's guide. *Psychon. Bull. Rev.* 12, 769–786. doi: 10.3758/BF03196772

Cowan, N. (1988). Evolving conceptions of memory storage, selective attention, and their mutual constraints within the human information processing system. *Psychol. Bull.* 104, 163 – 191. doi: 10. 1037/0033-2909.104.2.163

Cowan, N. (1995). *Attention and Memory: An Integrated Framework*. Oxford: Oxford University Press.

Cowan, N., Elliott, E. M., Saults, J. S., Morey, C. C., Mattox, S., Hismjatullina, A., et al. (2005). On the capacity of attention: its estimation and its role in working memory and cognitive aptitudes. *Cogn. Psychol.* 51, 42 – 100. doi: 10.1016/j. cogpsych.2004.12.001

Daneman, M., and Carpenter, P. (1980). Individual differences in working memory and reading. *J. Verb. Learn. Verb. Behav.* 19, 450 – 466. doi: 10.1016/S0022-5371(80)90312-6

Diamond, A. (2013). Executive functions. *Annu. Rev. Psychol.* 64, 135 –168. doi: 10.1146/annurev-psych-113011-143750

Dong, Y., and Cai, R. (2015). "Working memory in interpreting: a commentary on theoretical models," in *Working Memory in Second Language Acquisition and Processing*, eds Z. Wen, M. Mota, and A. McNeill (Bristol: Multilingual Matters), 63 – 79.

Dong, Y., and Liu, Y. (2016). Classes in translating and interpreting produce differential gains in switching and updating. *Front. Psychol.* 7: 1297. doi: 10.3389/fpsyg.2016.01297

Dong, Y., and Lin, J. (2013). Parallel processing of the target language during source language comprehension in interpreting. *Biling. Lang. Cogn.* 16, 682 – 692. doi: 10.1017/S1366728913000102

Ecker, U. K., Lewandowsky, S., Oberauer, K., and Chee, A. E. (2010). The components of working memory updating: an experimental decomposition and individual differences. *J. Exp. Psychol. Learn. Mem. Cogn.* 36, 170 – 189. doi: 10.1037/a0017891

Friedman, N. P., Miyake, A., Corley, R. P., Young, S. E., DeFries, J. C., and Hewitt, J. K. (2006). Not all executive functions are related to intelligence. *Psychol. Sci.* 17, 172 – 179. doi: 10. 1111/j. 1467-9280. 2006. 01681.x

Green, C. S., Strobach, T., and Schubert, T. (2014). On methodological standards in training and transfer experiments. *Psychol. Res.* 78, 756 – 772. doi: 10.1007/s00426-013-0535-3

Green, D. W. (1998). Mental control of the bilingual lexico-semantic system. *Biling. Lang. Cogn.* 1, 67 – 81. doi: 10.1017/S1366728998000133

Keiser, W. (1965). "Admission dans les Ecoles d'interprétation," in *Paper Presented at the AIIC Actas del Colloque Sur L'enseignement de L'interprétation de l'AIIC*, Paris, 3 – 8.

Köpke, B., and Nespoulous, J.-L. (2006). Working memory performance in expert and novice interpreters. *Interpreting* 8, 1 – 23. doi: 10. 1075/intp.8.1.02kop

Köpke, B., and Signorelli, T. M. (2012). Methodological aspects of working memory assessment in simultaneous interpreters. *Int. J. Biling.* 16, 183 – 197. doi: 10.1177/1367006911402981

Liang, J., Fang, Y., Lv, Q., and Liu, H. (2017). Dependency distance differences across interpreting types: implications for cognitive demand. *Front. Psychol.* 8: 2132. doi: 10.3389/fpsyg.2017.02132

Lilienthal, L., Tamez, E., Shelton, J. T., Myerson, J., and Hale, S. (2012). Dual n-back training increases the capacity of the focus of attention. *Psychon. Bull. Rev.* 20, 135 – 141. doi: 10.3758/s13423-012-0335-6

Liu, M., Schallert, D. L., and Carroll, P. J. (2004). Working memory and expertise in simultaneous interpreting. *Interpreting* 6, 19 – 42. doi: 10.1075/intp.6.1.04liu

Macnamara, B. N., and Conway, A. (2014). Novel evidence in support of the bilingual advantage: Influences of task demands and experience on cognitive control and working memory. *Psychon. Bull. Rev.* 21, 520 – 525. doi: 10.3758/s13423-013-0524-y

Marian, V., Blumenfeld, H. K., and Kaushanskaya, M. (2007). The language experience and proficiency questionnaire (LEAP-Q): assessing language profiles in bilinguals and multilinguals. *J. Speech Lang. Hear Res.* 50, 940–967. doi: 10.1044/1092-4388(2007/067)

McVay, J. C., and Kane, M. J. (2012). Drifting from slow to "d'oh!": Working memory capacity and mind wandering predict extreme reaction times and executive control errors. *J. Exp. Psychol. Learn. Mem. Cogn.* 38, 525–549. doi: 10.1037/a0025896

Mizuno, A. (2005). Process model for simultaneous interpreting and working memory. *Méta* 50, 739–752. doi: 10.7202/011015ar

Morales, J., Padilla, F., Gómez-Ariza, C. J., and Bajo, M. T. (2015). Simultaneous interpretation selectively influences working memory and attentional networks. *Acta Psychol.* 155, 82–91. doi: 10.1016/j.actpsy.2014.12.004

Morris, N., and Jones, D. M. (1990). Memory updating in working memory: The role of the central executive. *Br. J. Psychol.* 81, 111–121. doi: 10.1111/j.2044-8295.1990.tb02349.x

Noble, K. G., McCandliss, B. D., and Farah, M. J. (2007). Socioeconomic gradients predict individual differences in neurocognitive abilities. *Dev. Sci.* 10, 464–480. doi: 10.1111/j.1467-7687.2007.00600.x

Paap, K. R., Johnson, H. A., and Sawi, O. (2015). Bilingual advantages in executive functioning either do not exist or are restricted to very specific and undetermined circumstances. *Cortex* 69, 265–278. doi: 10.1016/j.cortex.2015.04.014

Padilla, P. (1995). *Procesos de Memoria y Atención en la Interpretación de Lenguas.* Ph.D. thesis, Universidad de Granada, Granada.

Padilla, P., Bajo, M. T., Canas, J. J., and Padilla, F. (1995). "Cognitive processes of memory in simultaneous interpretation," in *Topics in Interpreting Research*, ed. J. Tommola (Turku: University of Turku), 61–72.

Raven, J. C., Court, J. H., and Raven, J. (1977). *Manual for Raven's Advanced Progressive Matrices: Sets I and II.* London: Lewis&Co. Ltd.

Redick, T. S., Broadway, J. M., Meier, M. E., Kuriakose, P. S.,

Unsworth, N., Kane, M. J., et al. (2012). Measuring working memory capacity with automated complex span tasks. *Eur. J. Psychol. Assess.* 28, 164–171. doi: 10.1027/1015-5759/a000123

Redick, T. S., and Lindsey, D. R. (2013). Complex span and n-back measures of working memory: a meta-analysis. *Psychon. Bull. Rev.* 20, 1102–1113. doi: 10.3758/s13423-013-0453-9

Service, E., Simola, M., Metsaenheimo, O., and Maury, S. (2002). Bilingual working memory span is affected by language skill. *Eur. J. Cogn. Psychol.* 14, 383–407. doi: 10.1080/09541440143000140

Shelton, J. T., Elliott, E. M., Matthews, R. A., Hill, B., and Gouvier, W. D. (2010). The relationships of working memory, secondary memory, and general fluid intelligence: working memory is special. *J. Exp. Psychol. Learn. Mem. Cogn.* 36, 813–820. doi: 10.1037/a0019046

Signorelli, T. M., Haarmann, H. J., and Obler, L. K. (2012). Working memory in simultaneous interpreters: Effects of task and age. *Int. J. Biling.* 16, 198–212. doi: 10.1177/1367006911403200

Signorelli, T. M. (2008). *Working Memory in Simultaneous Interpreters*. Ph.D. thesis, CUNY, New York.

Soveri, A., Rodriguez-Fornells, A., and Laine, M. (2011). Is there a relationship between language switching and executive functions in bilingualism? Introducing a within group analysis approach. *Front. Psychol.* 2: 183. doi: 10.3389/fpsyg.2011.00183

Timarova, Š, Čeňkova, I., Meylaerts, R., Hertog, E., Szmalec, A., and Duyck, W. (2014). Simultaneous interpreting and working memory executive control. *Interpreting* 16, 139–168. doi: 10.1016/j.neuropsychologia.2017.01.008

Tzou, Y.-Z., Eslami, Z. R., Chen, H. C., and Vaid, J. (2012). Effect of language proficiency and degree of formal training in simultaneous interpreting on working memory and interpreting performance: evidence from Mandarin-English speakers. *Int. J. Biling.* 16, 213–227. doi: 10.1177/1367006911403197

Unsworth, N., Redick, T. S., Heitz, R. P., Broadway, J. M., and Engle, R. W. (2009). Complex working memory span tasks and higher-order cognition: a latent-variable analysis of the relationship between processing and storage. *Memory* 17,635 - 654. doi:10.1080/09658210902998047

Valian, V. (2015). Bilingualism and cognition. *Biling. Lang. Cogn.* 18,3 - 24. doi:10.1017/S1366728914000522

Xie, Z., and Dong, Y. (2017). Contributions of bilingualism and public speaking training to cognitive control differences among young adults. *Biling. Lang. Cogn.* 20,55 - 68. doi:10.1017/S1366728915000474

Zhang, W. (2008). A study of the effect of simultaneous interpreting on working memory's growth potential (In Chinese). *Mod. Foreign Lang.* 31,423 - 430.

方法谈：

实证类研究如何做到不止于描述层面？

本文通过研究案例重点介绍如何对采用实证方法特别是实验方法所收集的数据进行汇报与解读。论文的核心思想是，数据的汇报不能止于描述层面，而应紧扣研究问题，做到有理有据，以小见大，通过数据回应理论争议，深化认知。

研究案例考察的核心问题是语言经验如何影响执行功能。切入点是对比不同语言经验（连传训练 VS.一般外语学习）如何影响三个工作记忆任务的表现。语言经验影响执行功能的议题与当时学界关注的热点——双语优势息息相关。案例首先指出有关双语优势的研究结果不一致，指出导致不一致的重要因素之一是"问题的复杂性"——双语现象本身很复杂，囊括不同程度的语言转换与双语激活。类似地，口译译员的工作记忆优势也存在同样问题：口译本身很复杂，包括众多子过程与子成分；工作记忆也很复杂，也包括众多子过程与子成分。鉴于此，破局的关键是降低"问题的复杂性"。因此，有必要将这两个复杂过程进行分解，界定各自的子成分，然后考察其子成分之间的关系，而不仅仅是两者笼统的关系。

通过对连续口译任务的各个子成分进行了分析，我们认为：与普通外语学习中的听和说相比，连续传译的突出特点是需要快速准确地在目标语言中回忆源语信息。这个特点与工作记忆中的更新能力（updating）相匹配。工作记忆的更新能力指的是根据任务需求的变化,能够主动监控和修改工作记忆中的内容,涉及在工作记忆中添加、删除或修改信息的动态过程,以使其保持相关和最新。此外,口译要求译员以并行方式处理源语输入,即他们在处理源语的同时可能受到目标语言的影响,表明译员可能需要更高效的方式来处理源语言,从而能够更好地回忆细节并在言语工作记忆任务中表现更好。因此,我们提出以下假设:① 工作记忆的更新能力与连续口译的表现密切相关,连续口译训练可以增强更新能力;② 言语工作记忆广度可能与连续口译相关,连续口译训练可以增强言语工作记忆广度。

研究设计围绕这两个假设展开。核心自变量语言经验包括两个水平,操作化为连续传译组与一般外语学习组。工作记忆方面,采用 N-Back 任务测量更新能力,采用听力广度任务测量言语工作记忆广度,采用连续字母广度(letter running span)测量注意焦点(Focus of Attention, FOA)。为了确保研究结果的信效度,我们采取了两个措施:一是以"一般外语学习组"作为"连续传译组"的对照条件;二是将前测作为基线,同时匹配关键参数,保证两个组除了实验操纵外,在前测中没有差别。所有的设计都是为了确保后测数据的差异来源于实验操纵而不是其他混淆变量。

数据分析与解读围绕研究设计展开。首先,关注关键参数的匹配。从第 165 页表 1 可以看出,两组被试在年龄、外语水平、父母教育程度、智力、外语学习开始时间等关键参数上没有差别。此外,两组在三个工作记忆任务上的表现也没有统计学上的区别。这部分分析的结果表明,在前测时,两组被试可以视为同质的,为后测两组的比较奠定了坚实的基础。换言之,有了前测的基线,后测数据的差异就可以归因于实验操纵的不同。进一步的数据分析围绕两个方面展开:① 连续口译训练和一般外语训练在对工作记忆的影响上有何不同?② 工作记忆更新能力和言语广度与连续口译表现相关吗?分析结果主要有三点:① 在所有工作记忆指标中,仅前后测的 N-back 反应时间和前测听力广度与后测连续口译表现呈正相关;当将前测 N-back 反应时间和前测听力广度同时纳入回归模型时,N-back 反应时间显著预测后测连续口译表现,而听力广度的预测仅具有边际显著性;② 在 N-back 反应时间指标上,两组被试在后测中存在显著差异,连续口译组在后测中取得了显著进步,而对照组没有进步;而在 N-back 准确性指标上,两个群体在后测中均取得了进步;③ 在工作记忆广度的两个指标上,两个群体之间没有显著差异,两个群体在后测中的听力广度均有显著提高,而连续字母广度都没有改善。

就研究结果而言,最重要的发现是明确了工作记忆中的更新成分和连续口译之间的关系:更新效率可以预测连续口译的表现(见第169页表5),而连续口译训练可以增强更新效率(相比之下,一般外语训练则没有这种效果,见第167页表3)。这一发现回应了引言部分对连续口译任务的分析:在连续口译中,使用目标语回忆源语信息在准确性和速度方面要求高,相比之下,一般的外语学习中的听说并不具备相同的要求,而回忆的过程似乎与N-back任务中的更新过程非常相似。关于言语工作记忆广度与连续口译训练关系的第二个假设只得到部分支持:前测听力广度与连续口译表现相关,但当它与N-back反应时间指标一起进入同一回归模型时,预测效果仅具有边际显著性。

通过案例,我们可以看出:在报告数据时,我们不能仅停留在描述性的层面,而应该紧密围绕研究问题进行分析和解释,从细微之处看到更广泛的意义,并通过数据来回应理论上的争议。也就是说,每一步的分析背后都有明确的理论指导与目的。具体到本研究案例,第一步的数据分析旨在阐明在前测阶段对两组被试进行了关键参数的匹配,确保后测数据的差异可以归因于实验操纵。其次的分析旨在明确连续口译训练对工作记忆更新能力有积极的影响,表明更新效率可以预测连续口译的表现。相比之下,一般外语学习训练没有相同的效果。最后的分析则明确连续口译训练对工作记忆广度没有直接的影响,尽管前测的听力广度与后测的连续口译表现存在一定的相关性。

基于语料库的动词与构式关系研究*
——以 sneeze 及物动词用法的规约化为例

王仁强　陈和敏**

摘要：动词与构式的关系是构式语法中的一个热点问题,而类似于 Goldberg (1995) 经典例证 Pat sneezed the napkin off the table 中的 sneeze 在当代英语词库中是否已然是及物动词,是一个颇具争议的问题。本文结合语言使用理论及常规与拓展理论,基于五个大型的历时/共时英语语料库,以当代英语中 sneeze 及物动词用法的规约化为例,对动词与构式的关系问题进行研究。结果表明,词库与句法虽构成连续体,但二者的区别也不可忽视;动词与构式存在双向互动关系,动词本身的属性也会因在构式中反复使用而发生变化。鉴于 sneeze 及物动词用法具有超高的类型频率、较高的个例频率、久远的时间跨度和广泛的使用语域,该用法在当代英语中已经规约化,可以从言语层面句法中的用法抽象为语言层面词库中的用法,并录入大中型当代英语词典。研究发现,前人研究之所以出现结论偏差,一方面是因为没有使用自下而上的语料库方法,从而难以区分语言层面词库中的词类和言语层面句法中的词类,另一方面则是因为以偏概全的逻辑错误。

关键词：语言使用理论；常规与拓展理论；构式；动词；规约化

---

* 原载《外语教学与研究(外国语文双月刊)》2014 年第 1 期。《外语教学与研究》编辑部匿名评审专家以及广东外语外贸大学王初明教授、冉永平教授和湖南大学刘正光教授曾对本文提出过宝贵意见,特此致谢！文中任何错讹之处概由作者负责。

** 王仁强,四川外国语大学副校长、教授,博士生导师,博士后合作导师。兼任中国高等教育学会外语教学研究分会副理事长,中国辞书学会常务理事兼学术委员会委员,国内外多家重要期刊匿名审稿专家。重庆市学术技术带头人,重庆英才·创新领军人才,重庆市高校哲学社会科学协同创新团队和重庆市研究生导师团队带头人。主要从事词典学、认知语言学、对比语言学、语言类型学和语料库语言学研究,近年来聚焦词类问题与和量子语言学研究。

陈和敏,四川外国语大学硕士研究生,研究方向为词典学。

一、引　言

动词与构式的关系问题近年来受到越来越多的关注(Goldberg，1995，2006；Fauconnier & Turner，1996；Lakoff & Johnson，1999；Langacker，2005；Boas，2008；Barsalou et al.，2010；Herbst，2010)。Goldberg(1995：9—19)认为，不同构式中的动词意义基本保持不变，而完整表达式的意义差异多半源于不同的构式。比如，在 Pat sneezed the napkin off the table 这个句子中，致使移动构式[NP+V+NP+PP]具有独立于动词本身而存在的致使移动义，而 sneeze 出现在句中是构式压制的结果，致使移动构式把致使义传承给了 sneeze，其固有的不及物动词属性并没有改变。Fauconnier & Turner(1996)从概念整合理论的角度对上述结构进行了探讨，并基本认同 Goldberg 的观点。Lakoff & Johnson(1999：502)也认为 sneeze 基本上是一个不及物动词，本身不带宾语或方向副词，sneeze 出现在该句中并产生新义主要是致使移动构式(而非构式中词项)的贡献。不过，Langacker(2005：147—153)认为，Goldberg 所谓"构式意义最大化而动词意义最小化"的立场走向了极端：当 sneeze 用于致使构式的时候，sneeze 就涌现为致使动词，因而存在动词意义引申，但是 sneeze 的这个用法并未规约化，只是临时性用法。Barsalou et al.(2010：340)基本认同 Goldberg 有关构式压制的解释，认为不及物动词 sneeze 不像 push 那样可以直接带宾语，因而我们可以说 Melanie pushes the pillow，但不可以说 Melanie sneezes the pillow；而 Lisa sneezed the foam off her beer 之所以完全符合语法，是因为 sneeze 被嵌入致使构式中而获得了合理解读；最重要的是，当一个类似 sneeze 这样的不及物动词被插入致使构式中时，动词的及物特征就被压制到这个动词中，不及物动词因此获得了及物特征。Herbst(2010：243—245)认为，sneeze 在 She sneezed the foam off the cappuccino 中的及物动词用法尚未规约化，该用法不应收入词典，除非该用法得到更加频繁地使用。

遗憾的是，上述研究均为基于语感的理论思辨而非基于真实语料分析的实证研究。Pat sneezed the napkin off the table 这个例子本身是由 Goldberg 自创的，而 Melanie sneezes the pillow 这个不合语法的例子也是 Barsalou 等人杜撰的。那么，当代英语中 sneeze 的及物动词用法是否仅限于致使移动构式[NP+V+NP+PP]？Sneeze 的及物动词用法是否仅限于跟介词短语 off 搭配？

Sneeze 的及物动词用法始于何时,使用频率如何,使用范围如何? 换言之,当代英语中的 sneeze 是否已经衍生出规约化的及物动词用法?

虽然构式语法对新颖用法具有较强解释力,但其恒定意义假设(invariant meaning hypothesis)和压制理论并不能充分解释语言的历时演变(Bybee, 2010: 183—187)。有鉴于此,本文拟结合语言使用理论和常规与拓展理论,以五个大型的历时/共时英语语料库为数据基础,对当代英语中 sneeze 及物动词用法的规约化情况进行研究,以期深化对动词与构式以及词库与句法关系的研究。

二、研究设计

语言使用理论(Usage-based Theory)认为,语言从本质上讲是一个复杂适应系统,语言结构始终处于动态变化之中,语言结构是在使用中涌现出来的,而使用频率在语言结构的固化和规约化过程中扮演着重要角色(Langacker, 2000, 2004; Barlow & Kemmer, 2000; Bybee, 2001, 2010; Bybee & Hopper, 2001;王仁强,2011)。换言之,"语言使用与语言系统之间存在着辩证关系:语法不仅仅构成用于语言使用的知识库,其本身还是语言使用的产物"(Kristiansen & Geeraerts, 2013: 2)。前一个视角把使用事件视为语言系统具体的、实际的示例。据此,我们可以通过分析例示语言系统的使用事件洞察语言系统。而从后一个观点看,使用事件以一种动态的方式定义和不断重新定义语言系统。规约化指存在于一个语言社团全体成员脑子里的模式和常规,而规约化程度可通过语料库方法进行检测(Langacker, 2004: 49)。鉴于规约化体现为语言社团中的语言演变,基于语料库的语言特征变化调查除了考察该特征的语言联结模式之外,尚需考察其非语言联结模式,如语域分布、历时分布等(Biber, 2000: 289)。

常规与拓展理论(Theory of Norms and Exploitations)是著名词典学家兼语料库语言学家 Patrick Hanks 在其新著 *Lexical Analysis: Norms and Exploitations*(2013)中完整阐释的语言学理论。这是一个基于词库、语料库驱动、自下而上的语言学理论,因而与语言使用理论具有很好的兼容性。根据常规与拓展理论,每个词的规约允准用法只有通过概率方式界定,对其搭配和配价进行统计分析,最好采用多种统计方式,并运用多个语料库(Hanks, 2013: 382—383)。

有鉴于此，在综合考察各大语料库的语言代表性及其适用性之后，我们选取了英国国家语料库（British National Corpus，BNC）、当代美语语料库（Corpus of Contemporary American English，COCA）、《时代》杂志语料库（Time Magazine Corpus of American English，TIME）、历时美语语料库（Corpus of Historical American English，COHA）和英国网络语料库（British English Web Corpus，ukWaC）来检索 sneeze 做及物动词用法的实例，从使用频率（含个例频率和类型频率）、使用域以及使用年代等方面进行分析。其中，BNC 是一个封闭语料库，收录了自 20 世纪 80 年代至 1993 年的口语与书面语语料库，库容为 1 亿词。COCA、TIME 和 COHA 均由美国杨百翰大学 Mark Davies 教授研发，其中 COCA 涵盖了从 1990 至今的各种类型语料，为当今最大的免费使用的共时平衡语料库，库容为 4.5 亿词。TIME 收录了自 1923 年至 2006 年期间 Time 杂志上的全部文章，库容为 1 亿词。COHA 收录了自 1810 年至 2009 年的美语语料，库容为 4 亿词。ukWaC 由 Adriano Ferraresi 教授研发，全部语料来源于英国域名的网站，共收入超过 15 亿词。以上五个语料库中，BNC、COCA 和 ukWaC 为共时语料库，TIME 和 COHA 为历时语料库。

在数据收集处理过程中，我们首先从各个语料库中检索出 sneeze 做动词用法的所有实例，然后再人工筛选出其做及物动词的全部实例。接着对全部及物动词用法数据进行如下分析：对各个语料库中 sneeze 的及物用法进行统计，计算其个例频率；由于及物结构本身具有众多差异性，我们针对每个及物构式本身进行分析，考察 sneeze 在及物结构中出现的不同构式，分析其类型频率；最后统计 sneeze 及物用法出现的时间和语域，以期发现其历时演变和共时普及情况。

三、调 查 结 果

1. 个例频率

如表 1 所示，sneeze 做及物动词的用法在五个语料库中均有显现，共有 96 例，约占其动词用法总数的 2.1%。进一步分析得知，其在共时语料库中共 52 例，平均比例为 1.69%；在历时语料库中 44 例，平均比例约为 2.71%。尤为引人注意的是，在当今最大的共时美语语料库 COCA 与最大历时美语语料库 COHA 中的出现比例更高，分别是 2.58% 和 3.13%。

表 1　sneeze 及物动词用法在五大语料库中的分布

	及物用法		不及物用法		合　计
	词　频	百分比	词　频	百分比	
BNC	2	1.28	154	98.72	156
COCA	29	2.58	1 096	97.42	1 125
TIME	5	2.29	213	97.71	218
COHA	39	3.13	1 209	96.87	1 248
ukWaC	21	1.2	1 729	98.8	1 750
平均比例		2.1		97.9	
词频合计	96		4 401		4 497

2. 类型频率

如表 2 所示，sneeze 不仅出现在 Goldberg(1995)所论述的[NP+SNEEZE+PP+NP]中，还出现在[NP+SNEEZE+NP]、[NP+SNEEZE+NP+AdvP]、[NP+SNEEZE+NP+Adj]和[NP+SNEEZE+NP+NP]中。其中，[NP+SNEEZE+NP+AdvP]居首，共 33 例，占总数的 34.38%。其次是[NP+SNEEZE+NP]和[NP+SNEEZE+NP+PP]，分别是 28 例和 30 例，占总数的 31.25%和 29.17%。

表 2　Sneeze 在各类及物构式中的分布（类型频数）

	BNC	COCA	TIME	COHA	ukWaC	共计
SNEEZE+NP		11	1	10	6	28
SNEEZE+NP+PP	1	12	3	8	6	30
SNEEZE+NP+AdvP	1	4	1	19	8	33
SNEEZE+NP+Adj		1				1
SNEEZE+NP+NP		1		2	1	4
合　计	2	29	5	39	21	96

进一步调查 sneeze 做及物动词的不同构式，我们发现，sneeze 与部分词的共现呈现出一定规律性。在 33 例[NP+SNEEZE+NP+AdvP]中，sneeze sth off 共有 18 例，sneeze sth out 共 12 例，sneeze sth away 共 2 例，sneeze sth everywhere 有一例。其中,sneeze sth off 中,以 sneeze one's head off 这一用法最为突出。Sneeze sth out 中,sneeze one's heart/brain out 也较为突出。而在[NP+SNEEZE+NP+PP]中,sneeze 能与九个介词共现,Goldberg(1995)论述的与介词 off 共现的例子仅出现 1 例,而与 into、to、over 和 out of 的共现更为突出。详见表 3。

表 3 [NP+SNEEZE+NP+PP]构式中的介词共现频数

介词	into	to	over	out of	through	around	onto	off	from
词频	10	6	5	4	2	2	1	1	1

3. 历时分布

根据 COHA,sneeze 的及物动词用法最早出现在 1845 年 Henry William Herbert 的小说 *The Warwick Woodlands or Things as They Were There Ten Years Ago* 中,一共出现两次,并且刚好出现在两个连贯的段落中:

"Begging your pardon, Measter Archer,"…, when Measter McTavish *sneezed* me clean oot o' t' wagon!

"What's that? — what the devil's that?" cried I;…, and the next of his *sneezing* a man out of a phaeton.

如表 4 所示,160 余年来 sneeze 及物动词用法在 COHA 中稳步增长:

表 4 sneeze 及物动词用法在 COHA 中使用年代调查

时 间 跨 度	词 频
the 1840s—the 1900s	11
the 1910s—the 1950s	13
the 1960s—the 2000s	15

4. 语域分布

如表 5 所示,sneeze 的及物动词用法分布在 COCA 所收录的四大语域中,其中小说和杂志分布最多。

表 5　sneeze 及物动词用法在 COCA 中语域分布情况

	小　说	杂　志	学术期刊	口　语	合　计
词　频	14	12	1	2	29
百分比	48.28%	41.38%	3.45%	6.91%	100%

四、讨　论

1. 词类判断的标准、层面和程序

词类判断的标准、层面和程序存在一种错综复杂的关系。词类判断的标准出错、层面选错或程序出错都会导致词类判断的结果出错。

关于词类判断标准的问题，学界有诸多论述，但认知语法的最新研究表明，尽管词类判断中意义有着重要参考作用，但语法功能才是最终判断依据。Langacker(2009：240—241)指出，"一个词的语法行为才是判断其语法范畴的关键因素。概念内容是无法事先定为名词性内容或动词性内容的。常有的情况是，相同的词汇内容要么体现为不同的词，要么体现为兼类词的不同义项。因而，在实践中，一个词的词类是通过确定其所参与的构式来判断的"。其中，"所参与的构式"实际上体现的是其可以充当的语法功能，这体现了语言使用理论的基本主张，即语言知识是从使用中涌现出来的。其实，Langacker 在论证主要词类的语义刻画时，往往首先举出一个体现研究对象语法功能的构式，然后在分析其语义刻画基础上判断其词类属性。但这仅仅是言语层面句法中的词类属性，并不一定等同于规约化的语言系统层面词库中的词类，因而词类判断的标准必须结合词类判断的层面和程序。

关于词类判断的层面和程序，学界也存在重要分歧，但结论渐趋明朗。在汉语、英语、越南语、泰语等分析语或孤立语中，语法多功能现象比较突出(Robins, 1989：214)，由此触发了有关词类判断的层面和程序的探讨。针对古汉语字类与句子成分之间的不完全对应情况，马建忠(1898：8)提出"字无定义，故无定类"，实际上只认可古汉语句法层面的词类。黎锦熙(1924：6)在探讨汉语词类时指出，"凡词，依句辩品，离句无品"。换言之，在黎锦熙当时看来，现代汉语也是"词无定类"，词类只存在于句法中，因而也没有词类分层问题。但是，在《新著国语文法》1951年再版序言中,黎锦熙已经意识到词类分层问题,并指出:《新著国语文法》说"凡词,依句辩品"是对的,但"离句无品"之说是错的(黎锦熙,1992:序言,21)。基于索绪尔的语言学思想,Jespersen(1924:62)明确指出,"孤立地看,英语中很多词都可以兼属一个以上的词类;但在每个特定的应用中,它们都只能归属某个单一词类"。这是有关词类分层的最早研究,前者指语言层面词库中的词类归属,后者指言语层面句法中的词类归属,但Jespersen在指出两个层面词类区别的同时,并未明确指出它们之间是否存在联系。郭锐(2002:89—90)区分了现代汉语词汇(即词库)层面的词类属性和句法层面的词类属性,但他认为,"词汇层面的词性就是词语固有的词性,需在词典中标明;句法层面的词性是词语在使用中产生的,需要句法规则控制"。显然,郭锐的观点与Jespersen的观点类似,但明显割裂了词库层面词类与句法层面词类之间的关联。Dash(2005:140)指出,每个词从功能上讲有两个语境实体:一是脱离语境的词库实体,二是依赖语境的句法实体。尽管在词库层面,一个词因其具有多义的可能性而可以兼属多种词类,其最终的词类归属和意义取决于句法层面的使用语境。换言之,决定一个词拥有何种语法角色和意义的正是句法。由此观之,Dash(2005)在Jespersen(1924)的基础上有所发展,即一方面区分了词库层面和句法层面的词类,同时还指出了其中的有机联系(词库层面的词类源于句法层面的词类),但是句法层面的词类是否一定等同于词汇层面的词类却并不明晰。结合语言使用理论和语料库方法,王仁强(2010)提出,一个语言层面词库中的词的词类判断应该建立在使用模式调查的基础上,这有助于发现其无标记语法功能(即规约化用法),从而有效区分语言系统层面词库中的词类和言语层面句法中的词类。鉴于语言与言语存在辩证关系,语言演变呈现一种双螺旋结构(Hanks,2013:411),因此王仁强(2010)的观点既揭示了语言系统层面词库中的词类和言语层面句法中的词类区别,又指出了其中的有机联系:语言系统层面词库中的词类源于言语层面句法中的词类,但句法中的词类不完全等同于词库中的词类,只有在句法中体现了规约化的词类属性才等同于词库中的词类。鉴于"词汇常规用法可以视为语言系统的一部分,但这些常规用法只有通过大规模语料库分析方能发现"(Hanks,2013:350),因此王仁强(2010)的观点与常规与拓展理论的主张不谋而合。

2. Sneeze及物动词用法的涌现与规约化

根据王仁强(2010),可以肯定的是,上述语料库中sneeze接宾语的用法首先是言语层面句法中的及物动词,这一点与 Langacker(2005) 和 Barsalou *et al.*(2010) 的看法基本一致,而是否为语言系统层面词库中的及物动词尚待证实。

上述调查表明,sneeze 的及物动词用法在五个共时和历时语料库中均有一定的用例,但相对于其不及物动词用法,其及物动词用法的个例频率不够高;sneeze 及物动词用法的类型频率很高:涉及五类及物构式,其中[NP+SNEEZE+NP+PP]构式中就涉及九个不同的搭配介词;sneeze 及物动词用法最早出现在 1845 年,延续至今已有近 170 年的使用历史;在 COCA 中,sneeze 的及物动词用法使用域非常广泛,包括小说、杂志、学术期刊和口语,其中在小说中最具有凸显意义。根据 Langacker(2004:49) 和 Biber(2000:289),我们认为,sneeze 的及物动词用法已经具有较高的规约化程度。但是,相对于其不及物动词用法,其及物动词用法的个例频率毕竟并不高:在当今最大的共时美语语料库 COCA 与最大历时美语语料库 COHA 中的出现比例分别是 2.58% 和 3.13%。鉴于语文词典的处理对象是语言中词项的规约化用法(Hanks 1990:32),这是否说明 sneeze 及物动词用法的规约化程度尚未达到语言系统层面的词库中并收入词典呢?我们认为,情况并非如此,因为个例频率并不是规约化程度最重要或唯一的指标。

以 mother 和 father 为例,根据 COCA,mother 共有用例 193 481 条,其中动词用例 219 条,仅占 0.11%,而 father 共有用例 166 073 条,其中动词用例 905 条,仅占 0.54%。但是,在 2006 年出版的 *The American Heritage Dictionary of the English Language*(第 4 版)和 2011 年出版的 *The Oxford Advanced American Dictionary* 中,mother 和 father 两个词条在(语言社团)语言系统层面词库中均处理为名动兼类词。

鉴于个例频率促成个体词例的固化/规约化,类型频率促成更抽象图式的固化/规约化(Evans & Green, 2006:188),而类型频率与语言结构的能产性关系密切(Bybee, 2010:95),加之 sneeze 及物动词用法久远的时间跨度和广泛的使用语域,我们认为,sneeze 及物动词用法具有很高的规约化程度,可以考虑收入大中型语文词典。正如 Leech(2006:115) 所言,英语中有不少动词(如 open 和 finish)在不同语境中分别充当及物动词和不及物动词。有鉴于此,把 sneeze 视为在语言系统层面词库中兼属及物动词和不及物动词并不为怪。

3. 动词与构式的关系

上述调查表明,sneeze 的及物动词用法并非临时的新颖用法,而是规约化程度很高的用法,在当代英语语言系统层面词库中兼属及物动词和不及物动词。

有鉴于此,Goldberg(1995,2006)否认 sneeze 衍生及物动词义的观点,以及 Langacker(2005)、Barsalou et al.(2010)和 Herbst(2010)等人认为 sneeze 及物动词用法是新颖用法的观点都不成立。我们认为,他们的研究结论之所以会出现偏差,一方面是因为其结论并非基于语料库调查得出。虽然 Langacker(2005)正确指出 Goldberg(1995)所谓 sneeze 是否具有及物动词义这个问题的实质是看 sneeze 及物动词用法是否规约化,而规约化的程度可通过语料库研究来客观测量,但 Langacker 本人并未亲自实践。针对现有构式语法研究存在的问题,Boas(2008)也呼吁构式语法研究采取一种基于语料库的自下而上的研究路径方能走出困境。另一方面,还因为上述学者在研究中犯了一个以偏概全的逻辑错误:sneeze 在 Pat sneezed the napkin off the table 这个句子中的用法显得新奇并不等于它在所有致使构式实例中都是新颖的用法,更不等于其所有及物动词用法都是新颖的用法。

Goldberg(1995,2006)主张词汇对整个句子的意义应该减到最小,而将意义赋予构式,认为这样可以避免额外添加动词义。例(1)即是上文讨论的 Goldberg(1995:156)在说明致使移动构式存在的相关论述中列举的例子:

(1) Fred sneezed the napkin off the table.

她认为,此构式中的动词本身并不允准直接后接宾语,构式所以成立是因为致使移动构式的存在赋予它三个论元。在进一步论述中,她认为 sneeze 之所以是不及物动词,是因为本句两个述义 Sneeze(Fred, the-napkin)和 Off(the-napkin, the-table)中,第一个述义没有任何意义。然而,我们认为这个解释非常牵强。众所周知,当人们因为感冒或受到冷空气、粉尘、花粉等刺激而打喷嚏时,通常会有一股强烈的气流从鼻腔和口腔喷出,因而打喷嚏的过程是一个力量传递的过程,这与及物本身所传达的意义是一致的。而基于生活常识,除了气体和鼻涕之类的东西外,一般不会有其他物质能够从鼻腔或口腔中喷出,因而出现类似例(2)中 green mucus(绿色的鼻涕)这样的宾语就再自然不过了:

(2) You probably have not seen a baby *sneeze* green mucus because we sneeze for a variety of reasons, not just when we have colds. (COCA, 2000)

而且，正如表 5 所示，COCA 里的 sneeze 及物动词用法中，接近一半源于小说语域。以下 14 个例子就是从 COCA 小说语域中筛选出来的完整用法：

(3) It would also be nice if I shat golden ingots and *sneezed* harlots. (COCA，2010)

(4) Navin *sneezed* blue pollen onto his shirt. (COCA，2010)

(5) This incidental fact disturbs Salim and he begins feeling like one of the pet psychologists on the morning magazine shows in Montral, the ones who made him *sneeze* cereal-milk through his nose. (COCA，2007)

(6) He whined, sniffed, and *sneezed* a wet circle around her, then attempted a series of licks repelled by the hand of my wife. (COCA，2006)

(7) And then our pirate forebears arrived, swilling brandy and *sneezing* mainland diseases all over them. (COCA，2006)

(8) She'd sing a stupid solo part—the Waterfall, they called it— not even something she'd invented or planned to do who knows how many years ago when she'd had to *sneeze* her brains out. (COCA，2002)

(9) Eighty bucks? For standin' around all day? You used to *sneeze* eighty bucks. (COCA，2002)

(10) The sudden motion made me heave and *sneeze* an ungodly water, a fuliginous gray stew thick with tubes like black licorice. (COCA，2000)

(11) But I never wanted Arizona for the air conditioning. The coolers set me off. I *sneezed* pure rocket fuel for five minutes then pushed away from the fence, to walk along the track. (COCA，1997)

(12) So it was that, at age 60, King Shabaka, short-winded and feeling cheated, lived alongside but not exactly with his Queen, who — if the truth be told — often asked Allah to *sneeze* her

into the afterworld where her faith and loving kindness would be better appreciated. (COCA, 1996)

(13) He took a deep breath and the mingled dust went right up his nose and the next thing you know, he was *sneezing* sonnets. (COCA, 1994)

(14) Richie, it's easier to clap hands to shut off the television than it is to *sneeze* it off. (COCA, 1993)

(15) The Abbe's exasperation was now greater even than the time he *sneezed* a crucible of gold dust over the flames of an open hearth. (COCA, 1992)

(16) Lyman Mays prodded the fire with an iron poker until it *sneezed* a shower of sparks. (COCA, 1990)

研究表明,尽管 Goldberg(1995,2006)提及动词与构式的双向互动,但在实际论述中却过于强调构式对动词的单向压制,强调动词意义最小化,而忽略了动词由于在构式中反复使用而对其语法特征所产生的影响。"动词意义最小化"这个主张看似合理,实则与乔姆斯基"自上而下"的研究是一脉相承的(Boas,2008:126)。Michaelis(2006)采用"恒定意义假设"和压制理论来解释词汇意义和语法意义不兼容时新颖意义的涌现,其"恒定意义假设"与 Goldberg"动词意义最小化"如出一辙。但正如 Bybee(2010:183—187)所指出的那样,"恒定意义假设"和压制理论对创新用法具有很强的解释力,但并不能有效解释语言结构和意义在使用中可能发生的历时演变——创新用法的固化乃至规约化。语言使用理论认为,语法意义与语法形式都是由于反复使用而形成的(Bybee,2006:713),而语言单位的每次使用都会对其固化/规约化程度有正面影响(Langacker,1987:59)。

上述基于语料库的调查和基于百科知识的分析也能在理论上找到佐证。Fillmore(1982)认为,对词语或构式的理解应该基于认知框架,而认知框架的形成一方面源于个人经验,另一方面又经常受到社会文化意识的影响。在认知语法中,Langacker(2008)认为词的概念义并不能展现其用法的全貌,而应看其在相关认知域中的识解,其焦点与凸显角度不同就会表现为不同的用法。据此,我们认为,sneeze 所显现的不同用法可以用下图直观展现:

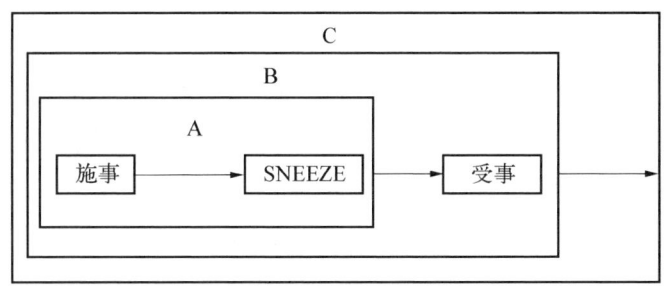

图 1　sneeze 动词用法的凸显

如图 1 所示,与 sneeze 相关的框架共有三种。框架 A 凸显 SNEEZE 动词本身,由此而产生类似 Fred sneezed 这样的句子。框架 B 凸显伴随 SNEEZE 而产生的物质,由此产出类似 Fred sneezed mucus 这样的句子。而框架 C 凸显了伴随 SNEEZE 这一动作所发出的气体对外界事物造成的影响和结果,因而出现类似 Fred sneezed the napkin off the table 这样的句子。

动词与构式关系的实质是词库与句法的关系,而词库与句法的关系问题在不同语言学流派中的观点有所不同。乔姆斯基等生成语言学派认为,词库与句法有严格的区分,但该模式中的词项信息往往是不充分的,这种自上而下的研究路径存在问题(Boas,2008:115—117)。Goldberg、Langacker 和 Croft 等所倡导的构式语法认为,词库与句法无严格的区分,二者构成连续体。Sinclair(2004:165)则认为,语法(句法)与词库相互渗透,不用严格区分。Boas(2008:120—126)深刻指出,尽管与乔姆斯基等生成语法相比,Goldberg 构式语法关于动词与构式互动的观点拥有不少优势,但也面临三大困境:① 有时并不清楚动词义与构式义的融合是怎样受到限制的;② 难以界定动词后论元的语义范围;③ 难以基于语义类别预测一个动词的论元范围。Boas 认为,之所以出现上述问题,是因为词项与有意义的语法构式的互动关系很难限制。他提议采取基于语料库的自下而上的研究路径来克服上述困难。鉴于常规与拓展理论是一个基于词库、语料库驱动、自下而上的语言学理论,Hanks(2013:390)指出,其对构式语法形成重要补充:构式语法旨在解释所有可能用法(包括特异用法),而常规与拓展理论则旨在解释规约化用法。本项基于语料库的研究表明,词库与句法的关系既非生成语言学派所主张的简单的二元对立,也非构式语法所倡导的二者构成连续体强调句法淡化词库的观点。

基于语言使用理论和常规与拓展理论,我们认为,鉴于语言是一个复杂适应系统,语言使用与语言系统存在辩证关系,语言演变呈现出双螺旋结构,语言系统层面词库中的用法虽然是词的用法潜势,但词库中的用法源于言语层面句法中规约化用法模式的抽象。换言之,只有通过语料库使用模式调查在言语层面句法中体现规约化用法的词类属性,才等同于语言层面词库中的词类。这样就既体现了词库与句法构成连续体,同时又强调了句法与词库之间的区别和联系。鉴于词典的收录对象是规约化的词汇单位及其意义和用法,表征的是语言层面词库中语言单位的意义潜势(Hanks, 2013: 87),言语层面句法中的词类和语言层面词库中的词类区分对于词典学之类的语言描写研究就显得尤为重要。因此,区分语言层面词库中的词类与言语层面句法中的词类,不仅有重要的语言学意义,而且还具有很强的应用价值。

五、结　　论

词库与句法虽构成连续体,但二者的区别仍不可忽视;动词与构式存在双向互动关系,恒定意义假设和压制理论不能完整解释语言的历时演变;语言使用理论和常规与拓展理论很好地解释了词项的词类属性规约化以及词项与构式的关系问题,而自下而上的语料库研究路径能有效克服构式语法研究的某些弊端。

参考文献

Barlow, M. & S. Kemmer (eds.). (2000), *Usage-based Models of Language*. Stanford: CSLI Publications.

Barsalou, L., C. Wilson & W. Hasenkamp (2010), On the vices of nominalization and the virtues of contextualizing. In B. Mesquita, L. Barrett & E. Smith(eds.). *The Mind in Context*. New York: The Guilford Press. 334-360.

Biber, D. (2000), Investigating language use through corpus-based analyses of association patterns. In M. Barlow & S. Kemmer(eds.). 2000. 287-313.

Boas, H. (2008), Determining the structure of lexical entries and grammatical constructions in construction grammar. *Annual Review of*

Cognitive Linguistics 6: 113 – 144.

Bybee, J. (2001), *Phonology and Language Use*. Cambridge: CUP.

Bybee, J. (2006), From usage to grammar: The mind's response to repetition. *Language* 82: 711 – 733.

Bybee, J. (2010), *Language, Usage and Cognition*. Cambridge: CUP.

Bybee, J. & P. Hopper(eds.). (2001), *Frequency and the Emergence of Linguistic Structure*. Amsterdam: John Benjamins.

Dash, N. (2005), *Corpus Linguistics and Language Technology*. New Delhi: Mittal.

Evans, V. & M. Green(2006), *Cognitive Linguistics: An Introduction*. Edinburgh: Edinburgh University Press.

Fauconnier, G. & M. Turner (1996), Blending as central process of grammar. In A. Goldberg (ed.). *Conceptual Structure, Discourse, and Language*. Stanford: Center for the Study of Language and Information. 1 – 22.

Fillmore, C. (1982), Frame semantics. In Linguistic Society of Korea(ed.). *Linguistics in the Morning Calm*. Seoul: Hanshin Publishing. 111 –137.

Goldberg, A. (1995), *Constructions: A Construction Grammar Approach to Argument Structure*. Chicago: The University of Chicago Press.

Goldberg, A. (2006), *Constructions at Work*. Oxford: OUP.

Hanks, P. (1990), Evidence and intuition in lexicography. In J. Tomaszczyk & B. Lewan-dowska-Tomaszczyk (eds.). *Meaning and Lexicography*. Amsterdam: John Benhamins. 31 – 41.

Hanks, P. (2013), *Lexical Analysis: Norms and Exploitations*. Cambridge, MA.: The MIT Press.

Herbst, T. (2010), Valency constructions and clause constructions or how, if at all, valency grammarians might *sneeze the foam off the cappuccino*. In H. Schmid & S. Handl (eds.). *Cognitive Foundations of Linguistic Usage Patterns: Empirical Studies*. Berlin: Walter de Gruyter. 225 – 255.

Jespersen, O. (1924), *The Philosophy of Grammar*. London: George Allen and Unwin Ltd.

Kristiansen, G. & D. Geeraerts(2013), Introduction: Context and usage in cognitive sociolinguistics. *Journal of Pragmatics* 52: 1-4.

Lakoff, G. & M. Johnson(1999), *Philosophy in the Flesh*. New York: Basic Books.

Langacker, R. (1987), *Foundations of Cognitive Grammar. Vol. I: Theoretical Prerequisites*. Stanford, CA.: Stanford University Press.

Langacker, R. (2000), A dynamic usage-based model. In M. Barlow & S. Kemmer(eds.). 2000. 1-63.

Langacker, R. (2004), Form, meaning and behavior. In E. Contini-Morava, R. Kirsner & B. Rodríguez-Bachiller (eds.). *Cognitive and Communicative Approaches to Linguistic Analysis*. Amsterdam: John Benjamins. 21-60.

Langacker, R. (2005), Construction Grammars: Cognitive, radical, and less so. In M. Cervel & F. de Mendoza Ibáñez(eds.). *Cognitive Linguistics: Internal Dynamics and Interdisciplinary Interaction*. Berlin: Mouton de Gruyter. 101-159.

Langacker, R. (2008), *Cognitive Grammar: A Basic Introduction*. Oxford: OUP.

Langacker, R. (2009), Constructions and constructional meaning. In V. Evans & S. Pourcel(eds.). *New Directions in Cognitive Linguistics*. Amsterdam: John Benjamins. 225-267.

Leech, G. (2006), *A Glossary of English Grammar*. Edinburgh: Edinburgh University Press.

Michaelis, L. (2006), Tense in English. In B. Aarts & A. MacMahon(eds.). *The Handbook of English Linguistics*. Oxford: Blackwell. 220-234.

Robins, R. (1989), *General Linguistics: An Introductory Survey*. London: Longman.

Sinclair, J. (2004), *Trust the Text*. London: Routledge.

郭 锐:《现代汉语词类研究》,商务印书馆2002年版。

黎锦熙:《新著国语文法》,商务印书馆1924年版。

黎锦熙:《新著国语文法》,商务印书馆1992年版。

马建忠:《马氏文通》,商务印书馆1898年版。

王仁强:《现代汉语词类体系效度研究——以〈现代汉语词典〉(第5版)词类体系为例》,《外语教学与研究》2010年第5期,第380—386页。

王仁强:"Usage-based theory(UBT): A milestone in American functionalism",《中国外语》2011年第6期,第83—89页。

方法谈:

如何提升语言学论文讨论和结论部分的站位?

在实证论文中,讨论部分是最难写但又是最关键的部分,很多论文被退稿往往就是因为讨论部分存在缺陷。在这个部分,研究者须结合相关理论对研究结果进行全面深入的讨论分析,引出关键问题并提出相关解释和解决方法。在讨论中,要让读者明白研究的价值和意义所在,并结合研究问题和引言中所涉及的研究背景对研究结果进行讨论。在讨论部分的结尾处,要对结果的意义进行概括或者给出结论,从而有助于向读者传达研究的核心发现或贡献。讨论部分一般涵盖以下内容:研究中最重要的发现,这些发现的意义,你的发现与其他研究有何关联,你的发现的局限性,对任何意外的、不清楚的或令人惊讶的结果进行解释,以及对后续研究的建议。需要注意的是,不要讨论任何论文中没有描述过的结果或数据。同理,除非数据支持你的结论,否则不要轻易下结论。

讨论部分要紧扣研究问题,并对研究结果进行解释和探讨。讨论部分是对结果的讨论,讨论内容应与引言部分的研究问题形成呼应。没有在引言部分提出问题,往往造成在讨论部分无话可说。本文的核心问题是:动词与构式的关系是什么?这是构式语法研究中的热点和难点问题。围绕这个核心问题还有两个连锁问题:一个是表层问题(即论文副标题所涉及的问题),同时也是构式语法研究中讨论动词和构式关系时常常提及的问题,即当代英语中sneeze带宾语是否是及物动词,以及如果是及物动词,其及物动词用法是否规约化?另一个是延伸的深层次问题,即在回答好动词与构式的关系问题的基础上回应词库和句法的关系问题。有鉴于此,本文的讨论分成三节进行:一是讨论词类判断的标准、层面和程序;二是讨论sneeze及物动词用法的涌现与规约化;三是讨论动词与构式关系,顺带延伸讨论词库和句法的关系。三个部分环环相扣,步步推进。

本文之所以首要讨论词类判断的标准、层面和程序，是因为词类问题是一个千年谜题①，词类判断的标准出错、层面选错或程序出错都会导致词类判断的结果出错。通过理论梳理强调了句法层面的（个体词）的词类在句法功能、语用功能（命题言语行为功能）和概念化语义之间的密切关联，同时还揭示了判断（社群）词库中（概括词）词类的关键是考察相关词类用法的规约化问题，即综合考虑相关用法的个例频率、类型频率、时间跨度和语域分布四项标准。这个部分其实实际上构成了王仁强系统阐释的双层词类范畴化理论②的雏形。双层词类范畴化理论运用了量子思维和超学科研究方法论的四大公理，有助于破解词类这个千年谜题。

在这个理论铺垫的基础上，第二节的讨论一方面指出语料库索引行中 sneeze 带宾语的个体词用法都是及物动词，且这种看法与 Langacker（2005）和 Barsalou 等（2010）的观点一致，但另一方面又结合结果部分所展示 sneeze 及物动词用法的个例频率、类型频率、时间跨度和语域分布等数据结果，最终判定当代英语中概括词 sneeze 的及物动词用法已经涌现并规约化，可以收入大中型语文词典。

第三节关于"动词与构式的关系"的讨论则指出，Goldberg（1995,2006）否认 sneeze 衍生及物动词义的观点，以及 Langacker（2005）、Barsalou et al.（2010）和 Herbst（2010）等人认为 sneeze 及物动词用法是新颖用法的观点都不成立。文章认为，这些学者的结论之所以会出现偏差，一方面是因为他们的结论不是基于语料库调查的结果（这是凸显了本文在研究方法上的重要创新），另一方面还因为他们在研究中犯了一个以偏概全的逻辑错误：sneeze 在"Pat sneezed the napkin off the table"这个句子中的用法显得新奇并不等于它在所有致使构式实例中都是新颖的用法，更不等于其所有及物动词用法都是新颖的用法。本文发现，尽管 Goldberg（1995,2006）提及动词与构式的双向互动，但在实际论述中却过于强调构式对动词的单向压制，强调动词意义最小化，而忽略动词由于在构式中反复使用而对其语法特征所产生的影响。据此，文章进一步指出，动词与构式关系的实质是词库与句法的关系。本项基于语料库的研究表明，词库与句法的关系既非生成语言学派所主张的简单的二元对立，也非构式语法所倡导的词库

---

① 王仁强：《科学主义词类研究的方法论困境》，《外语教学》2022 年第 1 期，第 9—16 页。
② 王仁强：《双层词类范畴化理论的超学科方法论》，《外语教学》2023 年第 1 期，第 8—16 页。

与句法构成连续体但强调句法而淡化词库的观点。鉴于语言是一个复杂适应系统，语言演变呈现出双螺旋结构，语言系统层面词库中的用法虽然是词的用法潜势，但词库中的用法源于言语层面句子中规约化用法模式的抽象。换言之，只有通过语料库使用模式调查在言语层面句子中体现规约化用法的词类属性才等同于语言层面词库中的词类。这样就既体现了词库与句法构成连续体，同时又强调了句法与词库之间的区别与联系。讨论部分最后强调了本项研究的特殊价值，即区分语言层面词库中的词类与言语层面句子中的词类，不仅有重要的语言学意义，而且还有很强的应用价值。

论文写作过程中，很多研究生难以理解结论和讨论部分有什么区别，这是因为讨论和结论往往会有一定程度的重叠叙述。一个很好的经验法则就是：你的结论是对你到目前为止所写全部内容的总结。换言之，结论是对论文进行升华的部分。在结论部分，你要提醒读者你前面写过什么，但是记住要有所选择：你可以重复你的研究问题和假设，重复你最重要的发现，指出你的研究对现有文献的贡献，确保你的结论在内容和语言上与引言一致，指出研究的局限性。与讨论部分要求相同的一点是：不要在结论中引入新论点或新数据。就这篇论文而言，结论部分在总揽全局的基础上重申了动词与构式的双向互动关系以及词库与句法的区别与联系，与此同时还指出恒定意义假设和压制理论不能完整解释语言的历时演变，强调本文所采用的语言使用理论和常态与拓展理论能够很好解释概括词的词类属性规约化以及词项与构式的关系问题，特别是基于语料库的自下而上的研究路径能够有效克服构式语法研究的某些弊端。

> 第三部分　欲善其事，先利其器

大规模计算机口试分析评分效果研究*

刘建达　吕剑涛**

摘要：基于计算机的外语考试和评分越来越多，以往研究大都涉及基于纸笔评分效果，对基于计算机的主观题评分效果研究不多。本文从评分一致性和分数维度差异两方面研究了大规模计算机口试分析评分的效果。通过对比整体评分法发现，分析评分法的评卷员行为一致性较好。评卷员使用整体评分法时未能较好地根据表达内容的完整性打分，而且容易出现集中趋势。进行分析评分时，评卷员在内容和语言分项上一致性较差。在准确度方面，评卷员给低水平考生评分要比给高水平考生评分好。

关键词：口语考试；分析评分；整体评分；评卷行为

一、引　　言

主观题的评分方法主要有整体评分法（holistic scoring）和分析评分法（analytic scoring）。整体评分要求评卷员对考生的答题质量进行全面的评估，给出一个整体分数；分析评分则要求评卷员对试题考查的每种技能给出单独的分数（Chi, 2001）。评分信度是两种评分法的关注重点，相关研究结果也不尽相

---

*　原载《现代外语（双月刊）》2015年第2期。本研究得到教育部人文社科重点研究基地重大项目"题组反应理论与英语试题库研究"（11JJD740012）资助。

**　刘建达，博士、教授、博士生导师。教育部"新世纪优秀人才培养计划"入选者。现任广东外语外贸大学副校长，国家教材委员会外语学科专家委员会委员，中国英汉语比较研究会语言测试与评价专业委员会会长，教育部大学英语教学指导委员会副主任委员。主要研究方向包括语言测试与评价和外语教育。

吕剑涛，广东外语外贸大学，博士，研究方向为语言测试、语用学。

同。Klein et al.(1998)发现两种评分法信度相当,对学生排名影响甚少。Barkaoui(2010a)使用定性分析法观察评卷员的表现,发现整体评分让评卷员更关注学生的答卷,而分析评分使评卷员更注意评分细则;Barkaoui(2011)的研究还显示整体评分具有更高评卷员间信度,分析评分虽出现更大评分差异,但评卷员内信度更高。穆倩倩(2010)认为,分析评分在测试低水平学习者的写作能力时有更高的评分信度,而整体评分则在测试高水平学习者时信度更高。一些研究则表明分析评分优于整体评分,这些研究发现分析评分法具有更高信度(Goulden,1994;洪佳敏,2010),能为教师提供更多信息(Bacha,2001),评分严厉度更稳定(Chi,2001),能更好地促进学生口语能力发展(Tuan,2012),很好区分出考试的写作能力(Wiseman,2012)等;Harsch & Martin(2013)的研究还表明整体评分会掩盖一些差异,尤其是评卷员如何使用各种评分指标的细节。当然,Xi(2007)也发现托福口试中分析评分实际上不能提供比整体评分更多的考生能力信息。冯蕾、高淑芬(2012)则建议写作评分宜整体评分和分析评分相结合。

总的来说,分析评分法使评卷员更注重考查技能的每个方面,具有更高的信度,但费时费力(Weigle,2002);整体评分法操作简单,效率较高,但评卷员的评分侧重点往往不同(Nakamura,2002)。在使用方面,试题强调考生的全面能力时,人们常用整体评分法;试题侧重检查考生对完成任务的各种技能的掌握情况时,分析评分更为合适(Klein et al.,1998)。实际运用中,整体评分法多用于大规模考试,因培训评卷员更为方便且评分速度相对较快;而分析评分法常用于课堂测试,因评分结果可帮助教师诊断学生的学习情况(Chi,2001)。

目前国内外的一些大规模考试都含有口语考试。雅思(IELTS)口试使用分析评分,主要包括流利连贯、词汇使用、语法使用和语音语调四个方面,关注语言质量(Brown & Taylor,2006)。托福(TOEFL-iBT)口试采用整体评分法,包含四项评价指标(综合描述、表达传递、语言使用和主题发展)(Alderson,2009)。大学英语四级考试口语考试(CET-SET)采用分析评分法,从语言准确性和范围、话语的长短和连贯性、语言灵活性和适切性,分四个等级对考生参与不同形式的口头交际的表现打分。英语专业四级口试也采用分析评分,从内容、语音语调、语法与词汇三个方面,分别评定考生等级(优秀、良好、及格、不及格)。

现有研究主要探讨写作考试的评分,讨论口试,特别是基于计算机口试评分的研究还很少。国内一些大型考试已增加口试,考试形式也由过去的考官和考生面对面考试改为基于计算机的人机对话考试。评分依据考生的答题录音进行,评分方式也由以前的当面打分改为在专门的计算机平台上打分,降低了评分耗时。英语口试一般需要人工评分,评分标准是影响评分结果的主要因素,而且评分带有一定的主观性,评分信度一直是人们关注的焦点。分析评分信度较好(Weigle, 2002),因此,有必要研究分析评分在大型计算机辅助英语口试中是否也具有较好信度。本文旨在回答以下三个问题:

(1) 分析评分与整体评分的结果是否有差异?
(2) 分析评分的评分员一致性如何?
(3) 分析评分的分数维度差异如何?

二、研究方法

1. 参与对象

本研究的数据为国内某大型计算机辅助英语口试的评分记录。参与该考试的考生为某省报考高校外语专业的高三学生,英语总体水平偏高。每年考试人数约为五万人。该考试为能力水平考试,分为两部分:听力和口语。口语部分第一题为模仿朗读,除了考查考生的语音语调,还考查考生模仿录音朗读的能力;第二题为口头表达,考查考生用英语进行思维和表达的能力,考生根据某一话题下的三个引导性问题进行叙述或讨论。由于英语表达能力是该考试考查的重点,本文仅讨论口头表达部分的评分情况。

考生使用专门考试软件参加考试,其口语录音被考试软件记录并上传至服务器,由评卷员在专门评分软件平台上打分。考生录音由电脑随机分配给每位评卷员。整体评分量表分为五个等级,每个等级从内容完整性、语言正确性、语音语调、流畅度四个方面进行描述;分析评分量表分别对四个方面进行描述,每个方面的描述分为五个等级,例如,语言正确性在每个等级的描述分别为:

(1) 能用合适的词汇、短语、语法结构组织话语;

(2) 基本能用合适的词汇、短语、语法结构组织话语,只有个别地方出现错误;

(3) 有时不能使用合适的词汇、短语、语法结构组织话语;

(4) 使用的词汇、短语、语法结构大部分不正确;

(5) 不能使用合适的词汇、短语、语法结构组织话语。

16位评卷员对5 216名考生口头表达部分进行评分。16位评卷员均为非英语本土语大学英语教师,其年龄、教龄各异,英语水平均达熟练程度,大部分为女性,平均分为两组,一组使用整体评分法评分,另一组使用分析评分法评分。该口试以往一直使用整体评分,大部分评卷员未有使用分析评分的经历。

2. 评分过程

正式评分前,对两组评卷员分别集中进行了培训。培训内容包括评分量表讨论和范文试评。要求组长掌握好其组员对评分标准的理解,由组长带动所有组员参与评分标准的讨论,组长从组员的反馈中了解组员对评分标准的理解。在讨论之初,评卷员认为分析评分比较耗时、复杂,且难操作,在对某个方面打分时,容易不自觉同时考虑其它方面。经过较长时间的讨论,评卷员逐渐熟悉分析评分量表。组长确保每位组员对评分标准达成共识后开展试评。为了帮助评卷员养成对每个方面单独打分的思维习惯,试评时选择了一些分项差异较大的范文,比如语音语调欠佳,内容较完整的范文。组长确保每位组员正确评价范文的情况下允许其正式评分。

培训后,8位评卷员对2 030名考生进行分析评分,其余8位评卷员对3 186名考生进行整体评分。每位评卷员的评卷量在150—400份试卷之间。为了研究不同评分方法结果的一致性,对部分试卷使用了两种评分法评分,部分试卷进行了双评,评卷结果通过SPSS和Facets(Linacre, 2012)软件进行分析。

三、结 果

1. 评分结果差异

分析表明,两种评分法下考生能力值的一致度不高,Pearson相关度为0.402。为了找出差异所在,我们将考生的整体评分和分析评分各分项得分进行多元回归分析。结果显示,分析评分法各项得分都有意义地解释了整体评分法得分的变化($p<0.01$)。内容分项的相关系数为0.284;语言分项为0.509;流畅度分项为0.873;语音语调分项为0.438。这表明评卷员使用整体评分量表时可能对流畅度考虑较多,对内容关注较少。该结果与已有研究结果类似,在使用

整体评分时评卷员总会根据自己的爱好偏重某些方面,尤其语言准确度(Barkaoui,2010b;Huang,2010)。Eckes(2012)就指出评卷员认为重要的部分往往评分较严厉,而不是很重要的部分偏宽松。Jin & Mak(2013)的研究也发现,在测试汉语口语能力时发音、词汇和语法起着最主要的作用。Sawaki(2007)发现某口语分析评分中,语法对整体分数的影响最高。

2. 评分员一致性

口试的评卷信度主要表现为评卷员一致性,包括评卷员间一致性(inter-rater reliability)和评卷员内一致性(intra-rater reliability)。评卷员间一致性指评分严厉度是否存在差异;评卷员内一致性指同一评卷员的严厉度是否受评分时段、疲惫度、评分对象等因素影响(Bachman,2000),由评卷员均方拟合统计量(Infit MnSq 和 Outfit MnSq)反映(Myford & Wolfe,2004)。如表1所示,8位分析性评卷员的分隔指数(15.09)、信度(0.99)以及8位整体评卷员的分隔指数(10.29)和信度(0.99)均表示评卷员的严厉度有差异。卡方检验显示,分析性评卷员间差异($\chi^2=1\,264.9$, df=7, $p<0.00$)和整体评卷员间差异($\chi^2=815.4$, df=7, $p<0.00$)均有显著统计意义,表明两组评卷员的严厉度都有明显差异。

表1 分析评卷员与整体评卷员一致性对照表

评卷员*	严厉度	加权		未加权	
		均方值	Z值	均方值	Z值
1	−0.17	0.89	−3.1	0.64	−0.4
2	−0.60	**1.48**	9.0	1.25	0.5
3	0.08	1.18	4.2	0.91	0.0
4	−2.19	**0.71**	−6.8	0.55	−0.1
5	−0.36	0.87	−3.5	0.89	0.0
6	0.74	0.90	−1.9	1.48	0.8
7	0.51	0.78	−5.7	1.25	0.5
8	0.73	1.00	0.0	1.24	0.5
平均值	−0.16	0.98	−1.0	1.03	0.2
标准差	0.96	0.25	5.3	0.33	0.4

分隔指数:15.09,信度:0.99;卡方值:1 264.9,d.f.:7,$p<0.00$.

续 表

评卷员*	严厉度	加权		未加权	
		均方值	Z 值	均方值	Z 值
9	0.05	0.39	−8.2	0.12	−8.0
10	−1.70	0.92	−0.9	0.84	−0.6
11	−0.43	1.42	5.6	3.68	8.8
12	−0.51	1.22	2.1	0.84	−0.6
13	1.47	1.47	4.2	1.32	1.4
14	−0.74	0.75	−2.8	0.60	−2.0
15	0.92	0.77	−2.8	0.45	−3.6
16	2.20	0.70	−5.2	0.90	−0.6
平均值	0.16	0.96	−1.0	1.09	−0.7
标准差	1.29	0.38	4.7	1.10	4.8

分隔指数：10.29,信度：0.99;卡方值：815.4,d.f.：7,$p<0.00$。

* 1—8 号评卷员使用分析评分法,9—16 号评卷员使用整体评分法。

当评卷员内一致性较高时,加权的均方拟合统计量的数值接近1,对于高风险考试的主观题评分(Yang, 2010),均方拟合统计量过大(非拟合)表示评分行为不符合模型预测,过小(过度拟合)表示评卷员集中使用评分量表的某些等级。两种评分方法下,加权的均方拟合统计量的平均值都接近1,但使用分析评分法的评卷员的内一致性略高。

评卷员2、11和13出现较明显的非拟合情况。评卷员2与模型预测结果差异较大的18项评分记录中,12项为语言分项,由此可见评卷员2未能较好判断考生的语言能力。评卷员11和13(整体评分法)的评分记录中也有较多与模型预测差别较大的记录,两位评卷员都提供了一些"不太可能"的评分。评卷员11偏宽松(严厉度−0.43),评卷员13偏严厉(严厉度1.47),对部分考生的分数定级存在明显偏差。

评卷员4、9的均方拟合统计量远小于1,两位评卷员可能过度使用了某些评分等级(Linacre, 2012)。统计分析表明(表2),评卷员4比较多使用等级四(内容、语言、流畅度、语音语调的次数分别为213、246、162、213,均接近或超过80%),尤其是对语言分项打分时,基本只使用等级四(92%);评卷员9

则过多使用等级三和四,使用次数分别为149(32%)和276(60%),两个等级加起来占了总数的92%。

表2 评卷员4和9使用各等级分数的次数

	评卷员4				评卷员9
	内容	语言	流畅度	语音语调	整体评分
等级一	0	0	0	0	0
等级二	2	1	0	0	10
等级三	4	12	38	8	149
等级四	213	246	162	213	276
等级五	49	9	68	47	32

3. 维度和等级差异

分析评分中,内容和语言分项双评记录的难度差异显著比语音语调和流畅度分项大。此外,内容和语言分项双评记录的难度值均有显著差异($p<0.05$),而流畅度和语音语调分项的双评记录难度差异并不显著($p>0.05$),因此造成评卷员间差异的最大来源是内容和语言。

测量误差决定试卷信度(Bachman,2000)。古典测试理论假定所有考生的测量误差相同,但Rasch模型可以为每个考生提供单独的标准测量误差,测量误差可以通过信息函数得出(余民宁,1993)。考试提供的信息越多,信度越高,测量误差越小(Baker,2001)。分析评分法各分项的信息量分布较均匀;而整体评分的信息函数在4—6 logits的范围内信息量几乎为0,说明考试对该范围考生的测量误差较大,评卷员不能很好地判断该能力水平段的考生。低能力水平考生的信息量比高能力水平考生的信息量高。由评分量表中各等级提供的信息量大小可发现,第一至三等级提供的信息量均比第四、五等级提供的信息量大,说明评卷员使用第一至三等级进行评分比使用第四、五等级更准确。评卷员对高水平考生的评卷准确度把握相对较差。

分析还发现,获得语言侧面等级五的人数相对较少(表3),反映出现今我国英语学习者比较难用适当的语言说话表达的特点。表4给出各维度间分数的相关度,各维度间相关度均不高,语言与其他三个维度的相关度相对较高,从某种程度反映出语言是考生在其他维度得分的关键因素。

表 3 获得各等级的人数

	等级一	等级二	等级三	等级四	等级五
内　　容	20	36	422	1 187	365
语　　言	13	68	822	1 082	45
流 畅 度	14	102	865	908	141
语音语调	9	33	475	1 295	218

表 4 各维度间分数的相关度

	语　言	流畅度	语音语调
内　容	0.451	0.404	0.388
语　言		0.479	0.503
流畅度			0.408

四、讨　　论

1. 分析评分结果与整体评分结果是否有差别？

分析评分结果与整体评分结果一致度不高，但评卷员使用两种评分方法评分时基本上都围绕内容、语言、语音语调及流畅度四个方面来进行。评卷员在使用整体评分量表时更多关注语言、语音语调和流畅度，对流畅度关注最高，对内容的关注度相对较低。原因可能是判断内容完整性费时耗力，是口试评分的难点。然而，内容完整性是判断口头表达很重要的一部分，所以使用整体评分量表时应要求评卷员加强对内容侧面的重视。

目前对口语考试评卷员行为的研究一般是基于研究者通过实验收集到的评分数据（吕长竑等，2008），使用真实考试数据研究评卷员行为的文献还不多。在正式口试评卷中，评卷员的工作量往往较大，由于考试具有较大风险，评卷员承受的压力也大，评卷员在这样的评卷条件下的评分行为、评分策略可能有所变化。例如，为了完成评卷任务，评卷员需要在短时间内评阅完多份试卷，由此造成的压力和评分策略和行为的改变还需进一步进行研究。

2. 分析评分的评分员一致性如何?

评卷结果总体上是可信的,但不同评卷员在使用两种评分方法时存在各种差异。要提高评卷员的评分质量,培训非常重要,及时的偏差分析结果反馈能有效提高评卷质量(Schaefer, 2008)。本研究中,可与评卷员2讨论语言分项各评分等级的描述,了解该评卷员是否已正确理解各等级描述,并试评数篇范文。可与评卷员11和13重评有问题的试卷,并找出评分失误的原因。在8位分析评分评卷员中,评卷员4最宽容,严厉度为-2.19(表1),因而应提醒该评卷员适当增加评分严厉度。评卷员9过多使用了第三、四等级,存在明显集中趋势。集中趋势是评卷员评分时采取的一个比较常见的安全策略,为了避免给出可能不恰当的极端分数,只使用中间等级分数(Myford & Wolfe, 2004)。可邀请评卷员9试评数篇分数较低和较高的范文,并与其讨论评分结果。

3. 分析评分的分数维度差异如何?

内容和语言差异明显比流畅度和语音语调差异大。有评卷员反映,判断考生是否回答了所要求的内容比较考验评卷员的记忆力,听的时间越长,越容易忘记考生前面的讲话,回过头再听又费时,操作麻烦。对语言项打分时,有的评卷员往往只根据考生的前面几句话作出判断。相反,考生的流畅度和语音语调很快可以判断准确,较为容易打分。因此,评卷员培训的重点应该放在内容和语言两个分项上,采取技术手段协助或必要时强制要求评卷员听完考生所有录音。

与整体评分相比,评卷员使用分析评分各等级准确度更高。但评卷员对高水平考生判断准确度不如低水平考生。评卷员的英语熟练程度可能是影响其评分误差的因素之一(Lee, 2009),英语水平不高的评卷员可能没法准确区分能力较高的考生。因此,整体评分法对评卷员的英语水平要求可能比分析评分高,需要进一步研究确认该推断。

考生最难获得最高等级分数的维度是语言。然而,数据分析结果显示语言在一定程度上决定了考生在其他侧面的分数。

五、结　　论

传统的做事测试的评卷方式是评卷员基于纸笔进行评分,随着现代技术的发展,基于计算机的评卷系统不断出现。研究也表明基于计算机的评卷不但有与纸笔评卷同样好的信度,而且可以提高评卷质量,更有利于评卷质量的监控,增强试卷分发的随机性、隐蔽性(Chuang et al., 2008)。本文使用真实考试数据,分析某大型计算机口语考试分析评分的效果。该口语考试举行集中评分,有利于对评卷员进行统一培训,评卷工作在数天内完成。评卷员在适当的培训后基本能较好适应和使用计算机评卷平台,使用分析评分比整体评分耗时较多,但在熟练掌握评卷技巧后,这种差距明显减少。进行整体评分时,评卷员未能足够关注话题陈述的完整性,评卷员在两种评分方法下都具有显著差异,使用分析评分时差异较小,评卷员内部一致性也较高,使用整体评分法时较易出现集中趋势;评卷员在内容和语言分项较难达成一致,对高水平考生评分的准确度较低。

今后评卷员培训应着重加强评卷员对内容完整性和语言准确性两方面的理解和判断,强调口试评分中更多关注考生进行信息表达的能力,而不只是语言形式和流利度。然而,在多次评卷员培训中,笔者发现无论如何强调信息表达的重要性,有些评卷员在讨论中还是不知不觉将注意力过多放在语言形式上,这可能与我国英语教学长期强调语言准确性学习有关。本研究结果表明,基于计算机口试评分使用分析评分较为合适:使用分析评分能逐步提高评卷员对信息表达能力的重视;提高英语教师培养学生用英语表达信息的积极性。分析评分能更好地帮助欠缺经验的评卷员以评分标准为依据评分,降低他们对能力做整体判断的要求,从而在一定程度上保证评分的内一致性(Barkaoui, 2011)。

显然,评卷员的评分行为在很大程度上受培训影响(Weigle, 2002),评卷员差异可能与不同的培训内容(Lumley, 2002)、培训方式(Elder et al., 2007)、培训本身的效用(Lim, 2011)有关。培训是提高评分信度的一个必要条件(Weigle, 1998)。目前,我国口试评卷员培训多采用评分前面对面培训,培训后马上开始评分工作。这样做虽然简捷,但忽略评卷员间的个体差异。另一做法是根据评卷员的个人需要制定培训计划,即评卷员个性化培训。实现个性化培训的方法有多种,例如可以根据评卷员的特征将评卷员分为若干小组,每个小组内根据评卷员特点安排不同的培训内容;或者建立网上培训系统,提前让评卷员通过网络接受培训。

本文只分析了16位评卷员的评分记录,并未结合评卷员的年龄、性别、性格等特点挖掘其评分规律,未能进一步提供解释评卷行为的各种定性数据。今后研究还需进一步探究造成评卷员差异的原因。

参考文献

Alderson, J. C. (2009), Test review: Test of english as a foreign language™: Internet-based test (TOEFL iBT®). *Language Testing* 26(4): 621-631.

Bacha, N. (2001), Writing evaluation: What can analytic versus holistic essay scoring tell us?. *System* 29(3): 371-383.

Bachman, L. (2000), *Fundamental Considerations in Language Testing*. Oxford: Oxford University Press.

Baker, B. F. (2001), *The Basics of Item Response Theory*. ERIC Clearinghouse on Assessent and Evaluation.

Barkaoui, K. (2010a), Variability in ESL essay rating processes: The role of the rating scale and rater experience. *Language Assessment Quarterly* 7(1): 54-74.

Barkaoui, K. (2010b), Explaining ESL essay holistic scores: A multilevel modeling approach. *Language Testing* 27(4): 515-535.

Barkaoui, K. (2011), Effects of marking method and rater experience on ESL essay scores and rater performance. *Assessment in Education: Principles, Policy & Practice* 18(3): 279-293.

Brown, A. & L. Taylor(2006), A world survey of examiners' views and experience of the revised IELTS Speaking Test. *Cambridge ESOL: Research Notes* 26: 14-18.

Chi, E. (2001), Comparing holistic and analytic scoring for performance assessment with many-facet Rasch model. *Journal of Applied Measurement* 2(4): 379-388.

Chuang, Y., L. L. Chen & M. C. Chuang (2008), Computer-based rating method for evaluating multiple visual stimuli on multiple scales. *Computers in Human Behavior* 24(5): 1929-1946.

Eckes, T. (2012), Operational rater types in writing assessment: Linking rater cognition to rater behavior. *Language Assessment Quarterly* 9(3): 270-292.

Elder, C., G. Barkhuizen, U. Knoch & J. von Randow(2007), Evaluating rater responses to an online training program for L2 writing assessment. *Language Testing* 24(1): 37–64.

Goulden, N. R. (1994), Relationship of analytic and holistic methods to raters' scores for speeches. *Journal of Research and Development in Education* 27(2): 73–82.

Harsch, C. & G. Martin (2013), Comparing holistic and analytic scoring methods: Issues of validity and reliability. *Assessment in Education: Principles, Policy and Practice* 20(3): 281–307.

Huang, J. & C. Foote (2010), Grading between the lines: What really impacts professor's holistic evaluation of ESL graduate student writing?. *Language Assessment Quarterly* 7(3): 219–233.

Jin, T. & B. Mak (2013), Distinguishing features in scoring L2 Chinese speaking performance: How do they work?. *Language Testing* 30(1): 23–47.

Klein, S. P., B. M. Stecher, R. J. Shavelson, D. McCaffrey, T. Ormseth, R. M. Bell, K. Comfort & A. R. Othman (1998), Analytic versus holistic scoring of science performance tasks. *Applied Measurement in Education* 11(2): 121–137.

Lee, H. K. (2009), Native and nonnative rater behavior in grading Korean students' English essays. *Asia Pacific Education Review* 10: 387–397.

Lim, G. S. (2011), The development and maintenance of rating quality in performance writing assessment: A longitudinal study of new and experienced raters. *Language Testing* 28(4): 543–560.

Linacre, J. M. (2012), *A User's Guide to FACETS: Rasch-Model Computer Program*. Chicago: MESA Press.

Lumley, T. (2002), Assessment criteria in a large-scale writing test: What do they really mean to the raters?. *Language Testing* 19(3): 246–276.

Myford, C. M. & E. W. Wolfe (2004), Understanding Rasch measurement detecting and measuring rater effects using many-facet Rasch measurement part II. *Journal of Applied Measurement* 5(2): 189–227.

Nakamura, Y. (2002), Effectiveness of paired rating in the assessment of English compositions. *JLTA Journal* 5: 61–71.

Sawaki, Y. (2007), Construct validation of analytic rating scales in a speaking assessment: Reporting a score profile and a composite. *Language Testing* 24(3): 355-390.

Schaefer, E. (2008), Rater bias patterns in an EFL writing assessment. *Language Testing* 25(4): 465-493.

Tuan, L. (2012), Teaching and assessing speaking performance through analytic scoring approach. *Theory and Practice in Language Studies* 2(4): 673-679.

Weigle, S. C. (1998), Using FACETS to model rater training effects. *Language Testing* 15(2): 263-287.

Weigle, S. C. (2002), *Assessing Writing*. Cambridge, UK: Cambridge University Press.

Wiseman, C. S. (2012), A comparison of the performance of analytic vs. holistic scoring rubrics to assess L2 writing. *Iranian Journal of Language Testing* 2(1): 59-92.

Xi, X. (2007), Evaluating analytic scoring for the TOEFL® Academic Speaking Test (TAST) for operational use. *Language Testing* 24(2): 251-286.

Yang, R. (2010), *A Many-Facet Rasch Analysis of Rater Effects on an Oral English Proficiency Test*. PhD Dissertation, Purdue University.

冯蕾、高淑芬:《评分方法在大学英语写作形成性评估中效应实证研究:整体评分与混合评分方法对比分析》,《北京交通大学学报(社会科学版)》2012年第3期,第126—131页。

洪佳敏:《英语写作测试中的评分者效应:整体评分和分项评分对比研究》,上海师范大学硕士学位论文,2010年。

吕长竑、宋冰、王焰、刘文丽、黎斌:《口语测试评分标准比较研究》,《外语教学与研究》2008年第6期,第440—446页。

穆倩倩:《分项评定法还是整体评定法?》,四川外语学院硕士学位论文,2010年。

余民宁:《试题反应理论的介绍(7)——讯息函数》,《研习资讯》1993年第6期,第5—9页。

方法谈：

定量研究的优势是什么？数据会说谎吗？

语言测试中的主观题评分是指需要人工评分的测试题目，如翻译、写作、口语等。在进行主观题评分时，评卷员需要根据一定的评分标准和判定规则对考生的答案进行评估，并给出相应的分数。而定量分析则是一种系统性的、以数据为基础的研究方法，可以对评卷员的评分行为进行量化的分析和评估。定量分析在语言测试主观题评分中具有诸多优势。例如，可以提高评分的客观性、一致性、和效率。定量研究可以通过建立明确的评分标准和判定规则，减少评卷员主观因素的影响，从而提高评分的客观性和准确性。同时，还可以通过对评卷员的评分行为进行量化的分析和比较，识别出评卷员之间的评分差异，并提供针对性的培训和指导，从而提高评分的一致性和可靠性。通过分析评卷员的评分行为，可以发现评分过程中存在的问题和瓶颈，并提出相应的改进措施，从而提高评分的效率和准确性。此外，通过对评分行为的量化分析和评估，可以发现评分中存在的偏差和不公正现象，并提出相应的纠正措施，保证评价的公正性和准确性。

本研究中，评卷员2、11和13都出现较明显的非拟合情况。评卷员2与模型预测结果差异较大的18项评分记录中，12项为语言分项，由此可见评卷员2未能较好判断考生的语言能力。评卷员11和13（整体评分法）的评分记录中也有较多与模型预测差别较大的记录，两位评卷员都提供了一些"不太可能"的评分。评卷员11偏宽松（严厉度－0.43），评卷员13偏严厉（严厉度1.47），对部分考生的分数定级存在明显偏差。评卷员4比较多使用等级四（内容、语言、流畅度、语音语调的次数分别为213、246、162、213，均接近或超过80%），尤其是对语言分项打分时，基本只使用等级四（92%）；评卷员9则过多使用等级三和四，使用次数分别为149（32%）和276（60%），两个等级加起来占了总数的92%。根据这些定量数据分析，我们可以有针对性地对评卷员进行区别培训。对评卷员11和13进行评分标准的再培训，对评卷员2这对语言这一评分项进行单独培训。针对评卷员4，则对分级差异，尤其是高分段的判断进行培训。所以说，定量研究可以帮助我们有针对性对不同的评卷员进行培训，从而提高评分的信度。具体操作上，可与评卷员2讨论语言分项各评分等级的描述，了解该评卷员是否已正确理解各等级描述,并试评数篇范文。可与评卷员 11 和 13 重评有问题的试卷,并找出评分失误的原因。评卷员 9 过多使用了第三、四等级,存在明显集中趋势,可邀请评卷员 9 试评数篇分数较低和较高的范文,并与其讨论评分结果。

然而,尽管定量研究在语言测试主观题评分中具有很多优势,数据能告诉我们很多信息,但也要注意定量分析的结果有可能受到一些数据无法告知的因素的影响,有时还需依靠经验进行综合判断。例如,评卷员可能会受到自身经验、知识水平、个人偏好等因素的影响,从而影响评分结果;评分标准的质量可能会导致不同评卷员对同一份答案给出不同的分数,从而影响评分结果的准确性;评分过程中的疲劳和误差可能会导致评卷员的注意力和判断力下降,从而影响评分结果的准确性,答案的难度和复杂度可能会导致评卷员的评分难度增加,从而影响评分结果的准确性;考生可能会受到情感因素的影响,如焦虑、紧张、压力等,从而影响其答案的质量和准确性,进而影响评分结果。定量分析倾向于将语言数据简化为数字和统计数据,这可能会忽略语言活动中语言现象的复杂性和多样性。例如,定量分析可能无法捕捉到语言交际中的非语言因素和语言使用的文化和社会背景。同时,定量分析的结果取决于数据的质量和可靠性。如果数据收集不当或存在偏差,那么定量研究的结论也可能存在偏差。此外,定量研究需要研究者在数据收集和分析过程中对一些变量进行控制,这可能会限制研究的范围和深度。定量分析还可能无法涵盖所有的语言现象,因为某些语言现象可能无法被量化。

因此,为减少数据"说谎"的影响,我们需要采取一些相应的措施,如建立明确的评分标准和判定规则、提供充足的培训和指导、加强评卷员的质量控制和监督、减轻评卷员的工作负担等。同时也需要采用多种评分方法和策略,如双评、多评、交叉评估等,以提高评分结果的准确性和可靠性。

"A More Inclusive Mind towards the World": English Language Teaching and Study Abroad in China from Intercultural Citizenship and English as a Lingua Franca Perspectives[*]

Fan (Gabriel) Fang, Will Baker[**]

Abstract: With the status of English as a global lingua franca (ELF), English is no longer the sole property of its Anglophone native English speakers (NES) problematising the current dominance of Anglophone cultures and NES in the field of English language teaching (ELT). The notion of intercultural citizenship education offers a critical alternative model in language education. To investigate how ELF, intercultural approaches and the concept of intercultural citizenship might be integrated within the field of ELT, a study was conducted in a university located in southeast China. Due to the large number of ELT learners and high degree of student mobility in China these are issue of much relevance in this setting. The research collected qualitative data through face-to-face interviews, email interviews and focus groups with students on study abroad programmes who have both ELT and first hand intercultural experiences. Many students spoke positively about aspects of intercultural citizenship, but classroom

---

[*] 原载 *Language Teaching Research* 2017, Volume 22, Issue 9。

[**] 方帆,英国南安普顿大学哲学博士(现代语言与应用语言学方向),师从 Jennifer Jenkins 教授,现为汕头大学教授(外国语言学与应用语言学),硕士研究生导师,爱思唯尔 2021、2022 年外国语言文学领域中国高被引学者。研究方向为社会语言学、应用语言学、英语教学、教师发展等。

Will Baker,南安普顿大学副教授,研究方向为应用语言学、社会语言学、语言教学。

instruction offered only limited channels for students to experience and understand intercultural communication and citizenship. In contrast, most of their understanding and experiences were gained outside the classroom during study abroad. Furthermore, many students spoke about the importance of English in their development of intercultural connections and citizenship. We conclude that more in-depth and critical approaches to teaching language, culture and intercultural communication in ELT are needed which foster and cultivate students' sense of intercultural citizenship.

Key Words: English as a Lingua Franca; Intercultural Communication; Intercultural Citizenship; ELT; China

Introduction

It has been widely recognized that as the English language has spread across the globe, it predominantly functions as a lingua franca (ELF)① facilitating communication between people from different lingua-cultural backgrounds. The number of non-native speakers of English (NNSEs) far outnumbers native speakers of English (NSEs). Thus, the position taken in this article is that NSE no longer control, nor should be arbiters, of the language. However, this pluricentric cultural and linguistic landscape is not currently reflected in ELT (English language teaching), where the traditional power relationship that privileges native models of language and Anglophone culture is still largely entrenched. The concept of *native speakerism* remains the dominant ideology in the field of ELT (Houghton & Rivers, 2013), while critical perspectives on language and culture instruction and alternative goals and approaches such as intercultural education and

---

① In this paper, ELF refers to the 'any use of English among speakers of different first languages for whom English is the communicative medium of choice, and often the only option' (Seidlhofer, 2011: 7).

citizenship (e.g. Byram, 2008; 2012; Byram et al., 2017) struggle to secure a position. In this paper, we argue that perspectives from ELF and intercultural education and citizenship offer a potentially fruitful, and so far under-explored, combination and alternative to the dominant ideologies of ELT. We relate this discussion to China and issues arising from the increasing role of English in education. This is followed by a presentation of data from a study illustrating core themes in intercultural communication, intercultural citizenship and English language education in China. Finally, implications regarding critical approaches to intercultural communication and citizenship in ELT are discussed.

ELF, intercultural citizenship and ELT

ELF studies can be seen as adding to post-structuralist perspectives on language and intercultural communication in critically investigating the concepts of language, culture, identity and communication in a manner that emphasises the fluidity of the relationships between them (Baker, 2015; Jenkins, 2015). This questions essentialist correlations between a language, culture, nation and identity. While the nation state still exerts a strong influence on all these areas, it is only one of many scales at which we can view these concepts. ELF studies have illustrated English used to create and negotiate cultural practices, references and identities that move between and across local, national and global scales as well as emergent and hybrid cultural practices and identities created in situ (Kaloscia, 2014; Baker, 2015; Zhu, 2015). Importantly, given the multilingual and multicultural nature of ELF communication (Jenkins, 2015), the boundaries between languages and cultures become blurred. In this sense, ELF communication is transcultural rather than intercultural communication, since it is not always clear which culture or language the communication is in-between (see also Kramsch, 2009). Thus, the 'trans' prefix more accurately represents this movement through and across communicative contexts as well as connecting to the similarly dynamic perspectives on language and communication adopted in translanguaging studies (e.g. Canagarajah, 2013; Garcia & Li, 2014; Li, 2016).

The presence of English in diverse transcultural and translingual settings, with the majority of its users employing it as an additional language, has profound implications for teaching. Firstly, there is no longer a clear target language/target culture correlation. As the use and ownership of English expands beyond the traditional Anglophone countries (typically the US, the UK and Australia in ELT), the relevance of focusing on varieties of English and cultural practices associated with these settings becomes harder to sustain. Secondly, given the diversity of English use the rationale for focusing on any one variety and setting for the language becomes problematic. Instead, if the goal of teaching is to communicate in English, then the focus must be on preparing learners for variety, change and adaptation. Key suggestions have included a focus on the processes of language learning and use (Seidlhofer, 2011) and a 'post-normative' pedagogy (Dewey, 2012, 2015) in which language forms are approached as adaptable and contextually varied rather than as a fixed code. Accompanying this is a wider perspective on the goals of language learning in which the typically narrow communicative competence of ELT, with its emphasis on linguistic competence, is expanded to include pragmatic competence (Jenkins, 2015) and intercultural awareness (Baker, 2015).

In many ways, this links to the arguments made in intercultural approaches to language education more generally (e.g. Byram, 1997, 2008; Kramsch, 2009). Here too, there has been a concern with expanding the notion of communicative competence, especially in the work on intercultural communicative competence (ICC) (Byram, 1997, 2008). Likewise, there has been a reconsideration of the native speaker as a model for language learners and advocating of an intercultural speaker as a more appropriate and attainable alternative with respect to ICC. Although, Byram remains agnostic on the question of linguistic competence in relation to native speakers and 'standard' language in ICC [personal communication and see introduction]. More recently, the discussion has been concerned with the notion of intercultural citizenship as a goal in language education (e. g. Byram, 2008, 2012, 2014; Byram et al., 2017; Lu & Corbett, 2012; Porto, 2014) and Byram's (2008: 187) definition of intercultural citizenship education given below, is well-cited in this literature.

1. Causing/facilitating intercultural citizenship experience, and analysis and reflection on it and on the possibility of further social and/or political activity, i. e. activity that involves working with others to achieve an agreed end;
2. Creating learning/change in the individual: cognitive, attitudinal, behavioural change; change in self-perception; change in relationships with Others (i. e. people of a different social group); change that is based in the particular but is related to the universal.

Intercultural citizenship here combines the international/intercultural and critical from earlier work in foreign language education and intercultural communicative competence with the emphasis on activity in the here and now in citizenship education (Byram et al., 2017: xxiii). Thus, intercultural citizenship involves going beyond learning *about* 'others' to a kind of learning which results in change in the individual and also produces activity in the community, where that community ranges from the local to the national and, crucially, the international and global.

Intercultural citizenship, as both goal and content for language education, would seem commensurable in many ways with the above discussion of ELF, which also emphasised the importance of identifying with multiple communities in language use that include, but also go beyond, the local and the national. However, to date, there has been little exploration of the cross-over between ELF studies and intercultural citizenship studies, a gap which this paper aims to address. In particular, it is important to recognize that language choices are not marginal issues, and perspectives on the 'appropriate' use of and ownership of English are crucial. Language learners are unlikely to identify with a language in which they feel inferior to an idealised native speaker and that they associate with a 'distant' Anglophone community to which they have little contact. Therefore, how the language being learnt is positioned, and the ideology that underpins this positioning, are central. At present though, approaches that emphasise the use of ELF for intercultural communication and the development of intercultural citizenship clash with the dominant ideology of Anglophone and idealised native speaker models of culture and language in ELT.

ELF, Intercultural Citizenship and student mobility

An area where many of these issues come to the fore is in student exchanges and mobility both during preparation for the time abroad and the sojourn itself. One of the often stated aims of student mobility is to develop students' intercultural awareness/competence and sense of intercultural/global citizenship (Baker, 2016; Beaven & Borghetti, 2015; Kinginger, 2013). At the same time, it has long been recognized that study-abroad experiences do not by themselves guarantee growth in intercultural awareness or the development of intercultural citizenship and appropriate support, evaluation and reflection are crucial to successful intercultural student exchanges (Byram & Feng, 2006; Jackson, 2012). While there is too little space here to deal with all the issues study abroad and student mobility give rise to, two concerns of relevance for this paper are the approach to language and the model of intercultural citizenship.

Firstly, much of the preparation for student mobility has traditionally assumed a correlation between the language of instruction in an institution, a local host community and a national culture and language. However, the increasingly international orientation of many higher education institutions (HEIs) means that such connections can no longer be taken for granted as diverse student and staff bodies make them highly multilingual and multicultural environments. This is particularly the case in Anglophone settings but also in internationally orientated universities that use EMI (English as a medium of instruction), where English most frequently functions as a lingua franca (Jenkins, 2014). Therefore, investigating student sojourners' study-abroad experiences in English using environments and their previous English language education is likely to prove a fruitful area for uncovering possible tensions and discrepancies in approaches to language and intercultural education and the development of intercultural citizenship.

Secondly, while Byram's critical and transformative approach to intercultural citizenship outlined above has received support in language education research (Byram et al., 2017), within education more generally there are a number of competing frameworks. In particular, the neoliberal perspective which emphasises the development of knowledge and skills to enable global mobility for employment and economic benefits has proved pervasive (Aktas et al., 2016). Neoliberal approaches in education, including in language teaching, rather than engaging with communities and social action as envisaged by Byram, may result in increased stratification of social divides to the benefit of cosmopolitan elites (Gray, 2010; Block et al., 2012). To date, there is insufficient empirical evidence to be able to draw conclusions on how educational institutions or individual students view intercultural citizenship. Furthermore, there is likely to be a great deal of variation between the different approaches, suggesting that this is an area of interest for further research.

English and intercultural citizenship in ELT in China

As already noted, given the large number of English learners and the extent of student mobility in China, particularly to Anglophone countries (Jenkins, 2014), issues around language use, language teaching, study abroad and intercultural citizenship are of great relevance. English has made remarkable gains in status during the last few decades particularly after the 2008 Beijing Olympic Games, 2010 Shanghai Expo and Guangzhou Asian Games and the

English teaching industry is booming (Fong, 2009). English is taught from kindergarten, to primary school, to secondary school, and as a compulsory subject in Chinese higher education to both English and non-English majors. It is estimated that there are currently over 400 million English learners in China (Wei & Su, 2012).

However, this English boom is not without controversy. Although some view the dominance of English as beneficial for generating future economic growth and accelerating China's engagement with the world (e.g. Chang, 2006), others have been more critical. As a country that highly values Confucianism and first language literacy (Deng, 2011, 2014; Fong, 2009), the popularity of English learning in China has generated 'identity anxiety among Chinese involved in learning English' (Gao, 2009: 57-58). Therefore, the notion of *zhongxue weiti*, *xixue weiyong* (中学为体, 西学为用: Chinese learning for essence (*ti*); Western learning for utility (*yong*)) is applied in English learning (Gao, 2009; Gil & Adamson, 2011). This perspective, on the one hand, allows access to the knowledge and opportunities that learning English provides, while on the other hand defends the learning of Chinese for culture and identity (Gil & Adamson, 2011: 24).

This second view can, however, only be regarded as a temporary solution, and in reality the use and learning of English is far more complex and cannot be explained simply in terms of *ti* and *yong*. It is important to realise that learning English in China is not merely a linguistic issue but is embedded in socio-political and ideological grounds between the English language and Chinese culture and identity. Current studies reveal the multiple roles and functions of English in China embracing pride in Chinese culture, but also rebellion against authority and increased global connectivity (Li, 2016; Ren et al., 2016). Crucially, research has shown that English is increasingly viewed less as the language of the other and more as part of the multilingual, or translingual resources of its users that 'transforms its users and their subjectivities, creating new spaces for social relations, social structures, and social cognition' (Li, 2016: 21). At the same time, the orientation towards a native speaker and Anglophone ideology is still strong, especially in ELT practices (Fang, 2016a, 2016b; Liu, 2016; Wang, 2013). Nonetheless, here too the picture is ambiguous with intercultural communicative competence and global orientations to English forming a core part of the national curriculum in both secondary schools and colleges, but appearing little understood by teachers (Liu, 2016). One of the few empirical studies in China to focus explicitly on intercultural citizenship reported that while university students generally had positive attitudes towards notions associated with intercultural citizenship, their understanding of the concept was still superficial and that more 'systematic' education in intercultural citizenship is needed (Han et al., 2017: 39). Han et al. (2017) conclude that given the relevance and interest in intercultural education and citizenship in China, more research is needed.

Methodology

To address the gaps identified in the previous literature review in relation to intercultural citizenship education, ELF, ELT and student mobility, we sought to investigate the experiences and attitudes of a group of Chinese learners/users of English who had recently returned from study abroad experiences. Four main research questions guided the analysis and presentation of the data here:

1. What are Chinese university student sojourners' experiences of ELT in relation to intercultural communication, competence and citizenship?
2. What are these students' experiences of intercultural communication in their study-abroad exchange programmes?
3. In what ways, if any, do student sojourners develop awareness of intercultural citizenship as a result of their study-abroad exchange programmes?
4. What is the relationship between students' perceptions and use of English and their perceptions of intercultural communication and intercultural citizenship?

This research was conducted in a provincial key university located in southeast China. The university has more than 7,000 students, and the English Language Centre, where this study took place, offers language courses to the whole university. As an international university, it provides various exchange programmes for students to study abroad. These exchange programmes aim for student sojourners to develop a sense of intercultural awareness through their experiences.

In terms of participant recruitment, snowball sampling was adopted (Schutt, 2014) through student contacts of the first author, based in China. As the focus is on intercultural citizenship and English in intercultural communication, the researcher recruited student participants who had studied abroad for at least four months as they have more experiences to draw on (see Table 1).

Table 1 Profiles of Participants

Participants	Gender	Major	Where	Length of Stay
Gary	M	English	Ireland	4 months
Laura	F	English	Canada	4 months
Lisa	F	Public Administration	Canada	4 months
Ava	F	English	Ireland	4 months
Hannah	F	English	Ireland	4 months
Lynn	F	Law	Canada	4 months
Andrew	M	Chemistry	New Zealand	5 months
Carter	M	Electronic Information	Canada, Hong Kong	5 months

Data collection involved an initial face to face semi-structured interview covering all four research questions; following this, six participants attended a focus group (Lisa, Hannah, Lynn, Andrew, Carter - and Sally[①]) to discuss the themes further. The researcher facilitated the focus group with minimum involvement to ensure that the participants could express their opinions in a

---

[①] Sally participated in the exchange programme to New Zealand for only one month and a half, and thus her interview data is not included.

relatively relaxing atmosphere. Finally, an email interview was conducted with the eight participants which specifically focused on intercultural/global citizenship① and their study abroad experiences. All the interviews and the focus group were conducted in Chinese Mandarin.

After data collection, Mandarin transcriptions of the recordings were produced. We adopted content analysis (Schreier, 2012) 'to explore the deeper meanings so as to add interpretive depth and breadth to the analysis' (Jenkins, 2014: 128) and to systematically organise the data. Initial coding based on the research focus and emergent themes was conducted by the first author through listening to the recordings with the transcription. The transcription was then input to *NVivo*. Next, a second level of coding was undertaken to group the data according to emergent, data-driven themes. After the initial two coding levels, the first author translated the coded data extracts. A final interpretative level of coding, drawing together the previous themes and research questions, was undertaken by both authors, which forms the basis of the themes presented below.

Findings

The findings from the interviews and focus groups are presented according to the four main themes related to emergent codes and the four research questions (RQ): *intercultural citizenship and education (RQ1), intercultural citizenship and study abroad experience (RQ2), intercultural citizenship and learning/change (RQ3), intercultural citizenship and ELF (RQ4)*.

Intercultural citizenship and education

For many Chinese university students the only opportunity to gain cultural knowledge and intercultural citizenship experience is through classroom

---

① How the terms 'intercultural', 'global' and 'citizenship' are translated is not a trivial matter (Feng, 2006) and we adopted both intercultural citizenship (跨文化公民身份) and global citizenship (全球公民身份) to maximise the changes of participants' familiarity with the terms. Indeed our initial translation of intercultural citizenship yielded little response from the participants whereas a later translation of global citizenship resulted in much more extensive data.

instruction in ELT. However, these student sojourners report a mismatch between their experiences of mainstream methods of ELT and their time abroad. As the examples below show, students felt that:

1. there was insufficient focus on the intercultural dimension in language education,

2. when it was dealt with, it was often at a superficial level,

3. the community and activity aspects of intercultural citizenship were missing.

Extract 1

> Hannah: It is not enough. It is possible that I read extensively in my major and delve deeply into some knowledge. […] However, we need more practical skills to deal with real-life experience abroad.

Extract 2

> Gary: Most cases have been discussed even when I was in high school […] They are quite artificial and I do not think I have learned much from the textbooks and classroom instruction.

Extract 3

> Lisa: Chinese students in primary and secondary school are not taught about community service and are not made aware of either intercultural citizenship or community service in nine-year compulsory education.

At the same time, however, all of the participants felt that education could and should form an important part of developing intercultural citizenship, as explained by Laura below.

Extract 4

> Laura: I think this should be one part of the education experience, because with the development of globalization, it's very important to have an international view, whose condition is to have understanding of other countries. Therefore, these kinds of activities are of necessity.

The students suggested a range of ways to do this including 'voluntary activities related to education and environmental protection' (Lynn, Sally); language-related services, such as an English corner (Laura, Hannah); and community activities organised by embassies or experiences of travelling abroad (Gary).

Intercultural citizenship and study abroad experience

Perhaps unsurprisingly, given the negative perceptions of formal instruction, most of the participants reported developing a greater understanding of intercultural competence/awareness and citizenship though their study abroad experiences. They discussed various intercultural experiences, which raised their levels of intercultural awareness/competence and citizenship as illustrated by Andrew and Sally below.

Extract 5

> Andrew: The most amusing experience is when the host prepared soup for us, and two students and I were sipping the soup with a 'siiiirrr' sound, like when we are eating noodle. The host says: 'why are you doing this. This is impolite', and one student responds: 'in my home country, sipping the soup means that it is very delicious'. I also agree with the last comment. The host then replies: 'no. It is not polite to do this here. You need to be quiet when eating'.
>
> Interviewer: What happened then?
>
> Andrew: We were then laughing together and let it pass.

Extract 6

> Sally: I do feel the international social environment. More than 70% students in my postgraduate class are international students, who are from China, India, Canada, and America, etc., and whose backgrounds like age and career are different. Teachers will discuss hot issues like the global environment with us. Besides, the courses are inclusive, because we will discuss the negative news of one country, but we will discuss the facts objectively, instead of attacking others.

Additionally, some of the students actively sought out intercultural citizenship experiences while abroad, undertaking a range of activities in the community.

Extract 7

   Lynn: I once joined the international student organization and went to local church gatherings to get to know their daily lives.

Extract 8

   Laura: I have attended volunteer work in hospital abroad. I sent the patients in the hospital some candies, cookies with warm smiles with other volunteers on Halloween. Also, I remember one of our volunteers played the piano for them, and we felt glad seeing the smiles on the patients' faces.

However, the responses here were uneven with students revealing different levels of experience and understanding of both intercultural competence/awareness and citizenship. While some participated in numerous activities and reported significant changes, others seemingly only developed a superficial understanding with little meaningful engagement with others as demonstrated with Ava's rather essentialised description below.

Extract 9

   Ava: Paris is not that romantic, and the subway there is dirty and smelly; Santorini is not that beautiful; the thieves in Italy are numerous and rampant; and the students abroad are not that aggressive answering questions in class like the movies show.

Even the same participants reported a range of experiences, for example, Laura who was so positive in extract 8 also felt that the differences in cultures were less than she had expected.

Extract 10

   Laura: Sometimes I was busy with my studies, essays and exams. I did not have time for social activities. At that time, I felt quite depressed, because I felt what I learnt here [in Canada] seemed to have no difference with that at home.

Intercultural citizenship and learning/change

A crucial part of developing intercultural citizenship is for intercultural experiences to lead to learning and change in the individual and this was part of many participants' experiences of studying abroad. The students reported being more open-minded and interested in engaging with others as well as being more tolerant of difference or 'variety' as Lynn describes in a particularly articulate example below.

Extract 11

> Lynn: I feel that all the changes that have happened to me are positive. First of all study, after a half-year exchange abroad, influenced by the foreign teaching and learning style, I found myself thinking more independently, and having a stronger desire to put forward questions and express my own ideas. What's more, I noticed the significance of equality and inclusiveness in intercultural communication. For instance, there are more chances for me to interact with organizations with different cultural backgrounds and communicate with people from different countries at school. Meanwhile, it will lead to some arguments or even conflicts, however, the key is to communicate equally and understand empathetically. These changes help me and others, because we will have a more inclusive mind towards the world, and also understand and respect variety.

Behavioral changes were also apparent as some students also continued to engage in or expressed a wish to engage in community activities when they returned to China.

Extract 12

> Laura: After I came back, I have taken part in the visit to the elderly in the community, which are the activities of the College Youth Volunteer

Organization.

Extract 13

> Sally: In the UK, many students will do the voluntary work after class spontaneously, inspired by their own interest and social responsibility, which changes me unconsciously, and makes me willing to be a volunteer.

However, other responses were more ambiguous in the extent to which they showed positive or deep changes in attitudes or behavior in individuals. For example, Ava felt that 'white people' (her categorisation) did not understand Chinese people or culture, by saying that in class 'when the teacher talks about Chinese, the white students really cannot understand'. Moreover, participants frequently characterised others by their nationality.

Extract 14

> Gary: I found that European students have a broad understanding of different countries, so they can fit in quickly. Besides, I think it is not only Chinese students who like to stay together, but French and German students also tend to gather together speaking their mother language. However, it is only based on my observation, which could be wrong.

Nonetheless, while such characterisation can lead to essentialism, being open to alternative perspectives is a way of avoiding stereotypes, as Gary appears to recognize in the final comment 'it is only based on my observation, which could be wrong'.

Finally, a number of participants focused on the personal benefits of study abroad and the changes it brought to them fitting in more closely with neoliberal, rather than critical educational, approaches to intercultural citizenship. So for example, Laura stated that 'The overseas experience has broadened my horizon, and meanwhile inspired me to chase the better lifestyle' but at the same time she also reported taking part in more communities activities (see extract 12), suggesting the two perspectives are not necessarily exclusive.

Intercultural citizenship and ELF

Lastly, language is not a trivial issue in intercultural communication and a number of the students explicitly discussed the relationship between language use and proficiency and their experiences of intercultural communication, as well as linking this to the development of intercultural citizenship. For instance, students in the focus group talked about the importance of being confident when speaking in English in order to develop a sense of ownership or identity through English.

Extract 15

> Carter: I think it is important to be confident when speaking English. I feel that Chinese people dare not speak English and would rather stay with Asian people because they are not confident in English. [...] I think it is important to be confident and learn to integrate with people there.
>
> Lynn: Yes, yes. It is important to learn to be involved in different social settings. I see many university students stay around with other Chinese students.
>
> Andrew: Yes yes many of them.
>
> Carter: Especially those who went abroad in a very young age [...] they have a strong sense of belonging.

For other students, English seemed to be a barrier to intercultural citizenship as for them it was closely associated with Anglophone countries (especially the US) and hence seen a threat to their national identity.

Extract 16

> Lisa: Since we have learned English for nearly 2 decades, we should use this to figure out how others think. But I never talk about this change to my friends even if I consider it important, because I am afraid of being accused of being pro-America.

Indeed, this association between English and Anglophone settings was often repeated, typically as an ideal and hence source of anxiety since as 'non-native' speakers they can never reach this ideal. These mixed attitudes to English and its relationship to identity and development are clearly expressed by Laura who, through the email interview, simultaneously links English to the type of positive personality changes and increased social connections associated with intercultural citizenship, and also to 'shame' in not being 'native like'.

Extract 17

> Laura: My personality does change, for I become more optimistic, and willing to talk with others. I feel like that English is very important after the overseas study. [...] My attitude changes. Firstly, I realise its significance, and at the same time, I am very grateful that I have learned this language. Commanding English makes it possible to communicate with people from different places, otherwise, I cannot know a group of good friends.

Extract 18

> Laura: I remember that I knew a teaching assistant, who once asked me how long had I learnt English, and I thought about it and found that I had learnt English for 8 years, then he said he would use the standard of 'native speaker' to judge my essay. I thought about it carefully and found out that I still did not have a great progress in English, and I feel ashamed of that.

Discussion and implications

Despite the increased prominence given to intercultural communication, ELF, globalization and citizenship in current policy and curricula in Chinese settings, this study, like previous research (e.g. Han et al., 2017; Liu, 2016), found little reference to these concepts in reported ELT practices. This resulted in a mismatch between the participants' experiences of intercultural communication while abroad and what was learnt in the classroom. Nonetheless, regardless of the lack of preparation, the findings here confirm existing research in showing study abroad as a largely positive experience in developing a sense of intercultural competence/awareness and citizenship (e.g. Byram & Feng, 2006; Byram et al., 2017; Jackson, 2012; Kinginger, 2013; Beaven & Borghetti, 2015) and all students reported changes in both attitudes and behaviours. However, as might be expected, the extent of changes reported by participants is not even, with some more profound than others, and stereotypes and essentialism still present. It is also not clear from this data to what extent participants developed a sense of cultural identification that went beyond the nation (however complex) and recognized the possibility of hybrid or liminal identifications at a range of scales including the local, national and global (Baker, 2015, 2016; Beaven & Borghetti, 2015). This may in part be due to the majority of experiences taking place in Anglophone settings where the link between a language, culture and nation appeared more straightforward, at least to these students. Nonetheless, as will be discussed in relation to ELF, it remains a concern that the link between English, and Anglophone linguistic and cultural practices often went unchallenged.

Importantly though, the findings clearly show that all participants were able to relate to the concept of intercultural citizenship and felt that it should and could form a valuable part of ELT. While we cannot generalise from this small scale study, another important finding appears to show that neoliberal approach to intercultural citizenship for individual gain (Aktas et al., 2016) and more critical community orientated approach such as those advocated by Byram et al. (2017) are not necessarily mutually exclusive. Some participants described both personal gains and opportunities from study abroad and a sense of intercultural citizenship alongside greater engagement and interest in wider communities.

Another key finding from this study was that many participants recognized, and were able to discuss at length, the importance of language, or specifically English, in intercultural communication and study abroad. English language proficiency, confidence and ownership were all discussed and related to the ability to develop a sense of identity and intercultural citizenship through

English. However, like previous research more generally and specifically in China, attitudes were quite mixed (Jenkins, 2007; Fang, 2016a; Ren et al., 2016; Wang, 2013). On the one hand, participants viewed English as the language that connected them to global communities and allowed them to develop a sense of intercultural citizenship. On the other hand, English was still associated with Anglophone settings. This association was seen by some as a threat to national identity, as well as positioning them negatively compared to the idealised Anglophone native speaker of English. As with intercultural competence/ awareness and citizenship, it is not clear to what extent participants developed a sense of language in intercultural communication that went beyond the national scale.

In terms of pedagogic implications, this study joins the growing body of research calling for a more explicit and systematic approach to intercultural education in language teaching (e.g. Baker 2015; Byram, 2008; Kramsch, 2009). The participants in this study appear to have developed their intercultural competence/awareness and sense of intercultural citizenship primarily through their own efforts during study abroad rather than through classroom instruction. This represents both a missed opportunity for a concrete goal in language learning beyond passing exams and also a failure to meet the needs of language learners. Furthermore, there still seems to be a strong attachment to national 'native speaker' conceptions of English in ELT leading to contradictory beliefs about its role as a global language among students. This is particularly concerning given that elements of intercultural competence, citizenship and ELF are present in current Chinese English language policy (Liu, 2016) and underscores the continuing gap between theory, policy and classroom practices.

While there is too little space here to offer detailed recommendations on how this gap might be addressed, it seems clear that both more and a greater variety of cultural content, as well as more intercultural education which focuses on preparation for intercultural communication, is needed. It would also be beneficial to introduce the concept of intercultural citizenship as this provides a framework to help make sense of student experiences of intercultural communication and, we believe, provide an alternative model and aim to the inappropriate native speaker 'standard'. Approaches which take greater account of the intercultural dimension to language education are not new, and there are many models to choose from (Byram, 2008; Byram et al. 2017; Kramsch, 2009). We argue that this needs to be combined with teaching English in a way that recognizes its role as a global lingua franca rather than principally as an Anglophone language. While this is a newer area of pedagogic research, studies are beginning to emerge (e.g. Bayyurt and Akcan, 2015) including some that have addressed Asian contexts (Baker, 2015; Galloway, 2013; Kirkpatrick, 2011). Nonetheless, with a few exceptions (Wen, 2015; Han et al., 2017), there has been little discussion directly related to China and even less empirical research and much more is needed.

Conclusion

Any conclusions drawn from this research must be tentative since it is a small scale study providing a snap shot in a single site. The findings are also reports of participants' perceptions rather than observations of classroom practices or intercultural interactions. Nonetheless, a number of key themes have emerged that may resonate in other settings. Most importantly, the participants' reports make clear the role experiences of intercultural communication in study abroad have in developing intercultural competence/awareness and a sense of intercultural citizenship. Participants reported changes in behaviour and attitudes leading to a greater understanding of other people and cultures, more openness to diversity and interest in wider communities. However, the depth of these changes appeared quite uneven, and for many, the understanding of 'others' seemed predominantly focused at the national scale in terms of identity, culture and language. A clear mismatch emerged between formal classroom instruction and experiences during study abroad with the majority of students' development of intercultural competence and citizenship taking place in study abroad. There were also mixed understandings and attitudes to ELF, but all participants emphasized the importance of language (English) in experiences of intercultural communication and citizenship. At present, there is little research in China on these topics, and given the increasing role of English in education as well as the large number of Chinese students studying abroad, further research is urgently needed.

Acknowledgements

This research is supported by the Ministry of Education Project of Key Research Institute of Humanities and Social Sciences at Universities in P. R. China (Project No. 15JJD740007), and Young Creative Talents Project of Social Sciences at Universities in Guangdong Province (Project No. 2015WQNCX034).

We would like to thank all the student participants of this study. We are also grateful to the anonymous reviewers and editors for their comments and feedback on the earlier version of this article. Any lack of clarity and any omissions remain entirely our responsibility.

References

Aktas, F., Pitts, K., Richards, J. C., & Silova, I. (2016). Institutionalizing global citizenship: A critical analysis of higher education programs and curricula. *Journal of Studies in International Education*, 1–16.

Baker, W. (2015). *Culture and Identity through English as a Lingua Franca: Rethinking Concepts and Goals in Intercultural Communication*. Berlin: De Gruyter Mouton.

Baker, W. (2016). English as an academic lingua franca and intercultural awareness: Student mobility in the transcultural university. *Language and Intercultural Communication*.

Bayyurt, Y., & Akcan, S. (Eds.). (2015). *Current Perspectives on Pedagogy for ELF*. Berlin: De Gruyter Mouton.

Beaven, A., & Borghetti, C. (2015). Editorial: Intercultural education for student mobility. *Intercultural Education*, 26(1), 1–5.

Block, D., Gray, J., & Holborow, M. (Eds.). (2012). *Neoliberalism and Applied Linguistics*. Abingdon: Routledge.

Byram, M. (1997). *Teaching and Assessing Intercultural Communicative Competence*. Clevedon: Multilingual Matters.

Byram, M. (2008). *From Foreign Language Education to Education for Intercultural Citizenship: Essays and Reflections*. Clevedon: Multilingual Matters Ltd.

Byram, M. (2012). Conceptualizing intercultural (communicative) competence and intercultural citizenship. In J. Jackson (Ed.), *The Routledge Handbook of Language and Intercultural Communication*. London: Routledge, 85–97.

Byram, M. (2014). Twenty-five years on – from cultural studies to intercultural citizenship. *Language, Culture and Curriculum*, 27(3), 209–225.

Byram, M., & Feng, A. (Eds.). (2006). *Living and Studying Abroad*. Clevedon: Multilingual Matters.

Byram, M., Golubeva, I., Han, H., & Wagner, M. (Eds.). (2017). *From Principles to Practice in Education for Intercultural Citizenship*. Bristol: Multilingual Matters.

Canagarajah, S. (2013). *Translingual Practice: Global Englishes and Cosmopolitan Relations*. London: Routledge.

Chang, J. (2006). Globalization and English in Chinese higher education. *World Englishes*, 25(3/4), 513–525.

Deng, Z. (2011). Confucianism, modernization and Chinese pedagogy: An introduction. *Journal of Curriculum Studies*, 43(5), 561–568.

Deng, Z. (2014). Confucianism, modernization and Chinese pedagogy (Part Two): Continuing the conversation. *Journal of Curriculum Studies*, 46(3), 301–304.

Dewey, M. (2012). Towards a post-normative approach: Learning the pedagogy of ELF. *Journal of English as a Lingua Franca*, 1(1), 141–170.

Dewey, M. (2015). Time to wake up some dogs! Shifting the culture of language in ELT. In Y. Bayyurt & S. Akcan (Eds.), *Current Perspectives on Pedagogy for ELF*. Berlin: De Gruyter Mouton, 121–134.

Fang, F. (2016a). Investigating attitudes towards English accents from an ELF framework. *The Asian Journal of Applied Linguistics*, 3(1): 68–80.

Fang, F. (2016b). 'Mind your local accent': Does accent training resonate to college students' English use? *Englishes in Practice*, 3(1): 1–28.

Feng, A. (2006). Contested notions of citizenship and citizenship education – The Chinese case. In G. Alred, M. Byram & M. Fleming (Eds.), *Education for Intercultural Citizenship: Concepts and Comparisons*. Clevedon: Multilingual Matters, 86–105.

Fong, E. T. Y. (2009). English in China: Some thoughts after the Beijing Olympics. *English Today*, 25(1), 44–49.

Galloway, N. (2013). Global Englishes and English Language Teaching (ELT) – Bridging the gap between theory and practice in a Japanese context. *System*, 41(3), 786–803.

Gao, Y. (2009). Sociocultural contexts and English in China: retaining and reforming the cultural habitus. In: J. Lo Bianco, J. Orton, & Gao Y., (eds.). *China and English: Globalization and the Dilemmas of Identity*. Bristol: Multilingual Matters, 56–78.

García, O., & Li, W. (2014). *Translanguaging: Language, Bilingualism and Education*. Basingstoke: Palgrave Macmillan.

Gil, J., & Adamson, B. (2011). The English language in Mainland China: a sociolinguistic profile. In A. Feng, (Ed.), *English Language Education across Greater China*. Bristol: Multilingual Matters, 23–45.

Gray, J. (2010). *The Construction of English: Culture, Consumerism and Promotion in the ELT Global Coursebook*. Basingstoke: Palgrave Macmillan.

Han, H., Li, S., Hongtao, J., & Yuqin, Z. (2017). Exploring perceptions of intercultural citizenship among English learners in Chinese universities. In M. Byram, I. Golubeva, H. Han & M. Wagner (Eds.), *From Principles to Practice in Education for Intercultural Citizenship*. Bristol:

Multilingual Matters, 25 – 44.

Houghton, S. A., & Rivers, D. J. (Eds). (2013). *Native-speakerism in Japan: Intergroup Dynamics in Foreign Language Education*. Bristol: Multilingual Matters.

Jackson, J. (2012). Education abroad. In J. Jackson (Ed.), *The Routledge Handbook of Language and Intercultural Communication*. London: Routledge, 449 – 463.

Jenkins, J. (2007). *English as a Lingua Franca: Attitude and Identity*. Oxford: Oxford University Press.

Jenkins, J. (2014). *English as a Lingua Franca in the International University: The Politics of Academic English Language Policy*. London: Routledge.

Jenkins, J. (2015). Repositioning English and multilingualism in English as a Lingua Franca. *Englishes in Practice*, 2(3), 49 – 85.

Kaloscia, K. (2014). *Communities of Practice and English as a Lingua Franca: A Study of Erasmus Students in a Central-European Context*. Berlin: DeGruyter Mouton.

Kinginger, C. (Ed.). (2013). *Social and Cultural Aspects of Language Learning in Study Abroad*. Amsterdam: John Benjamins.

Kirkpatrick, A. (2011). English as an Asian lingua franca and the multilingualmodel of ELT. *Language Teaching*, 44(2), 212 – 224.

Kramsch, C. (2009). *The Multilingual Subject*. Oxford: Oxford University Press.

Li, W. (2016). New Chinglish and the Post-Multilingualism challenge: Translanguaging ELF in China. *Journal of English as a Lingua Franca*, 5(1), 1 – 25.

Liu, H. (2016). *Language Policy and Practice in a Chinese Junior High School from Global Englishes Perspective*. PhD, University of Southampton.

Lu, P., & Corbett, J. (2012). An intercultural approach to second language education and citizenship. In J. Jackson (Ed.), *The Routledge Handbook of Language and Intercultural Communication*. London:

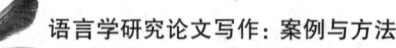

Routledge, 325-329.

Porto, M. (2014). Intercultural citizenship education in an EFL online project in Argentina. *Language and Intercultural Communication*, 14(2), 245-261.

Ren, W., Chen, Y. & Lin, C. (2016). University students' perceptions of ELF in mainland China and Taiwan. *System*, 56, 13-27.

Schreier, M. (2012). *Qualitative Content Analysis in Practice*. London: Sage.

Schutt, R. K. (2014). *Investigating the Social World: The Process and Practice of Research*, (8th ed). Thousand Oaks: Sage.

Seidlhofer, B. (2011). *Understanding English as a Lingua Franca*. Oxford: Oxford University Press.

Wang, Y. (2013). Non-conformity to ENL norms: A perspective from Chinese English users. *Journal of English as a Lingua Franca*, 2(2), 255-282.

Wen, Q. (2015). Teaching culture(s) in English as a lingua franca in Asia: Dilemma and solution. *Journal of English as a Lingua Franca*, 5(1), 155-177.

Wei, R., & Su, J. (2012). The statistics of English in China. *English Today*, 28(3), 10-14.

Zhu, H. (2015). Negotiation as the rule of engagement in intercultural and lingua franca communication: Meaning, frame of references and interculturality. *Journal of English as a Lingua Franca*, 4(1), 63-90.

 方法谈：

质性研究的优势是什么？如何让人信服？

社会科学研究的实证研究，需要遵从一定的研究方法，对语言学研究特别是应用语言学的实证研究也不例外。笔者第一次接触语言学的研究方法，是在英国攻读硕士阶段的一门必修课上，当时对语言学研究方法几乎是一无所知，通过这门课程，便开始了解到应用语言学数据收集的步骤与分析方法，以及量化与质性研究的区别。加之,我硕士研究生修读的课程,更加关注语言与社会研究,后来博士的研究聚焦于社会语言学,因此后来的研究兴趣也更加偏向于质性研究。但是,对于量化与质性研究在数据收集与分析等方面,我不认为它们是对立的。反而更应该是互补的,也就是方法论说的"三角互证",但是"三角互证"是否一定要通过量化与质性研究这一所谓的"混合法"研究来达成,也是质性研究本身进一步探讨的话题。

量化与质性研究从认识论上的区别,在此我不进行具体探讨,就肖小穗(2021)对质化研究的根源探讨指出:"质化研究根源于一个人文主义批评的学术传统。"(p. 113)假设雨后,一辆车开过水坑溅起一摊水到路人身上,量化研究关注的可能是车速与溅起的水花大小的联系,以及水花大小与水花同路人的距离是否会导致路人被水花溅到。但是对于质化研究,这些变量似乎并不那么重要。质化研究更加关注的是,司机当时决定把车开到水坑的想法,是选择减速还是加速,路人被水花所溅以后的行为和心理,司机把车开过水坑的行为和心理。所以说,质化研究是一个以人为本的研究,它重在关注事物本身,强调深入探究事物的本质。

就应用语言学来说,语言学习和心理规律可能可以通过量化研究得出一定的结论,但通过质性研究可以基于个体差异对个性化学习进行深入的阐释(Griffiths & Soruç, 2020)。质性研究的优势在于对现象背后的解读和对个体的关注,对语言习得的文化性、社会性等进行解读,其更加偏向求异,深入探究,有自身的主观性,但又承认社会研究中的主观性;研究者作为社会参与者,通过观摩、交谈、采访、日志等方式进行田野调查,寻求事件的原因,从而探讨事件背后的意图和本质(肖小穗,2021)。例如探讨外语学习课堂焦虑或者外语学习愉悦感,量化研究关注的是引起焦虑和愉悦的变量,如教师、同伴、测试等关系,但缺乏了解变量背后的因素和学生产生焦虑或者愉悦的原因。例如,课堂焦虑对外语学习动机不一定是负相关的关系,焦虑的产生也许可以促进外语学习动机;同理,愉悦对外语学习动机不一定是正相关关系,愉悦也许也会导致学习动机的下降。外语学习焦虑也许不是成绩差的原因(Sparks, Ganschow & Javorsky, 2000),通过外语学习动机研究如何实现"理想二语自我"和"实际自我"(Dornyei, 2005)的关系,这背后的原因就需要质性研究通过不同的方式对其背后的原因进行分析。质性研究通过话语呈现,可以进一步从资料本身探讨语言学和语言教育的社会因素,例如学生可能会谈及同伴的性格、成绩给自身造成的焦虑,以及老师和家长的鼓励或批评带来的愉悦或者焦虑。

质性研究在探究事件和行为背后的原因有着自身的优势，但是在方法论层面，质性研究的科学性和系统性还没有被人们熟知，相比量化研究，质性研究没有成熟的问卷，呈现出的多元的数据也需要从不同层次进行编码解读，其研究过程和量化研究相比可能需要进行不断地重构、修改，而数据收集也不一定存在一个所谓的终点(end point)。对于质性研究来说，数据收集的样本量分析及其饱和度(saturation)，需要研究人员做出判断，从而提高质性研究的透明度、可靠性和认可度(谢爱磊，陈嘉怡，2021)。如何做一项让人信服的质性研究，是值得进一步探讨的问题。

虽然没有固定的步骤，但是我认为质性研究需要前期缜密的计划，并在数据收集的过程中严格地遵循，其间不断地进行反思与总结，并做好下一步数据收集的计划。质性研究的人群抽样需要有针对性，例如目的抽样(purposive sampling)作为质性研究较为常用的抽样方法，旨在探究一个特定群体的文化、思维与生活方式等内容，其中这一群体需要符合一定的筛选标准。而滚雪球抽样(snowball sampling)也是以一定的标准通过研究对象进行介绍，可以在较短的时间内募集到一定符合研究需求的研究对象(参照 Fang & Baker, 2018)。在数据收集过程中，研究者一般也是田野调查的参与者，但是如何把握研究者的"参与度"，则需要其在不断反思总结之后形成田野调查熟悉与敏感度，从而提升数据收集的有效性。质性研究的样本收集更多是聚焦于样本的典型性，反映了研究群体的特征，这一点和量化研究的代表性是不一样的。这一点，对于不熟悉质性研究的人来说，可能对其样本抽样存在一定的误区。以本导读案例为例，我通过滚雪球抽样进行研究对象的收集，在明确研究对象特征和标准的前提下，让受访者进行推荐，加上研究人员的筛选，可以保证选取的研究对象标准较为一致(参照 Fang & Baker, 2018)。

质性研究的样本量，也是一个经常被提及的问题。我认为，一项好的质性研究，不是单纯看其样本量，甚至可以说质性研究的成功与否并不是由它的样本量决定的。以本文研究作为案例分析，在本文案例中，我们招募了六位参与者，但是，质性研究更重要的是其数据的深度，本文案例用了面对面访谈、焦点小组以及邮件访谈等方式进行数据收集，有较为充分的数据作为支撑。另外，当研究者认为数据可以支撑后续分析，且对一个事物或者问题的阐释可以在多方面、多维度分析的基础上进行时，研究者可以选择在一项研究中报道和研究问题最为相关的那一部分数据。当然,研究者手头的数据一定要比在文章所呈现的要多得多,这也给研究者提出了另一个挑战,即质性研究数据的分析与解读。

我时常听到人们讨论质性研究的复杂性与挑战性,谈及数据的杂乱,从而无从进行分析。质性研究对于资料分析的工具如 NVivo、MAXQDA,都是可以对不同的质性数据进行整理。但是和量化研究不同的是,质性研究现阶段的分析工具,其实是帮助研究者进行编码与数据分类,其具体过程还是要研究者亲力亲为进行分析,而编码分析是一个循环的过程,可能需要基于研究问题进行归纳式(inductive)分析,这个过程中,研究者基于研究问题有一定的编码框架;与此同时,质性研究的魅力在于编码还可以来源于数据本身,即基于数据进行演绎式(deductive)分析,可以通过二级甚至三级编码凝练出与研究相关的新主题。以本文为例,文章探讨学生在海外交换学习到回国的跨文化公民身份构建研究,我们对编码过程进行了较为详细的介绍:初级编码是基于研究的目的和研究问题从较为宏观的层面进行列举,我们把数据录入 NVivo 软件进行二级编码;二级编码则是基于数据本身呈现的主题。两轮编码过后,我们把和文章相关的数据摘要进行翻译、整合,再解读后呈现出文章的最终分析主题。

质性资料的分析与解读是决定研究成功与否、可信服与否的关键环节。所以,质性研究的编码环节是十分重要的,不能草草为之。编码本身也是具有主观性的,这不可避免,也无需刻意避免。所以,如何保证编码的有效性,也是质性研究过程中需要注意的问题。我认为,质性研究让人信服的另外一个重要的方面,是编码的一致性。研究者可以在自身编码的基础上,另外邀请了解研究性质的、经验丰富的研究者独立进行编码(也可以作者间都各自进行编码),与研究者的编码进行对比,在对比编码相似度之后,通过进一步讨论凝练出质性分析的数据主题。如果对数据编码采取这一步骤,也可以提升编码者之间的信度,从而提升研究资料的可靠性。

诚然,在一个论文中是很难把质性研究的方方面面进行全面的呈现。从较为宏观的角度,本文的作用是希望让更多的人对质性研究感兴趣,同时消除对质性研究的一些偏见。质性研究基于解释主义进行研究(陈向明,2006),不仅解释"是什么",还探讨人们"怎么做",以及解释事物背后的"为什么"。对研究方法来说,没有孰优孰劣之分,更重要的是研究者如何根据研究问题和研究目的制定相关的研究方法。如果一定要说质性研究的优势,那可能是其"解释性"与"批判性"(Lune & Berg, 2017)。质性研究需要研究者在遵循研究伦理的前提下,聚焦于研究本身进入田野或者设计相关问题进行数据收集,同时又可以跳出研究对收集到的数据进行解读,再回到研究中间进行数据的重构、解读与研究者的反思和再研究。可以说,质性研究的另一个优势,是数据的可持续性与延展性。只要掌握了数据的分析方法,学会整理与统筹数据,质性研究可以做得既有深度又有价值。对语言学和应用语言学来说,与人进行较为深入且多维度的沟通交流,可以更加全面了解语言学习背后的心理、文化、社会、价值和身份认同等多种因素,这也恰恰是现阶段语言学和应用语言学研究所关注的人文和社会转向。

参考文献

Dörnyei, Z. (2005). *The Psychology of the Language Learner: Individual Differences in Second Language Acquisition*. New Jersey: Lawrence Erlbaum Associates.

Fang, F., & Baker, W. (2018). 'A more inclusive mind towards the world': English language teaching and study abroad in China from Intercultural citizenship and English as a lingua franca perspectives. *Language Teaching Research*, 22(5), 608–624.

Griffiths, C., & Soruç, A. (2020). *Individual Differences in Language Learning: A Complex Systems Theory Perspective*. Basingstoke: Palgrave Macmillan.

Lune, H., & Berg, B. L. (2017). *Qualitative Research Methods for the Social Science*. Harlow: Pearson.

Sparks, R. L., Ganschow, L., & Javorsky, J. (2000). Déjà vu all over again: A response to Saito, Horwitz, and Garza. *The Modern Language Journal*, 84(2), 251–255.

陈向明:《质的研究方法与社会科学研究》,教育科学出版社2006年版。

肖小穗:《质化与量化研究(Qualitative and Quantitative Research)》,《中国传媒海外报告(China Media Report Overseas)》2021年第2期,第111—126页。

谢爱磊、陈嘉怡:《质性研究的样本量判断——饱和的概念、操作与争议》,《华东师范大学学报(教育科学版)》2021年第12期,第15—27页。

Syntactic Complexity in Adapted Extracurricular Reading Materials[*]

Lei Lei, Yaqian Shi[**]

Abstract: Extracurricular reading is important for language learning since it is not just beneficial for vocabulary and grammar acquisition, but also useful for other aspects such as reading comprehension. Previous research has focused on the role of linguistic features such as syntactic complexity in adapted textbooks, while little attention has been paid to that in other reading materials such as extracurricular ones. This study examined the syntactic complexity in adapted extracurricular reading texts at five difficulty levels based on five machine learning algorithms. The results showed that the adapted texts differed significantly across the five levels in terms of syntactic complexity, with large effect sizes. In addition, three indices of syntactic complexity, i. e., DC/T, MLS, and CN/C, were found to well distinguish texts at different levels. The findings of the present study have significant implications for the adaptation of language learning materials such as extracurricular reading texts and test materials.

Keywords: Extracurricular reading materials, Syntactic complexity, Machine learning, Text adaptation

---

[*] 原载 *System* 113 (2023)。

[**] 雷蕾,上海外国语大学语料库研究院教授、博士生导师。研究方向为:语料库语言学、语言数字人文、学术英语等。
施雅倩,华中科技大学外国语学院讲师。

1. Introduction

Language materials that are adequately adapted for its target learners are important for language learning (Chen & Meurers, 2019; Sung et al., 2015). Such materials enable learners to understand the texts, motivate them to read more, and accordingly improve their language skills (Krashen, 2004; Rodrigo, 2016, pp. 66 – 86). One issue that adapters may carefully consider in adapting the materials is the factor of linguistic complexity (Mesmer et al., 2012). They attempt to re-edit the materials in order to make the language adequately complex at lexical, syntactic, and textual levels for the target learners (Bailey & Heritage, 2014). In addition, to address the issues of objectivity and replicability in the process of material adaptation, linguistic benchmarks for material adaptation are needed.

Linguistic benchmarks are important (Jin & Lu, 2018) since without such benchmarks, adapters may heavily rely on their experience and expertise (Allen, 2009; Crossley et al., 2012). For example, Green and Hawkey (2012) investigated the adaptation process of test materials for academic reading tests by four experienced teachers. They found that the four teachers largely depended on their own experience and intuition and considerably varied in their adaptation strategies, which was problematic and might lead to inconsistency in the adapted materials (Crossley et al., 2012; Green & Hawkey, 2012). To address the issue, it is necessary to develop benchmarks for learning material adaptation, particularly those at lexical and syntactic levels since lexical and syntactic modifications are often needed in adaptation (Jin et al., 2020; Vajjala & Meurers, 2012). As for lexis, a number of word lists such as *Academic Word List* (Coxhead, 2000) have been developed based on large-scaled textbook corpora. These lists consider the distribution of their included words at different grade levels, which can serve as lexical benchmarks for the adaptation of learning materials.

Compared with lexis, syntax has received less attention and syntactic benchmarks for adaptation are scarce. One possible reason for it is that syntax, particularly syntactic complexity, is more complicated since it is a multidimensional construct that can be measured from numerous perspectives (Lu, 2010). More importantly, syntactic features such as clauses, noun phrases, and T-units were more difficult to be automatically identified due to technical issues. As a result, most previous studies manually analysed a few syntactic features based on small datasets (Ortega, 2003). Syntax has thus been less investigated and syntactic benchmarks are more scarce than lexical ones.

Syntactic complexity is important for learning materials adaptation since it is an important part of linguistic complexity (Bulté & Housen, 2014) and syntactic modification is one of the most frequently used strategies in materials adaptation (Green & Hawkey, 2012). Given the importance of syntactic complexity and the scarcity of syntactic benchmarks in text adaptation, we intend to investigate the adapted texts from the perspective of syntactic complexity. More specifically, we aim to examine how the adapted extracurricular reading materials at different levels differ from one another in terms of syntactic complexity. Such differences can reveal the relationship between text level and syntactic complexity. More importantly, the results may provide significant insights into the development of syntactic benchmarks for text adaptation.

1.1 Syntactic complexity in adapted materials

A key step concerning the development of syntactic benchmarks is to ascertain how the adapted materials for various target learners differ from one another in terms of syntactic features, particularly syntactic complexity (e.g., Crossley et al., 2012; Jin et al., 2020; Zarco-Tejada, 2019). To this end, many studies have investigated the syntactic complexity features of the adapted materials, which will be elaborated on below.

The factor of syntactic complexity in material adaptation has been explored largely from two perspectives summarised as follows. One line of research is to explore the differences of syntactic complexity in adapted textbooks at different levels (e.g., François, 2009; Jin et al., 2020; Sung et al., 2015; Zarco-Tejada, 2019). One example is Crossley et al. (2007) that compared adapted textbooks with authentic texts in terms of three indices of syntactic complexity, and significant difference was found in the use of noun phrases and the number of constituents per word between adapted textbooks and authentic texts. Another example is Zarco-Tejada (2019), who investigated the features of syntactic complexity of adapted textbooks at A2, B1, and B2 levels in the Common European Framework of Reference (CEFR). He found that the examined adapted textbooks at the three levels varied significantly in some syntactic features such as the number of main clauses. Similarly, Jin et al. (2020) explored the syntactic complexity of the adapted textbooks at 12 levels of primary and secondary grade levels in China. They found that all eight measures of syntactic complexity that they had examined showed significant between-level differences, five of which were significant predictors of grade levels. Their results provided significant insights into teaching/learning materials adaptation.

Another line of research is to explore the differences of syntactic complexity in adapted extracurricular materials at different levels (e.g., Allen, 2009; Crossley et al., 2012). For example, Allen (2009) investigated the use of relative clauses in news texts adapted from the *Guardian Weekly*, a British periodical, at elementary, intermediate, and advanced levels. The results showed that the number of non-restrictive relative clauses increased from elementary to advanced levels. Based on the same data used in Allen (2009), Crossley et al. (2012) examined their between-level differences in terms of three indices of syntactic complexity, i.e., the mean number of words before the main verb, the mean number of high-level constituents per word, and the uniformity and consistency of the syntactic constructions. Significant differences were found between elementary-intermediate and elementary-advanced levels in terms of the number of words before the main verb.

1.2 The machine learning approach to text classification

Although previous studies on adapted materials have revealed some of their linguistic features, they are probably methodologically limited since they only adopted some traditional analyses such as correlation analysis and frequency analysis. As a result, it remained unanswered how effective these linguistic features could be to distinguish the adapted materials at different levels.

Recently, the machine learning approach has increasingly been employed to classify the text levels of the adapted materials (e.g., François, 2009; Jin et al., 2020; Sung et al., 2015). Machine learning algorithms such as Multinomial Logistic Regression, Support Vector Machine, Naïve Bayes, Generalized Linear Model, and Deep Learning have been frequently used in such tasks, which will be introduced below. First, Multinomial Logistic Regression is an extension algorithm of Logistic Regression that can handle multilevel response variables (El-Habil, 2012). One of its advantages is that the produced model is more intuitively interpreted since it uses odds ratios as estimators for the explanatory variables (Petrucci, 2009). Therefore, Multinomial Logistic Regression has been widely used in text level classification (e.g., François, 2009; Jin et al., 2020). For example, François (2009) used it to classify the levels of textbooks based on their lexical and grammatical features. The results showed that it could accurately classify 38% of the textbooks. Nevertheless, it should be noted that Multinomial Logistic Regression is sensitive to the issue of multicollinearity and variable redundancy (Lee et al., 2013; Ranganathan et al., 2017). Hence, we should select the most useful and less correlated variables as predictors when we adopt Multinomial Logistic Regression for the classification task.

Second, Support Vector Machine is a flexible algorithm that represents different classes in a hyperplane in a multidimensional space (Srivastava & Bhambhu, 2010). The hyperplane is then generated iteratively to minimize the error (Bhavsar & Panchal, 2012), and the hyperplane that is most capable of generalization for classification is selected. Support Vector Machine performs better on small samples than on large samples (Liu et al., 2012). Therefore, we should take the sample size into consideration when we use it. Support Vector Machine has been used in text classification due to its satisfactory performance. For example, Sung et al. (2015) adopted Support Vector Machine to classify the grade levels of textbooks based on multilevel linguistic features that included word, semantics, syntax, and cohesion features, which achieved an accuracy of 71.75%.

Third, Naïve Bayes is a probability algorithm that assigns the most likely class label to a document that is represented as a set of feature vectors based on the Bayes theorem (Granik & Mesyura, 2017). The fundamental assumption of Naïve Bayes is that all features or predictors are mutually independent (Granik & Mesyura, 2017), which limits the applicability of the algorithm. One obvious advantage of Naïve Bayes is that it works efficiently with a small amount of training data (Zulfikar et al., 2017). Therefore, it has been used in text classification due to its simplicity and relatively good performance (Chen et al., 2009). For example, Leroy et al. (2008) used Naïve Bayes to classify the difficulty levels of online health information based on their vocabulary features, which reached an accuracy of 98%.

Fourth, Generalized Linear Model is a generalization of linear regression that allows for a non-normal distribution of the response variables, such as Exponential, Gamma, and Poisson distributions (Fox, 2016). As a result, Generalized Linear Model is highly flexible and has been used in areas such as text classification (Eyheramendy & Madigan, 2007). Given its effectiveness in classification tasks, Generalized Linear Model is also used in our study. However, the algorithm is very sensitive to outliers and thus we should detect and remove outliers when we use it for text classification (Kuhnt & Pawlitschko, 2005).

Last, Deep Learning is a more sophisticated algorithm that imitates the workings of the human brain and automatically creates patterns for classification (Goodfellow et al., 2016). It performs well in intricate structures in high-dimensional data and thus increasingly gains popularity in various tasks such as topic classification, translation, and sentiment analysis (Lecun et al., 2015). However, one disadvantage of Deep Learning is that it works like a black box and hence it is not easy to interpret its results (Castelvecchi, 2016). Therefore, we may need to carefully explain the results. Given its satisfactory performance in previous studies, Deep Learning is also used in this study.

In summary, we will employ five machine learning algorithms, i.e.,

Multinomial Logistic Regression, Support Vector Machine, Naïve Bayes, Generalized Linear Model, and Deep Learning to classify the adapted texts at various levels and to identify the most predictive indices of syntactic complexity. The reason for using the five algorithms is that they include both traditional algorithms and more sophisticated ones. The use of both traditional and more sophisticated algorithms allows us to make a more reasonable comparison of their performance in the classification tasks. Traditional algorithms such as Multinomial Logistic Regression, Support Vector Machine, and Naïve Bayes have been frequently used to classify levels of adapted materials and they obtained varying accuracies (e.g., 34% (Jin et al., 2020) vs. 71% (Sung et al., 2015)). However, it may not be fair to compare their performance since these algorithms were employed in different classification tasks such as those at different levels and based on various linguistic features (e.g., François, 2009; Jin et al., 2020; Sung et al., 2015). Therefore, we used the traditional algorithms for the classification tasks and compared their performance. We also included more sophisticated algorithms such as Deep Learning in our study since it obtained good performance in other classification tasks (e.g., 95.76% in medical text classification tasks (Prabhakar & Won, 2021)). We hypothesized that Deep Learning also performed well in our classification tasks, which might shed light on the selection of machine learning algorithms for similar tasks in future research. Generalized Linear Model is also included in our study due to its effectiveness and satisfactory performance in classification tasks.

1.3 Issues of previous studies

Although previous research has contributed much to our understanding of the syntactic features in various genres of adapted texts, they may be limited at least from three perspectives.

First, many studies concerning the syntactic complexity of adapted materials focused on adapted textbooks (e.g., Jin et al., 2020; Sung et al., 2015; Zarco-Tejada, 2019), while less attention has been paid to the adaptation of other types of language learning materials such as extracurricular texts (except for a few studies such as Allen (2009) and Crossley et al. (2012)). In fact, extracurricular reading texts are particularly important for successful language teaching/learning due to the significant roles they play in language learning. First, most of the learners' reading activities take place out of class, and extracurricular reading seems an indispensable part of language learning (Kuimova & Ukhov, 2016; Pfost et al., 2013). Second, extracurricular reading contributes significantly to learners' language development. For example, extracurricular reading is found beneficial for vocabulary acquisition (Suk, 2017) and grammar competence improvement (Ponniah, 2018).

Second, except for some studies such as Vajjala and Meurers (2012), many studies on adapted extracurricular reading texts examined only a narrow range of indices of syntactic complexity. For example, Allen (2009) investigated the use of relative clauses in adapted news texts. As discussed earlier, syntactic complexity includes multiple dimensions or constructs, and a fuller picture of the features of syntactic complexity in adapted materials is needed to paint.

Third, most studies used only one or two traditional algorithms such as Multinomial Logistic Regression and Support Vector Machine to classify the adapted materials at different levels, which resulted in varying accuracies (e.g., François, 2009; Jin et al., 2020; Sung et al., 2015). To compare and triangulate the validity of different machine learning algorithms, it is necessary to adopt several machine learning algorithms that include both the traditional and the more sophisticated ones for text classification.

2. Measurement of syntactic complexity

Syntactic complexity refers to the variation and sophistication of the grammatical structures in language productions (Housen & Kuiken, 2009; Lu, 2011; Norris & Ortega, 2009). It is considered as a multidimensional construct that includes a wide range of aspects such as length of production, coordination, and subordination (Norris & Ortega, 2009). Therefore, many different measures have been proposed to quantify syntactic complexity, such as length of production units at clausal, sentential, and T-units' levels (Ortega, 2003).

More recently, tools for the automatic analysis of syntactic complexity have been developed, such as the Tool for the Automatic Assessment of Syntactic Sophistication and Complexity (Kyle, 2016) and the Syntactic Complexity Analyzer (SCA) (Lu, 2010, 2011). These tools can automatically calculate the syntactic complexity of a text, which are useful for the quantitative analyses of large-scale language data and thus they have been widely employed in many different studies (e.g., Lei et al., 2023; Lu & Ai, 2015; Wu et al., 2020). In this study, we will use the tool of Syntactic Complexity Analyzer (SCA) (Lu, 2010) to automatically analyse the syntactic complexity of adapted extracurricular reading texts at different levels. The reasons for using it are as follows.

First, the tool SCA was developed based on the results of previous studies regarding syntactic complexity (Ortega, 2003). More specifically, SCA includes the indices that were either found useful for discriminating learners of different proficiency levels or recommended in the previous studies.

Second, it measures five dimensions of syntactic complexity, i.e., length of production, overall sentence complexity, amount of subordination, amount of coordination, and phrasal complexity (see Table 1 for the details). Therefore, it can comprehensively analyse the syntactic complexity of a text.

Table 1 Indices of syntactic complexity used in the study (modified from Lu and Ai (2015) and Jin et al. (2020)).

Measure	Code	Description
Length of production		
Mean length of sentence	MLS	Number of words divided by number of sentences
Mean length of T-unit	MLT	Number of words divided by number of T-units
Mean length of clause	MLC	Number of words divided by number of clauses
Overall sentence complexity		
Clauses per sentence	C/S	Number of clauses divided by number of sentences
Amount of subordination		
Clauses per T-unit	C/T	Number of clauses divided by number of T-unit

continued

Measure	Code	Description
Complex T-unit ratio	CT/T	Number of complex T-units divided by number of T-units
Dependent clauses per clause	DC/C	Number of dependent clauses divided by number of clauses
Dependent clauses per T-unit	DC/T	Number of dependent clauses divided by number of T-units
Amount of coordination		
Coordinate phrases per clause	CP/C	Number of coordinate phrases divided by number of clauses
Coordinate phrases per T-unit	CP/T	Number of coordinate phrases divided by of T-units
T-unit per sentence	T/S	Number of T-units divided by number of sentences
Phrasal complexity		
Complex nominals per clause	CN/C	Number of complex nominals divided by number of clauses
Complex nominals per T-unit	CN/T	Number of complex nominals divided by number of T-units
Verb phrases per T-unit	VP/T	Number of verb phrases divided by number of T-units
Non-finite elements		
Non-finite elements per clause	NFE/C	Number of non-finite elements divided by number of clauses

Third, SCA has been widely used in previous studies and its validity has been proven (e.g., Bi & Jiang, 2020; Jin et al., 2020). For example, Polio and Yoon (2018) evaluated the validity and reliability of SCA by comparing the results based on SCA with the hand-coded results of 30 essays. They found that the indices of syntactic complexity produced by SCA were highly related with the hand-coded ones. The results indicate that SCA is a reliable and valid tool for automatically analysing the syntactic complexity of a text.

3. Aims of this study

To address the issues of previous studies in section 1.3, the present study aims to examine syntactic features of adapted extracurricular reading texts at different levels in terms of syntactic complexity based on a topic-, genre-, and size-balanced corpus. To be specific, the purpose of the study is two-fold. First, it intends to examine the features of syntactic complexity of adapted extracurricular reading texts at various difficulty levels. Second, it aims to identify the indices of syntactic complexity that can well classify texts at different levels based on both traditional and more sophisticated algorithms. The research questions that this study attempts to answer are as follows.

RQ1. Do the adapted extracurricular reading texts at different levels significantly differ from one another in terms of syntactic complexity? If yes, what are the differences?

RQ2. What indices of syntactic complexity can well classify the adapted texts at different levels?

4. Methods

In this section, we will first describe the data used in the study and then the procedures of data processing.

4.1 Data

The data used in the study are adapted news texts downloaded from Newsela (https://newsela.com). Newsela is an educational website that provides reading texts to learners at different proficiency levels. All texts provided by Newsela are adapted based on authentic news stories from well-known periodicals such as *The Guardian*, *The New York Times*, and *The Washington Post*. Writers and editors at Newsela will first closely examine the content and quality of the original news stories before they adapt them. They take into account issues such as balance, objectivity, and tone when they select news stories and deliberately avoid bias. Then, professional adapters at Newsela adapt each news story into five texts at various difficulty levels, varying from 2 to 12. The difficulty levels of 2 – 12 correspond to the grade levels under the educational system of K-12 in the United States that refers to kindergarten to 12th grade. The texts at levels of 2 - 12 mean that students at that grade or higher than that grade can read and comprehend them. When adapting the texts, they consider linguistic features such as lexical and syntactic ones. For example, when simplifying a text, they may split a complex sentence into several shorter, simpler ones, and rewrite a sentence with easier words and simpler syntactic structures (Agnello, 2021). As a result, any learner reader, regardless of her/his proficiency level and reading ability, can access the same content at the level that is suitable to her/him (Agnello, 2021). In addition, Newsela publishes reading texts across more than 20 genres every day and these texts are of various topics, such as politics, economics, cartoons, sports, music, and games. A wide variety of topics and genres offer readers many options and thus readers at different ages can choose the texts they are interested in. For example, readers at 7 years old may be interested in cartoons, so they can read the adapted cartoon texts at the lowest level. Readers at 14 years old may be interested in both cartoons and sports, and they can read those adapted texts at their appropriate levels. The aforementioned features of the Newsela texts make them particularly appropriate for the present study since (a) the linguistic difficulties of a group of five adapted texts, either lexical and syntactic ones, are different, and (b) more importantly, other factors that might affect the use of language in a text are controlled (e.g., genres, contents, and topics).

A reading text was collected from Newsela and included in this study if: (a) it belonged to one of the three subjects, i.e., ELA (English for Language Arts), Science, and Social Studies, and (b) it was adapted into the following five reading levels, i.e., 3, 5, 7, 9, and 12. Levels 3, 5, 7, 9, and 12 were selected for two reasons. First, since most of the authentic news stories in Newsela were adapted into five texts at levels of 3, 5, 7, 9, and 12, the selection of adapted texts at these five levels allowed us to collect a fairly large number of texts for our research. Second and more importantly, the selected five levels cover a wide range of levels, ranging from Grades 3 to 12, which makes it possible for a fuller description of the extracurricular reading materials at various levels. In other words, the two criteria were used to select texts from Newsela in order to secure a wide variety of topics and levels. With each subject at each text level 150 texts, a total of 2 250 texts were collected in this study.

4.2 Data processing

The Newsela texts were processed as follows. First, the Newsela texts were analysed with Syntactic Complexity Analyzer (Lu, 2010). Then, non-finite elements per clause (NFE/C) was also included since previous studies found it useful for measuring non-finite elements/subordination (Jin et al., 2020). NFE/C was calculated by subtracting one from the measure of verb phrases per clause (Jin et al., 2020). That is, a total of 15 indices of syntactic complexity were produced for each Newsela text.

Second, outlier texts were detected and removed from the data. A text was identified as an outlier and removed if one or more of its indices of syntactic complexity were three standard deviations away from the mean (Shiffler, 1988). A total of 124 texts were hence removed and the remaining 2 126 ones were used for the subsequent analyses (see Table 2 for the statistics of the remaining 2 126 texts).

Table 2 Statistics of the adapted reading texts with outliers removed.

Text level	Subject			Total Texts	Total Words
	ELA	Science	Social Studies		
3	150	149	150	449	211 800
5	150	150	150	450	313 557
7	150	148	148	446	372 539
9	148	143	146	437	385 147
12	123	108	113	344	345 790
Total	**721**	**697**	**707**	**2 126**	**1 628 833**

Third, tests of one-way multivariate analysis of variance (MANOVA) and one-way analysis of variance (ANOVA) were used to determine whether the adapted texts at different levels significantly differed from one another in the indices of syntactic complexity. When the results were significant, Games-Howell post hoc tests were used to examine significant differences between paired levels.

Fourth, machine learning approach was taken to identify the indices of syntactic complexity that were most useful for the classification of the adapted texts at different levels. Spearman's rank correlation was first performed to examine the correlation between each index of syntactic complexity and the text level (Jin et al., 2020). We used the Spearman's rank correlation rather than Pearson's correlation because the text levels are ordinal scale data and the number of texts at the five levels are not normally distributed. Indices that are strongly or moderately correlated with text level (i.e., $rho > 0.4$) (Akoglu, 2018) were identified as potential predictor variables for machine learning. Then, five machine learning algorithms, i.e., Naïve Bayes (NB), Generalized Linear Model (GLM), Multinomial Logistic Regression (MLR), Deep Learning (DL), and Support Vector Machine (SVM), were used for the classification of the adapted texts into different levels. It should be noted that the model used for Deep Learning is feed-forward artificial neural network with complex multilayers (RapidMiner, 2019). The reason for using this model is that it can imitate the working process of human neuron and has been found to be effective for various tasks of classification, clustering, and prediction in many fields (Abiodun et al., 2018).

The classification task was performed as follows. First, the data were randomly split into the training and testing data. The split ratio between the training and testing data was set at 6∶4. Such a ratio has been used in many previous studies and proven to be useful (e.g., Moustafa & Slay, 2016). The training data were used for building a model based on the five machine learning algorithms. Then, the testing data were applied to evaluate the classification performance of the trained model. Th evaluation metric of accuracy is used to assess the classification performance of the models (Tripathy et al., 2016). It measures the proportion of correctly classified texts level in each algorithm.

This metric was calculated based on the following equation:

$$accuracy = \frac{TP + TN}{the\ total\ number\ of\ classified\ cases}$$

where TP (True Positive) refers to the number of samples that were positive and correctly classified as positive and TN (True Negative) is the number of examples that were negative and correctly classified as negative (Tripathy et al., 2016). The binary classification aims to identify whether an unknown item belongs to a specific category. If yes, it is positive. Otherwise, it is negative. For example, a classification task is to decide whether an animal is a dog. If the algorithm identifies it as a dog, the result is positive. If the algorithm identifies it not as a dog, it is negative.

Last, we conducted feature ranking based on their average weights in the five algorithms (Sun et al., 2013; Zaharie et al., 2007). We first extracted the weights of the 15 indices of syntactic complexity in the five machine learning algorithms and then calculated their average weights based on the following formula:

$$AW_i = 0.2 \times W_{NB} + 0.3 \times W_{GLM} + 0.1 \times W_{MLR} + 0.3 \times W_{DL} + 0.2 \times W_{SVM}$$

where AW_i is the average weight of an index, and W_{NB}, W_{GLM}, W_{MLR}, W_{DL}, and W_{SVM} are its weights in the five algorithms. The weights in the formula, i.e., 0.2, 0.3, 0.1, 0.3, and 0.2, were determined by the performance of the five algorithms. Generalized Linear Model and Deep Learning performed best among the five algorithms, with an accuracy of over 90%. Thus, they were assigned 0.3. Naïve Bayes and Support Vector Machine performed well, with an accuracy of over 80%. They were hence assigned 0.2. Multinomial Logistic Regression achieved an accuracy of less than 37% and thus was assigned 0.1. For example, the weights of the index DC/T in the five algorithms were 0.122, 0.065, 0.145, 0.109, and 0.141, respectively. Thus, its average weight was 0.119 ($0.122 \times 0.2 + 0.065 \times 0.3 + 0.145 \times 0.1 + 0.109 \times 0.3 + 0.141 \times 0.2 = 0.119$). Based on the average weights of the 15 indices, we identified the indices that were most useful for the classification of the adapted texts at different levels.

The tests of machine learning algorithms were performed in RapidMiner, a software that offers an integrated environment for data preparation, machine learning, and text mining (Chisholm, 2013). RapidMiner was selected in the study for three reasons. First, the educational version of RapidMiner is freely available. Second, it is user-friendly. More importantly, RapidMiner has been used in many studies and its validity has been proved (Tripathi et al., 2015).

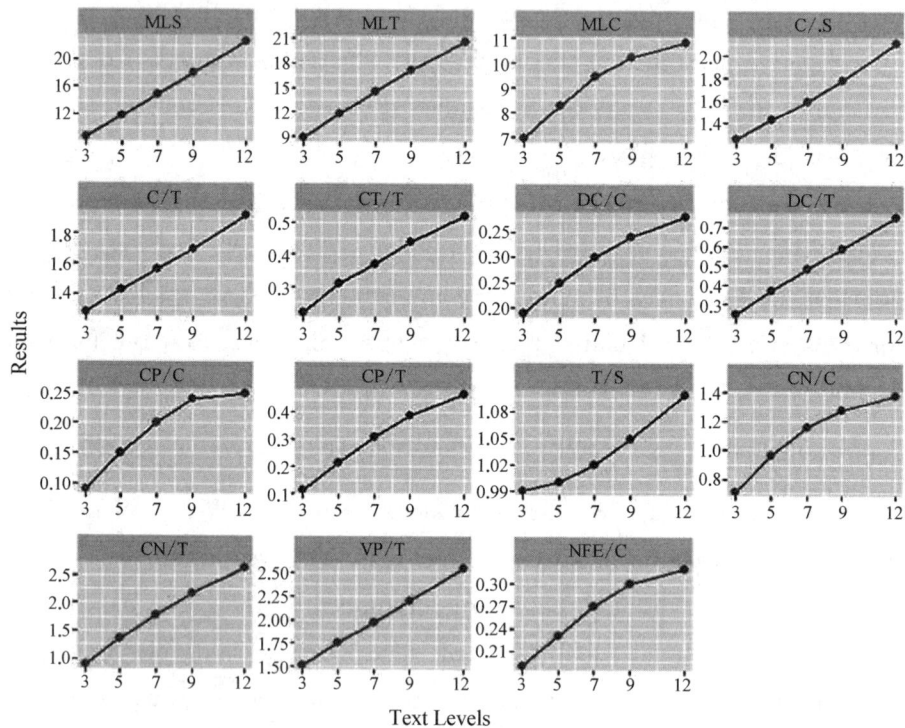

Fig. 1　The growth patterns of the 15 indices of complexity by increasing text levels.

5. Results

5.1 Descriptive statistics

The descriptive statistics of the 15 indices of syntactic complexity at five text levels are presented in Fig. 1 (see Table S1 in Supplementary Material for specific statistics). It was found that the 15 indices increased linearly across the five levels. For example, MLS (Mean Length of Sentence) grew from 8.74 words per sentence at text level 3 to 22.61 at text level 12. The results indicated that when the difficulty level of a text increased, its syntactic complexity in terms of the 15 indices increased correspondingly.

5.2 Results of MANOVA and ANOVA

The result of MANOVA shows significant differences of the adapted texts in syntactic complexity at different levels, with a moderate effect size ($F=98.795$, $p.<0.001$, $\eta_p^2=0.41$). The results of ANOVA (see Table S2 in Supplementary Materials for statistics) showed that the indices of syntactic complexity were significantly different across the text levels, with large effect sizes ($\eta_p^2=[0.230, 0.940]$). Results of Games-Howell post hoc tests indicated that all indices of syntactic complexity, except for CP/C, differed significantly across the text levels (see Table S3 in Supplementary Material for statistics).

5.3 Results of correlations and machine learning algorithms

The results of Spearman's rank correlations (see Table S4 in Supplementary Material for statistics) showed that the 15 indices were significantly correlated with the text level ($rho>0.4$, $p.=0.000$), with eight correlations having very large effect sizes ($rho>0.8$). Therefore, all indices were to be included as potential predictor variables for the classification of text levels in the follow-up machine learning analyses.

The results of text classification based on the five machine learning algorithms (see Table S5 in Supplementary Material for statistics) showed that Deep Learning and Generalized Linear Model performed best in classifying the adapted texts at different levels, with an accuracy of 93.8% and 91.1%. Support Vector Machine and Naïve Bayes also performed well with an accuracy of 85% and 83.9%. However, the performance of Multinomial Logistic Regression, with an accuracy of 36.8%, was not comparable to those of the other four algorithms.

The unsatisfactory performance of Multinomial Logistic Regression may be attributed to two factors. The first factor is its sensitivity to multicollinearity. That is, if the predictors (indices of syntactic complexity in this case) are strongly correlated, Multinomial Logistic Regression will be less accurate (Ranganathan et al., 2017). The results of Pearson's correlations (see Table S6 in Supplementary Material for statistics) showed that many indices were highly correlated ($r>0.8$), which might partly explain the low accuracy of Multinomial Logistic Regression. Another factor that is closely related to the first one is the redundancy of variables or features, that is, too many variables may affect the performance of Multinominal Logistic Regression (Lee et al., 2013). We will return to this issue below.

The weights of the 15 indices in the five algorithms and their average weights were calculated (see Table S7 in Supplementary Material for statistics) and the results reveal some points of interest. First, DC/T and MLS were probably two most predictive indices since their average weights ranked first and second in the list. The finding indicated that they were highly distinctive syntactic features in classifying adapted reading texts at different levels. Second, MLT, C/S, C/T, and CN/C might also well classify the texts because their average weights ranked high. Other indices might contribute moderately to the classification task due to their lower ranks in the models. To summarise, six indices, i.e., DC/T, MLS, MLT, C/S, C/T, and CN/C, were probably significant indices for classifying the adapted texts at different levels.

Let us get back to the issue of the low performance of Multinomial Logistic Regression. First, to address the issue of redundancy in predictor variables, we could use a smaller group of predictors, and theoretically, the aforementioned six significant indices could serve as candidate predictors of the text levels. However, the issue of multicollinearity still existed with the six indices since MLS was strongly correlated with MLT ($r=0.8$), while DC/T, C/T, and C/S were strongly correlated with each other ($r>0.8$). To address the multicollinearity issue, we decided to only use DC/T, MLS, and CN/C as the predictor variables, and conducted the machine learning for the experiment the second time. The results (see Table S8 in Supplementary Material for statistics) showed that the performance of three machine learning algorithms, i.e., Naïve Bayes, Multinomial Logistic Regression, and Support Vector Machine, significantly improved. In particular, the performance of Multinominal Logistic Regression improved with the three predictor variables, increasing from 36.8% to 88%. It is also worth noting that except for Multinominal Logistic Regression, the remaining four algorithms all reached an accuracy of over 90% when DC/T, MLS, and CN/C were used as the predictor variables.

6. Discussion

6.1 Syntactic complexity at different text levels

The study first explored the differences of syntactic complexity in adapted reading texts at different levels, and the results revealed some points of interest. First, the adapted reading texts at various levels were significantly different from each other in all the 15 indices of syntactic complexity, with large effect sizes. Second, all the 15 indices of syntactic complexity were positively related with the text level. The result confirmed the importance of syntactic complexity in text adaptation (Jin & Lu, 2018). In other words, the syntax of a text should be carefully considered when a text is adapted to better match the proficiency levels of the target learners.

Third, all the indices were significantly different across the text levels except for CP/C (Coordinate Phrases per Clause). To be specific, CP/C was not significantly different between levels 9 and 12, which indicated that CP/C reached its ceiling at grade 9. One possible reason is the earlier acquisition of coordination in language learning (Norris & Ortega, 2009). Coordination may be learned at earlier stages of language learning, and beginner learners largely depend on coordination to express their ideas (Jiang et al., 2019). However, as their language proficiency increases, learners may grasp other more complex syntactic means such as subordination and noun phrases and use less coordinate clauses. As a result, CP/C significantly increased in texts of relatively low levels and reached its ceiling at higher level, level 9 in this case. Interestingly, the result is not entirely consistent with that reported in previous studies such as Jin et al. (2020), who found that CP/C still exhibited significant differences between texts at high levels such as 10 and 12. One possible reason for such an inconsistency is the data used in the two studies. The data used in our study are adapted extracurricular reading texts while those in their study are adapted textbook texts. Textbooks are developed for a fairly general purpose of language teaching and lay the foundation for language learning. Hence, textbooks at higher levels may still use many simple structures as detected by indices such as CP/C. In contrast, extracurricular reading texts aim to further facilitate leaners' language learning beyond textbooks since they are developed based on authentic texts that are linguistically and culturally more difficult (Buendgens-Kosten, 2013). Therefore, extracurricular reading texts may use more complex syntactic structures rather than coordination, particularly when the texts are adapted for learners at a higher level of language proficiency.

6.2 Indices of syntactic complexity for classifying text levels

The study used 15 indices of syntactic complexity for classifying texts at different levels based on five machine learning algorithms. The results showed that three indices of syntactic complexity, i.e., DC/T, MLS, and CN/C, could serve as distinctive features that well classified the levels of the adapted reading texts. The findings are partly consistent with those in previous studies such as Jin et al. (2020), which found that MLS and DC/T were most predictive of text levels.

DC/T is a measure of the dependent clauses per T-unit, which measures the subordination dimension. Our results are similar to Jin et al.'s (2020) in that they also found that subordination was useful for the classification of adapted texts at various levels. In addition, subordination was also found to be an effective indicator of the proficiency levels of learners, particularly of the beginners and intermediate learners (Jiang et al., 2019).

MLS refers to the mean length of sentences, expressed in number of words. Although MLS is the coarsest-grained indices of the syntactic complexity (Jin et al., 2020), it helps discriminate the text levels of the adapted reading texts. This finding was also in line with learners' development of syntactic complexity. For example, MLS was found to be positively correlated with learners' language proficiency (Alexopoulou et al., 2017; Lu, 2010). That is, learners at higher proficiency levels tend to produce longer sentences.

CN/C is an indicator of complex nominals per clause, which measures the dimension of phrasal complexity. Our results are in line with previous findings and confirm that phrasal complexity is an effective indicator of language development (Biber et al., 2016; Yoon, 2017). In other words, advanced learners are more likely to express their complex ideas with increased phrasal complexity.

6.3 Machine learning approach to text classification

The study employed five machine learning algorithms for the classification of adapted texts at different levels. Several points are worth noting as regards the results.

First, the five machine learning algorithms that were employed in this study performed well in the classification of adapted texts at different levels. In the first experiment when all 15 indices were used as predictor variables, four algorithms, i.e., Naïve Bayes, Generalized Linear Model, Deep Learning, and Support Vector Machine, achieved an average accuracy of 88%. Multinomial Logistic Regression achieved an accuracy of 36.8%. In the second experiment when three indices, i.e., DC/T, MLS, and CN/C, were used as predictor variables, Naïve Bayes, Generalized Linear Model, Deep Learning, and Support Vector Machine achieved an accuracy over 90%. The remaining algorithm, i.e., Multinomial Logistic Regression, achieved an accuracy of 88% in the second experiment. Of course, our results seem satisfactory in that the accuracies in our study (approximately 90%) are much higher than 20%, the accuracy of a random assignment. However, it should be noted that it may not be fair to compare our results with those in previous studies though the accuracies of classifications in our study seem much higher (90% versus 34.1% (Jin et al., 2020)). The satisfactory performance of these algorithms may be attributed to the data used in this study. Each news story was adapted into five texts of various levels while its main content remained the same. That is, the confounding factors that might affect the use of language in a text such as genres, contents, and topics were controlled. Without these confounding factors, the five machine learning algorithms performed well in classifying the adapted texts in our study, though Multinomial Logistic Regression only did so when the predictor variables were reduced to the top 3.

Second, more attention should be paid to the selection of machine learning algorithms. This study conducted two experiments. In the first experiment, 15 indices of syntactic complexity were used as the predictor variables. In the second experiment, only three indices with most predictive power were selected as predictor variables. The results of the two experiments showed that the performance of some traditional algorithms such as Multinomial Logistic Regression was significantly improved in the second experiment (from 36.8% to 88%). It indicated that we should carefully consider the requirements of various machine learning algorithms and select the most appropriate variables for them. For example, some traditional algorithms such as Multinomial Logistic Regression were sensitive to multicollinearity and variable redundancy. Therefore, more attention should be paid to the issue of multicollinearity and variable selection when they are used for classification.

Third, Multinomial Logistic Regression is not comparable to the other algorithms in terms of classification accuracy. Similar to the results of previous studies (e.g., François, 2009; Jin et al., 2020), it obtained a lower accuracy in the first experiment when all 15 indices of syntactic complexity were used as predictor variables. Although the accuracy of Multinomial Logistic Regression was significantly improved in the second experiment, its accuracy was still lower than those of the other algorithms. Therefore, researchers may consider more sophisticated algorithms such as Deep Learning and Generalized Linear Model when they employ machine learning methods for text classification purposes in future research.

To summarise, the study has adopted five machine learning algorithms to classify the adapted texts at various levels, with satisfactory performance. The results indicate that the machine learning approach is promising for text classification tasks. In addition, the method is also effective in identifying the indices of syntactic complexity that can well classify texts at different levels.

6.4 Implications for text adaptation and pedagogy

The results in our study have some implications for text adaptation. First, we have identified three indices of syntactic complexity, i.e., DC/T, MLS, and CN/C, that can well classify the adapted texts at various levels. The three indices measure three dimensions of syntactic complexity, i.e., subordination, length of sentence, and phrasal complexity. The results indicate that three dimensions of syntactic complexity, i.e., subordination, length of production, and phrasal complexity, may significantly affect the syntactic complexity of a text and they are probably the key issues in the adaptation of extracurricular reading materials. Given their significance in both text classification and syntactic complexity development, adapters may pay special attention to them when they adapt texts into those of various levels. As the text level increases, the texts should include more subordinate clauses and noun phrases as well as longer sentences to meet the demands of learners at higher levels. More importantly, it is necessary to incorporate them into the benchmarks of syntactic complexity. However, it should be noted that it is not enough to take into account only these three dimensions since the results were obtained only based on our experimental dataset and may need further verification in other datasets. Hence, adapters should consider all syntactic dimensions in text adaptation since indices at other dimensions may also contribute to the syntactic complexity of a text.

Second, as discussed earlier, one important reason for the higher classification accuracy obtained in this study lies in the data used. The data were balanced in terms of genres, contents, and topics since each news text was adapted into five texts of various levels while its main content remained the same. The results indicate that the differences of syntactic complexity between adapted texts of various levels may be more easily adjusted when other confounding factors that may affect the use of language in a text such as genres, contents, and topics are controlled. Therefore, when adapting language test materials, adapters can also adapt one text into several ones of various difficulty levels, particularly for a diagnostic test (Lee, 2015) or an adaptive test (Frey & Seitz, 2009). Such test materials may more accurately assess the language proficiency of learners.

This study also has important pedagogical implications. Our findings may help language instructors obtain a better understanding on the relationship between the difficulty level of a reading text and its syntactic complexity. More importantly, the findings can help instructors prioritize the learning of different syntactic dimensions for learners at different proficiency levels. For example, our results show that CP/C significantly increases at earlier stages of language acquisition and then reaches its ceiling at the level of 9. As discussed earlier, one possible reason for this is the earlier acquisition of coordination in language learning (Norris & Ortega, 2009). In other words, coordination may be learned first, and beginner learners largely depend on coordinate clauses to express their ideas (Jiang et al., 2019). Therefore, instructors may need to focus more on coordinate clauses when their target learners are beginner and/or intermediate learners. They should select the language materials with coordination and explicitly teach them how to use such syntactic structures with examples to ensure that the target learners fully grasp coordination. On the other hand, instructors should select language materials with more complex structures such as subordinate clauses and complex nominals when their target learners are those at a higher proficiency level.

7. Limitations and future research

This study is limited in several aspects. First, the study focuses on one genre, i.e., news. Future research may investigate adapted texts of other genres (e.g., novels) since syntactic complexity varies across different genres (Polio & Yoon, 2018). Second, the six dimensions of syntactic complexity investigated in the study concern syntactic elaboration. However, syntactic complexity consists of syntactic elaboration and syntactic diversity (Bi & Jiang, 2020). Future research may examine syntactic diversity to paint a fuller picture of differences of syntactic complexity between adapted texts at different levels. Third, the study examines the adapted texts at five different levels. Nevertheless, the proficiency levels of learners are much more varied and fine-grained. Therefore, future research may investigate the adapted texts at more fine-grained levels, which will further reveal how the syntactic complexity of a text changes as its level gradually increases.

Fourth, the difficulty levels of the adapted texts are objectively determined by readability assessment. Such an approach may be inadequate since individual differences may also contribute to their difficulty levels. In other words, students' perceived difficulty of an adapted text may differ from its objectively defined difficulty level. For example, an adapted text at level 3 may be perceived as level 5 by students. Therefore, future research can investigate the relationship between students' perceived difficulty of the adapted reading texts and their syntactic complexity features. Finally, instructors may do classroom research to test the feasibility and applicability of stratified teaching when the same original text is adapted into several ones of various levels while their genres, contents, and topics are kept unchanged. Students in the same class may vary from one another in terms of their language proficiency levels, and hence the stratified teaching may also be required. One possible solution is that instructors can provide students with different versions of the same text which are at corresponding difficulty levels. Students can thus select a text that fits their proficiency levels while participating in the same discussion in class. Such an approach may enhance students' interest in language learning and improve their classroom performance. For example, for students at lower proficiency levels, they may read adapted texts at the intermediate levels and complete the basic tasks. In contrast, students at higher proficiency levels may further their study by reading texts at higher levels and completing more advanced tasks. Research with the foregoing design is needed to examine the effect of such a stratified teaching on students' performance and language development.

Acknowledgements

This work was supported by Huazhong University of Science and Technology Double First-Class Funds for Humanities and Social Sciences. The authors would like to thank the anonymous reviewers and the editor for their insightful comments and suggestions.

Appendix A. Supplementary data

Supplementary data to this article can be found online at https://doi.org/10.1016/j.system.2023.103002.

References

Abiodun, O. I., Jantan, A., Omolara, A. E., Dada, K. V., Mohamed, N. A., & Arshad, H. (2018). State-of-the-art in artificial neural network applications: A survey. *Heliyon*, *4*(11), Article e00938.

Agnello, E. (2021). Simplified but not the same: Tracing numeracy events through manually simplified Newsela articles. *Numeracy*, *14*, 1–18. https://doi.org/10.5038/1936-4660.14.2.1375.

Akoglu, H. (2018). User's guide to correlation coefficients. *Turkish Journal of Emergency Medicine*, *18*, 91–93. https://doi.org/10.1016/j.tjem.2018.08.001.

Alexopoulou, T., Michel, M., Murakami, A., & Meurers, D. (2017). Task effects on linguistic complexity and accuracy: A large-scale learner corpus analysis employing natural language processing techniques. *Language Learning*, *67*, 180–208. https://doi.org/10.1111/lang.12232.

Allen, D. (2009). A study of the role of relative clauses in the simplification of news texts for learners of English. *System*, *37*, 585–599.

https://doi.org/10.1016/j.system.2009.09.004.

Bailey, A. L., & Heritage, M. (2014). The role of language learning progressions in improved instruction and assessment of English language learners. *Tesol Quarterly*, *48*, 480–506. https://doi.org/10.1002/tesq.176.

Bhavsar, H., & Panchal, M. H. (2012). A review on support vector machine for data classification. *International Journal of Advanced Research in Computer Engineering & Technology*, *1*(10), 2278–1323.

Biber, D., Gray, B., & Staples, S. (2016). Predicting patterns of grammatical complexity across language exam task types and proficiency levels. *Applied Linguistics*, *37*, 639–668. https://doi.org/10.1093/applin/amu059.

Bi, P., & Jiang, J. (2020). Syntactic complexity in assessing young adolescent EFL learners' writings: Syntactic elaboration and diversity. *System*, *91*, Article 102248. https://doi.org/10.1016/j.system.2020.102248.

Buendgens-Kosten, J. (2013). Authenticity in CALL: Three domains of 'realness'. *ReCALL*, *25*(2), 272–285. https://doi.org/10.1017/S0958344013000037.

Bulté, B., & Housen, A. (2014). Conceptualizing and measuring short-term changes in L2 writing complexity. *Journal of Second Language Writing*, *26*, 42–65. https://doi.org/10.1016/j.jslw.2014.09.005.

Castelvecchi, D. (2016). Can we open the black box of AI? *Nature News*, *538*(7623), 20. https://doi.org/10.1038/538020a.

Chen, J., Huang, H., Tian, S., & Qu, Y. (2009). Feature selection for text classification with Naïve Bayes. *Expert Systems with Applications*, *36*(3), 5432–5435. https://doi.org/10.1016/j.eswa.2008.06.054.

Chen, X., & Meurers, D. (2019). Linking text readability and learner proficiency using linguistic complexity feature vector distance. *Computer Assisted Language Learning*, *32*, 418–447. https://doi.org/10.1080/09588221.2018.1527358.

Chisholm, A. (2013). *Exploring Data with RapidMiner*. Birmingham, UK: Packt Publishing.

Coxhead, A. (2000). A new academic word list. *Tesol Quarterly*,

34, 213-238. https://doi.org/10.2307/3587951.

Crossley, S., Allen, D., & McNamara, D. (2012). Text simplification and comprehensible input: A case for an intuitive approach. *Language Teaching Research*, *16*, 89-108. https://doi.org/10.1177/1362168811423456.

Crossley, S., Louwerse, M., McCarthy, P., & McNamara, D. (2007). A linguistic analysis of simplified and authentic texts. *The Modern Language Journal*, *91*(1), 15-30. https://doi.org/10.1111/j.1540-4781.2007.00507.x.

El-Habil, A. M. (2012). An application on multinomial Multinomial Logistic Regression model. *Pakistan Journal of Statistics and Operation Research*, *8*(2), 271-291. https://doi.org/10.18187/pjsor.v8i2.234.

Eyheramendy, S., & Madigan, D. (2007). A flexible Bayesian generalized linear model for dichotomous response data with an application to text categorization. In *Complex Datasets and Inverse Problems*. Institute of Mathematical Statistics, 76-91.

Fox, J. (2016). *Applied Regressions Analysis and Generalized Linear Models*. Retrieved from https://us.sagepub.com/en-us/nam/applied-regression-analysis-and-generalized-linear-models/book237254.

François, T. L. (2009). Combining a statistical language model with Multinomial Logistic Regression to predict the lexical and syntactic difficulty of texts for FFL. In *Proceedings of the EACL 2009 Student Research Workshop*. Athens, Greece: Association for Computational Linguistics, 19-27. https://doi.org/10.3115/1609179.1609182.

Frey, A., & Seitz, N. N. (2009). Multidimensional adaptive testing in educational and psychological measurement: Current state and future challenges. *Studies In Educational Evaluation*, *35*, 89-94. https://doi.org/10.1016/j.stueduc.2009.10.007.

Goodfellow, I., Bengio, Y., & Courville, A. (2016). *Deep Learning*. Massachusetts: MIT Press.

Granik, M., & Mesyura, V. (2017). Fake news detection using Naive Bayes classifier. In *IEEE First Ukraine Conference on Electrical and Computer Engineering*, 2017, 900-903.

Green, A., & Hawkey, R. (2012). Re-Fitting for a different purpose: A case study of item writer practices in adapting source texts for a test of academic reading. *Language Testing*, *29*, 109–129. https://doi.org/10.1177/0265532211413445.

Housen, A., & Kuiken, F. (2009). Complexity, accuracy, and fluency in second language acquisition. *Applied Linguistics*, *30*, 461–473. https://doi.org/10.1093/applin/amp048.

Jiang, J., Bi, P., & Liu, H. (2019). Syntactic complexity development in the writings of EFL learners: Insights from a dependency syntactically-annotated corpus. *Journal of Second Language Writing*, *46*, Article 100666. https://doi.org/10.1016/j.jslw.2019.100666.

Jin, T., & Lu, X. (2018). A data-driven approach to text adaptation in teaching material preparation: Design, implementation, and teacher professional development. *Tesol Quarterly*, *52*, 457–467. https://doi.org/10.1002/tesq.434.

Jin, T., Lu, X., & Ni, J. (2020). Syntactic complexity in adapted teaching materials: Differences among grade levels and implications for benchmarking. *The Modern Language Journal*, *104*, 192–208. https://doi.org/10.1111/modl.12622.

Krashen, S. (2004). *The Power of Reading: Insights from the Research* (2nd ed.). Englewood, Colorado: Libraries Unlimited.

Kuhnt, S., & Pawlitschko, J. (2005). Outlier identification rules for generalized linear models. In *Innovations in Classification, Data Science, and Information Systems*. Berlin: Springer, 165–172.

Kuimova, M. V., & Ukhov, S. A. (2016). Some benefits of extracurricular reading in foreign language teaching. *Ponte*, *72*, 276–280. https://doi.org/10.21506/j.ponte.2016.4.39.

Kyle, K. (2016). *Measuring Syntactic Development in L2 Writing: Fine Grained Indices of Syntactic Complexity and Usage-based Indices of Syntactic Sophistication* (Doctoral Dissertation). Atlanta, Georgia State: Georgia State University.

Lecun, Y., Bengio, Y., & Hinton, G. (2015). Deep learning. *Nature*, *521*, 436–444. https://doi.org/10.1038/nature14539.

Lee, Y. W. (2015). Diagnosing diagnostic language assessment. *Language Testing*, *32*, 299–316. https://doi.org/10.1080/10543406.2012.756500.

Lee, K., Ahn, H., Moon, H., Kodell, R. L., & Chen, J. J. (2013). Multinomial multinomial logistic regression ensembles. *Journal of Biopharmaceutical Statistics*, *23*, 681–694. https://doi.org/10.1080/10543406.2012.756500.

Lei, L., Wen, J., & Yang, X. (2023). A large-scale longitudinal study of syntactic complexity development in EFL writing: A mixed-effects model approach. *Journal of Second Language Writing*, *59*, Article 100962. https://doi.org/10.1016/j.jslw.2022.100962.

Leroy, G., Miller, T., Rosemblat, G., & Browne, A. (2008). A balanced approach to health information evaluation: A vocabulary-based naïve Bayes classifier and readability formulas. *Journal of the American Society for Information Science and Technology*, *59*(9), 1409–1419. https://doi.org/10.1002/asi.20837.

Liu, X., Gao, C., & Li, P. (2012). A comparative analysis of support vector machines and extreme learning machines. *Neural Networks*, *33*, 58–66. https://doi.org/10.1016/j.neunet.2012.04.002.

Lu, X. (2010). Automatic analysis of syntactic complexity in second language writing. *International Journal of Corpus Linguistics*, *15*, 474–496. https://doi.org/10.1075/ijcl.15.4.02lu.

Lu, X. (2011). A corpus-based evaluation of syntactic complexity measures as indices of development. *Tesol Quarterly*, *45*, 36–62. https://doi.org/10.5054/tq.2011240859.

Lu, X., & Ai, H. (2015). Syntactic complexity in college-level English writing: Differences among writers with diverse L1 backgrounds. *Journal of Second Language Writing*, *29*, 16–27.

Mesmer, H. A., Cunningham, J. W., & Hiebert, E. H. (2012). Toward a theoretical model of text complexity for the early grades: Learning from the past, anticipating the future. *Reading Research Quarterly*, *47*, 235–258. https://doi.org/10.1002/RRQ.019.

Moustafa, N., & Slay, J. (2016). The evaluation of network anomaly detection systems: Statistical analysis of the UNSW-NB15 data set and the comparison with the KDD99 data set. *Information Security Journal: A Global Perspective*, 25(1-3), 18-31.

Norris, J. M., & Ortega, L. (2009). Towards an organic approach to investigating CAF in instructed SLA: The case of complexity. *Applied Linguistics*, 30, 555-578. https://doi.org/10.1093/applin/amp044.

Ortega, L. (2003). Syntactic complexity measures and their relationship to L2 proficiency: A research synthesis of college-level L2 writing. *Applied Linguistics*, 24, 492-518. https://doi.org/10.1093/applin/24.4.492.

Petrucci, C. J. (2009). A primer for social worker researchers on how to conduct a multinomial Multinomial Logistic Regression. *Journal of Social Service Research*, 35(2), 193-205. https://doi.org/10.1080/01488370802678983.

Pfost, M., Dörfler, T., & Artelt, C. (2013). Students' extracurricular reading behavior and the development of vocabulary and reading comprehension. *Learning and Individual Differences*, 26, 89-102. https://doi.org/10.1016/j.lindif.2013.04.008.

Polio, C., & Yoon, H. J. (2018). The reliability and validity of automated tools for examining variation in syntactic complexity across genres. *International Journal of Applied Linguistics*, 28, 165-188. https://doi.org/10.1111/ijal.12200.

Ponniah, J. (2018). The robustness of incidental grammar acquisition through reading. *Journal of Asia TEFL*, 15, 882-889. https://doi.org/10.18823/asiatefl.2018.15.3.25.882.

Prabhakar, S. K., & Won, D. O. (2021). Medical text classification using hybrid deep learning models with multihead attention. *Computational Intelligence and Neuroscience*. https://doi.org/10.1155/2021/9425655.

Ranganathan, P., Pramesh, C., & Aggarwal, R. (2017). Common pitfalls in statistical analysis: Measures of agreement. *Perspectives in Clinical Research*, 8, 187-191. https://doi.org/10.4103/picr.PICR_123_17.

RapidMiner. (2019). *RapidMiner 9 operator reference manual*. Retrieved from https://docs.rapidminer.com/latest/studio/operators/.

Rodrigo, V. (2016). Graded readers: Validating reading levels across publishers. *Hispania*. 99 https://www.jstor.org/stable/44112826.

Shiffler, R. E. (1988). Maximum Z scores and outliers. *The American Statistician*, 42, 79-80. https://doi.org/10.1080/00031305.1988.10475530.

Srivastava, D., & Bhambhu, L. (2010). Data classification using support vector machine. In *Proceedings of International Conference on Tools with Artificial Intelligence*, 3-6. https://doi.org/10.1109/ICTAI.2010.9.

Suk, N. (2017). The effects of extensive reading on reading comprehension, reading rate, and vocabulary acquisition. *Reading Research Quarterly*, 52, 73-89. https://doi.org/10.1002/rrq.152.

Sung, Y. T., Lin, W. C., Dyson, S. B., Chang, K. E., & Chen, Y. C. (2015). Levelling L2 texts through readability: Combining multilevel linguistic features with the CEFR. *The Modern Language Journal*, 99, 371-391. https://doi.org/10.1111/modl.12213.

Sun, X., Liu, Y., Xu, M., Chen, H., Han, J., & Wang, K. (2013). Feature selection using dynamic weights for classification. *Knowledge-Based Systems*, 37, 541-549. https://doi.org/10.1016/j.knosys.2012.10.001.

Tripathi, P., Vishwakarma, S. K., & Lala, A. (2015). Sentiment analysis of English tweets using RapidMiner. In *Proceedings of 2015 International Conference on Computational Intelligence and Communication Networks*. Kolkata, India: Institute of Electrical and Electronic Engineers, 668-672. https://doi.org/10.1109/CICN.2015.137.

Tripathy, A., Agrawal, A., & Rath, S. K. (2016). Classification of sentiment reviews using n-gram machine learning approach. *Expert Systems with Applications*, 57, 117-126. et al., 2016.

Vajjala, S., & Meurers, D. (2012). On improving the accuracy of readability classification using insights from second language acquisition. In *7th workshop on the innovative use of NLP for building educational application*. Montreal, Canada: Association for Computational Linguistics, 163-173. Retrieved from http://www.bbc.co.uk/bitesize.

Wu, X., Mauranen, A., & Lei, L. (2020). Syntactic complexity in English as a lingua franca academic writing. *Journal of English for Academic Purposes*, *43*, Article 100798.

Yoon, H. J. (2017). Linguistic complexity in L2 writing revisited: Issues of topic, proficiency, and construct multidimensionality. *System*, *66*, 130-141. https://doi.org/10.1016/j.system.2017.03.007.

Zaharie, D., Lungeanu, D., & Holban, S. (2007). Feature ranking based on weights estimated by multi-objective optimization. In *Proceedings of IADIS first European Conference on Data Mining*. Lisbon, Portugal: International Association for Development of the Information Society, 124-128.

Zarco-Tejada, M. A. (2019). Automatic profiling of L2-simplified texts: Identifying discriminate features of linguistic proficiency. *Digital Scholarship in the Humanities*, *34*, 661-675. https://doi.org/10.1093/llc/fqy067.

Zulfikar, W. B., Irfan, M., Alam, C. N., & Indra, M. (2017). The comparison of text mining with Naive Bayes classifier, nearest neighbor, and decision tree to detect Indonesian swear words on Twitter. In *2017 5th International Conference on Cyber and IT Service Management (CITSM)*. IEEE, 1-5.

方法谈：

语料库语言学可以帮我们做什么？

一、语料库语言学是什么？

语料库是根据研究需要收集、整理的文本集合，而语料库语言学则是利用语料库数据和方法探索语言现象和规律的研究领域（Cheng，2011；McEnery & Hardie，2012）。在语料库语言学发展初期，囿于语料收集不便等因素的限制，研究者提出了语料库建设的代表性和平衡性等原则（Ädel，2020）。比如，关于语料库的代表性原则，在建设英国国家语料库（British National Corpus，BNC）时，开发者会考虑该库既要包括笔语文本又要包括口语文本，而笔语部分则需要包括报纸、杂志、期刊、图书、未发表信函等尽可能多样化文体的文本(Aston & Burnard,1998),以确保收入该库的语料具有广泛的代表性。又如,关于语料库的平衡性原则,英国国家语料库在建设时制定了严格的文本抽样原则与抽样比例(Aston & Burnard,1998),以保证样本的平衡性,避免由于收录某类样本过多或过少而使得样本比例失衡。

近年来,计算机技术日新月异快速发展,通过网络收集数据越来越便利,数据储存和数据处理愈发便捷,很多研究开始在语料库中收录尽可能多的文本,有些甚至收录几乎全样本数据,这促使我们开始重新认识语料库建库的代表性和平衡性原则。比如,当代美国英语语料库(Corpus of Contemporary American English,COCA)收录的语料包括口语、小说、杂志、报纸、网页等八大类十多亿词次文本[1];作为监控语料库(Monitor corpus)的网络新闻语料库(News on the Web,NOW),从2010年开始建库至今,每日从互联网自动爬取报纸和杂志文本,每月新增30万余篇新文章,约1.8亿至2亿词次数据,到2023年8月该库数据规模已达178亿词次。[2] 又如,Lei & Wen(2020)研究了英语句法在过去两百余年间的变化情况,发现句法存在逐渐简化的趋势。该研究采用1790至2017年间美国年度国情咨文所有文本进行探索,是收录所有可能样本的全样本案例。另一个典型的全样本语料库案例是Card et al.(2022)。该研究采用1880年至今20余万篇美国国会演讲和五千余篇总统发言样本,研究了关于移民议题政治演讲的情感倾向,发现美国政治人物关于移民的演讲或发言越来越正面,但呈现两党分化的极性趋势。该研究采用1880年至今几乎所有国会演讲文本,是典型的全样本研究。

二、语料库语言学研究方法与基于语料库的科学研究

以伯明翰大学John Sinclair等学者为代表的研究者认为语料库语言学是一门独立的学科(Sinclair,1991),而以兰卡斯特大学诸学者为代表的研究者则认为语料库语言学更多是方法取向,即语料库语言学还并不能成为一门独立的学科,而仅是一种方法论;换言之,语料库语言学更多的是给研究者提供了充分运用语料数据对语言现象进行描述并总结语言规律的机会。上述争议也产生了语

---

[1] 关于COCA语料库说明,参见 https://www.english-corpora.org/coca/help/coca2020_overview.pdf。

[2] 关于NOW语料库说明,参见 https://www.english-corpora.org/now/。

料库语言学到底是"基于语料的"(Corpus-based)还是"语料驱动的"(Corpus-driven)之分野(详细讨论参见 Tognini-Bonelli,2001)。

如果搁置上述争议,研究者们发现,语料库语言学的确具有明显的方法论属性,研究者通过对语料数据的探索,为他们的研究理论或假设获取丰富的实证数据支撑。传统的语料库语言学多采用检索行(Jeaco,2021;Wulff & Baker,2020)、词表(Gardner & Davies,2014;Lei & Liu,2016;Rayson & Potts,2020)、关键词(Bednarek,2012;Miller,2020)、搭配词/多词共现/短语(Hardy & Colombini,2011;Wulff & Baker,2020)等方法对语言现象进行描述和研究。研究者也开发了本地桌面工具〔如 WordSmith(Scott,2022)、AntConc(Anthony,2022)、LancsBox(Brezina & Platt,2023)〕或在线检索工具(如 BNC① 和 COCA② 在线检索平台)辅助学者运用上述方法进行研究。

另外,随着技术的发展,研究者们也开发了功能更强大的工具来辅助学者的研究。比如,TreeTagger(Schmidt,1994)可以对文本进行词性赋码,Stanza(Qi et al.,2020)和 spaCy(Honnibal & Montani,2017)可以对文本进行词性赋码、句法分析、命名实体识别等常见的自然语言处理任务。又如,学者专门开发了针对特定语言特征分析任务的工具,如词汇复杂度分析工具(Kyle & Crossley,2015;Lu,2012)、句法复杂度分析工具(Kyle,2016;Lu,2010)、文本连贯性分析工具(Crossley et al.,2019)等。

基于成熟的方法属性和强大的研究工具,语料库已成为语言学研究不可或缺的一部分。语言学研究各分支学科均广泛采用语料库方法进行探索,如语言本体研究(Hyland & Jiang,2016;Lei & Wen,2020)、二语习得研究(Laufer & Waldman,2011;Lei,2012)、外语教学研究(Flowerdew,2009;Lei & Qin,2022)、社会语言学研究(Bamman et al.,2014;Shi & Lei,2021)、语言数字人文(Zhu & Lei,2018;雷蕾,2023)等。与语言学研究紧密相关的翻译研究(Hu,2016;Liu et al.,2022)和文学研究(Brooke et al.,2016;Jockers & Mimno,2013)也越来越多使用语料库方法进行探索。

三、案例分析

本小节将以本文为例,展示如何利用语料库数据和方法进行语言学相关研

---

① https://www.english-corpora.org/bnc/.
② https://www.english-corpora.org/coca/.

究。首先,我们将介绍该研究的目的。然后,我们将详细介绍该研究的方法,包括语料库的构建和语料的分析处理。最后,我们将汇报该研究的主要结果。

(一)研究目的

该研究旨在探究不同难度等级的课外阅读改编文本的句法差异。具体而言,该研究有两个研究目的:

(1)探究不同难度等级的课外阅读改编材料在句法复杂度上的差异特征。

(2)利用机器学习方法识别出对文本难度等级具有较强预测力的句法复杂度指标。

(二)研究方法

1. Newsela 语料收集。

本研究所用的语料是来自 Newsela 网站[①]的课外阅读材料。Newsela 是一家教育网站,旨在为不同水平的语言学习者提供课外阅读材料。选择 Newsela 收集语料主要有两个原因:第一,Newsela 提供的阅读文本是由专业改编团队根据真实文本改编而来,改编时会考虑文本的词汇、句法结构等方面的特征;第二,Newsela 的阅读材料通常被改编成五个难度等级,比如 3、5、7、9、12。也就是说,一篇文章会被改编成五篇难度不等的文章,而其主要内容和主题保持不变。难度等级不同并且句法结构有所差异使得 Newsela 文本尤其适合本研究的目的。

为了排除其他因素干扰、保证研究结果可靠性,纳入研究的阅读材料须同时满足以下两个条件:① 属于 ELA(English Language Arts)、科学(Science)、社会(Social Studies)三个类别中的一类;② 改编后的五个文本难度等级分别为 3、5、7、9 和 12。以上两个条件能保证尽可能多地收集到一个体裁、难度等级平衡的语料库。最终,本研究总共收集了 2 250 篇文本。

2. 语料处理。

Newsela 语料收集完毕后主要进行了如下分析处理:

(1)基于语料库的句法分析:利用句法复杂度分析器[Syntactic Complexity Analyzer (Lu, 2010)]分析每篇 Newsela 文本的句法结构。该分析器生成 14 个句法指标,涵盖了句法复杂度的五大维度(即长度、整体句子复杂度、从句、并列句和短语复杂度)。另外,根据先前研究发现(Jin et al., 2020),该研究还将从句

---

① https://newsela.com.

包含的非限定成分数量(Non-finite elements per clause)这一指标纳入研究。鉴于此,每篇文本总共生成了 15 个句法复杂度指标。

(2) 剔除异常文本:当该文本中有句法指标的平均值超过"均值±3 个标准差"(Shiffler,1988)时就认为是异常文本,需要剔除。

(3) 统计分析:利用多元方差分析和一元方差分析探究不同难度等级的课外阅读改编文本在 15 个句法复杂度指标上是否存在显著差异。如果存在,进行事后配对检验,查看具体哪些等级之间存在显著差异。同时,利用相关分析对这些句法指标与文本难度等级之间的相关性进行分析,挑选出与文本难度等级具有显著强相关的指标,作为下一步分析的候选指标。

(4) 机器学习方法:基于上一步提取的句法复杂度候选指标,我们利用五种机器学习算法(即朴素贝叶斯、广义线性模型、多元逻辑回归、支持向量机和深度学习)进行文本难度等级分类。根据分类表现结果和各个指标在分类任务中所占的权重,识别出对文本难度等级具有较强预测力的句法指标。

(三) 研究结果

该研究主要有如下发现:

(1) 不同难度等级的课外阅读改编文本在这 15 个句法指标上均存在显著差异。难度等级和各个句法复杂度指标之间存在显著的正相关关系。换言之,随着文本难度等级的增加,各个维度的句法复杂度基本呈显著上升趋势。

(2) 基于句法复杂度和机器学习算法的文本难度等级分类表现良好,平均准确率在 90% 左右。

(3) 根据各个句法指标在分类任务中所占的权重,识别出了三个对文本难度等级具有较强预测力的句法复杂度指标,它们分别衡量的是长度、从句和短语层面的句法复杂度。

以上研究发现对阅读材料的改编有重要参考意义,能够帮助改编者了解影响难度等级变化的主要句法特征,对他们未来的改编活动有重要借鉴意义。同时,该研究发现也有助于改编标准的制定,从而保证改编文本的质量和一致性。另外,本研究也证明了机器学习算法在改编文本难度等级分类研究中的有效性,为未来研究开拓了新的研究思路。

四、结语

本研究主要介绍了语料库语言学的概念、语料库语言学研究方法以及基于语料库的科学研究。另外,我们还通过案例分析展示了语料库在科学研究中的具体应用。在本文中,研究者根据研究目的专门构建了 Newsela 语料库,在确保体裁、难度等级平衡的情况下尽可能多地收集文本语料。之后,利用基于语料库的文本分析方法、统计分析方法以及机器学习方法进行了数据处理和分析。该研究是语料库语言学应用的一个典型案例,展示了如何根据研究目的收集语料和分析语料,为相关研究假设提供实证数据支撑。同时,它也证明了新技术新方法在语料库研究中应用的可能性,进一步拓展了语料库研究方法。语料库研究方法不再局限于传统的检索、搭配等方面,诸如机器学习等自然语言处理领域的新技术也是进行语料分析的有效手段,有助于进一步挖掘语料背后的语言规律。

参考文献

Ädel, A. (2020). Corpus compilation. In M. Paquot & S. T. Gries (Eds.), *A Practical Handbook of Corpus Linguistics*. Springer International Publishing, 3–24. https://link.springer.com/10.1007/978-3-030-46216-1_1.

Anthony, L. (2022). *AntConc* [Computer software]. Waseda University.

Aston, G., & Burnard, L. (1998). *The BNC Handbook: Exploring the British National Corpus with SARA. Edinburgh Textbooks in Empirical Linguistics*. Edinburgh Univ. Press.

Bamman, D., Eisenstein, J., & Schnoebelen, T. (2014). Gender identity and lexical variation in social media. *Journal of Sociolinguistics*, 18(2), 135–160. https://doi.org/10.1111/josl.12080.

Bednarek, M. (2012). "Get us the hell out of here": Key words and trigrams in fictional television series. *International Journal of Corpus Linguistics*, 17(1), 35–63. https://doi.org/10.1075/ijcl.17.1.02bed.

Brezina, V., & Platt, W. (2023). *#LancsBox* [Computer software]. Lancaster University.

Brooke, J., Hammond, A., & Hirst, G. (2016). Using models of lexical style to quantify free indirect discourse in modernist fiction. *Digital Scholarship in the Humanities*, fqv072. https://doi.org/10.1093/llc/fqv072.

Card, D., Chang, S., Becker, C., Mendelsohn, J., Voigt, R., Boustan, L., Abramitzky, R., & Jurafsky, D. (2022). Computational analysis of 140 years of US political speeches reveals more positive but increasingly polarized framing of immigration. *Proceedings of the National Academy of Sciences*, *119*(31), e2120510119. https://doi.org/10.1073/pnas.2120510119.

Cheng, W. (2011). *Exploring Corpus Linguistics*. Routledge. https://www.taylorfrancis.com/books/9781136628153.

Crossley, S. A., Kyle, K., & Dascalu, M. (2019). The tool for the automatic analysis of cohesion 2.0: Integrating semantic similarity and text overlap. *Behavior Research Methods*, *51*(1), 14–27. https://doi.org/10.3758/s13428-018-1142-4.

Flowerdew, L. (2009). Applying corpus linguistics to pedagogy: A critical evaluation. *International Journal of Corpus Linguistics*, *14*(3), 393–417. https://doi.org/10.1075/ijcl.14.3.05flo.

Gardner, D., & Davies, M. (2014). A new academic vocabulary list. *Applied Linguistics*, *35*(3), 305–327. https://doi.org/10.1093/applin/amt015.

Hardy, D. E., & Colombini, C. B. (2011). A genre, collocational, and constructional analysis of RISK. *International Journal of Corpus Linguistics*, *16*(4), 462–485. https://doi.org/10.1075/ijcl.16.4.02har.

Honnibal, M., & Montani, I. (2017). *spaCy: Natural Language Understanding with Bloom Embeddings, Convolutional Neural Networks and Incremental Parsing* [Computer software]. https://spacy.io/usage.

Hu, K. (2016). *Introducing Corpus-based Translation Studies* (1st ed.). Berlin: Springer.

Hyland, K., & Jiang, F. (2016). Change of attitude? A diachronic study of stance. *Written Communication*, *33*(3), 251–274. https://doi.org/10.1177/0741088316650399.

Jeaco, S. (2021). Concordance line sorting in *The Prime Machine*. *International Journal of Corpus Linguistics*, *26*(2), 284–297. https://doi.org/10.1075/ijcl.18056.jea.

Jin, T. A., Lu, X., & Ni, J. (2020). Syntactic complexity in adapted teaching materials: Differences among grade levels and implications for benchmarking. *The Modern Language Journal*, *104*(1), 192-208. https://doi.org/10.1111/modl.12622.

Jockers, M. L., & Mimno, D. (2013). Significant themes in 19th-century literature. *Poetics*, *41*(6), 750-769. https://doi.org/10.1016/j.poetic.2013.08.005.

Kyle, K. (2016). *Measuring Syntactic Development in L2 Writing: Fine Grained Indices of Syntactic Complexity and Usage-based Indices of Syntactic Sophistication* [Unpublished doctoral dissertation]. Georgia State University, Atlanta.

Kyle, K., & Crossley, S. A. (2015). Automatically assessing lexical sophistication: indices, tools, findings, and application. *TESOL Quarterly*, *49*(4), 757-786.

Laufer, B., & Waldman, T. (2011). Verb-noun collocations in second language writing: A corpus analysis of learners' English: Verb-noun collocations in L2 writing. *Language Learning*, *61*(2), 647-672. https://doi.org/10.1111/j.1467-9922.2010.00621.x.

Lei, L. (2012). Linking adverbials in academic writing on applied linguistics by Chinese doctoral students. *Journal of English for Academic Purposes*, *11*(3), 267-275. https://doi.org/10.1016/j.jeap.2012.05.003.

Lei, L., & Liu, D. (2016). A new medical academic word list: A corpus-based study with enhanced methodology. *Journal of English for Academic Purposes*, *22*, 42-53. https://doi.org/10.1016/j.jeap.2016.01.008.

Lei, L., & Qin, J. (2022). Research in foreign language teaching and learning in China (2012-2021). *Language Teaching*, 1-27. https://doi.org/10.1017/S0261444822000155.

Lei, L., & Shi, Y. (2023). Syntactic complexity in adapted extracurricular reading materials. *System*, *113*, 103002. https://doi.org/10.1016/j.system.2023.103002.

Lei, L., & Wen, J. (2020). Is dependency distance experiencing a process of minimization? A diachronic study based on the State of the Union addresses. *Lingua*, *239*. https://doi.org/10.1016/j.lingua.2019.102762.

Liu, K., Liu, Z., & Lei, L. (2022). Simplification in translated Chinese: An entropy-based approach. *Lingua*, *275*, 103364. https://doi.org/10.1016/j.lingua.2022.103364.

Lu, X. (2010). Automatic analysis of syntactic complexity in second language writing. *International Journal of Corpus Linguistics*, *15*(4), 474–496.

Lu, X. (2012). The relationship of lexical richness to the quality of ESL learners' oral narratives. *The Modern Language Journal*, *96*(2), 190–208.

McEnery, T., & Hardie, A. (2012). *Corpus Linguistics: Method, Theory and Practice. Cambridge Textbooks in Linguistics*. Cambridge University Press.

Miller, D. (2020). Analysing Frequency Lists. In M. Paquot & S. T. Gries (Eds.), *A Practical Handbook of Corpus Linguistics* (pp. 77–97). Springer International Publishing. https://link.springer.com/10.1007/978-3-030-46216-1_4.

Qi, P., Zhang, Y [Yuhao], Zhang, Y [Yuhui], Bolton, J., & Manning, C. D. (Eds.) (2020). *Stanza: A Python Natural Language Processing Toolkit for Many Human Languages*. https://nlp.stanford.edu/pubs/qi2020stanza.pdf.

Rayson, P., & Potts, A. (2020). Analysing keyword lists. In M. Paquot & S. T. Gries (Eds.), *A Practical Handbook of Corpus Linguistics* (pp. 119–139). Springer International Publishing. https://link.springer.com/10.1007/978-3-030-46216-1_6.

Schmidt, H. (Ed.) (1994). *Probabilistic Part-of-speech Tagging Using Decision Trees*.

Scott, M. (2022). *WordSmith Tools* [Computer software]. Lexical Analysis Software.

Shi, Y., & Lei, L. (2021). Lexical use and social class: A study on lexical richness, word length, and word class in spoken English. *Lingua*, *262*. https://doi.org/10.1016/j.lingua.2021.103155.

Shiffler, R. E. (1988). Maximum Z scores and outliers. *The American Statistician*, *42*(1), 79–80. https://doi.org/10.1080/00031305.1988.

10475530.

Sinclair, J. M. (1991). *Corpus, Concordance, Collocation: Describing English Language*. Oxford university press.

Tognini-Bonelli, E. (2001). *Corpus Linguistics at Work. Studies in Corpus Linguistics*. John Benjamins.

Wulff, S., & Baker, P. (2020). Analyzing Concordances. In M. Paquot & S. T. Gries (Eds.), *A Practical Handbook of Corpus Linguistics* (pp. 161-179). Springer International Publishing. https://link.springer.com/10.1007/978-3-030-46216-1_8.

Zhu, H., & Lei, L. (2018). British cultural complexity: An entropy-based approach. *Journal of Quantitative Linguistics*, 25(2), 190-205. https://doi.org/10.1080/09296174.2017.1348014.

雷蕾:《语言数字人文:"小帐篷"理论框架》,《外语与外语教学》2023年第3期,第64—73页.

复杂理论视角下任务复杂度对二语口语表现的影响*

郑咏滟　刘飞凤**

摘要：本研究从 Robinson 的"认知假设"切入，旨在考察中国学习者口语表现中的任务复杂度效应。基于《中国学生英语口笔语语料库》中的八级口语语料库，我们对三年的口语独白任务重新进行任务复杂度分类，并针对低、中、高任务复杂度的口语语料进行了计量语言学分析。结果表明，学习者口语词汇复杂度各指标随着任务复杂度升高显著变化，但是整体词频结构维持稳定，说明口语词汇系统作为复杂自适应系统，与任务环境的认知需求产生互动适应。本研究从宏观层面揭示任务复杂度和学习者语言行为间的深层联系，结果显示数据驱动型语言学研究可为现有二语习得研究开拓疆域，运用计量手段可为系统研究语言复杂性提供新思路。

关键词：任务复杂度；词汇复杂度；复杂自适应系统；计量语言学；语料库

一、引　　言

近三十年来，基于任务的二语习得研究方兴未艾，学习者的认知能力和任务复杂度之间的互动关系成为核心议题。Robinson 将基于任务的研究分为任务

---

* 原载《现代外语（双月刊）》2020 年第 3 期。本文为国家社科基金一般项目"中国外语环境下学习者书面语的动态系统发展研究"（18BYY113）的阶段性成果。

** 郑咏滟，应用语言学博士，复旦大学外文学院教授、博士生导师、博士后合作导师，现任外文学院副院长。2021 年国家级重大人才工程青年学者，爱思唯尔 2021、2022 年外国语言文学中国高被引学者，中美富布赖特高级研究学者（2016/2017），复旦大学外文学院多语研究创新团队带头人。研究领域：第二语言习得、复杂动态系统理论、双语及多语发展。

刘飞凤，上海中学教师，研究方向为应用语言学。

产出、任务难度和任务复杂度三个维度,其中最受关注的是任务复杂度,即任务的内在认知要求,包括对语言学习者在注意力、记忆力、推理能力以及其他信息加工过程中的要求(Robinson,2001,2007)。国内外学者针对已有成果展开了元分析(例如Jackson & Suethanapornkul,2013;邢加新、罗少茜,2016),然而学习者语言产出中的任务复杂度效应并未达成定论。更重要的是,大多实证研究遵循二语习得传统的实验范式从微观层面操纵任务复杂度,数据量较小,使用的语言复杂度衡量指标庞杂,很难从整体上把握任务复杂度对学习者语言产出的影响。

本研究旨在探索中国外语学习环境下学习者语言习得和发展规律,尝试衔接语料库语言学、计量语言学和基于任务的二语习得研究。国外已有学者率先使用自然语言处理技术分析学习者作文语料库中的任务复杂度效应(Alexopoulou et al.,2017),显示出衔接语料库和二语习得研究的潜力。本研究试图借助计量语言学科学分析手段,对现有的学习者口语语料库(文秋芳等,2008)重新分析,从宏观层面考察任务复杂度对学习者口语复杂特征表现的影响,以此探索数据驱动的语言学研究和传统二语习得研究之间的协同效应,以期展示大数据研究范式在二语习得研究中的前景。

二、文 献 回 顾

1. 认知任务复杂度对学习者语言复杂度的影响

Robinson(2001,2007)将任务复杂度细分为"资源消耗型"(resource-dispersing)和"资源指引型"(resource-directing)两个维度。"资源消耗型"维度包括有无准备时间、是否为单一任务、有无背景知识,沿此维度提高任务复杂度会导致注意力分散,语言产出的复杂度、准确度、流利度会产生竞争和制约。"资源指引型"包括任务涉及的因素多少、是否为此时此地、有无推理、立场选定,沿此维度提高任务复杂度会使学习者注意力更加集中在具体语言形式上,提高语言产出的复杂度和准确度,降低流利度。

国外认知任务复杂度的实证研究起初围绕学习者口语产出展开,但之后重心逐渐转向书面语研究。相反,国内任务复杂度研究大多集中在写作产出任务(如刘兵等,2017),口语研究较为零散,如何莲珍、王敏(2003)。因此,本研究着重探讨口语产出中的任务复杂度效应。Jackson & Suethanapornkul(2013)和邢加新、罗少茜(2016)对已有口语研究展开元分析,发现 Robinson 的"认知假设"仅得到部分印证。Jackson & Suethanapornkul(2013)选取的九个口语独白任务中任务复杂度对口语产出的句法复杂度有负面影响($d=-0.02$),对词汇复杂度有正面影响但效应值很小($d=0.03$)。邢加新、罗少茜(2016)选取的11项国内研究中,口语任务复杂度对口语句法复杂度的积极影响更明显,对流利度的负面效应更明显,但是在词汇复杂度方面书面语的效应量大于口语任务效应量。任务复杂度对口语产出的词汇有一定积极影响,但不具有显著意义。

以上两项元分析说明现有口语任务研究尚待完善。首先,现有研究通常采用单因素变量,缺乏对多个因素变量的统一考察。例如,Jackson & Suethanapornkul(2013)的分析发现国外口语任务大多采用"此时此地"($+/-$here-and-now)单变量,仅有两项研究采用了"有无推理"($+/-$ reasoning)变量(如 Ishikawa,2008),从未纳入"立场选定"($+/-$ perspective taking)变量。邢加新、罗少茜(2016)发现国内的口语任务大多采用"有无推理"变量,也缺乏"立场选定"变量。Robinson(2001)强调任务复杂度应该被视作一个连续体,因此需要从多个变量入手考察口语任务复杂度效应。其次,现有研究均以控制性的实验范式为方法,实验数据有限。何莲珍、王敏(2003)的早期研究收集了48名大一学生的口语数据,而 Ishikawa(2008)的数据只包含24名日本学习者。近年来随着语料库语言学和计量语言学的飞速发展,二语习得研究者或能从数据驱动的研究范式获取灵感,更全面、深入地探索任务复杂度对口语产出的影响。本研究即为这个方向的尝试。

2. 复杂自适应系统语言观

基于语言事实,来自不同语言学分支的语言学家,包括应用语言学和二语习得(Larsen-Freeman & Cameron,2008 等)、计量语言学(Liu,2018)等,纷纷认同语言是一个复杂自适应系统的观点。复杂自适应系统语言观为衔接二语习得研究和计量语言学奠定了语言哲学基础。

复杂理论框架下语言被视作一个复杂动态系统,系统各成分间相互联结、交互变化,在一定外部条件刺激下语言系统会通过自组织行为适应环境给予的压力,涌现出新的语言结构、状态或功能。语言系统的词汇、句法、语篇等不同层面在同一系统内,存在互相支持和竞争(郑咏滟,2018);受省力原则支配,不同层面需要协同起来完成交际目的(刘海涛,2017)。同时,复杂系统也具有适应性。所谓"适应"即系统通过自组织过程适应外部环境而出现新的结构、状态或功能(Liu,2018)。换言之,语言使用者可以通过"软组装"各类资源(包括自身的认知资源、语言资源和环境给予的资源)对外界环境刺激做出反应,涌现出更高级的语言行为(Larsen-Freeman & Cameron,2008;郑咏滟,2018)。"认知—互动"视角的二语习得研究者将任务视作学习者协商、理解语言意义的微环境(Robinson,2007),因此任务内在的认知复杂度可以被视作任务环境对学习者内在认知资源的刺激,而学习者产出语言复杂度则是学习者通过调配自身认知资源和语言资源而做出的适应性语言行为。这点为从复杂理论角度探讨任务复杂度效应提供了理据。

计量语言学以文本为研究对象,聚焦文本的整体特征。文本被视作语言系统和语言参与主体(即语言使用者)之间相互作用的产物(刘海涛,2017)。计量语言学认为语言系统是个由人驱动的复杂自适应系统,所以文本计量指标中体现的语言结构会随着语言使用者认知资源的变化而变化。基于此,计量语言学通过计算文本计量指标探索语言系统的自适应机制和语言演变的动因,采用数学手段对大规模文本的整体特征做出科学性描述,以此对传统实验范式的基于任务的二语习得研究提供补充(刘海涛,2017)。近年来已有学者尝试结合计量语言学与应用语言学研究。例如,Ouyang & Jiang(2017)基于横断面学习者语料库使用文本计量手段说明齐普夫定律的有关参数能够很好反映本族语者和同年级二语学习者写作产出的句法复杂度或水平差异,指出计量手段对二语习得研究同样是有效的手段。基于此,我们认为计量语言学常用的文本计量手段可以丰富现有的学习者语言复杂度测量指标,从宏观层面揭示任务复杂度和学习者产出语言之间的深层联系。

三、研究设计

基于以上回顾,本研究将学习者口语产出的词汇使用视作一个复杂自适应子系统(郑咏滟,2018),考察词汇协同子系统和任务环境之间的互动关系。研究问题如下:第一,口语独白任务中随着任务复杂度增加,学习者口语词汇计量指标是否产生变化? 具体产生何种变化? 第二,口语文本计量指标之间是否存在互动关系? 这种关系是否随着任务复杂度递增而变化?

1. 语料文本

本研究语料来自文秋芳等(2008)编著的《中国学生英语口笔语语料库》(2.0

版)的八级口语语料库,来源于 2003—2007 年间全国英语专业八级口试。由于英语专业八级考试的对象是高校英语专业四年级学生,他们可以视作中高级水平学习者。

在专业八级口试中,每位考生需完成三项任务,其中第一、二项任务为口译任务,第三项任务是就指定话题进行评论,是一项口语独白任务。该项任务给考生出一个具体话题,并提供相关的背景材料,考生有一定准备时间,然后根据背景信息在相应的时间限制内就指定话题表达观点。

考虑到任务条件的一致性(即同一类型的口语独白任务)和语料数据的均衡性,本研究选取 2004、2005、2007 年这三年的第三项口语独白任务,详见表 1。

表 1 2004、2005、2007 年专业八级口试任务话题

年 度	话 题	文本文件数	形符数	因果推理	立场选定	任务复杂度
2004	Suggestions for the 2008 Beijing Olympics	187	53 203	+	−	中
2005	China's Employment Market Challenged by More Graduates	188	71 791	−	−	低
2007	Pets or not?	185	52 923	+	+	高
合 计	/	560	177 917			

注:−表示几乎没有,+表示有。

2. 任务复杂度分类

就给定话题进行评论属于典型的口语独白任务,因此该口语语料库可以视作一个任务语料库。但是,任务复杂度的设定并非语料库建设的初始目的,因此我们无法仿照任务研究常用的实验范式,直接通过控制任务复杂度变量来考察语言复杂度。尽管如此,我们仍可以依据 Robinson 的任务复杂度分类框架(Robinson,2007)中对"资源指引型"维度的定义判定以上三个口语任务内在的认知复杂度。同时,为了弥补以往研究多使用单一维度变量而从未使用"立场选定"变量的缺憾,我们决定选取与评论这一任务类型密切相关的两个变量:因果推理,即是否只需要传递信息(−),还是需要确立事件关联并试图给出理由来支持个人的观点(+);立场选定,即是否只需要表达本人对一事件的立场(−),还是需要纳入多方立场进行论证(+)。参照以往研究的做法,两位作者分别根据

定义对三个口语任务进行判断,并经过协商达成一致。三个口语任务按照任务复杂度,呈现低(2005 年)、中(2004 年)、高(2007 年)三个水平,递次升高(见表1)。

3. 计量指标和数据分析

词汇复杂度又称词汇丰富度,一般包括词汇多样性、词汇密度和词汇难度。二语习得研究中常用的词汇复杂度指标,例如词汇频率概览(LFP)(Laufer & Nation, 1995),均为外源性指标,即通过与外部语料库(例如 BNC 或 COCA)的词频比对来区分高频词和低频词。但是,计量语言学建立在齐普夫分布的概率论基础上,旨在计算语言单位的使用概率,采用数学手段探讨语言的内在结构和规律,捕捉文本中语言复杂度的涌现。因此,计量语言学指标基于语言使用者自身产出语言的词频进行计算,能够从内源性角度描述词汇使用,从而揭示词汇协同子系统在应对外界认知复杂度改变时做出的自适应反应。

结合二语口语文本特征,我们选取六个常用的词汇计量指标进行文本分析。

第一,平均形符长度(average token length):按照字母数来衡量单词内部复杂度的指标,可以反映文本的用词风格。

第二,类符形符比例(Type-token ratio,TTR)。这是最常用的反映词汇多样性的基本衡量指标。由于 TTR 的计算受到文本长度的影响,本研究计划采用 MATTR 进行计算,通过移动窗口的运行可以有效避免文本长度的影响。本研究采用 MATTR 软件(http://ai1.ai.uga.edu/caspr/)默认以 500 词作为一个标准窗口进行文体特征分析的设置进行计算。取值越高,词汇多样性程度越高。

第三,h 点(h-point):h 点指的是文本中词的秩频分布的一个临界点。词的秩频分布计算方式如下:将文本中每个词(例符)按照其频次降序排列,并按照 1 到 V 的顺序依次编号。每个频序 r 都对应着一个频次值 f(r)。h 点就是词的秩频分布上 r=f(r)的那个点,在自然语言文本中 h 点一般位于频序相邻的两个词之间(刘海涛,2017),此时文本 h 值为频序相邻的两个词对应 h 值的均值。h 点之前的词大多为功能词,其后的词大多为实义词,h 点的取值可以反映文本中词汇使用的丰富度,h 点取值越小,词汇丰富度越高。

第四,R_1:这也是词汇丰富度指标。基于 h 点对文本中的实词(例符)的比例进行估算得出 R_1。首先需要计算出文本中词的秩频分布 f(r)得出相应的累计概率分布(cumulative probability distribution)F(r)。F(r)是频序从 1 到 r 的词所累计的概率,也就是这些词的总频次占文本形符总数的比例。如果 h 点之前均为功能词,那么 F(r) 就是功能词在文本中所占的比例。然而事实上,h 点之前也可能存在实词,h 点之后也可能存在功能词。因此可以对 F(h) 进行校正(刘海涛,2017),结果为 $F(h) - h^2/2N$(N 为字符数),为 $1-(F(h)-h^2/2N)$ 表明文本中实词所占的比例越大,因此词汇丰富度也越高。

第五,作者视野(Writer's View)。这是计量语言学一个特有的指标。上文提到 h 点是文本中实词与功能词的分界点,可以视为作者掌握文本中实词与功能词使用的平衡点。h 点与秩频分布的起点和终点组成一个三角形,其中以 h 点为顶点的角度(以弧度计)就是作者视野(刘海涛,2017)。

第六,Λ 值(Lambda 值)。这个指标可以描述词频结构的稳定性,是文本中词的秩频分布的欧式长度进行计算的,文本规模对 lambda 取值的影响甚微,Λ 值越高,文本词频结构越复杂。该值可以有效区分文本体裁(刘海涛,2017)。Λ 值可视作语言产出词汇复杂度的整体结构。

本研究使用计量文本 QUITA 软件(Quantitative Index Text Analyzer)进行文本分析,并使用 R 语言 3.5.1 版本进行推论性统计分析。

四、结　果

1. 不同任务复杂度下学习者口语词汇复杂度

研究问题一探讨口语词会表现中的任务复杂度效应。结果显示,随着任务复杂度升高,所有计量指标均呈现出明显差异。下图是运用 R 语言制作的学习者口语表现中平均形符长度、MATTR、h 点、R_1、作者视野、Λ 值在低、中、高(左至右)复杂度下的小提琴图。

图 1(a)显示三个任务环境下的学习者口语平均形符长度:低任务复杂度 $=4.35,SD=0.26$;中任务复杂度 $=4.33,SD=0.27$;高任务复杂度 $=4.08,SD=0.23$。随着任务复杂度升高,平均形符长度降低,且具有显著差异($F=-0.020,p<0.001$),事后多重比较显示低、中任务复杂度间差异不显著,低、高任务复杂度和中、高任务复杂度间差异明显。这有可能是因为高复杂度环境下学习者更多认知资源指向词汇使用其他方面,只能暂时使用更短的单词满足即时交际的需要,这与计量语言学对词汇协同子系统的预测一致(刘海涛,2017)。

图 1(b)呈现三个任务环境下学习者口语词汇多样性 MATTR 分布特征:

低任务复杂度=0.43,$SD=0.05$；中任务复杂度=0.40,$SD=0.06$；高任务复杂度=0.44,$SD=0.06$。随着任务复杂度升高，MATTR 值先降再升。方差检测显示有显著差异($F=28.16, p<0.001$)，事后多重比较也表明两两间差异显著。另外，从图 1(b)中还可以看出，高任务复杂度下 MATTR 值离散程度更高，表明高任务复杂度刺激出更具差异性的个体表现，出现词汇多样性的最高值。

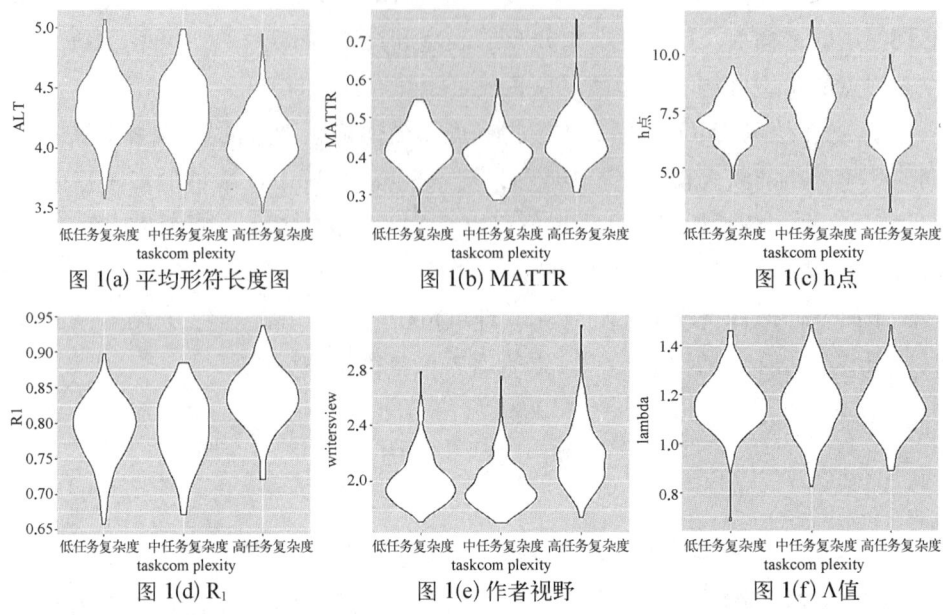

图 1(a) 平均形符长度图　　图 1(b) MATTR　　图 1(c) h 点

图 1(d) R_1　　图 1(e) 作者视野　　图 1(f) Λ 值

图 1　不同任务复杂度条件下口语词汇复杂度指标的分布

图 1(c)呈现三个任务环境下学习者口语词汇 h 点分布特征，从功能词角度反映文本丰富度变化：低任务复杂度=7.09,$SD=0.92$；中任务复杂度=8.08,$SD=1.20$；高任务复杂度=6.93,$SD=1.09$。方差检测显示有显著差异($F=62.59, p<0.001$)，事后多重比较表明低、中任务复杂度和中、高任务复杂度之间差异显著，而低、高任务复杂度间不存在显著差异。h 点值越高表明功能词越多，词汇丰富度越低。因此，口语词汇丰富度随着任务复杂度升高而先降再升。

图 1(d)呈现三个任务环境下学习者口语文本 R_1 分布特征，从实词角度反映文本丰富度变化：低任务复杂度 $R_1=0.79$,$SD=0.04$；中任务复杂度 $R_1=0.79$,$SD=0.05$；高任务复杂度 $R_1=0.84$,$SD=0.04$。方差检测显示差异显著($F=63.3, p<0.001$)，事后多重比较显示主要是高任务复杂度分别显著高

于低、中任务复杂度。这表明从实词角度反映的词汇丰富度在高任务复杂度环境中尤其明显。

图1(e)呈现三个任务环境下学习者口语文本作者视野分布特征,体现文本中使用者对实词和功能词的把握。作者视野在低任务复杂度为2.02($SD=0.17$),中任务复杂度1.98($SD=0.17$),高任务复杂度2.18($SD=0.22$)。方差检测显示差异显著($F=61.05, p<0.001$),事后多重比较显示主要是高任务复杂度分别显著高于低、中任务复杂度,说明学习者对实词和虚词的把握能力在高任务复杂度下显得尤为突出。此外,在低、中任务复杂度环境下,作者视野数值分布较为集中,而在高任务复杂度下该值离散程度较高,说明高任务复杂度环境刺激出口语用词方面更大的个体差异。

图1(f)显示三个任务环境下 Λ 值的分布特征:低任务复杂度 Λ=1.17, $SD=0.11$;中任务复杂度 Λ=1.16, $SD=0.12$;高任务复杂度 Λ=1.16, $SD=0.11$。方差检测显示不具有显著差异($F=0.288, p>0.05$)。这说明三个任务环境下学习者口语词频的总体结构稳定,并未随着任务复杂度增高而变化。

2. 不同任务复杂度环境下词汇计量指标间的关系

为了回答研究问题二,我们依次计算了低、中、高任务复杂度环境下六个词汇计量指标间的相关性,并运用 R 语言 corrplot 软件包进行了数据可视化(图2)。具体相关性的显著性检测结果见附录。

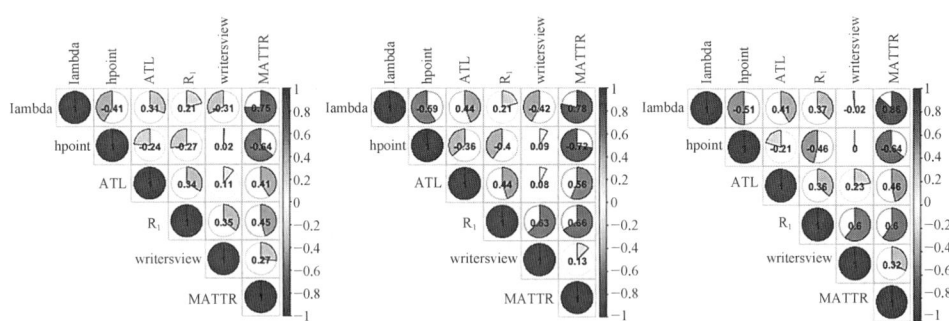

图2 不同任务复杂度下词汇计量指标的相关关系

篇幅所限,本节就重点发现汇报结果。第一,词汇多样性 MATTR 值和 Λ 值显著正相关。相关性随任务复杂度升高,在高任务复杂度环境下达到强相关($r_{低任务复杂度}=0.75, p<0.05$;$r_{中任务复杂度}=0.78, p<0.05$;$r_{高任务复杂度}=0.86, p<0.05$)。第二,词汇多样性 MATTR 值和 h 点(从功能词角度的词汇丰富度)

显著负相关（$r_{低任务复杂度}=-0.64$，$p<0.05$；$r_{中任务复杂度}=-0.72$，$p<0.05$；$r_{高任务复杂度}=-0.64$，$p<0.05$），此处 h 点的值越低表明词汇丰富度越高；词汇多样性 MATTR 值与 R_1 值（从实词角度的词汇丰富度）显著正相关（$r_{低任务复杂度}=0.45$，$p<0.05$；$r_{中任务复杂度}=0.66$，$p<0.05$；$r_{高任务复杂度}=0.60$，$p<0.05$）。两组数值结合说明词汇多样性和词汇复杂性存在显著正相关性，但这种相关性与任务复杂度并不存在线性关联，而是在中任务复杂度环境下达到顶点。第三，R_1 值（从实词角度的词汇丰富度）和作者视野显著正相关，但是在低任务复杂度环境下相关性较低：$r_{低任务复杂度}=0.35$，$p<0.05$；$r_{中任务复杂度}=0.63$，$p<0.05$；$r_{高任务复杂度}=0.60$，$p<0.05$。第四，尽管 h 点、R_1 和作者视野在计算的时候有一定关系，但是置于任务复杂度框架中，三者并无显著相关性，说明这三个指标分别指向词汇复杂度不同方面。

五、讨 论

本研究从 Robinson 的"认知假设"切入考察中国学习者口语表现中的任务复杂度效应。分析结果为认知假设提供了有力验证。以往针对口语任务的元分析（Jackson & Suethanapornkul，2013；邢加新、罗少茜，2016）表明任务复杂度对口语复杂度仅有微弱的积极效应，Robinson 的"认知假设"仅得到部分验证。本研究结果显示，选取的 6 个词汇计量指标中除了 Λ 值不具有显著差异外，其他指标均随任务复杂度升高而显著变化，任务复杂度效应显著。其中，平均形符长度随着复杂度正常而显著降低，而词汇多样性指标 MATTR 值、词汇丰富度 R_1 值和作者视野都在高任务复杂度环境下达到了最高值。由此可见，在逐步增加认知任务复杂度的情况下，学习者的确将注意力更多分配给了具体的词汇形式，产出了更多样、更丰富的词汇，并且在功能词和实词方面显示出更强的把控力，但在平均词长方面却有损失，符合 Robinson 的"认知假设"的预测。下文将从计量方法、任务复杂度变量、复杂自适应系统三个方面对研究结果展开讨论。

首先，本研究揭示的任务复杂度在口语词汇使用的显著积极效应与以往元分析结果不一致，可能是由于本研究采用的是数据驱动的计量语言学指标。以往实证研究均采用实验范式，通过控制任务复杂度变量考察语言复杂度的变化，遵循一一对应的因果关系论，且数据量较小。本研究尝试另辟蹊径，从计量语言学角度出发重新分析现有学习者语料库数据，从近 18 万词的口语数据中甄别语言模式。这种结合数据驱动的研究手段和二语习得研究的新范式在学习者书面语研究中已证明是一个有效途径(Alexopoulou et al.,2017),本研究显示在口语研究方面同样适用。此外,本研究采用了更加细致的词汇计量指标来体现词汇协同子系统的变化,通过数学方式描绘学习者口语词汇使用的整体涌现,或许更能捕捉语言形式的细微变化。计量语言学可以为二语习得研究贡献更多细致的语言测量指标,比如本研究使用的 h 点、R_1 和作者视野等指标在不同任务复杂度环境下具有显著区分度。

其次,本研究结果与以往结果不同也可能由于我们采用了"有无推理"和"立场选定"的双因素复杂度变量。事实上,低、中任务环境的唯一差别就是"有无推理",结果表明平均形符长度、R_1 和作者视野这三个指标在低、中任务复杂度环境中均不具有显著差异。由此推断,单因素的推理变量对语言复杂度的效应并不明显,这就解释了以往口语研究元分析得出的结论。本研究首次纳入"立场选定"变量考察任务复杂度效应。高任务复杂度的话题"Pets or not?"乍看之下属于简单话题,更贴近学生日常生活,但由于纳入了"立场选定"变量,需要学生从不同角度进行论述、推理、例证,深度参与到更高级别的审辨性思维活动,刺激学习者使用出最多样、最丰富的词汇,说明"立场选定"变量对学习者提出了最高的认知要求。尤其考虑到本研究使用的是英语专业八级口语测试的数据,英语专业四年级学生应已处于高级语言水平,所以认知要求越高,越能促使他们注意语言形式,突破原有局限,拓展自身语言库存,和 Robinson 的"认知假设"一致。

第三,本研究结果发现平均形符长度、词汇多样性和丰富度呈现竞争关系,词汇多样性和词汇丰富度间的显著正相关与任务复杂度并不存在线性关联,而是在中任务复杂度环境下达到顶点。此外,体现文本整体词频结构 Λ 值在不同任务复杂度环境下保持稳定,这些都说明随着认知要求的变化,词汇协同子系统中的不同组成部分也在随之变化,符合复杂自适应系统的特点。复杂自适应系统具有一套自我调节机制,能够维持系统自身动态平衡(Larsen-Freeman & Cameron,2008)。刘海涛(2017)指出,在一个平衡的词汇系统中,使用频率高的词长度通常比较短,这是语言中的统计规律。但如果一个较长的词突然频率增加,其词汇协同子系统则会做出反应,暂时缩短该词的长度满足实际交际需求,这是系统适应能力的具体表现。本研究结果也提出佐证。当认知任务复杂度升高时,学习者将更多资源分配给了更多样和丰富的用词,但却无法兼顾词长,可见出现了资源重新调配,语言整体行为涌现出新模式和新特征。同样,基于系统的全面联结性,系统中不同组成成分的关系也会随着外在环境的变化而变化(Larsen-Freeman & Cameron,2008),因此中任务复杂度环境催生出词汇多样性和词汇丰富度的最大程度平衡,互为增长,但是该互动模式在高任务复杂度环境却似乎显出减弱趋势。或许在以后研究中加入更多任务复杂度变量可以进一步探索词汇多样性和词汇丰富度的关联。我们还发现即使任务复杂度变化,Λ值(表示文本整体词频结构)仍然保持稳定,说明细分的口语词汇指标对不同的外界环境刺激做出反应后很可能产生自组,最后达到稳定结构。这也说明口语文本的词汇协同子系统的成分力量可能并不一致,某些特征从宏观角度产生了"抵消"作用,促成Λ值稳定性。

六、结　　论

本研究结果表明任务复杂度对学习者口语表现具有显著影响,不同任务复杂度对学习者的认知资源提出不同要求,学习者也通过重新调配认知和语言资源做出反应,词汇协同子系统相应变化。本研究试图将语料库和计量语言学已取得的丰硕成果应用到二语习得研究中,表明数据驱动型语言学研究可以为二语习得研究开拓更广阔前景。语料库语言学、计量语言学等新兴技术能够丰富、细化二语习得研究现有分析手段和工具,增强相关研究实操性和科学性。

本研究结果也有一定教学启示。为了加强学生口语词汇多样性和丰富度,锻炼实词和功能词的把控能力,在平时的口语训练中应依据学生语言水平和教学实际情况增加任务复杂度变量,尤其应重视"立场选定"这一变量,以此设计口语辩论活动,应能取得良好效果。

当然,由于本研究尚处于探索阶段,研究方法、计量指标的选取尚待改进。本研究没有采用严格控制的实验范式,对任务复杂度的分类属于事后分析,也缺乏对产出语言的各种控制。我们也认识到学习者在标准测试中的表现可能也受到了测试环境和条件的影响。尽管如此,本研究表明对已有的学习者语料库进行多角度分析可以成为拓展二语习得研究疆域的新途径,亟待未来研究纳入更多视角,进一步探索中国外语环境下学习者语言习得规律。

参考文献

Alexopoulou, T., M. Michel, A. Murakami & D. Meurers. (2017), Task effects on linguistic complexity and accuracy: A large-scale learner corpus analysis employing natural language processing techniques. *Language Learning* 67(S1): 180-208.

Ishikawa, T. (2008), The effect of task demands of intentional reasoning on L2 speech performance. *The Journal of Asia TEFL* (5): 29-53.

Jackson, D. O. & S. Suethanapornkul. (2013), The Cognition Hypothesis: A synthesis and meta-analysis of research on second language task complexity. *Language Learning* 63(2): 330-367.

Larsen-Freeman, D. & L. Cameron (2008), *Complex Systems and Applied Linguistics*. Oxford: Oxford University Press.

Laufer, B. & L. S. P. Nation (1995), Vocabulary size and use: Lexical richness in L2 written production. *Applied Linguistics* 16: 307-322.

Liu, Haitao (2018), Language as a human-driven complex adaptive system: Comments on "Rethinking foundations of language from a multidisciplinary perspective". *Physics of Life Reviews* 26-27: 149-151.

Ouyang, J. & J. Jiang (2017), Can probability distribution of dependency distance measure language proficiency of second language learners? *Journal of Quantitative Linguistics* (2): 1-19.

Robinson, P. (2001), Task complexity, task difficulty, and task production: Exploring interactions in a componential framework. *Applied Linguistics* 22: 27-57.

Robinson, P. (2007), Criteria for grading and sequencing pedagogic tasks. In M. P. Garcia Mayo (ed.). *Investigating Tasks in Formal Language Learning*. Clevedon, UK: Multilingual Matters, 7-27.

何莲珍、王敏:《任务复杂度、任务难度及语言水平对中国学生语言表达准确度的影响》,《现代外语》2003年第2期,第171—179页。

刘兵、王奕凯、Zhang, Jun Lawrence:《任务类型对在线英语写作任务准备和产出的影响》,《现代外语》2017年第1期,第102—113页。

刘海涛:《计量语言学导论》,商务印书馆2017年版。

文秋芳、梁茂成、晏小琴:《中国学生英语口笔语语料库》,外语教学与研究出版社2008年版。

邢加新、罗少茜:《任务复杂度对中国英语学习者语言产出影响的元分析研究》,《现代外语》2016年第4期,第528—538页。

郑咏滟:《高水平学习者语言复杂度的多维发展研究》,《外语教学与研究》2018年第2期,第218—230页。

方法谈:

跨学科研究方法如何助力语言学研究?

语言学自诞生之日起就是一个具有高度学科交叉特性的研究领域,应用语言学作为其一大主要分支也具有较强的跨学科属性。美国密歇根大学著名应用语言学家Diane Larsen-Freeman教授(2012)对"多学科"(multidisciplinary)、"跨学科"(cross-disciplinary)、"超学科"(transdisciplinary)做出如下区分:"多学科"路径强调采用不同学科的视角来解决共同问题,但是这种路径难以摆脱"添加式"的学科思维,缺乏学科间的有效融合。"跨学科"路径有效回应了学科互动的需求,在跨学科研究中往往会需要一个具体的学科落脚点,同时某一学科会占主导地位。"超学科"路径更适合解决当今世界错综复杂的现实问题,超学科范式下的应用语言学研究强调从不同视角、不同语言和不同情境探索现实的语言问题,因此是一种以问题为导向的研究范式,超越了学科界限内的理论和方法。

正因为如此,应用语言学的跨学科趋势和超学科转向是未来发展的必然趋势。应用语言学研究者也意识到了本学科面临的问题。由一群知名的应用语言学研究者组成的The Douglas Fir Group 2016年在学界顶级期刊 *The Modern Language Journal* 上发表了一篇题为"多语世界第二语言习得的超学科框架"的观点性文章(Douglas Fir Group, 2016)。该文明确指出:

> 附加语言学习者在教育、多语、多文发展、社会融入和全球化、科技化、的多样跨国环境中的语言表现过程中有许多亟待解决的需求,第二习得/发展研究必须能够应对这些需求带来的种种挑战(Douglas Fir Group, 2016:24)。

人的发展是应用语言学领域的核心问题,而为了解决这个问题,学界需要能够容忍不确定性,采用一种去中心化的视角去寻求跨越多个学科边界的解决办法(Hiver & Al-Hoorie,2022)。应用语言学的跨学科趋势和超学科转向将重点放置在问题驱动的框架和实践,根本目的在于"用对社会有用的、具有人文关怀的方式来解决问题"(Douglas Fir Group,2016:24)。举例说,随着近年来大规模的移民迁徙,移民家庭儿童的语言发展成为应用语言学前沿研究问题。但是为了全面理解这个问题,我们就不能仅仅调用语言学的知识,更需要教育学、社会学、心理学,甚至政治学等学科共同参与的知识融合。因此,如果仅仅使用结构主义语言学或认知语言学来理解移民家庭儿童如何维持祖传语,如何有效习得社会主流语言,那么得出的结论难免片面,也很难真正从实践层面帮助这个群体取得长足的语言发展,以更公平的方式获取教育资源、茁壮成长。因此,如果要从根本上探究应用语言学研究的核心问题,那么必须积极采用跨学科(甚至超学科)的路径,采用多元的视角、方法、手段找到解决问题的方案。

复杂动态系统理论(Complex Dynamic Systems Theory)(de Bot & Larsen-Freeman,2011;Larsen-Freeman & Cameron,2008)正是一个适合推进应用语言学范式转移的跨学科路径。该理论最开始起源于自然科学,在生态学、气象学、数学等学科有长足发展,直到1997年由美国密歇根大学教授Diane Larsen-Freeman教授引入应用语言学领域(Larsen-Freeman,1997)。有趣的是,在Larsen-Freeman教授提出该观点后,整个学界经历了将近10年的沉寂,直到2007年荷兰格罗宁根大学的学者联合起来发文讨论双语动态系统发展(de Bot,Lowie,& Verspoor,2007),才真正预示着复杂动态系统理论在应用语言学领域的兴起。该理论经历了25年的发展,如今已经成为应用语言学领域不可忽视的一股力量,在学习者语言发展、学习者个体差异、学习者与环境互动等多个方面都产出了非常丰硕的成果(郑咏滟,2020)。复杂动态系统理论由于其内在的语言哲学和系统性思维,自带一套具有鲜明特色的研究方法,而且这些研究方法也和传统的研究方法有很大差别。从复杂动态系统理论切入的跨学科应用语言学研究远非一蹴而就的易事。

我最早接触到复杂动态系统理论是在2010年读博期间。当时我研究的话题是二语词汇的长期发展,数据中既有认知心理的视角,又涉及社会文化因素。当时的学界还处于一种认知心理vs.社会文化割裂的状态,因此亟须找到一个理论框架能够弥合两个学派之间的分歧。复杂动态系统理论的出现对我来说犹如灵光乍现。当时相关的论著还比较少,中文相关的材料也十分稀缺,在理解相关理论的时候觉得困难重重,诸如"迭代""互适""分叉""分形"等概念对文科背景的研究者而言十分陌生。这就涉及跨学科理论和方法在应用语言学研究中的第一大困难:概念艰涩、体系庞杂。攻破这个最大的难点之后,才开始了真正意义上的跨学科研究。之后我发表了一系列的复杂动态系统理论视角下二语习得和发展研究。2020年发表在《现代外语》上的论文——《复杂理论视角下任务复杂度对二语口语表现的影响》(郑咏滟、刘飞凤,2020),是又一次用复杂理论和计量语言学助力考察二语口语发展的跨学科尝试。以下将以本文为例阐释跨学科方法助力语言学研究的重点和难点。

首先,在引入跨学科理论和方法时,需要全面、系统把握跨学科概念,并审慎评估在本学科中的适用性。复杂动态系统理论中的核心概念是"软组装"(soft-assembly),指的是语言使用者通过"软组装"各类资源(包括自身的认知资源、语言资源和环境给予的资源)对外界环境刺激做出反应,涌现出更高级的语言行为。"软组装"最初来自发展心理学,用于描述婴儿大动作的发展(Thelen & Smith, 1994)。这个跨学科概念对应用语言学研究者来说显然不易把握。但是通过深入理解该概念的起源和当时提出该概念时的语境,我们能够发现,它实际上是与先天学派的"硬连接"(hard-wired)对应。Thelen 和 Smith 认为婴儿学会用手够物的动作并不是一项事先编入的程序(硬连接),而是根据任务要求、自身发展水平和当时当地的情景条件而做出的临场反应(软组装)。通过全面把握该概念的内涵,我们认为可以用这个概念解释学习者如何与环境资源进行协商和互适,因此就用到了实证研究中,考察学习者口语表现和任务认知负担之间的"适应"过程。

使用跨学科理论和方法时要明确究竟解决什么问题。虽然我们都明白使用跨学科的方法很可能会促成学科的方法创新,促进学科的范式转移,但是仍然容易引起一些混淆。例如,我们可以用神经科学的方法来解决语言问题,但是最终结论的落脚点应该是语言学的核心问题,而不是神经医学的问题。因此,在借鉴跨学科的实证研究中,我们需要时刻保持警醒,清晰知晓我们要解决的是本学科的核心问题。例如,在本文中,我们从二语习得核心问题"任务复杂度"出发,通过回顾 Robinson 的"认知假设"中存在的不一致结果,提出需要使用语料库和计量语言学的分析手段来弥补现有的二语习得认知假设研究以控制性的实验范式为主、数据量偏小的不足。换句话说,我们使用跨学科的理论视角也好,创新方法也好,都是为了解决任务复杂度对口语表现多维度影响这一本学科的核心问题。最终得到的结论也能够从数据驱动的角度、科学的计量方法中刻画学习者口语词汇使用的整体涌现模式。

在使用跨学科的理论与方法时，也注意与语言学本体论之间的适配性，避免"水土不服"。例如，如果我们使用的是复杂动态系统理论的观点来研究学习者语言，那么再继续使用传统的结构主义语言观显然不合时宜。事实上，社会语言学和人类语言学的最新观点均对结构主义提出挑战，将语言重新定义为一种实践，语言是特定社会和文化背景下涌现出的行动形式（Li Wei, 2018）。Thibault（2011）提出，语言不是脱离实体的抽象形式，而是一种巧妙的价值化和语境化的实践行为，语言通过借鉴和连接不同社群的文化传统，最终能够超越空间和时间的限制。由此可见，语言并不是一套现成的、固定的语码等待人们去使用；相反，语言是被实时创造的，是使用者根据现时现地的交际需求顺化各类语言和非语言的资源产生的实践——本质上说这就是复杂动态系统倡导的涌现论和整体论观点。因此，当我们使用复杂动态系统理论的跨学科视角和方法时，必须重新拷问自身对语言本体论的深层次认识。否则，有可能理论视角具有跨学科创新性，研究方法却仍然墨守成规；也有可能虽然使用了跨学科的创新研究方法，但是最终的理论方面仍然止步不前，未有推动。在本文，我们旗帜鲜明地提出语言是一个人驱的复杂自适应系统（Liu, 2018），这个语言本体观为我们从复杂动态系统的"软组装"概念切入、衔接二语习得研究和计量语言学研究奠定了语言哲学基础。与之相呼应，计量语言学将文本视作语言系统和语言参与主体（即语言使用者）之间相互作用的产物，文本计量指标中体现的语言结构会随着语言使用者认知资源的变化而变化，这又为本研究采用计量语言学的指标测量学习者口语产出提供了充分理据，使我们得以从宏观层面以数据驱动的方式洞悉任务复杂度和学习者产出语言之间的深层模式。

篇幅所限，本文难以从各个方面展现跨学科理论和方法如何能够推动语言学发展。语言学本身是一个包含了诸多分支的学科，从形式语言学、认知语言学、功能语言学、心理语言学到应用语言学、社会语言学、人类语言学、语料库语言学和病理语言学，不一而足。如此丰富的分支恰恰体现出语言学研究的多面性和交叉性。由于本人的学识所限，本文的讨论仅限于应用语言学。但是，希望能够通过本篇导读，让大家认识到跨学科理论与方法并非能够解决所有问题的灵丹妙药。相反，在实践操作过程中仍然会遭遇诸多挑战。在使用跨学科理论与方法展开语言学研究时，要全面、系统把握跨学科的概念内涵，着力解决本学科的核心问题,并审慎考量跨学科理论方法与语言本体之间的适配性。如今整个人文社会学科都在经历深刻的跨学科转向,学科的边界日益模糊,随着人工智能的兴起和语言大模型的迅速发展,语言学将更深入参与到跨学科、超学科的研究中。

参考文献

de Bot, K., & Larsen-Freeman, D. (2011). Researching second language development from a dynamic systems theory perspective. In M. Verspoor, K. de Bot, & W. Lowie (Eds.), *A Dynamic Approach to Second Language Development* (pp. 5-23). Amsterdam: John Benjamins.

de Bot, K., Lowie, W., & Verspoor, M. (2007). A dynamic systems theory approach to second language acquisition. *Bilingualism: Language and Cognition*, 10(1), 7-21.

Douglas Fir Group. (2016). A transdisciplinary framework for SLA in a multilingual world. *Modern Language Journal*, 100(Supplement), 19-47.

Hiver, P., & Al-Hoorie, A. H. (2022). Transdisciplinary research methods and complexity theory in applied linguistics: introduction to the special issue. *International Review of Applied Linguistics*, 60(1), 7-22. doi: 10.1515/iral-2021-0020.

Larsen-Freeman, D. (1997). Chaos/complexity science and second language acquisition. *Applied Linguistics*, 18(2), 141-165.

Larsen-Freeman, D. (2012). Complex, dynamic systems: A new transdisciplinary theme for applied linguistics? *Language Teaching*, 45, 202-214.

Larsen-Freeman, D., & Cameron, L. (2008). *Complex Systems and Applied Linguistics*. Oxford: Oxford University Press.

Li Wei. (2018). Translanguaging as a practical theory of language. *Applied Linguistics*, 39(1), 9-30. doi: 10.1093/applin/amx039.

Liu, H. (2018). Language as a human-driven complex adaptive system: Comments on "Rethinking foundations of language from a multidisciplinary perspective" by T. Tong et al. *Physics of Life Reviews*, 26-27, 149-151.

Thelen, E., & Smith, L. (1994). *A Dynamic Systems Approach to the*

Development of Cognition and Action. Cambridge, MA: MIT Press.

Thibault, P. J. (2011). First-order languaging dynamics and second-order language: The distributed language view. *Ecological Psychology*, 23(3), 210-245.

郑咏滟、刘飞凤:《复杂理论视角下任务复杂度对二语口语表现的影响》,《现代外语》2020年第3期,第365—376页。

郑咏滟:《复杂动态系统理论研究十年回顾与国内外比较》,《第二语言学习研究》2020年第10辑,第84—98页。

基于多元读写理论的课堂教学设计：
以英语语言学课程为例[*]

冯德正[**]

摘要：本文提出以多元读写理论为指导的英语语言学课堂教学设计，以功能语言学及物性分析为例详细介绍了课堂教学的各个步骤，并根据教学过程和教学效果讨论了其对语言学教学的启示。研究发现，多元读写理论是解决语言学课程长期存在的枯燥、理论脱离实际等问题行之有效的方法，不仅可以提高学生的兴趣与课堂参与，而且可以训练学生应用语言学知识解决现实问题以及进行语言学学术研究的能力。

关键词：多元读写教学法；课堂教学设计；英语语言学课程；行动研究

一、引　　言

为了应对日益多模态、多媒体化的课堂教学，New London Group(1996)提出"多元读写教学法"(multiliteracies pedagogy)，探讨如何改变传统教学方式，有效利用多媒体资源，培养学生的多元读写能力。在国内，近几年来多元读写研究迅速发展。一方面，多元读写理论框架及其对中国英语教育的启示得到全面介绍与阐释（如朱永生，2008；葛俊丽、罗晓燕，2010；张德禄，2010；韦琴红，2013），另一方面，研究者开始将多元读写教学法应用于大学英语教学并通过实证研究考察其实际效果（如张义君，2011；王梅，2012；宋庆伟，2013；张德禄、刘

---

[*] 原载《中国外语》2017年第3期。
[**] 冯德正，新加坡国立大学博士，现为香港理工大学英文与传意学系副教授，博士生导师，专业英语交际研究中心主任，主要研究方向为多模态语篇分析、传播与交际研究、语言教学等，近期研究主要关注多模态中国话语及其国际传播。

睿,2014;张义君、徐巧林,2015)。然而,就研究方法而言,很多研究侧重教学效果的实证分析,对教学设计和实施过程则语焉不详甚至避而不谈。因此,很难说课堂只是用了多模态资源还是用了多元读写教学法(如宋庆伟,2013;朱静,2016)。有的研究即使对教学步骤进行了阐释,但每个步骤的执行是否完全符合多元读写教学法的理念仍值得商榷。其中的难点是如何实现真正的明确指导,只有个别研究借助语言学理论建立元语言系统设计学习过程(如张德禄、刘睿,2014)。就研究对象而言,虽然研究者都是语言学者,但迄今尚没有研究对语言学课程进行多元读写理论探讨。正如王扬(2004)指出的,综观外语界的各类学术期刊,绝大多数外语教学论文都集中在听、说、读、写的研究上,而对英语专业高年级相关专业知识课程的教学研究与探讨却寥寥无几,对英语语言学课程教学的研究和讨论更是屈指可数。王扬(2004:57)认为"这是一个值得外语界重视的问题,应该引起我们的注意和思考"。

从20世纪80年代英语语言学课程开设伊始,老一辈学者就指出该课程的一些突出问题,如"枯燥乏味、深奥难懂"(胡壮麟,1987:3),"我们对语言学的意义和用途讲得不够"(刘润清,1987:4),并提出切实有效的改进建议。黄希哲(1987:6)指出,语言学教学"在传授知识的同时,还要着眼于培养智力和能力。语言学从不同的角度、在不同的层次上、以不同的方法对语言现象进行观察、对比、分析、归纳、演绎,总结出语言的规律和体系"。杨朝光(1987:8)指出,理论部分的讲解要多采用启发式和归纳法,通过诱导提问和讨论的方式,让学生动脑、动口,积极参加课堂活动,尽量避免填鸭式教学。那么,三十年后,这些问题有没有得到解决,老一辈学者的建议有没有得到实施呢?答案是否定的。司文会(2009:179)指出,"学生学习兴趣弱、课堂沉闷、教学与实践相脱节、教学效率低"等问题依然是语言学课程的突出问题。刘艳峰(2014)发现62%的学生认为语言学是一门枯燥乏味、抽象深奥的学科。就教学方法而言,"不少高校在英语语言学的教学中一直沿袭传统的以教师为中心的知识灌输模式,忽略对学生自主学习能力和创新能力的培养"(刘艳峰,2014:56)。李燕飞、冯德正(2017)通过对高校语言学课程教学多媒体课件大赛获奖PPT的分析发现,大部分PPT仍体现了以教师为中心的知识传授,而对学生的分析和应用能力重视不足。因此,我们亟须借助先进的教学理论对语言学教学进行改革,真正体现语言学课程对培养学生语言意识、分析技能、思维模式的重要作用,而迄今为止,对语言学教学改革的探讨大都停留在理论层面(如王扬,2004;鞠玉梅,2007a;司文会,2009;

刘艳峰,2014),而用理论指导课堂教学实践的行动研究则屈指可数(如吴格奇,2005;鞠玉梅,2007b;余盛明,2014)。在此背景下,本研究尝试将多元读写理论应用于语言学教学,通过真实课堂教学案例的设计与分析,提出可行的语言学教学方法,并讨论其对语言学教学的启示。

二、多元读写教学法与教师行动研究

行动研究作为教育研究的一种方式,以其研究性和实践性的有效融合被认为是教师发展的最佳途径(申继亮,2006;李晓媛、俞理明,2007;王蔷,2001)。Richards(1998)指出,行动研究包括两个要素:一是研究要素,即对课堂教学进行分析与反思,这也是大部分学者所指的行动研究(如王蔷,2001;徐锦芬、李斑斑,2012);二是行动要素,即在发现问题的基础上用相关理论对课堂教学进行改造。与国外研究相比,我国外语界行动研究在教学中的覆盖面不够大,教师进行具体研究实践方面还有些欠缺(李晓媛、俞理明,2007:50)。很多学者通过对大学英语行动研究现状进行调查发现行动研究在我国大学英语教师的教学中没有得到足够重视,多数教师对行动研究不理解或实践力较差(如陈陆健,2012;徐锦芬、李斑斑,2012;王毅、黄仕会,2016)。而与教学反思相比,基于语言学理论的教学实践(即行动要素)显得更为薄弱。田贵森、王冕(2008)指出,高校教师的相关研究实际操作方法与应用性研究有待加强,尤其是有些文章专业性太强,使得广大不熟悉相关理论的一线外语教师望尘莫及(廖传风,2011:59)。就语言学课程而言:一方面,教学实践需要理论指导。正如廖传风(2011:58)所指出的,"外语教育的改革与创新,包括外语教学理念、教学方法等的改革与创新需要先进的语言学理论作指导,特别需要先进的语言学理论在外语教学实践中应用研究成果的指导";另一方面,语言学研究者不能仅仅纸上谈兵,在进行理论探讨的同时,需要进行行动研究,将理论应用到真实的课堂教学中,考察其实效。因此,将国际上最新的教育理论(如多元读写理论、语类教学法等)本土化并应用于课堂教学,开展行动研究,提出行之有效的教学模式是新媒体时代加快语言学教学改革,全面推动外语教师专业化发展的重要途径,也是行动研究发展的方向。下面我们将简要介绍多元读写理论作为教学法的主要内容。

自《多元读写教育学:设计社会未来》(New London Group,1996,以下缩写为"NLG")发表以来,多元读写成为教育学与多模态研究的热点。近十几年来,大量相关专著与论文集应运而生（如 Cope & Kalantzis，2000；Kalantzis & Cope，2005；Cole & Pullen，2010；Mills，2011）。多元读写教学法包含以下四个要素：

（1）实景实践（situated practice）。也就是说，英语教学应置于真实语境中。如果我们的教学目的是让学生在交际、写作等实践中熟练运用知识，那么我们必须让他们沉浸在真实的实践中（NLG，1996：84）。这与系统功能语言学的符号观是一致的。系统功能语言学认为语言是一种社会符号，其意义来源于其在交际过程中的社会功能（Halliday，1994）；而语言交际不可能在真空里进行，它必须发生在一定的场合或语境里。

（2）明确指导（overt instruction），其内容主要是多模态设计资源的元语言系统。多元读写理论用"设计"这一概念取代"语法"蕴含着教学法的两个重要转变：第一，从语言的"法则"到其他符号系统的"法则"（如视觉语法），将设计意义的资源从语言扩展到图像、手势等多模态符号；第二，从语法为中心到语义为中心，即读写能力训练不是对语法规则的重复操练，而是明确指导学生如何在真实语境中创造性地建构意义。

（3）批评框定（critical framing）。NLG（1996）强调，读写能力与社会价值观、文化与意识形态是不可分割的，而批评框定就是使学生在实景实践中通过教师的明确指导，了解（多模态）语篇中的价值观与意识形态，例如教材、广告或电影中的消费主义、性别歧视等。需要指出的是批评框定并不是让学生持负面态度对事物进行批判，其核心是培养学生的分析能力，使其能够对语篇及其蕴含的社会文化现象进行客观理性的分析。

（4）转化实践（transformed practice）。转化实践是指学生在新的社会文化语境中应用所学知识的过程，而该过程中独立解读与建构多模态语篇的能力即是多元读写能力。Kalantzis & Cope（2005）指出，成功的转化实践包括"适当性"与"创新性"两个方面，也就是说，学生不仅能够熟练运用所学知识，而且能够超越所学知识，创造性地解决新问题。

这四个要素并非是线性的步骤，而是互相作用，共同实现多元读写能力。转化实践的前提是学生理解语篇建构的元语言并具备分析能力，亦即明确指导与批评框定两个步骤。同时，转化实践也应该是在真实语境中的实践。下面我们将探讨如何将相对抽象的概念应用到课堂教学设计中。我们选取的是笔者所讲授的以功能语言学为主要内容的一门课中的及物性分析一课，授课安排为两课时授课(lecture)加一课时的讨论课(seminar)，受众为 27 位英语专业的大四学生。

三、课堂教学设计实例：及物性分析

系统功能语言学中的及物性分析是较为抽象的内容。笔者第一次讲授该理论时，根据课程要求，使用 Halliday(1994)作为教材，根据教材所提供的例子阐释每一种过程的含义。然而，根据教学过程和学生反馈，笔者发现三个突出问题：① 内容枯燥，与真实生活脱节，难以吸引学生的兴趣；② 学生不知道为何要进行及物性分析，分析有什么用途；③ 课堂教学是以教师为中心的知识传授，而不是训练学生使用语言学知识解决问题的技能。这也是语言学课程的普遍问题(胡壮麟，1987；司文会，2009；刘艳峰，2014)。课程结束后笔者对教学方法进行了反思并开始研究多元读写教学法，发现该教学法的原则恰好解决上述教学问题。在研读大量多元读写教学法理论与教学实践后，笔者尝试改造课堂教学设计，并应用于教学实践。下面我们详细介绍改造后的教学过程。

1. 实景实践

实景实践要求教师不是选取教材中无语境的、孤立的句子作为例子，而是搜集真实语料作为教学素材。当时的一个热点问题是跨栏运动员刘翔在伦敦奥运会上退赛，各国媒体都对此进行了报道。因此，教师选取该事件作为教学素材，在课堂上首先播放伦敦奥运会 110 米栏项目的视频，然后给学生看来自中国新华网和美国 CNN 的两篇英文报道(文本一与文本二)。学生分组讨论两篇报道的立场有何不同并指出哪篇报道来自中国。教师随后指定几个小组分享他们的结论与理据。由于没有相关训练，学生只能根据自己的直觉与主观印象判断哪篇报道来自中国，每个小组只能指出两三条语言特征的不同。很多学生对自己的表现不满意，认为没有分析工具，无从下手，急切想知道到底哪篇报道来自中国以及如何通过系统分析得出令人信服的结论。这样一来，教师不仅给了学生动手分析的机会，更激发了学生对学习理论的兴趣。因此，除了使用生动的多模态资源，实景实践要求将传统语言学教学中先讲理论，然后"为理论找语言现象"，变为从语言现象出发，"为语言现象找理论"。这种问题驱动而不是理论驱动的教学方法是多元读写理论的基本特征，也是解决语言学课程长期存在的问题的有效途径。

文本一：Defending Olympic champion Liu Xiang pulled out of the men's 110 m hurdles first round Monday morning at the Beijing Olympics.//(2) In the last heat of the first round, Liu quit the race [[after a false start of Dutchman Marcel van der Westen]]. (3) He limped off the track, [[obviously being troubled by a foot injury]]. (4) Liu's coach Sun Haiping said in a post-race press conference,//(5) "His right heel injury has been a long problem since six years ago, even before the Athens Olympics." (6) "On Aug. 16, we arrived at the Olympic village, (7) medical experts analyzed Liu's injury (8) and specified (9) there was a problem on Liu's Achilles's tendon," (10) Sun said.

文本二：Liu Xiang pulled out of the Olympics [[before clearing his first hurdle on Monday, clutching his right leg in pain in front of a stunned crowd at the Bird's Nest]]. (2) Liu barely got out of the blocks//(3) and immediately started hobbling in the first heat. (4) Something snapped in his physical resistance after months of uncertainty about an inflamed hamstring. (5) He had competed rarely this year//(6) and in June saw [[his world record fall to Dayron Robles of Cuba]]. (7) Trouble immediately showed//when he warmed up. [[Stopping after two hurdles in the warm-up]], (8) he crouched down//(9) and walked gingerly back to the starting area.

2. 明确指导

此时,讲解理论的时机已经成熟。教师对Halliday(1994)的过程类型与参与者进行了详细讲解并举例说明,如表1所示。NLG(1996：86)指出,明确指导并不意味着将知识直接灌输给学生,而是一种积极的干预与引导,需要科学有效的指导方法。教师要首先引导学生积极思考,尝试意义建构,在学生最需要的时候根据实际情况给予及时的、明确的指导,然后逐渐减少指导,使学生能够独立建构意义(NLG,1996;Mills,2011)。因此,教师随后与学生一起对儿童图画书中的过程进行分析。采用图文并茂的图画书不但可以提高学生的兴趣,而且能够引导学生分析不同语类的真实语料。讲解过程是以教师为中心的知识解构(deconstruction),而分析儿童图画书则是师生共同建构知识(co-construction)。在共同建构阶段,教师通过提问和反馈(即包含 Initiation, Response, Feedback 的 IRF 结构, Sinclair & Coulthard, 1975)引导学生积极思考,加深对理论的理解,为下一步独立分析奠定基础。

表1 Halliday(1994)的过程类型与例示

Field of experience	Process type	Example
Doing	Material	He crashed his car
Happening	Material	Accidents happen
Behaving	Behavioural	He's still breathing
Consciousness -		
Internal	Mental	He saw the accident
External	Verbal	He said there was an accident
Being	Relational	He was OK
Having	Relational	He only had minor injuries
Existing	Existential	There was an accident

图1 儿童图画书例子的过程分析

3. 批评框定

Kalantzis & Cope(2005)将批评框定分为功能性分析和批评性分析两部分。就语言学课程而言,前者是指学生能够使用语言学理论对语料进行描述性分析,并能对语篇特征进行归纳与总结;后者是指学生能够对语料进行阐释性分析,即挖掘语篇特征所体现的作者身份、立场及其背后的心理、社会、文化因素。在本课例中,教师让学生再次进行分组讨论,对上述两篇报道的参与者(动作发出者)和过程进行分析并汇报他们的发现。在此基础上,他们重新讨论两篇报道的立场。教师随后对每组进行提问(每组一句)。经过实景实践和明确指导两个步骤,学生在此步骤中大都能准确分析报道中的参与者与过程类型。教师随后对错误的分析进行纠正,总结分析结果,对及物性框架进行巩固(consolidate)。

(1) 功能性分析。

就参与者(动作发出者)而言,新华社报道中,十个小句中有三句是刘翔,两句是孙海平,两句是医生,一句是名词化"his right heel injury",一句是"we"(Sun & Liu),还有一句是关系过程的"there"。而在 CNN 的报道中,九个小句中有七句是以刘翔为动作发出者,其余两句为"something"和"trouble"。如表2所示。动作过程的选择与参与者密切相关,新华社报道有六个物质过程,但其中只有两个与刘翔直接相关(pull out, quit),另外只有一个行为过程(limped off);而 CNN 的报道中有五个直接与刘翔退赛场景相关的行为过程,另外七个物质过程中有六个(如 pull out, compete)的动作发出者是刘翔。如表3所示。

表2 参与者类型

	刘翔	其他人	名词化	物质名词
Xinhua	3	5	1	1
CNN	7	0	0	2

表3 动作过程类型

	Material	Behavioral	Verbal/Mental	Relational
Xinhua	6	1	2	2
CNN	7	5	1	1

(2) 批评性分析。

学生需要在此基础上归纳两篇报道对参与者及过程的选择之间差别的本

质。总体来说,新华社报道倾向于"解释",而CNN报道侧重"描述"。前者尽量减少主人公的参与与其动作过程,使因果关系与责任变得模糊;而后者则通过占多数的参与者刘翔(78%)突显因果关系与责任,强调刘翔是唯一的责任者。这一抽象化(abstraction)过程是从描述到阐释的重要步骤。教师进一步引导学生理解造成差别的深层原因,对报道进行批评性分析。讨论之后,教师简单介绍 van Dijk(1995)关于"自己人"和"外人"的理论,即自己人的负面事件通常会轻描淡写(如稀释关注焦点、侧重解释等),而外人的负面事件则会渲染强调(如话题化、聚焦细节等)。基于对两篇报道不同立场的理解,教师进一步指出所有新闻报道都不是对事实的客观还原,而是反映了作者立场与意识形态的意义建构,培养学生的批判意识。教师同时强调这种批评意识不是主观的批判,而是基于语言学知识的系统、理性分析。这样一来,学生不仅树立了批判意识、掌握了分析工具,而且可以认识到语言学知识与日常生活密切相关,提高学习兴趣。

4. 转化实践

转化实践是指学生将所学知识应用到新的语篇分析中。在该课程设计中,转化实践的目标有两方面:一是将语言学知识用到生活中,改变思维方式,客观、理性地分析问题;二是通过分析真实语篇训练学术写作能力。转化实践主要由讨论课和课程作业实现。在一小时的讨论课中,教师仍然选用当时的社会热点问题作为素材,教师选取来自不同地区的两篇报道让学生分组讨论完成以下任务:① 分析报道中的参与者与过程类型并列表总结其不同;② 解释不同语法选择所体现的立场与态度;③ 阐释导致不同立场的深层原因并提出自己的建议。在讨论课上,学生一方面可以独立运用所学知识分析身边的热点事件,认识到语言学理论与现实生活密切相关,另一方面可以学习语言学研究与学术论文写作的思路,即分析什么(语料),怎么分析(理论框架),有什么发现(语篇特征),为什么会有这些特征(阐释深层原因)。

在原来的课程设计中,前六周将概念意义、人际意义与组篇意义等框架学习完后,第七周是期中考试,包括概念解释,句子分析以及给定文本的元功能分析,其目的是考查学生对知识的掌握,而不是运用知识解决实际语言问题。改变教学方式后教师将期中考核改为2 000字的论文。论文包括四个步骤:选择语料,确定分析框架,进行描述性分析,阐释语篇特征背后所体现的态度、立场、文化。这四个步骤一方面对应多元读写理论的实景实践、明确指导、功能性分析、批评性分析四个要素,另一方面对应学术写作的引言、研究方法、分析过程与结果、讨论四个基本组成部分。因此,这种考核方式作为转化实践使学生不仅能够独立使用语言学知识解决他们感兴趣的语言问题,而且能够训练他们的学术写作能力。

经过每周一次的讨论课训练,学生不再惧怕论文写作,而是享受探索的过程。下面是课程结束后两个学生的反馈:学生一指出,该课程使她第一次感觉到过去所学的理论是有意义的,使她觉得理论与现实生活是密切相关的。她说"I start to see things differently now",说明该课程已经改造了她的思维方式,她将可以在生活中运用所学知识对事物进行客观分析。这是转化实践最重要的标志。学生二所讲的则是转化实践的另一方面,即学术写作。她指出,她学会了如何写作学术论文,而且在这个过程中,她是被自己的好奇心驱动,而不是被迫。其结果是她拿到了大学四年来的第一个优秀。这也说明,该学生过去没有拿到优秀不光是自己的问题,教师不能激发学生兴趣,没有引导学生进行学术写作,也负有不可推卸的责任。

学生一:It felt like for the first time, in forever, all the theories that I have been studying for the past 3 years become something that make sense. Your class is the first class I feel somehow — connected. The connection is not only with what we learnt in class but other things in life also. I start to see things differently now(… smile)

学生二:Thanks for getting me to develop more interest in linguistics and acquire much more knowledge than ever before. I do feel I have learnt a lot during the writing and about how to write, it's just like I'm driven by my curiosity and interest to finish this paper, instead of being forced to write it. And I've received my very first A grade in the term paper from you, and more importantly, my very first A grade in all the papers.

四、讨论与启示

英语教育研究者与语言学者早已认识到语言学的重要性,也对语言学课程的教学目标和教学模式做了深入探讨。早在英语语言学课程设置之初,胡壮麟(1987:2)就指出,"作为语言专业的学生,不掌握有关语言的专门知识,不合情理",并强调语言学课程应该培养学生分析、综合、推理、批判的能力。如今,将以"教师为中心"的传统教学模式改为"以学生为主体"的先进教学模式,使语言学理论与学生日常英语学习相联系,培养学生应用语言学知识解决实际问题的能力已是学界共识(如王扬,2004;吴格奇,2005;鞠玉梅,2007a;余盛明,2014;李燕飞、冯德正,2017)。这些共识与多元读写理论的原则高度一致,后者可以为语言学课程改革提供有效的理论支持。本研究通过真实的课堂教学分析发现,多元读写理论可以解决语言学课程长期存在的学生兴趣低、理论与现实脱节、教师满堂灌等问题,使该课程成为最受学生欢迎、最"有用"的课程之一。其效果主要表现在以下三个方面:① 学生反馈。第一次授课时该课程的学生评分为 4 分(满分为 5 分),其后的几年评分为 4.5—4.8 分,成为学生最喜爱的课程之一。很多学生认为"the subject is among my favorite subjects I've ever taken throughout my 4 years university study";② 课堂表现。小组讨论使学生改变了被动听讲、玩手机等习惯,积极参与讨论;③ 学习效果。如转化实践一节所述,该课程不仅使学生对语言学知识感兴趣,而且学习到如何进行语言学研究与学术写作,并能将知识运用到生活中去。

　　该研究为英语专业本科和研究生语言学教学提供了很多有益启示:首先,在教学内容上,将传统语言学教学中先讲理论,然后"为理论找语言现象",变为从语言现象出发,"为语言现象找理论",将语言学理论与现实生活密切联系,引发学生对理论的兴趣。其次,在授课方式上,讲授与讨论有机融合。王扬(2004)提出传授型和讨论型相结合的方法,但没有说明如何结合。在多元读写框架内,教师和学生的角色非常清楚。多元读写课堂以学生为中心,但教师发挥设计者的作用,选择合适的情境引发学生讨论,设置恰当的问题引导学生理解概念,明确指导如何进行功能性与批评性分析。再次,在教学目标上,从知识灌输到训练分析方法转变,将语言学教学与学术英语教学相结合。考核方式从记忆知识要点变为考查学生使用语言学知识解决实际问题的能力。语言学具有科学研究的性质,对于训练学生的语言学习和研究的科学方法、严谨的思维和创新意识具有重要的意义(司文会,2009:179)。因此,教师在教学与考核过程中除了关注语言学知识的掌握与应用,还要有意识地对语言学研究与学术论文写作的方法进行指导。最后,在教师发展上,将语言学/语言教学理论研究与教学实践相结合。

教师行动研究要求教师不仅能够反思、分析自己的教学,而且能够将语言学理论应用到教学实践,并分析其效果。这样不仅能改进教学,而且能发展语言学理论,是教学与科研有效结合、互相促进的有效途径。

五、结　　语

为了适应当今社会对英语专业人才的要求,解决英语语言学课程长期存在的问题,语言学者必须借助其理论优势推进语言学教学改革。作为这种改革的尝试,本文首次将多元读写理论引入功能语言学课程教学,详细介绍了课堂教学设计的各个步骤,并根据教学过程和反馈信息对语言学教学提出建设性意见。实践证明,多元读写理论是解决语言学课程枯燥、理论脱离实际等问题行之有效的方法,不仅可以提高学生的兴趣与课堂参与,而且可以训练学生应用语言学知识解决现实问题以及进行语言学研究与学术写作的能力。该研究为教师使用多元读写教学法进行课堂教学实践与行动研究提供了详细的理据与操作方法。我们期待多元读写教学法能被广泛应用于语言学和其他学科教学,改变以教师为中心的知识灌输,提高学生运用语言学知识分析问题与进行学术写作的能力,同时在教学中验证、发展多元读写理论。

参考文献

Cole, D. R. & Pullen, D. L. (eds). (2010), *Multiliteracies in Motion: Current Theory and Practice*. London: Routledge.

Cope, B. & Kalantzis, M. (eds). (2000), *Multiliteracies: Literacy Learning and the Design of Social Futures*. South Yarra, VIC: Macmillan.

Halliday, M. A. K. (1994), *An Introduction to Functional Grammar*. London: Arnold.

Kalantzis, M. & B. Cope, (2005), *Learning by Design Guide*. Melbourne: Common Ground.

Mills, K. A. (2011), *The Multiliteracies Classroom*. Bristol: Multilingual Matters.

New London Group. (1996), A pedagogy of multiliteracies: Designing social futures. *Harvard Educational Review*, (66): 60-93.

Richards, J. C.（1998）, *Beyond Training: Perspectives on Language Teacher Education*. Cambridge: Cambridge University Press.

Sinclair, J. M. & M. Coulthard,（1975）, *Towards an Analysis of Discourse: The English Used by Teachers and Pupils*. London: Oxford University Press.

van Dijk, T. A.（1995）, Ideological discourse analysis. http://www.discourses.org/.

陈陆健:《大学英语教师行动研究现状分析》,《广西民族大学学报(哲学社会科学版)》2012年第1期,第183—186页。

葛俊丽、罗晓燕:《新媒介时代外语教学新视角:多元识读教学法》,《外语界》2010年第5期,第13—19页。

胡壮麟:《"语言学"在英文系扎根》,《外语教学与研究》1987年第2期,第2—3页。

黄希哲:《谈谈英语专业语言学教学》,《外语教学与研究》1987年第2期,第6—7页。

鞠玉梅:《关于高校英语专业语言学课程教学的思考》,《外语与外语教学》2007年第8期,第31—33页。

鞠玉梅:《以多媒体网络技术为基础的语言学导论课程研究性教学模式的构建》,《外语电化教学》2007年第4期,第3—6页。

李晓媛、俞理明:《国外行动研究趋势及其对中国外语教学研究的启示》,《外语教学》2007年第2期,第48—52页。

李燕飞、冯德正:《PPT课件设计与语言学知识建构:多元读写教学法视角》,《电化教育研究》2017年第5期,第95—100页。

廖传风:《系统功能语言学在外语教学中应用研究综述》,《山东外语教学》2011年第6期,第53—60页。

刘润清:《英文本科学生应必修"语言学引论"》,《外语教学与研究》1987年第2期,第3—4页。

刘艳峰:《基于网络自主学习的英语语言学课程教改探索》,《外语教学》2014年第3期,第56—59页。

申继亮:《教学反思与行动研究——教师发展之路》,北京师范大学出版社2006年版。

司文会:《任务型教学模式启发下的英语语言学课程教学改革》,《黑龙江史志》2009年第24期,第179—180页。

宋庆伟:《多模态化与大学英语多元读写能力培养实证研究》,《外语研究》2013年第2期,第55—59页。

田贵森、王冕:《功能语言学在中国的应用研究与发展》,《北京科技大学学报(社会科学版)》2008年第2期,第98—103页。

王梅:《多模态与多元文化读写能力培养实证研究》,《外语教学》2012年第1期,第66—69页。

王蔷:《行动研究课程与具有创新精神的研究型外语教师的培养》,《国外外语教学》2001年第1期,第1—7页。

王扬:《高校英语专业语言学课程教学初探》,《外语研究》2004年第5期,第57—60页。

王毅、黄仕会:《大学英语教师教学反思现状调查——以Bartlett教学反思过程为依据》,《外语研究》2016年第5期,第70—75页。

韦琴红:《多元识读理论解读》,《杭州电子科技大学学报(社会科学版)》2013年第4期,第59—62页。

吴格奇:《"语言学导论"课程教学行动研究与教师知识体系的反思》,《国外外语教学》2005年第2期,第32—36页。

徐锦芬、李斑斑:《中国高校英语教师教学反思现状调查与研究》,《外语界》2012年第4期,第6—15页。

杨潮光:《语言理论课也要有实践性》,《外语教学与研究》1987年第2期,第8—9页。

余盛明:《试论英语专业知识课的使命与教学模式——以"语言学导论"课为例》,《中国外语》2014年第5期,第4—11页。

张德禄:《多模态外语教学的设计与模态调用初探》,《中国外语》2010年第3期,第48—53、75页。

张德禄、刘睿:《外语多元读写能力培养教学设计研究——以学生口头报告设计为例》,《中国外语》2014年第3期,第45—52页。

张义君:《英语专业学生多元识读能力实证研究》,《外语界》2011年第1期,第45—52页。

张义君、徐巧林:《文本阅读模式探索——基于多元识读能力的培养实践》,

《首都经济贸易大学学报》2015年第5期,第116—120页。

朱静:《大学英语多元识读能力培养模式探究——基于PPT课堂展示的视角》,《教育学术月刊》2016年第1期,第106—111页。

朱永生:《多元识读能力研究及其对我国教学改革的启示》,《外语研究》2008年第4期,第10—14页。

 方法谈:

行动研究中如何基于问题阐释论文的研究价值?

学术论文写作往往离不开这样五个核心要素,即研究的出发点、研究的理论基础、研究方法、数据分析的过程与结果以及对研究结果的阐释。在不同的研究范式内,每一个要素都有一定的"套路"可以遵循。了解这些"套路"对研究生或初学者而言至关重要,就像学习书画时的"临摹"一样。然而,问题是很多初学者不知道该模仿什么以及如何进行有效模仿,抓不住最本质的方法,有时会导致"画虎不成反类犬"。本书为解决这一问题提供了很好的思路,根据不同选题提供"临摹"案例,并且更重要的是,对案例中关于论文写作的核心要素进行详细阐释,帮助初学者抓住问题的本质、明确了解该如何模仿、提高学术写作水平。本着这一原则,本方法谈将简要介绍多模态教学研究的几个核心要素与论文写作的方法。

首先是研究的出发点。一篇实证的研究论文通常需要由"问题"驱动,即"这个研究是为了解决什么问题"。这通常是引言部分的内容,也是最难写的,需要写作者去构思一个"故事",而不是像分析一样只是去呈现结果。这个"问题"从哪里来呢?其来源主要包括两个方面,即社会与文献。这就要求我们首先对我们生活的环境保持敏锐的观察,发现"问题"。但是,这时候的"问题"只是常识性的,不是学术性的。这就要求我们去研读相关文献,看看这个"问题"是不是被研究过了,前人用了什么方法,有什么发现,有什么不足等。这样我们就能更了解问题的本质与研究的价值,并且据此提出我们具体的研究问题。现在我们以本文为例来看引言是如何提出问题并阐释该研究的价值的。本文关注的是英语专业语言学课程枯燥乏味、与实践脱节、学生不感兴趣的问题。为了证明这一问题是普遍存在的,文章引用了大量相关文献,包括名家论述与最新的实证研究。就研究空白而言，文章指出，为了应对日益多媒体化的课堂教学，多元读写教学研究近几年迅速发展，但尚没有对语言学教学的研究。因此，我们尚不了解应该如何有效设计多模态资源，让语言学课变得更加有趣、有用。为了弥补这一空白并解决语言学教学的实际问题，本文开展了基于多元读写教学法的行动研究。这样一来，引言解决了三个关键问题：研究要解决的问题、研究的前沿评述以及研究的理据与价值。

接下来就是我们怎么去解决问题，即研究的理论框架与方法。首先我们需要搞清楚我们的研究范式，比如是质性的，量化的，还是混合的，因为这对一篇文章的研究设计具有决定性的影响。主流的多模态分析用的就是质性的话语分析方法。但是随着学科的进一步发展，越来越多的学者呼吁对大量数据进行实证分析，以使其结果更具普遍性。但我们介绍的这篇文章显然是质性的行动研究，因此研究不需要有个假设，不需要设计实验去验证假设，不关注客观性、普遍性等问题。我们研究的目的是对某一个案进行系统、详细、深入的分析，以揭示其内在的复杂性。这种系统分析就要求我们有一个分析框架。本文的框架就是多元读写教学法，因为其分析的课堂教学就是根据这一理念进行设计的。本文的目的在于呈现该理念在课堂教学中是如何实施的，亦即将课堂教学视为一个多模态语篇，考察教师如何有效使用多模态资源实现教学目标。分析过程需要注意的是总结提炼最显著的特征并选取典型的例子进行详细分析。例如，在本文中，一个基本的教学原则就是从理论出发，用例子解释理论，到从实例出发，为解释现象寻找理论的转变。文章考察了教师在课堂的不同阶段如何设计多模态资源。也就是说，并不是使用了多模态资源就一定比不使用要好，而是要看如何使用。教师需要使用多模态资源建构真实情景，解构抽象知识，并让学生对多模态话语进行分析，提高学生的分析能力。分析需要有框架、有层次、有步骤，而不是自己任意发挥。由于多模态语篇的复杂性，我们需要借助多元读写、社会符号学等框架去考察意义的特征及其多模态建构。这种系统分析需要让读者对多模态课堂教学有新的认识，而不是为了分析而分析，只是用一些术语与框架去包装一些显而易见的常识。

最后就是如何去阐释分析过程中出现的显著特征。我们不能停留在对现象的分析描述，而是需要对这些现象进行理论性、批评性的讨论与解读。这种讨论一般要包含两个层面：一是分析中发现的话语特征的交际功能；二是这些特征背后所体现的教学法、教育政策、社会文化等特征。我们对研究发现的解读通常需要另一个领域的理论。例如,如果我们研究的是课堂话语,那我们就需要多模态话语分析的理论进行系统描述,同时用教育学、心理学等领域的相关理论去阐释我们的发现。这就使得我们的研究具有跨学科性。这种不同学科理论的互补与融合也是创新的重要途径。同时,这种解读也可以让我们进一步探讨研究如何为解决引言提出的问题提供新的方法,有什么价值,有什么问题,下一步研究怎么做,等等,形成闭环。

综上所述,一篇好的论文需要针对某一问题,需要研究者对前沿文献有整体把握,了解自己的研究范式与研究方法。分析需要有系统的框架,提炼显著特征,能对某一(多模态)语篇现象提供新的认识与启示。这样我们的研究才能既有理论或方法上的创新性,也有现实的应用价值。当然,我们探讨的只是一种研究范式,不一定适用于所有的论文写作。作者应该根据自己的研究问题、研究范式、研究方法等选择合适的"临摹"对象。

后　　记

在我们步入语言学研究的大门之时，就要思考和选择研究方法。语言是一种复杂的现象，既具有自然属性，也具有社会性质，既具有人文主义传统，也与自然科学密不可分。语言学研究，总体解决是什么、怎么做、为什么的问题，在内容上涵括语言、民族、社会、符号、意义，不一而足，在取向上融合思维、文化、结构、认知、心理，复杂动态，在视角上凸显异域、本土、母语、外语，交融互鉴，在立意上体现本体论、方法论、认识论、价值论……步步深入。随着人工智能和信息技术与语言研究的融合，语言学的跨学科交叉研究日益突显，因此语言学的研究方法各具特色，日新月异。工欲善其事，必先利其器，选择合适的研究方法至关重要。

在实际研究中如何选择方法视研究目的而定。为了论述观点、验证假设、构建模型，语言学研究在方法上需要考虑研究信度和效度，择法而用，兼容并蓄，百花齐放，在质性研究和量化研究的相辅相成中扬帆远航。演绎、归纳、溯因，相伴相随；人文主义、实证主义、自然范式、科学范式，皆得其所；现象学、诠释学、叙事学、人种志，洞见存在；差异、关联、聚敛、发散，异曲同工；问卷、观摩、采访、日志，三角互证；文献分析、扎根理论、田野调查、个案研究，实事求是。语言学研究方法与学术论文撰写此唱彼和、互为表里。引言与研究问题、文献述评与研究理据、论文主体与框架和方法、结果分析与阐释，环环相扣、浑然一体，恰如编排精巧、简繁得当的乐章，不绝如缕，直至尾声。

行百里者半九十，师法前辈同行的研究和论文撰写案例，当属不二法门。是为本书编委会选取 16 个相关案例，为青年学者和研究生们提供可操作的指南的初衷。

在编排上，我们坚守严谨的学术标准和循序渐进的理念，力求将最适合、最优质的学术内容呈现给初入语言学研究大门的诸位。希望本书成为您的良师益友，带您走进科研入口，成为你在语言学研究中泛海远行、渐入佳境的小帮手。

本书得以出版，首先感谢语言学界专家学者的大力支持，胡壮麟、朱永生、陆俭明、俞理明、韩建侠、黄国文、潘文国、魏在江、张吉生、曾用强、董燕萍、刘玉华、蔡任栋、王仁强、陈和敏、刘建达、吕剑涛、方帆、Will Baker、雷蕾、施雅倩、郑咏滟、刘飞凤、冯德正诸师慷慨授权赐稿，并欣然允诺并按时完成了导读文字，不仅铸成了本书的内容，更使得我们有幸体悟了他们的科研心路和学术风采，确是循循善诱，春风化雨。感恩之情，难以言表。

本书还得到了《外语教学与研究》《语言教学与研究》《中国语文》《现代外语》《外国语》《中国外语》《外语与外语教学》《外语界》，以及 *System*、*Language Teaching Research*、*Frontiers in Psychology* 等期刊的鼎力支持，同意将已经刊发的优秀论文收入本书中，在此表示感谢。

厦门大学的杨信彰教授欣然应允作序，他学术造诣深厚，爱护后学，为本书增添了学术价值和人文关怀。我们深感荣幸，也期待读者能够从中受益。

感谢本书专家委员会的师长和学界名师们的指点和建议。他们高屋建瓴的学术视野、跨学科的学术造诣、富有创造力的教育智慧和经验使得本书严谨、深入、切题。

本书两位主编唐青叶、张新玲和两位副主编朱音尔、李晓媛分别为博士生、硕士生、本科生开设语言学和语言学方法论课程，在发挥各自研究和教学专长编撰此书的同时，也从中获益匪浅。

感谢上海大学研究生院对本书的出版资助，上海大学出版社责任编辑贺俊逸老师对文稿勘误，给予了大力帮助，在此表示衷心感谢。

上海大学外国语学院语言文化与世界文明博士生张稳同学从中国知网下载并认真核对和审读了所选论文，在此一并致谢。

衷心希望本书能助力语言学研究者。书中如出现谬误，则是编者的责任，请批评指正。

本书编写组
2024 年 5 月